Buchner Bründler

Buildings II 2007–2020

Edited by Ludovic Balland

With texts by Tibor Joanelly, Urs Stahel, Franziska Schürch, Isabel Koellreuter, and Oliver Schneider

PARK BOOKS

N° 068 Garden Tower p. 66 p. 169

N° 090　Peninsula Housing Development　**p. 71**　**p. 185**

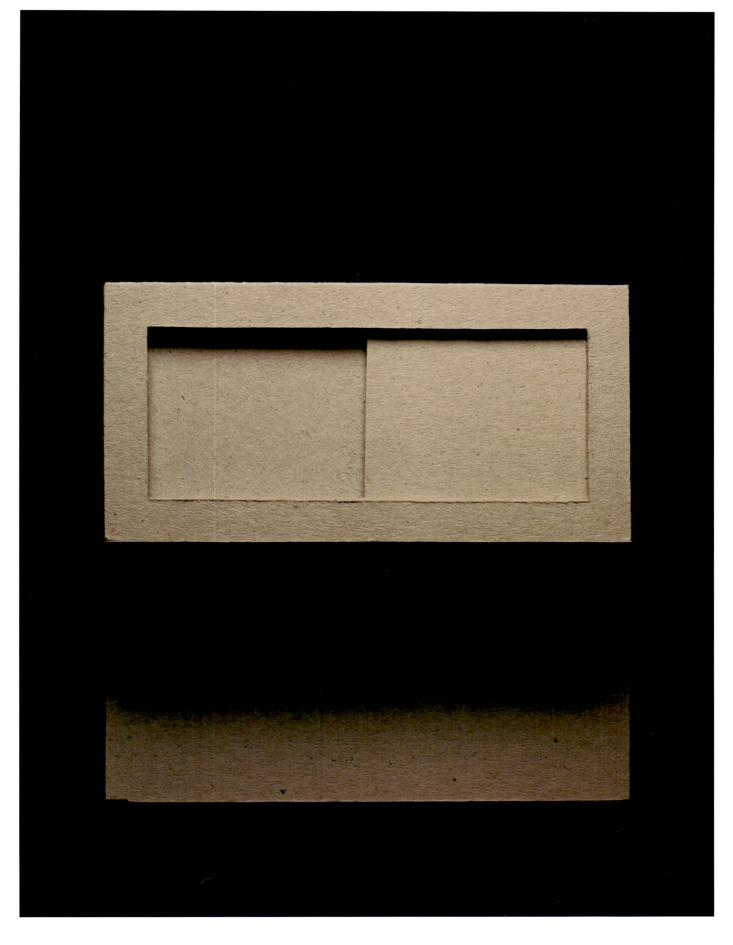

N° 113 Hotel Nomad **p. 74** **p. 199**

N° 123 Tièchestrasse Housing Development **p. 80** **p. 217**

N°147 Hertenstein House p.86 p.235

N°149 Credit Suisse Place Bel-Air Headquarters   **p. 93** **p. 249**

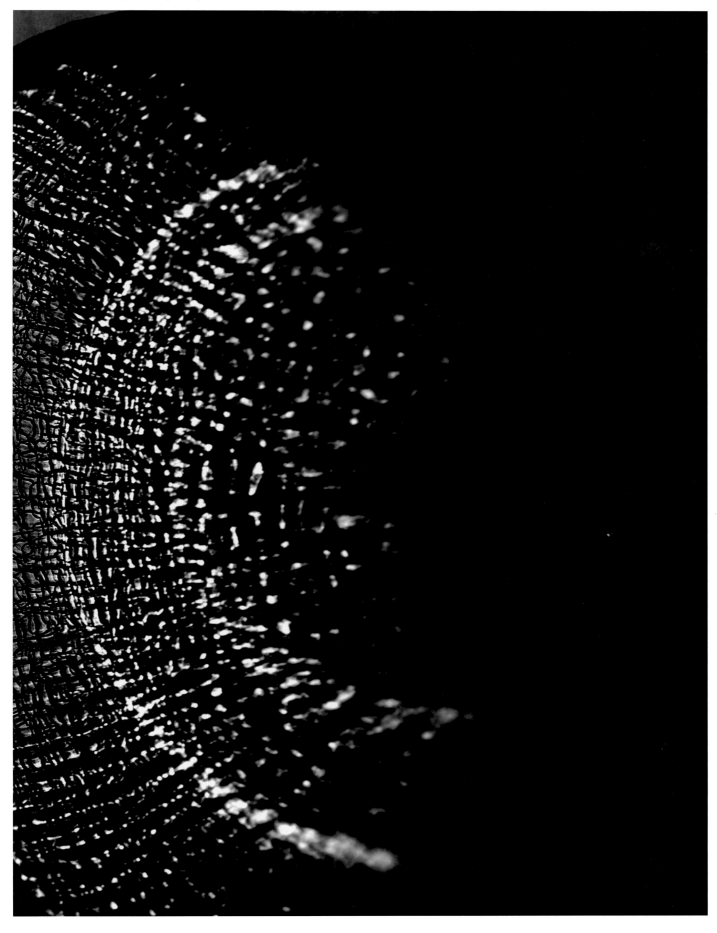

N° 174 Amthausquai Residential and Commercial Building p. 98 p. 265

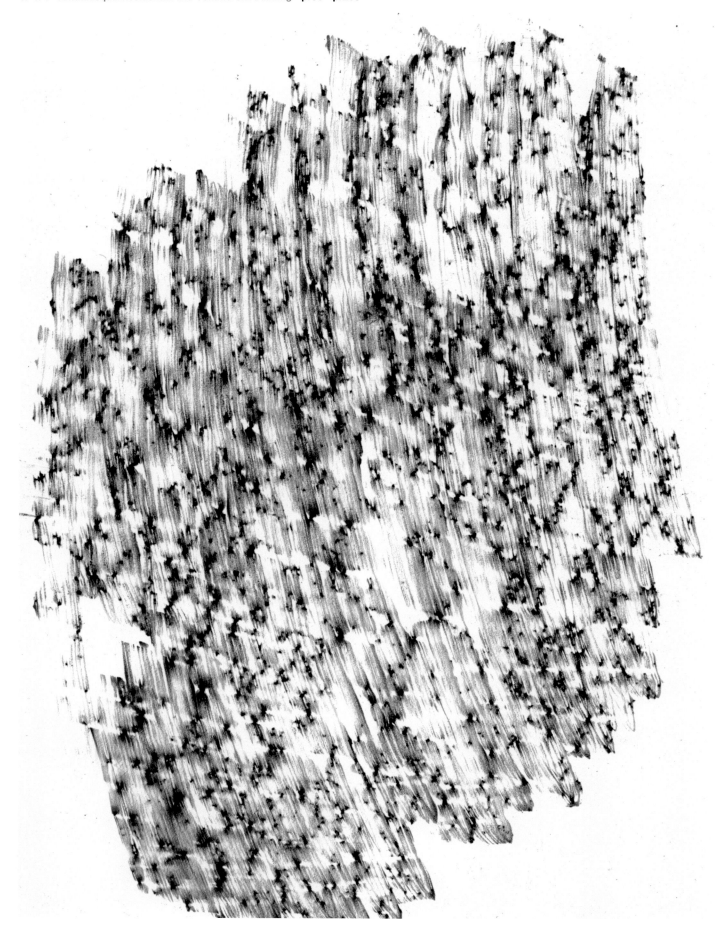

N° 179 Lörrach House **p.103** **p.281** Contents 11

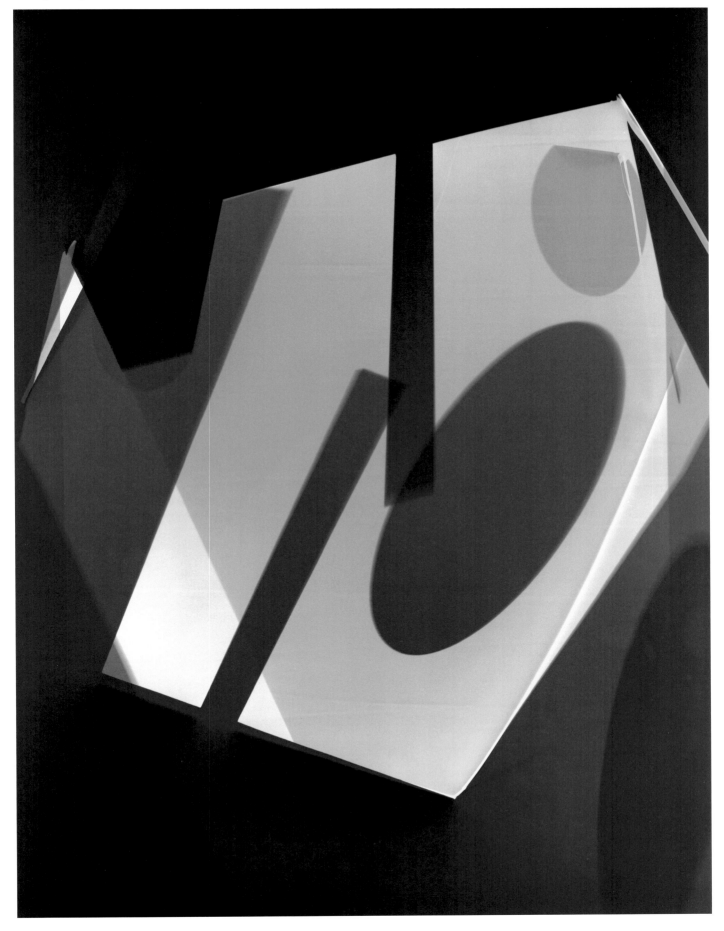

N° 207 Casa Mosogno p. 120 p. 313

N° 212   Münchenstein House   p. 132   p. 329

N° 224 Kirschgarten House p.138 p.343

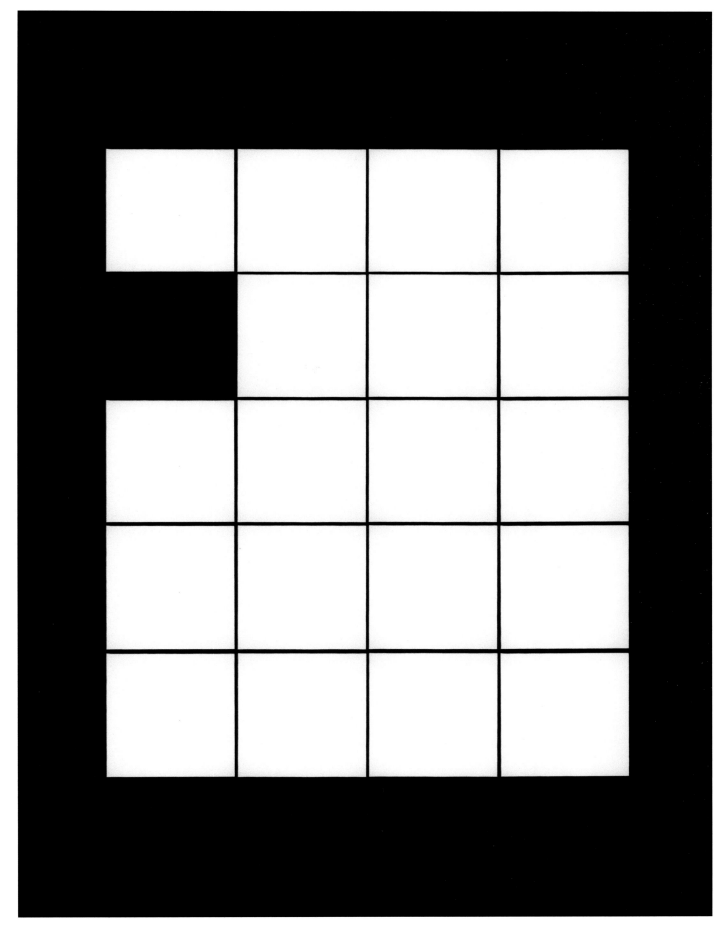

N° 249 Cherry Storehouse Nuglar   p. 143   p. 359

N° 260 **Missionsstrasse House** **p. 155** **p. 379**

Buchner Bründler

Buildings II

Edited by Ludovic Balland

Overview Buildings and Projects

N° 068	Garden Tower	66	169
N° 090	Peninsula Housing Development	71	185
N° 110	Kahlstrasse House		405
N° 113	Hotel Nomad	74	199
N° 123	Tièchestrasse Housing Development	80	217
N° 131	Hubackerweg House		408
N° 141	Kreuzlingen House		410
N° 145	Chienbergreben House		413
N° 147	Hertenstein House	86	235
N° 149	Credit Suisse Place Bel-Air Headquarters	93	249
N° 165	Reception Building Syngenta		415
N° 169	Parkhotel Bellevue		418
N° 174	Amthausquai Residential and Commercial Building	98	265
N° 175	Meilen House		420
N° 179	Lörrach House	103	281
N° 185	Eisenbahnweg Housing Development		423
N° 187	AUE Basel		426
N° 188	Zahnradfabrik Rheinfelden Development		428
N° 189	Rosentalturm Messe Basel		430
N° 190	Sekundarstufenzentrum Burghalde Baden		431
N° 198	Lindt Chocolate Center Kilchberg		432
N° 202	Conversion St. Alban Rheinweg		435
N° 205	Cooperative Building Stadterle	107	297
N° 206	Tulière Football Stadium Lausanne		436
N° 207	Casa Mosogno	120	313
N° 208	Stapferhaus Lenzburg		438
N° 209	Natural History Museum and State Archives Basel		440
N° 210	Kunsthaus Baselland		442
N° 212	Münchenstein House	132	329
N° 213	WDR-Filmhaus		445
N° 215	Stedtli Site Development		448
N° 216	Campus Biel		449
N° 217	Greifensee House		451
N° 219	Accademia di architettura		453
N° 220	Guesthouse Universität Hamburg		456
N° 224	Kirschgarten House	138	343
N° 232	Wendelmatte Greppen		459
N° 234	Swiss Tropical and Public Health Institute		460
N° 236	Studio Basel Bruderholz		462
N° 239	Railroad Station Building Altdorf		464
N° 240	Urban Development Horburg		467
N° 241	High-rise Heuwaage		470
N° 243	Bahnhof Nord Kloten		472
N° 244	Town Hall and Archaeology Museum Pully		473
N° 246	Fürigen Area		475
N° 247	Housing Development Rötiboden		478
N° 248	Swiss Ambassador's Residence Algiers		481
N° 249	Cherry Storehouse Nuglar	143	359
N° 250	Allschwil House		483
N° 252	Clinic Arlesheim Campus		486
N° 253	Papieri Area		487
N° 254	Gruner + Jahr Development		489
N° 255	Forum UZH		491
N° 260	Missionsstrasse House	155	379
N° 262	Pratteln Municipal Center		494
N° 264	Swiss Embassy Addis Ababa		495
N° 267	Culture Center Alpenstrasse Interlaken		496
N° 268	Laurenz-Carré Cologne		498
N° 270	Banque Pictet		501
N° 271	Stiftung Blindenheim		504
N° 276	Grossalbis Housing Development		507
N° 278	Webergut Zollikofen		508
N° 280	Tower at Jannowitz Bridge Berlin		510

Foreword	Daniel Buchner, Andreas Bründler	23
Vertigo	Ludovic Balland	25
Vielfalt / Variety	Tibor Joanelly	41
F & A—A Few Fantasies, A Few Aberrations	Urs Stahel	56

Workshop   65

Selected Buildings   167

Chronology of Projects   401

Further Buildings and Projects   405

Appendix   513

Foreword

This book elucidates our creative work of the last ten years. The main focus consists of a selection of buildings that are presented in detail, accompanied by a supplementary section that we consider as an atlas.

The concept refines the experiences we gathered from our first comprehensive book publication, *Buchner Bründler Buildings*, which was compiled to accompany the eponymous exhibition at ETH Zurich. At the time, the exhibition and the book were conceived as separate entities that mutually supplemented and enriched one another.

Derived from a selection of buildings, large-scale models were specially produced, primarily in concrete, generating a physical spatial presence as actual artifacts. This correspondingly led in the first monograph to a clear-cut distinction between the built and the projected, with a focus on visually conveying the built works.

This second book project likewise explores the same mediatory dialogue, allowing us to not only reflect on our own works, processes, and methodologies but also leading to the question which approximations of reality, which intellectual perspectives and visual languages, could be interwoven in order to successfully do so.

Following on from the first volume, the aim of *Buchner Bründler Buildings II* is to elaborate this intention further. In a renewed joint effort with Ludovic Balland this led to an editorial dialogue, culminating in the devising of interpretive visual compositions.

The post-production processes were mainly chosen in order to provide a more in-depth representation of the characteristic features and conceptual catalysts of the respective individual architectural project. The examinations of the selected buildings from an external viewpoint expand the classic image sequences to form a dialogical principle.

The depiction of architecture is tied to composition and the momentum of time. The chosen methodology creates layers of association that establish a multitude of new interpretations.

Daniel Buchner, Andreas Bründler

Vertigo

Ludovic Balland

This second monograph on the work of Buchner Bründler Architekten has been designed and used as an editorial workshop. An editorial workshop that facilitates interpretation and evaluation of the existing photographic documentation of the buildings, encourages experimentation with various forms of text and photograph, and thus enables the development and production of exclusive new content and images.

Architectural monographs rarely involve the production of new visual material because they're usually retrospective, so the documentation's already been done. This documentation of the architecture often conforms to certain standard expectations: spaces have to be comprehensively presented and photographed from eye level, exterior views have to show as much of the building as possible, certain details of the facade are picked out—this is photography in the service of architecture.

A workshop is a space equipped with tools and machinery. It's a space that lets you spread things out, develop them, make mistakes, experiment. Essentially it's a creative space. It could also be called a drafting room. But unlike the digital drafting process, which generally has the aim of constructing the perfect embodiment of some future reality, in an editorial workshop the studies, experiments, and "intermediate spaces" of the design remain visible.

In the workshop set up for the production of this book we used various media as tools for experimenting and to shift the main focus onto the production of images. The resulting visual material was then used as a basis for retrospective analysis of the buildings, for reconsidering and reflecting on the architecture. This approach complemented and refined the editorial presentation of the individual projects, and before long the book had become an analytical tool that would accompany us throughout the editing process. Having foreknowledge of the image production allowed us to work independently of local conditions and remotely from the buildings. We see the resulting images as new lenses for reading the architecture.

Let's start with a fuller description of the tools in this workshop: drawings, photographs, plans, texts, models—the hardware. In a workshop you tend to see certain specific actions being carried out—first in a definite sequence, second in predefined places. In the process of laying out this project we tried to identify and define the sequence of media used in the making of each building. It soon became clear that the media used were usually deployed as follows:

Ⓐ CONCEPTION

| writing/texts | sketches/drawings | models/renderings | photo/video |

Ⓑ PLANNING

| material samples | models/renderings | working drawings/details | writing/texts |

Ⓒ CONSTRUCTION

| building materials | writing/texts | photo/video |

Ⓓ DOCUMENTATION

| writing/texts | illustrations | photo/video |

What's striking here is that the media employed in the conception phase Ⓐ are similar to those used for documentation Ⓓ. The intention is the same, so the sequence ends in much the same way it started. We understand this process figuratively as a spiral—a spiral of development.

The media in this sequence are directed toward specific objectives. In Ⓐ the image or text is an abstract idea, like a dream, a projection for the future users of the building. The planning phase Ⓑ is focused on continual refinements to the realizability of the project.

In a sense, Ⓐ and Ⓑ belong together because the building has not yet been built. If Ⓐ is the image of a dream, then the function of Ⓑ is perhaps that of a daydream. But the actions carried out during Ⓑ are actually a function of efficiency and numbers. Hardly a daydream. So how do Ⓐ and Ⓑ produce coherent images if they're so inherently contradictory? How do these opposed objectives come together to generate a singular vision? This formula tends to produce an impossible synthetic image—a conflict. Dreams, and perhaps also visions, are the result of actual experiences which, though we may have lived through them in reality, are edited by some inscrutable process in our minds and thus inscribed as narratives that are far from reality. Since this media spiral of development ends where it started, the media used must be mutually dependent and closely related. The sketches, plans, photographs, and working drawings have to be able to function and communicate together.

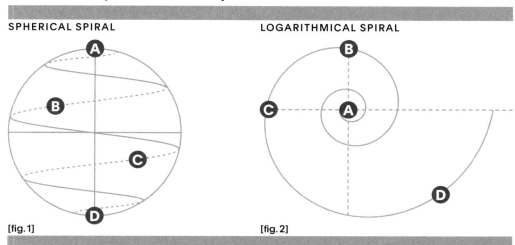

[fig. 1]   [fig. 2]

But there are different types of spiral. The "spherical spiral" [fig. 1] connects north and south; seen from above, these two extremities coincide in a point, which is a perfect analogy for the mutual dependence of media. The "logarithmical spiral" [fig. 2] moves ever further from the center, from its source. What would happen if phases Ⓐ, Ⓑ, and Ⓒ were to become detached from one another? Though all three phases lie on the same curve, the purpose of the built building needn't necessarily correspond to the source, the sketch, the original concept. As with the logarithmical spiral, which extends to infinity—vertigo. In our case the making of models and the ultimate construction of the building would have to be justified by the sketches and visions, not by the working drawings. Similarly, the images from phase Ⓓ on this generative infinity spiral—perhaps a utopian spiral—wouldn't have to reflect the reality of the images that have been sought and intimated in phase Ⓐ. These days the documentation phase Ⓓ, which usually consists of texts and photographs, often serves as a body of evidence.

Imagine for a moment what kind of architecture these various phases and their corresponding media might produce if they could somehow exist independently of one another on the same curve. The result would be a radical transformation. In a conversation published as *Pictures of Architecture: Architecture of Pictures*, Jacques Herzog described the need to find an alternative medium for thinking about and ultimately building architecture (at that point he wasn't in a position to participate in the architectural market) in these terms:

> While looking for alternatives, we came across video, which nobody was using in architecture at the time. Video images are interesting because they relate to real life. As in photography, their pictorial reality expresses things and acts that look real, so suddenly we found ourselves with a tool that would allow us to express our ideas on architecture in a contemporary form even without a concrete commission—and much more successfully than by using classical means of representation like models, plans and drawings.[1]

What we see in these stills from the film *Lego House*[2] by Herzog & de Meuron is not architecture. It's a storyline, a narrative. And in this sense, because it's a narrative, the visible architecture that we see in these stills of an interior is of no relevance.

Spirals of Development

Again, what would it be like if the discourse at the conception phase **Ⓐ** could be taken on its own terms? What if there was just a debate about the concept, a debate about the narrative, and ultimately a debate concentrating on the vision itself? Away from the numbers, away from working drawings and real economics. Imagine the color and candor that this sort of discussion might generate. Yet without being political, for politics has only one objective—power—whereas architecture's only objective is to build.

And what would it be like if planning and building could be considered on their own terms? What if they were able to operate independently of the architectural drawings while still adhering to the vision? Without wanting to please or appease the investors, without falling back into the untenable cycle of economic efficiency, instead reverting to the real possibilities of planning and building, to the real ecological and topological possibilities, and not least to the individual requirements of the inhabitants—as with the Quinta Monroy project, a housing estate for low-income families in Iquique, a Chilean port town bordering the Atacama Desert, erected by Alejandro Aravena between 2003 and 2004. Here the residential units were planned with an area of 70 square meters, but they were left half built so that the new residents could finish and extend them in line with their own requirements and financial means. These later additions gave the individual residents the opportunity to shape their own living spaces and thus helped to reinforce the connections between the people and their homes.

ELEMENTAL, Quinta Monroy, an incremental housing project, Iquique, Chile, 2004, photograph by Tadeuz Jalocha (above), photograph by Estudio Palma / Cristobal Palma (below)

On this spiral of development, then, how can the expression of an architectural idea maintain any distance from reality as represented and built? Is this exercise even possible in a society that's shaped by capital and apparently incapable of distancing itself from the dictates of efficiency? What modes of representation come close to reality anyway? In a book series entitled *Portraits*, the Swiss architectural practice Made In have attempted to analyze cityscapes not in terms of function and other measurable criteria but rather by showing, in the words of O. M. Ungers, a transcendental aspect, that of the idea upon which the actual design is based: "There are three levels of reality exposed: the factual reality—the object; the perceptual reality—the analogy; and the conceptual reality—the idea, shown as the plan—the image—the word."[3]

Even a brief retrospective view of architectural representation reveals the astonishing wealth of detail and precision expended, for instance on the theme of surface in the planning of St Peter's in Rome in Bramante's drawings.[4] Although the means of representation are limited to drawing, their quality and complexity creates an incredibly real representation of the unbuilt architecture. In the name of optimization, detailed visualizations such as these would ultimately be replaced—i.e. radically impoverished—by numbers and straight lines.

The remarkable thing about this spiral of development is that the object, once built, is generally represented and documented via the medium of photography, sometimes in drawings and illustrations, certainly also in writing. The spiral comes full circle. But what kind of images are these? How do they differ from the first images, those produced before the building was built? What do these new images communicate? What purpose do they serve? In this freefall of perception, where the finished building ends up bearing an uncanny resemblance to the renderings made before construction, it seems there's no longer any clearance or latitude, no intermediate space between dream and reality. Can we say the idea no longer exists if it perfectly matches the reality? Or is it the other way around? Where a building is the perfect realization of a sketch or a vision, as at Quinta Monroy, then we can say that architecture is no longer relevant; it's just an object, a space that becomes architecture by virtue of its inhabitants—and only though them—with each inhabiting it in their own way, in line with their own requirements and financial means.

Virtual Spaces

This is exactly where we want to pick up. With this dematerialization of architecture. Which begs some important questions: What sort of space do we live in? What kind of walls define it? Are they real or could the spaces also be virtual in our new age? Where does the virtual space lie in terms of our perception and our spiral of development?

The reality of the internet has created virtual spaces of action where power structures and visual relationships are subject to constantly changing mechanisms. How does the idea of space expand into digital channels? What are the visual codes and recording devices that come with this expansion? Since 2007, Google Maps has been using 3D cameras to photograph every street in the United States for its Street View service. Though the aim was to create a visual street directory from the perspective of the road user, the result is a catalog of commercial and residential spaces that now comprises more than 170 billion images and includes most of the buildings in the world.[5]

Similar levels of excess are evident in the way the internet represents the more intimate realm of interiors and private spaces. We've been using webcams to transmit stills and video ever since the 1990s. Initially these cameras were used externally, but with faster internet connections they were moved inside to our interior spaces: studios, places of work, private residences, and so on. Images of interior spaces and the people who inhabit them have multiplied exponentially and have now become a standard mode of communication.

My living space, which is closely connected to my person, dissolves and becomes interchangeable. It's become digital. With the pandemic and the global lockdown, digital space has taken on a new dimension, a new imperative. This little screen on my smartphone, now effectively an extension of my arm, is actually a potential meeting place. It allows me to escape solitude and confinement by establishing new digital connections and facilitating all manner of exchange and interaction. My living space and my social space are now equivalent to the dimensions of a 120 film (6 × 9 centimeters). The way we read and interpret these spaces has also completely changed: the museum—long understood as a stable and sacred space—has become accessible to all. The intimate private realm, having already been prized open by the webcam, is now expanding exponentially.

Is there anyone or anything that hasn't been photographed during the pandemic? Perhaps the public realm—which was suddenly empty. Like photographs from the American Wild West in the 1860s, devoid of human life and often also without architecture, our pictures of the public realm from the year 2020 are without people. It was as though everyone had just disappeared. We were so used to seeing the city full of people. But the people were still there—and just meters away, within the walls of their buildings.

Kurt Caviezel, *The USERS*, 2000–2020

Emilio Morenatti, Empty streets in Barcelona, 2020
John Vachon, "Abandoned Farmhouse, Ward County, North Dakota," 1940
William Bell, "Headlands North of the Colorada River Plateau," 1872, *Wheeler Survey*

Post-Construction

Back to our workshop and the permanent metamorphosis of representation, the creation of space, its agents, its residents, its destroyers. Structurally this book is divided into three main sections. The third main chapter, "Further Buildings and Projects," p. 405 presents various media from the development stages **Ⓐ** to **Ⓓ** from the Buchner Bründler archive, each of them given equal weight on the pages. The first two main chapters—"Workshop" p. 65 and "Selected Buildings" p. 167 act as a resonator between the architects' existing archive materials, from phase **Ⓓ** of the developmental spiral (documentary photography only), and the retrospective images we produced in the form of photograms, technical shots, portraits, model photography, and so on. The projects are edited in identical sequence in both chapters.

Let's now retrace our steps on the spiral of development. Starting with the built object and its various aspects, we set out to look for images that consciously keep their distance from the reality of the building and/or reinterpret that reality. Sometimes this brings us right back to **Ⓐ**, the first phase of the cycle, where the image represents just a fragment of some plausible reality. A place where many things are still unclear. A place where many things are still speculative. A place where the abstract nature of representation shows its real beauty and where accidents, multiple exposures, and superimpositions can happen. The medium of photography—also like the photocopy in the inquiry by Alexander Rosenkranz for the *Hotel Nomad* p. 74—enables precisely what architecture cannot do: the duplication of a motif. The already existing architecture, including its concepts, the surfaces, and spatial aspects, was an interpretational template with which we could adopt a specific mode of representing it.

Until we'd discovered and experimented with these specific modes of representation, our approach to each project was identical. It was a case of filtering out the essence of each building retrospectively. "Postmortem" was our working title. Retrospectively immersing yourself in the creative process is a complex task; between the original idea and its realization there are several intermediate stages that can sometimes demand purely pragmatic decisions out of necessity. The advantage of retrospectivity is being able to concentrate on essentials. Each of the fourteen buildings selected for comprehensive representation in this book was presented to us by the architects in the form of anecdotes, drawings, sketches, visualizations, and photographs. A distillation of the most relevant themes provided the basis for appropriate photographic treatment and for the selection of objects, material samples, models, and so on that would be required. The buildings existed, but in the workshop we were forced to work from memory. The theme of "retrospective design" may be trivial and technically anachronistic, but it was significant in that it produced the foundations that operated as our mode of investigation. Rediscover.

Imprints

The photogram technique is particularly well suited to visualizing space in the architectural context. On the one hand, the photographic paper serves as the site or the ground plan of the building. On the other, the photogram is an imprint of light and can be compared to a cast. All sorts of transparent surfaces can be pictured with a high degree of precision and in a way that captures the granulation of light at very high resolutions, as with the various glass finishes at the *Credit Suisse Headquarters* p. 93, p. 249.

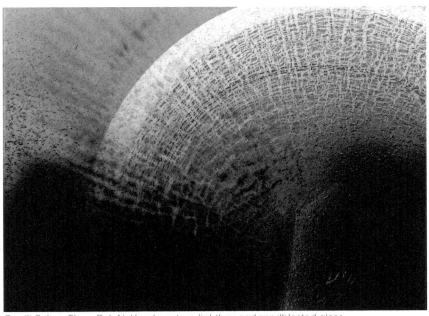

Credit Suisse Place Bel-Air Headquarters, lightbox and sandblasted glass,
Ludovic Balland, Annina Schepping, Hans-Jörg Walter, 2019

Lörrach House, layered Plexiglas, Annina Schepping and Hans-Jörg Walter, 2019

Missionsstrasse House, external walls of photographic paper, Annina Schepping and Hans-Jörg Walter, 2021

For the *Lörrach House* p. 103, p. 281 the different widths of the ground plan were simulated in sheets of Plexiglas then exposed on photographic paper. This enabled the visualization of spatial sequences and the creation of new spaces. For the *Missionsstrasse House* p. 155, p. 379 the external walls of an existing model (scale 1:33) were replaced with photographic paper. This experiment looked at the incidence of light on the interior and in the lightwells at two corners of the building—the architectural model as camera obscura.

Models

Designing and building a model is surely one of the easiest ways of generating space while minimizing expenditure of time and resources. Similarly, model photography is the most immediate and cost-effective means of capturing space. For our representation of the *Cherry Storehouse Nuglar* p. 143, p. 359, developed and realized in collaboration with Lilitt Bollinger, the construction of a model was used as a basis for explaining the development of the conversion. The architects used readily available materials to simulate and explain their scheme for the building. The material limitations and the spontaneity of the process ensured that the result was pared down to bare essentials. Here I think the interaction between the four hands was especially interesting—the way they respond to one another, the way they remove and reposition certain pieces of wood, constructing, amending, discussing. This series of photographs is a retrospective visualization of the building and its salient spatial features, but it also represents some of the personal interactions that took place during the decision-making process.

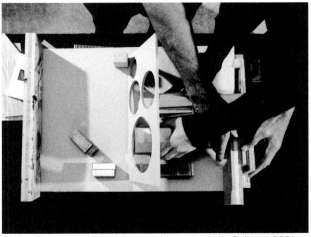

Cherry Storehouse Nuglar, assemblage, Ludovic Balland, 2021

Portraits

There were two projects for which the presence of the inhabitants was particularly important: the **Cooperative Building Stadterle** p. 107, p. 297 and especially the **Casa Mosogno** p. 120, p. 313. Having purchased a group of buildings in Mosogno, the new owners decided they wanted to preserve many of the objects that were found on site. These included countless wine bottles, wicker baskets, old tools, house keys, toys, and a confessional—a veritable miscellany of objects. First we took all these objects from the coach house and laid them out on the meadow in front of the main building. Then we sorted them according to size, function, and material—the sheer quantity was impressive. Having laid them all out we made a selection of what seemed the most significant objects. Lastly we placed the objects on a wall in the courtyard and photographed them individually. This wall above the local woods and the Isorno River, restored and extended by Buchner Bründler, served as our photographic studio. In some small way, these objects are connected to the building and the site. The light and the woods bear witness to the locality. The objects communicate their relationship to the house through the markings of use that they bear, through their geographically specific functions, through their colors and their age. The renovation was heavily influenced by the desire to visualize the history of the building, its uses, and its various inhabitants. And so the traces of this history are legible on the walls of the summer room. The photographed historical objects also bear witness; they prompt us to imagine them in their original places, in rooms that no longer exist.

The results of the various visualizations are like drafts—post-construction drafts. The requirement for an exact reconstruction of the rooms was quite irrelevant here. There were several visual accidents, bad exposures, inappropriate scales. In an age of readymade solutions, fast publishing, and rapid distribution, we're often confronted with nothing but the finished product. The creative process behind it usually goes unseen. And in these times, when the pandemic has fundamentally altered the way we read space and continues to call into question our received values about media, space, and society, we also need to question standard approaches to the visual representation

Casa Mosogno, inventory of everyday objects left behind by previous inhabitants, Ludovic Balland, 2020

of architecture. Architecture should no longer be regarded as an efficient, economical solution, as a product-oriented result. It ought to be a platform for research and experimentation into the way we want to read, write, and design space. Which creative spiral will we follow? The qualities of space aren't inherent in the representation of space; they depend on the imaginative resources than can be deployed to create them.

Spirals of Time

In the process of editing this publication we have always sought to foster retrospective understanding and critical dialogue. Sometimes, where architectural photography came up against its limits, new spatial sequences have come to light. Precise material photography has revealed new surfaces, new dimensions, a new sense of scale. A scale where you could quite plausibly be in the mountains, in the desert, or on the Moon.

The idea of taking a retrospective view of each project and its creative spiral in order to see and understand it differently had to be related to the site. Franziska Schürch, Isabel Koellreuter, and Oliver Schneider considered the history of the site of each new house and conversion from four different perspectives: *politics*, *economics*, *culture*, and *religion*. Depending on the information available, these four "interpretive lenses" were differently weighted. In some cases these journeys into the past went back a hundred years, in others it was more like a thousand. The scope of each investigation was determined by the events that shaped the history of the site. The motivation behind these studies was the desire to create a new context for understanding how each site evolved into what it is now—and to retrace our steps on the spiral of time.

---

[1] *Pictures of Architecture—Architecture of Pictures: A Conversation between Jaques Herzog and Jeff Wall,* moderated by Philip Ursprung (Vienna and New York, NY: Springer, 2004), 29.
[2] See ibid., 12. The film was a contribution to the exhibition *L'architectur est un jeu…magnifique,* Centre Georges Pompidou, Paris July 10 to August 26, 1985: film still.
[3] O. M. Ungers, "Morphologie: City Metaphors", in *Portraits 1: Airport Prison* (Zurich: Made in ETH, 2011), 29.
[4] See https://digi.ub.uni-heidelberg.de/diglit/serlio1544/0026 (accessed 8 Feb. 2022).
[5] See https://de.wikipedia.org/wiki/Google_Street_View#Verfügbarkeit (accessed 7 March 2022).

Vielfalt / Variety **Tibor Joanelly**

The catalog of works in this book has the quality of an atlas. It collects different projects, their common denominator perhaps being variety or multiplicity. Whereby "atlas" is actually the wrong word, because an atlas always collates items under a particular aspect, following particular criteria and intentions, and sets them in a particular context. Here, on the other hand, the presentation of the projects reminds one more of a kind of cabinet of curiosities in which the large and the small, old and new, the strange and the familiar directly encounter each other. This is not unlike the example of the famous (and perhaps also in an architectural context already somewhat overly quoted) classification of things by Jorge Luis Borges. In it, widely disparate things are brought together in a "logical" framework. In the adaptation of a "certain Chinese encyclopedia" animals are grouped, according to Borges, as follows:

> (a) those that belong to the Emperor, (b) embalmed ones, (c) those that are trained, (d) suckling pigs, (e) mermaids, (f) fabulous ones, (g) stray dogs, (h) those that are included in this classification, (i) those that are trembling as if they were mad, (j) innumerable ones, (k) those drawn with a very fine camel's hair brush, (l) others, (m) those that have just broken a flower vase, (n) those that resemble flies from a distance.[1]

This juxtaposition of unequal species and the overlapping of categories are typical for architectural design. Borges' enumeration contains everything that makes a design what it is: possession, status, culture, science, organisms, things, events, and myths. Behind such an assemblage of dissimilarities there *must* be a sort of designing hand, a discerning authorship. If, in the case of this quoted cosmos, it is unclear who or what guided the designing pen—"the Emperor of China"—this becomes all the more naturally evident in the case of a monograph. Foremost the monograph designs the work.

In fact designers trace a sort of map in their minds based on the existing and imagined material, and the atlas supplies precisely something like a survey—

also for those outside the minds of Daniel Buchner and Andreas Bründler and their co-workers. What this book makes accessible is a kind of open cabinet.

Viel-Faltungen / Multi-foldings

The word "*Vielfalt*" (variety), which Andreas Bründler uses again and again, has an ontological aspect, in other words something that talks directly to the existence of architecture.

Besides the mostly emphatic "*Viel*" (many), representing a collection of widely differing things, is also a "*Falten*" (folding), which more points to the manner in which—the how—something gets collected. This becomes all the more apparent when one—precisely because it perhaps sounds strange to a German (not an English) reader—associates this with the French word "*multiplicité.*" *Multiplicité* is closely tied to "multiply," and with this to the Latin *multiplicāre/multiplex*, also giving it something in the sense of "manifold," and thus corresponding to *plicāre, plectere (plexum)*, i.e. "to fold, fold up, intertwine."[2]

In short: to design is to fold. Or to be even more exact: fold up. In certain respects this statement is naturally trivial, because as a matter of fact every design—however modest the task—is about reconciling various things. And this is achieved by making things smaller, hence for example by folding them up—as in a magician's trick with a magic hat.[3]

The metaphor of folding, for instance a towel or a piece of paper, has a profound resonance: it describes an absolutely archaic action. And regarding philosophy—with an aside to mathematics—it also describes very clearly what happens in the process. The French philosopher Michel Serres uses the metaphor of a folded handkerchief to explain his concept of topology. Topology is the "doctrine of the position and arrangement of geometric entities in space," which due to its abstractness has to date remained a little-tapped mathematical seam for architecture. Thus Serres:

> If you take a handkerchief and spread it out in order to iron it, you can see in it certain [two-dimensional] fixed distances and proximities. If you sketch a circle in one area, you can make out nearby points and measure far-off distances. Then take the same handkerchief and [fold or] crumple

it, by putting it in your pocket. Two distant points are suddenly close, even superimposed. If, further, you tear it in certain places, two points that were close together can become very distant. This science of nearness and rifts is called topology....[4] Accordingly an architectural design can be seen as a topological manipulation in which various things are positioned in a new context, in new proximity: far-away materials are "folded into" the construction (the rift is not the topic here), and in the process they possibly touch but do not coalesce. (To be exact, the process of design also requires mediated objects "between the folds" of the handkerchief. This becomes lucid for example with constructional connections, such as nodes, which either rely on mediating structural elements, or the structural elements are modified so that they fit together.[5]) Just like constructional elements and materials, rooms too—as well as memories, ideas, concepts, and images—are folded into each other via conscious actions and thus brought into proximity with each other, making construction also similar to philosophizing. In the process of designing, through assembling variety in the anticipated architectural object, things are relocated, they are given new meaning.

Garden

The assembling of images likewise implies the visual quality of this invested meaning. And when this concerns the image of the surroundings, the visual sense that orientates itself on it, then the metaphor of the landscape-designed garden is close at hand. Andreas Bründler points directly to such a reference when, for example, discussing the **Missionsstrasse House** p.155, p.379 conversion. Here the architects joined the two separate

N° 260   Missionsstrasse House

parts of the former carriage-house by means of a building-high circular cut-out in the fire-protection wall, fully in the style of the artist Gordon Matta-Clarke. The space itself is enriched by numerous interventions, and based on the varying perspectives and impressions of depth the result can indeed be described as architecture designed as landscaped or even "gardened."

Like landscape pictures, quite often landscaped gardens are structured as visual spaces, with the actual landscape space emerging between the foreground and the background as in a theater. Like in stage design, in the designed landscape space the process of participation situates the viewer, virtually or latently, in the progression of a potential action; while in tracing the structures of the foreground and background, the eye performs the work of the actual body moving *transversally* through the space.[6]

What is "produced" in a landscape picture, respectively in a designed landscape space, as a stage-scenery-like graduation and spatial delineation using bushes, planted borders, and trees, can be effected in architecture using corresponding architectural objects—through load-bearing structures, fittings and fixtures and furniture, vertical and horizontal lines—all of which adjust the space to a certain degree and around which the viewer's gaze seeks its way into the depths. The greater, the more opulently and intelligently these things are composed, the more the spatial feeling is accentuated.

In the aforementioned conversion, this effect of depth and space is heightened almost to an extreme. Here not only the new binding joists and the remnants of the erstwhile firewall between the two parts of the building define a type of primary spatial-visual frame (an effect that is above all generated by the "encroachment" of the remaining wall sections to the left and right at the spatial edges), but moreover the fragments of the firewall mark a sort of middle between the side facade facing the garden and the functional volume next to the entrance. And in the center of the space thus spanned also "hangs" the chimney, and with it a virtual spherical spatial volume is delineated and suggested by the round "cut-out" in the firewall.

Through the direct perception of this virtual sphere—this author was reminded of the spatial perception experienced on entering the Pantheon in Rome—

numerous things happen, as if in a private garden, and much more than outside in the real garden.

The living space presents itself as an opulent visual overlapping, condensation, and staging of architectural elements. This type of visual enrichment does indeed have an equivalent in the history of landscape architecture, not least in connection with the remodeling or "improvement" of landscaped gardens. In his *Red Books*, the English landscape gardener Humphry Repton (1752–1818) developed a type of documentary technique with which he could persuade his clients to undertake the improvements that he saw as aesthetically necessary.[7] This happened by showing the situation before and after the intervention, often in the form of *foldout* images, giving the presentation and the subsequent studying of the projects by the client a playful aspect.

These improvements also went hand in hand with a perceptual intensification, whereby Repton's work resembled a process of precisioning, touching up, and enhancement by adding new elements—for instance plant borders or even a pond or a bridge—or the subtraction of existing structures in order to reveal things that were hidden, such as a distant church spire. The upshots of his interventions were always a reinforcement of spatial ambience, a sort of spatial ladder, the steps of which were intended to lead to the foreground or the background.

Compositions

In this context one could also speak of the composing of landscape pictures. Design as composing against the backdrop of the existing is thus also symbolic for the work of Buchner Bründler, including in an ontological sense. "Composition" ultimately also means that something first emerges through the act of addition, whereby at a material level it is crucial that one operates in full knowledge of the specific visual impacts that things have. In the act of composing, as it is meant here, pre-existing or new structures—walls, concrete beams, steel supports, wooden beams and fittings—all find expression as what they are, and only coalesce through the act of assembly in a temporal process. As in a drawing, which, seen as a material object, above all mediates the traces of the drawn narration. (Or as in this text, assembled out of a sum of smaller episodes and sections, all of them with their own declarations and up to now leading independent existences.) In that very process, authorship emerges not from a transcendental, somehow authoritarian, and permanently subject-centered concept, but rather far more out of an inner necessity in the composition—out of the things that are joined, out of their potential to mutually connect with each other.

The buildings shown in this book recognizably belong to Buchner Bründler, but nevertheless in their variety they always mirror the diversity of the assemblages and the backgrounds from which they emerge.

Authorship

When we talk about authorship, it becomes necessary to delve a little into architectural history. Architectural theory has wrestled with the term since the 1960s, and even today it is never clear what the status of the relationship between works, designers, and the collective is.

Actually it is astonishing that authorship largely failed to play a role in the linguistic turn in architecture in the 1970s, or for that matter was in fact suppressed in favor of a whatever kind of collective subject. One reason perhaps lies in Roland Barthes' 1968 verdict of the "death of the author," given in a critique of literary criticism and coupled with a message that could ultimately be politically understood and exploited.[8] Barthes denied literature (read: architecture) the prevailing personification that made language (and building) a closed system orbiting around the author. Authorship, so the inference, was the suppressed or repressed other in the linguistic turn, which in the twilight of postmodernism examined the sign and put it center-stage.[9] (Perhaps this was precisely the reason that for example Aldo Rossi turned away from semiotics in the early 1980s, and with his *Scientific Autobiography* began to search for design contentment in *both* his own experience *and* archetypical images.[10])

But authors were never dead. What Barthes describes with the term "modes of writing" as an abstract, self-referential, non-authorship-dependent system (and which was then correspondingly adopted as such) in fact possesses, in literature but to a far greater extent in architecture, an unequivocal personal signature.[11] This equally applies when the artistic object can be deconstructed independently of authorship.

Something similar pertains when we talk about architecture: as Barthes argued—and here the author of this text is in total agreement—criticism is in literature, as it is in architecture, an anamorphosis of the work,[12] i.e. a cleverly arranged projection: in architecture from the medium of space to that of language.

It is therefore always interesting to listen carefully when architects speak about their *own* work, because their phrases and words shed light on a highly individual linguistic character of their own architecture. The author of these lines is convinced that parallels exist between speaking and designing, and this even more so when building, as with Buchner Bründler, has discovered its own language that points far beyond the realm of the spoken— a (in an ideal sense) self-referential language of an individual architecture that reshapes the actions and thinking of a whole office, of an entire work.

When Daniel Buchner therefore refers, for example, to layerings and intertwinings, then this initially serves as a description of that which is visible and touchable in their own work. But it also implies a type of fundamental purpose, an intention that lies behind many design endeavors and is then actually materialized in the buildings. The two words "layerings" and "intertwinings" represent a kind of fundamental feeling for their own architecture, a tonality that primes everything.

If one elaborates this idea further, what quickly becomes illuminated behind both words is variety, a feeling for space more involving multiplication and addition than subtraction or abstraction—an accumulation and proliferation of spatially effective elements, which in their entirety allow something akin to depth to arise. This becomes manifestly clear for instance in the grid- or lattice-like roof structures in the **Kirschgarten House** [p.138, p.343] in Binningen,

N° 224 Kirschgarten House

its roof aprons framing the field of vision and "materializing" the space, but equally in many other projects in which elements (mostly load-bearing ones) are segmented, divided, dispersed, and then consolidated again. The twin columns on the exterior walkway of the **Cooperative Building Stadterle** p.107, p.297 ultimately likewise fit this context.

When experiencing it, this kind of (one could say mannerist or ornamental) entrée to phenomenal space excites a direct feeling in the viewer that he or she is bodily encapsulated in, perhaps slightly like in a well-tended garden when one moves close to and back and forth between various shrubs, flowers, and trees. The tableau that surrounds a *transversally* moving person encompasses that person. The space literally unfolds around or around about that person, or to again express it differently it is unfurled through movement and contemplation. That the intensity of this reciprocal effect is reinforced by "layerings" and "interwinings," that in the process material quality is directly transformed into spatial quality, is an explicitly intended corollary.

What is interesting in this context is that this spatial feeling can be "objectified" with reference to a specific creative period in the career of the Basle artist Thomas Hauri. It arose in 2011 as the thematic background to his work, and naturally Buchner Bründler have critically looked at Hauri's work. However, the great difference between painterly and architectural space lies in the distance of, respectively, the immersion in that which is experienced. Whereas Hauri's pictures, in contrast to their very animated and warm application of paint and color scheme, appear cold and abstract (and here the echoes of Malevich's or El Lissitzky's compositions), so Buchner Bründler's spaces appear more warm, despite the cold concrete, and encapsulating in the sense described above.

N° 205   Cooperative Building Stadterle

N° 147   Hertenstein House

How? Because the linguistic character of Buchner Bründler's spaces is, as intimated, highly personal, personalized too, and despite this remain comprehensible, legible, and transparent.

And nonetheless the space exceeds the language. It also shows that the semioticians of the 1970s were wrong: the architectural signs created by Buchner Bründler are so ambiguous and multi-layered that the word "sign" becomes practically redundant. The design, the space—"it"—proliferates, elaborates itself, evolves in the sense of "unfolding"; "it" generates itself out of itself (from the hands of the architects and their co-workers and the project participants, the wishes and needs of the client, the strictures of the building regulations, etc.).

Concrete

One of the important signatures of authorship for Buchner Bründler is exposed concrete—at least to date. Reinforced concrete is a strange building material: unlike say wood, it has no intrinsic form, and the form scope in its fabrication and finishing are too open to talk of a specific substance that assists in lending appearance. From thinly stretched shells to massive beams, concrete can perform any task. Buchner Bründler have applied the material in almost all of their projects, making it, by analogy, also into a supporting material for their work. In so doing they have not formally adhered to any single lineage in the rich tradition of concrete processing, although some projects follow their own, inherently formal criteria that the architects have always refined into an individual type of syntax.

But one theme would appear to have been followed more persistently for some time now: concrete, cast in the form of sculpted beams, such as in the **Hertenstein House** [p. 86, p. 235] (which has an identifiable predecessor in the private residence in Binningen from 2009) or indeed the house in Kirschgarten from 2018.

In these projects, the often freely suspended beams fuse monolithically into a grid or a web, which as said possesses a spatial impact. Unlike timber constructions, and similarly to the Brutalist formalisms of Le Corbusier or Kenzo Tange, this involves the outright celebration of a type of isomorphism, i.e. a sameness of form that highlights the continuity of material and space (a characteristic that also applies to "more straightforward" concrete buildings in which, for instance, exposed concrete walls encase fluid rooms).

To a certain extent this sort of isomorphism is an antithesis to the already mentioned motif of variety, although it simultaneously reaffirms the many-folded: one and the same material can adopt the most contrasting forms without really altering its substance.

In fact isomorphic design also allows the problem of architectural space to be formulated abstractly— as neatly demonstrated in the **Lörrach House** p.103, p.281, which is actually a "Räumling" (a space piece)[13]—for example as methodologically pursued by the Japanese architect Kazuo Shinohara in the houses during his short "second style."[14] However, in Buchner Bründler's buildings this isomorphic frame is always reshaped by further themes and raw materials, such as wood or glass, creating in turn an impression of variety.

Having said this, as a pure building material reinforced concrete has fallen out of fashion in terms of its poor sustainability performance. And in this context, above all two other projects provide clear insights into the relation between the parts and their whole, perhaps even providing a vision of the future: the Stadterle and the conversion of the **Cherry Storehouse Nuglar** p.143, p.359, the latter in collaboration with Lilitt Bollinger. In both buildings the architectural language is, in the actual sense of the word, elementary: their building elements are divorced from one another and "merely" joined by screws and the like. Via the assembled material, the spatial opulence is in reality heightened, likewise appearing as a construction in an ontological sense.

The two design trajectories sketched out here— isomorphism and construction—represent two basically different design approaches. In the case of Buchner

N° 179 Lörrach House

N° 249 Cherry Storehouse Nuglar

N° 212 Münchenstein House

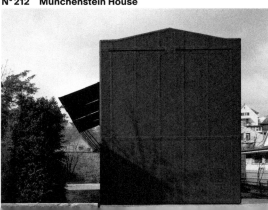

Bründler, both of them result in a similar spatial variety or opulence, sometimes unexpectedly or even reciprocally in the sense of the postulated dichotomy. Some of the timber buildings (and timber buildings are genuinely constructed), for instance the **Münchenstein House** p. 132, p. 329 or the **Tièchestrasse Housing Development** p. 80, p. 217 in Zurich, instead seem to be more "joined" in an isomorphic sense: constructional joints are suppressed and not visible; the relief or the figure of the facades reveals nothing about the way in which they are made; and nonetheless, aesthetically the buildings adhere to the principle of variety.

And vice-versa there are buildings composed of individual elements and that yet still entail isomorphisms. Thus the **Casa Mosogno** p. 120, p. 313 follows a "constructional" logic of individual things, and even the concrete is elementarily treated in the sense of its object character: a roof fascia (out of which nonetheless a spout "grows"), the staircase as an isomorphic sculptural object, a bench, the flue of the fireplace. These things are counterpointed in isolation and reinforced by a gigantic, resolutely constructed steel frame that bears the quarry stones of the chimney flue and the corrugated iron roof.

Social Sculpture

Foldings, compositions. Perhaps it has to do with the times, perhaps with the current interests of the essay's author in the correlations between architectural and social aesthetics, but in Buchner Bründler's work the design practices, understood in the widest sense, also, or especially, shine a light on social sculpture, as emerged for example via the negotiation processes in the Stadterle housing cooperative.

From an anthropological perspective, aesthetic and social practices can indeed be equated, based on

N° 123 Tièchestrasse Housing Development   N° 207 Casa Mosogno

the premise that the processes of aesthetic and social configuration are similar. Both domains are rooted in composition as a highly typical form of human action. Composition means assembling the existing things together with vocations and aligning them with each other, without them thereby loosing their identity. The more recent use of what is a term from the field of art to also apply to social, or to be more precise social-objective assemblages—above all by the French sociologist of technology and science Bruno Latour[15]—emphatically draws attention to the fact that the aesthetic and the social are structurally interconnected in the sense that the aesthetic is molded by social practices and the social through material and aesthetic things in equal measure.

It is therefore logical, both in architectural design and in social dealings, to assemble all these things "on the table," spread them out, sift through them, and to weave them together through active effort into an evident framework—just as with the "certain Chinese encyclopedia" cited to begin with.

Under the aspect of variety dealt with here, these observations suggest taking a somewhat more precise look at one particular term, as mentioned to the author by a sociologist, namely "social planning."[16] This somewhat fraught term means the production and combination of the material and the social, and has historical models in architecture as well. Alone the scale and social composition of Charles Fourier's *Phalanstère* in the early 19th century was based on a precise calculation of variety: the 1,620 inhabitants were to be selected so that they not only could provide the required professional and social basis for autonomous and self-administered undertakings, rather they were moreover meant to represent society as a whole.

Needless to say the Stadterle housing cooperative is worlds away from any such static, socio-technical notions. Instead, variety and individuality—as clearly manifested in the colorful mix of furniture on the walkway galleries—were ultimately constitutive elements for the cooperative and were incorporated right from the beginnings in the founding and project processes, only to then flourish in long and multifaceted negotiations. In this the architectural project and its authors played a catalyst function.

The architectural form of the Stadterle—the specific type of livable open-air walkways, its industrial-image materialization, the systematized and shelf-like architectural language—reacts programmatically, and above all also in terms of content, to the lived variety of the cooperative, albeit it in a very architectural way. The building is thoroughly aestheticized, architecturally controlled and saturated, thus forming a vis-à-vis to the ups and downs of the lives housed here, yet at the same time emerging from them, connected to them.

No wonder that seen from outside the Stadterle appears as a vessel, as the embodiment and staging of the exuberant lives lived within it. During the design process, its co-evolving form reproduced the social in a type of projective mimesis, as an anticipatory metamorphosis of the topos of variety discussed here.

Stealth

Perhaps this is also a similar correspondence discoverable between the work and authorship of Daniel Buchner and Andreas Bründler. At a personal level, the author of this text met both of them at an early stage on his path as a critic and their path as architects, namely when he was asked to write about one of their first projects. In order to describe the multifaceted massing of the vertical extension of an existing house in Lupsingen, the author strove to make an analogy with an (at the time ulta-modern) US Stealth combat aircraft. This hit a chord with the architects, and the intention of the text was to make an association with the "surreptitious," non-conformist lifestyle of the clients.[17] But secretly, the current author also saw an equivalence in the impression made by the two young architects—dressed in black hip hop clothes—and with it to a lifestyle that clearly deviated from the norm amongst creative architects at the time. This otherness indicated wide-ranging interests beyond the horizon of the drawing board, ones that the architects still follow: music making, cycling, kite surfing, motorbike maintenance ….[18]

If this text started by mentioning an atlas at the same time as querying the principle behind its collation, and because the catalog of works in this book simply follows a time and not a content narrative, nonetheless the presentation of any works adheres to undisclosed selection and classification criteria. Undetected and unconsciously, curating ones own oeuvre follows the architects' own interests and preferences—but also indirectly the decisions made by clients and other project participants. In the process, the definitions set by Ludovic Balland regarding design *and* content that contribute to the form of this book assume a similar *explicating* task as this text does: it is about finding pictures for a non-linguistic background. The author of this text has talked about the design of gardens or "social composing" in housing cooperativess—the impulse for these ideas came during numerous discussions with Andreas Bründler and Daniel Buchner at their office table and on the move while viewing the buildings. The clue to the question of the architects' intentions that was pursued came from the repeated mention of words such as "variety," "layerings," and "intertwinings"—words that the current writer recognized as a continuous endeavor behind their works. Ultimately these terms were fortified by the facticity of the works: one building speaks a language of depth of color, another of interwoven rooms, of condensed horizontal and vertical lines in space, or yet another of the accumulated objects of those who use it. All of these are traces of variety and breadth—generated from the endeavor to fold the manifold things of this world topologically into what is in the last resort an aesthetic composition and into new contextual meanings.

1   Jorge Luis Borges, "The Analytical Language of John Wilkins," in *Other Inquisitions*, trans. Ruth L.C. Simms (Austin, TX: University of Texas Press, 1964), 101–105, here 103.
2   See *Kluge: Etymologisches Wörterbuch der deutschen Sprache* (Berlin/New York: De Gruyter, 2002), 636.
3   This leaves aside both the idea that a design can magically unfold a whole world and that a design miniaturizes the world, neither of which are followed up on here.
4   Michel Serres with Bruno Latour, *Conversations on Science, Culture, and Time*, trans. Roxanne Lapidus (Ann Arbor, MI: University of Michigan Press, 1995), 60.
5   See "Fügen in Holz," *werk, bauen + wohnen* 5 (2019), whole issue.
6   The word "transversal" originates from the essay *Proust and Signs* by Gilles Deleuze, first published in French in 1964, and plays an important part in the work of the Japanese architect Kazuo Shinohara (1925–2006). See Tibor Joanelly, *Shinoharistics: An Essay About a House* (Zurich: Kommode Verlag, 2020).
7   The author's thanks go to Albert Kirchengast for this information.
8   Roland Barthes, "The Death of the Author," in *Image – Music –Text*, trans. Stephen Heath (New York, NY: Farrar, Straus and Giroux, 1977), 142–48.
9   See Bruno Reichlin and Fabio Reinhart, "Die Aussage der Architektur: Werk-Umfrage über Architektur und Semiotik – Teil 1," *werk* 4 (1972): *Was bedeutet Architektur?*, 242–55; "Die Aussage der Architektur: Werk-Umfrage über Architektur und Semiotik – Teil 2," *werk* 6 (1972), 384–85.
10   Aldo Rossi, *A Scientific Autobiography*, trans. Lawrence Venuti (Cambridge, MA: MIT Press, 1982).
11   See Roland Barthes, *Writing Degree Zero*, trans. Annette Lavers and Colin Smith (Farrar, Straus and Giroux, 1968).
12   See Roland Barthes, *Criticism and Truth*, ed. and trans. Katrine Pilcher Keuneman (London and New York, NY: Continuum, 2007), 32.
13   The term was coined by Andrea Deplazes. See Heinz Wirz (ed.), "Räumlinge: Valentin Bearth & Andrea Deplazes," *De Aedibus* 1 (1999).

14   This refers to the buildings created from 1970 to 1974, characterized by an extremely enhanced abstract spatial character. Similarly to Picasso, Kazuo Shinohara divided his own work into four periods, which he called "styles." See *werk, bauen + wohnen* 12 (2015): *Kazuo Shinohara*. Andrea Deplazes asked his students to analyse one of these houses, the House in Higashi-Tamagawa, as an assignment.

15   See Bruno Latour, "Ein Versuch, das 'Kompositionistische Manifest' zu schreiben," Munich, 2010, online under http://www.heise.de/tp/artikel/32/32069/1.html (accessed August 18, 2021).

16   This information about the relation between social composition and "social planning" was kindly mentioned in a discussion with Christina Schumacher.

17   Tibor Joanelly, "Regelmässig arbiträr," *werk, bauen + wohnen* 6 (2001), 52–53.

18   In Daniel Buchner's explanations some of these activities can be seen as characterizations of their own work: "making music means discovering sound forms and shaping them, the key thing in doing it being the performing—outwardly, but also inwardly, the act of sharing." With motorbikes the thing that interests him is the archaic mechanics and engineering, "and then obviously experiencing this crazy momentum, being exposed."
As in architecture and in music, the feeling of imminence is counterpoised by the possibility to "perform," to find the really good line. This "manual skill" aspect is also apparent in its extreme form in kite surfing: according to Buchner it is "likewise a balancing act, a permanent improvement, practice; it requires untiring patience. You come ever closer to attaining your own potential perfection, and at the same time you push the challenge level onward. A kite is a *bundle* of energies, it generates huge forces that you strain yourself to shape into controlled dynamics."

F&A—A Few Fantasies, A Few Aberrations

Urs Stahel

I

What would have become of photography without architecture? What, for that matter, architecture without photography? Both are purely fictitious questions, naturally, because the connection was and is amazingly strong. But perhaps they are enlightening, or at least entertaining questions? We'll see. But first, very slowly, let's begin at the beginning.

What quickly becomes apparent is that architecture acted, so to say, as the toddler's walking frame for photography. The first known photograph in photographic history was created in 1826 on a windowsill. It shows what Nicéphore Niépce saw from the window of his study in the country manor Le Gras, and was taken with an exposure time of around eight hours on a format of 16.5 × 21 centimeters. To achieve this, Niépce used a camera obscura and a coating of light-sensitive asphalt as a chemical substance. He called the technique heliography.

And then? What happened next? The first picture by Louis Jacques Mandé Daguerre, the inventor of the daguerreotype, the charmingly original and non-copyable small metal plate, mostly encased in richly colored velvet, showing a view of the Boulevard du Temple in Paris. What we recognize are houses and a street lined by rows of trees. And other than that? Nothing. Wait, yes: a single person with his foot resting on some sort of water-pump and apparently taking a rest. The picture appears as if it was taken in the early morning, the streets almost entirely empty. But that would be mistaken. Due to the long exposure time, anything moving failed to engrain itself on the light-sensitive layer, so that qua time and speed were simply overlooked or erased.

For his part, William Henry Fox Talbot, in his first negative-to-positive process, the calyotype or talbotype (which later, as a principle, dominated photography until digitization), had a penchant for house facades, with a leaning ladder stretching up to the first story, or with a besom in front of an open barn door. Magical stasis, as if it were siesta time. Finally Maxime du Camp, who in 1852 captured the Great Sphinx and the Pyramids of Giza on behalf of the French government, unperturbed in themselves and reposing in an architectural garden laid out in time immemorial and forever more, in the garden of the giants.

Yes, photography and architecture! Architecture and photography! Motionless, sculptural architecture gave the infant pictorial technique a helping hand in taking its first faltering steps. Completely unequivocally. Architectures simply stood there, without whining, without complaining. They were far more concrete than the landscapes disappearing into the horizon, above which the passing clouds would practically rub out the sky in the photographic coating. They allow things to be approached, stepped back from, a frontal or side view, elevations, bird's-eye views—only for X-ray views it was still a couple of decades too early. Light and shadow were so sharp that the verisimilitude of 3D, of volumes, diffused across the flat negative or positive. Architecture, building volumes, geometrical brick piles helped photography step-by-step to find its footing. They provided the pretense that everything would turn out right with this new pictorial technique, even if it was a little too slow to begin with, and it still appeared pretty amorphous.

Otherwise, for quite a while, prospects would have looked rather dim for photography. Perhaps the principle would have even become forgotten, it could be speculated, because other than mistiness, blurriness, and emptiness, to begin with nothing would have remained. What is sure is that it would never have come to the unbelievable act that the French state purchased the principle from Daguerre, granted him a lifelong appanage, and then gifted it to the world: free of charge, non-copyrighted, but also minus any guarantee, just like that, so that it could spread around the world as quickly as possible—in an unsurpassable triumphal procession, as we now know today.

And architecture, what about it? It certainly didn't have to worry about an existential crisis. A building is a building, and such a great existential necessity—either for habitation, commerce, or manufacturing—that it would have emerged with or without pictorial representation. That's how easy things are sometimes, at least at the first stage of existence. But then they very quickly became/become considerably more complicated, also in its case.

It's absurd, I'll admit, but I always have the feeling that, in parallel to image creation, architecture in the last 150 to 200 years has become all the more tenuous, thin-skinned, fragile, transparent. The longer the thinner, the thinner the more figurative, the more figurative the more transparent. No thick, solid walls any more, instead glass and steel as construction materials. No squatness, nothing stooped any more, rather an upright gait, and upright stance. Skinny, elongated, thin-skinned, like the demands of fashion, the dictates of capital. Maximum allure, maximum utilization. Nowadays architecture is so much an image that we're all familiar with it even without ever having seen it. So much an image that it is snatched up at first glance, at the first amount, without ever having even stepped inside it. So persistently and so much an image that it can also have long been torn down again. Didn't something used to stand here on the corner? Architectural photography, it appears, has jostled its way itself, bit by bit, to usurp the building and the idea of simple use; has swaddled it, lulled it. The current state of affairs can be clearly pinpointed: There is architecture and the image of architecture. Two intoxicating realities, two different ontological modes. Reality 1 and Reality 2. And amazingly we nowadays often read both of them as screens.

II

Back to the beginning again, but askew. What is this actually all about?

In fact architecture and photography could hardly be further apart from one another. On the one side a real, palpable, tangible, built space which one can look into, walk into, which one can perambulate. We see it, touch it, feel it, and enter it. By entering it, we also occupy it, we are inside it, stretch ourselves out, put it to use, own it, "contaminate" it. Our whole body, our being, reacts to the space, smells the still-fresh concrete, the coating of the parquet; our hands stroke across the surfaces of the still-bare, dewy materials, tear off the rustling protective film; we hear the echo of our steps, the clanging, soft or muffled echo of sounds, of movements. Our bodies, our motions, invigorate the architectural mass, they consummate its intention to provide us with shelter and scope. Scope for living, scope for working; space to relax, space to regenerate; school rooms, research, healing, or festive rooms. It is there, stands there, graspable, immoveable, for ages.

In today's world we'd also say: analog, concrete, regardless of whatever digital techniques were used to draw and develop it.

On the other side is photography. Divided, for quite some time now, between analog and digital. Since the first birth pangs of its invention, an almost immaterial "thing," flat, level, transparent, a glass plate, a film sheet, a film roll, a paper sheet, nowadays a data volume, which unfolds itself colorfully and illuminated from behind on our screens. Photography seems so immaterial that Oliver Wendell Holmes, the Boston physician, lawyer, writer, already wrote, with futuristic extravagance, in 1859:

> Form is henceforth divorced from matter. In fact, matter as a visible object is of no great use any longer, except as the mould on which form is shaped. Give us a few negatives of a thing worth seeing, taken from different points of view, and that is all we want of it. Pull it down or burn it up, if you please. We must, perhaps, sacrifice some luxury in the loss of color; but form and light and shade are the great things.... [1]

He describes photography not as form and material, rather as pure form—banished onto a negligibly thin medium. In his extravagant fantasy the material world can subsequently be dispensed with.

Here, therefore, material *and* form; and there, form *minus* material. The contradistinction couldn't be expressed more pointedly: Ontologically, architecture and photography are two entirely different planets. And nonetheless they are closely connected to each other; that we know, that we've understood earlier here; namely intimately and multiply. Holmes himself writes:

> There is only one Coliseum or Pantheon; but how many millions of potential negatives have they shed,—representatives of billions of pictures,—since they were erected! Matter in large masses must always be fixed and dear; form is cheap and transportable. We have got the fruit of creation now, and need not trouble ourselves with the core. [2]

Unbelievable what the guy had already formulated as early as 1859! Even then—photography was just twenty years old—there were apparently millions of negatives of the Coliseum and the Pantheon as the basis for billions of images, so how many more of them are there today, printed and digital, whizzing around the globe in the age of multimedia, the replica, as Jean Baudrillard formulated it, in the "*Simulationsmoderne*", the era of simulation.

Baudrillard understood society as being totally saturated, compounded, determined by media: "Everywhere socialization is measured by the exposure to media messages. Whoever is underexposed to media is desocialized or virtually asocial."[3] And more pithily in the shorthand diction of Michael Wetzel, a Baudrillard connoisseur:

> The world becomes *the cause* of its photographic and cinematic reproduction, and the images from around the whole world supplant the image of the world. One could say: image-being acquires a primacy over being. New medias and computer technologies have catapulted us into this zone of indifference between being and appearance, reality and image. The world of the simulacra absorbs appearance and liquidates the real.[4]

This reads, precisely 130 years later, as radically as if it were a later version of Oliver Wendell Holmes, simply with a slightly more theoretically declension. The images from around the whole world supplant the image of the world, and simultaneously eradicate the real!

Despite their opposing natures, there are obviously relationships between them, including painful ones. On this, once again Oliver Wendell Holmes: "Every conceivable object of Nature and Art will soon scale off its surface for us. Men will hunt all curious, beautiful, grand objects, as they hunt cattle in South America, for their skins, and leave the carcasses as of little worth."[5] Here Holmes describes—*avant la lettre*—with what unbelievable energy we will smother the world of the real, of material, with a world of images, how we will plaster our planet with images as if we wanted to practically shrink-wrap it in an overlay of pictures, how with time we will also accord depictions more value than the depicted, how the image finally divorces itself from its object and obtains it own unique significance. His comparison with the hunt for skins, with skinning, with flaying the skin off its object, and throwing away the cadaver is a painful affair—physically too.

And to be fair, one of the hunting grounds, one of the trophies of the photographic safari, was architecture. As said, to begin with for the banal reason that architecture is immobile, it stands, doesn't move, patient and attractive. But then also because the play with built geometry successfully harmonizes with that of seeing, of perspective, with the monocular central perspective of photography. Immobile architecture was and is an attractive didactic drama for photography: captured with alplanatic objective lenses and without converging vertical lines, perfectly mitered, the geometrical volumes compressed into a flat rectangle. With the focus on the vanishing point, with sufficient depth of field and contrast-enhancing filters (nowadays part of the postproduction), that stresses the plasticity of the building, the textured facades, shot from different angles, elevated or from a worm's-eye view, in order, as required, to lend the architectural volume more standing and vehemence. Architecture helped photography to comprehend the image area and dimensional depth as an interconnected system, as a plaything in photographic composition and form.

    And, once again, now the equation in reverse. As a global rule: 50 percent content, 50 percent communication (or is it 10 or 90 percent?). The project has been planned, building permission granted, and construction is underway. Here photography acts, on the one hand, as a tool of documentation, communication, promotion, vis-à-vis the clients, the authorities, the later occupants, in journals and online platforms; and on the other to try and stay the unstoppable march of time, to thwart forgetting. There's only one Coliseum, but in reality billions of pictures of it. There are very few buildings that survive for a hundred or hundreds of years, but probably pictures, or at least a few pictures of them. Systems of rates of financial return are ratcheted up all too rapidly nowadays, meaning that architects quite understandably endeavor to have a say in the image of their buildings, to co-define it. Classic architectural photography is their amenable instrument, their assistant, obliged to follow their instructions, freeze-framing the building when the clock hits zero, as soon as the building is complete, cleaned, and the keys are about to be handed over—just before the building becomes occupied and is for the first time transmogrified. Only in this very narrow window of opportunity does the building show what the architects imagine it to represent, what they conceived it to be: as a lucid structure; as a serene, sedate setting; or as a powerful icon, as a piercingly luminous lantern. A moment of rapture before the architecture becomes "utilized," before—as Roland Barthes once formulated it addressing the subject of trousers, where the trousers only become trousers by being worn—becoming, in other words, actual architecture, a functioning, living, pulsating building.

For this reason, almost all architectural photography—if it's not social photography or doesn't aspire to be art—duplicates architecture in its perfection, in the form of a (as yet) idle reification, devoid of people, devoid of use, as the purest possible visual realization of a particular, personal, perhaps also contemporarily idealized idea. But the control is also so rigid because architects precisely feel, indeed meticulously know, that images speak their own language, that they prompt other discourses than just the physical experience of architecture, because they sense how photography transmutes volumes and structures into planes, distills material and form into pure symbols, into pixels, and how it, in doing so, transforms, accentuates architecture, namely by enlarging, diminishing, deforming, heightening, or lessening it—but in whatever case has the capacity to spread, to scatter it, far and wide. How architecture can coagulate to become a symbol and a mythos. How, at a certain juncture, the image can, as said, have more force than the real architecture.

III

Renderings, in this context, are something like the ultimate control over the image—a kind of photography 4.0. They're design and idealization rolled into one, an advertizing platform and iconography together. A new form of a self-fulfilling prophecy that in the last resort makes built reality superfluous. At last, Mr. Holmes, here we are! And in its coequal, the field of design is ablaze—the screens are over-glowing! The flip side of the coin is that the designs, precisely because they seem so detailed and consummate, represent an unobtainable gold standard of reality, an eternal springtime. Renderings run the danger of duplicating architecture so radically, so absolutely, that the subsequent built space may seem strangely insipid and anemic. Rendering: crisp and cool. Reality: dreary and susceptible to failure?

IV

The photographic work of Ludovic Balland and his team in this book follow a completely different trajectory. It's not an Icarus-like flight of fantasy; it's not dazzlingly gaudy, pompous. Instead it turns back, reverts, and hazards a visual analysis, a visual commentary. It seems to treat the built architecture as one huge resonator, whose vibrations echo in different ways in different photographic materials. The result is a visual conversation that wants to simultaneously mirror the design and reality, idea and material, the built and the used. A bold, ambitious, but, as we ourselves can discern on these pages, auspicious endeavor.
Full stop.

1 Oliver Wendell Holmes, "The Stereoscope and the Stereograph," *The Atlantic Monthly* 3, no. 20 (June 1859), https://www.theatlantic.com/magazine/archive/1859/06/the-stereoscope-and-the-stereograph/303361 (accessed January 5, 2022).
2 Ibid.
3 Jean Baudrillard, *Simulacra and Simulations* (Ann Arbor: University of Michigan Press, 2002), 80.
4 Michael Wetzel, "Paradoxe Intervention: Jean Baudrillard und Paul Virilio—Zwei Apokaliptiker der neuen Medien," in Ralf Bohn and Dieter Fuder (eds.), *Simulation und Verführung* (Munich: Fink, 1994), 139–54 (emphasis added).
5 Holmes, "Stereoscope".

Workshop

Ludovic Balland and Annina Schepping

N° 068	Garden Tower	66
N° 090	Peninsula Housing Development	71
N° 113	Hotel Nomad	74
N° 123	Tièchestrasse Housing Development	80
N° 147	Hertenstein House	86
N° 149	Credit Suisse Place Bel-Air Headquarters	93
N° 174	Amthausquai Residential and Commercial Building	98
N° 179	Lörrach House	103
N° 205	Cooperative Building Stadterle	107
N° 207	Casa Mosogno	120
N° 212	Münchenstein House	132
N° 224	Kirschgarten House	138
N° 249	Cherry Storehouse Nuglar	143
N° 260	Missionsstrasse House	155

N° 068 **Garden Tower** 66

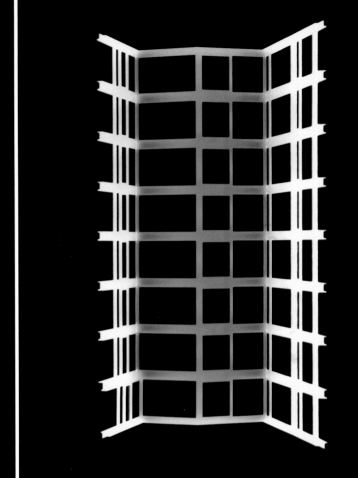

Segmentation of the 3D-printed building framework into individual layers; photograms, each 30.3 × 40.2 cm   [1] Floor and building load-bearing structure   [2] Window frontage
[3] Balconies with incorporated planters, joined with metal brackets   [4] Overlay of all three layers   [1–5, 10/11] © Ludovic Balland, Anina Schepping, Hans-Jörg Walter

[5] All building layers enveloped with lattice

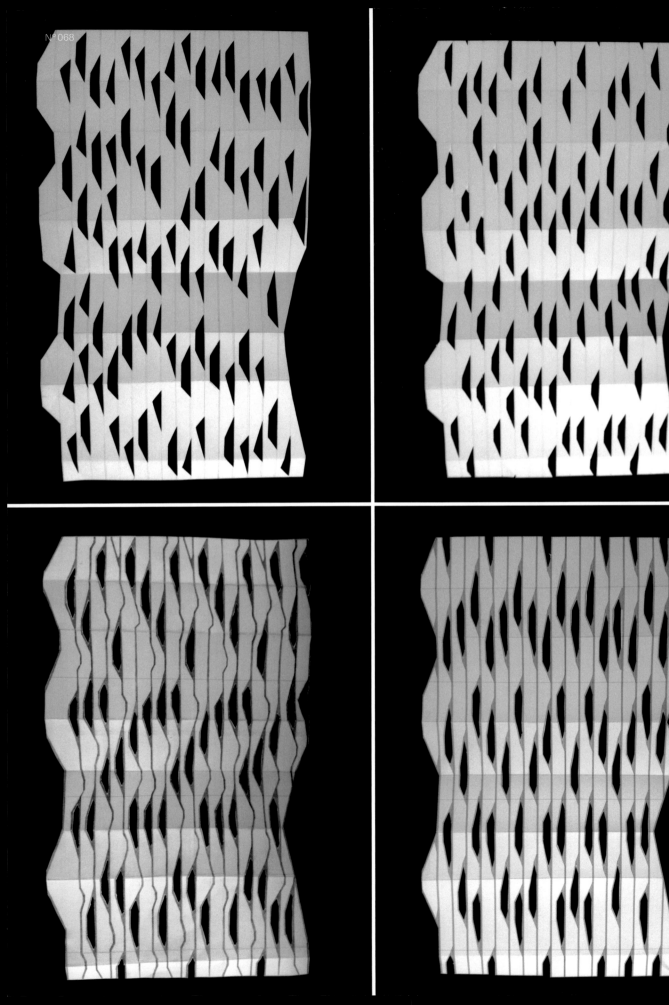

[6–9] Facade development with opening variations © Buchner Bründler Architekten

Garden Tower

[10] Outer building layer; photogram, 31.9 × 43.8 cm

Garden Tower 70
Selected Buildings
→ p. 169

[11] Outer building layer and greenery: Kirlian photographs combined with photogram, 30.3 × 40.2 cm

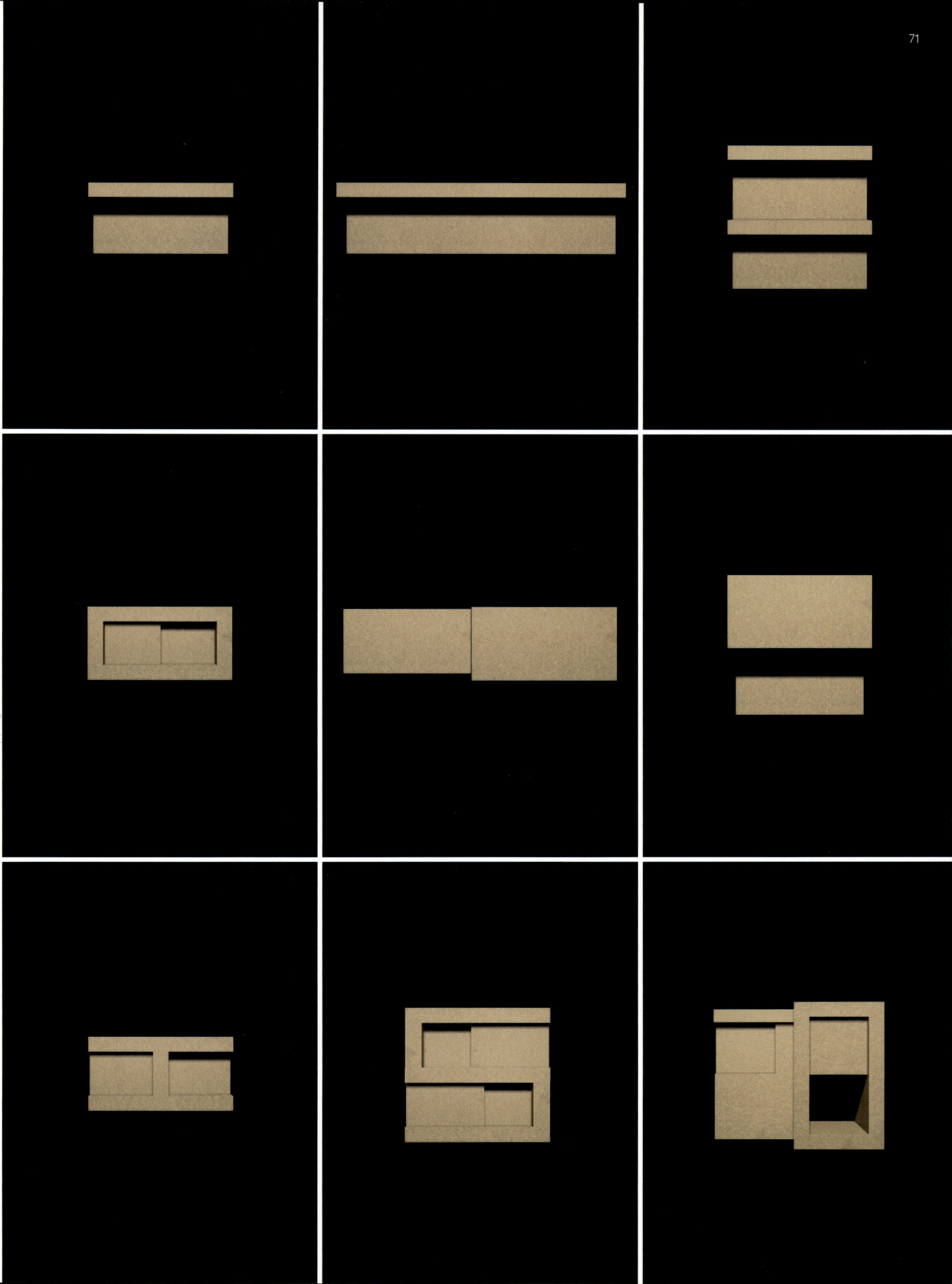

N° 090
Peninsula
Housing
Development

[1–27] Shadow directions of nine different facade elements; 3D visualization © Annina Schepping, Frederik Sutter

N° 090

72

Peninsula Housing
Development
Selected Buildings
→ p. 185

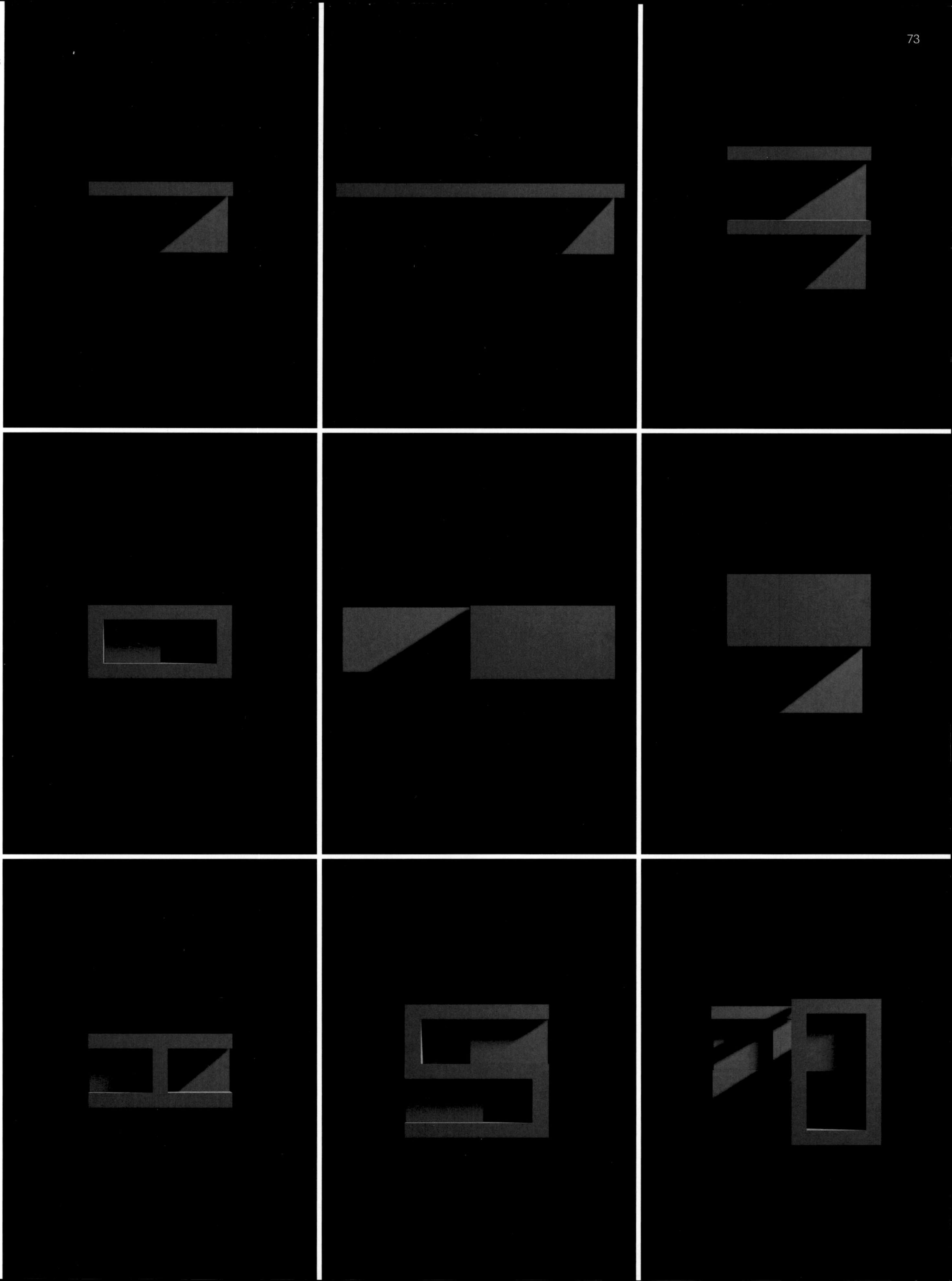

Hotel Nomad

[1–12] Xerox-montage with Konica Minolta Bizhub C220, 29.7 × 42 cm, 2021 © Alexander Rosenkranz

Hotel Nomad

Hotel Nomad
Selected Buildings
→ p. 199

[1] View, east

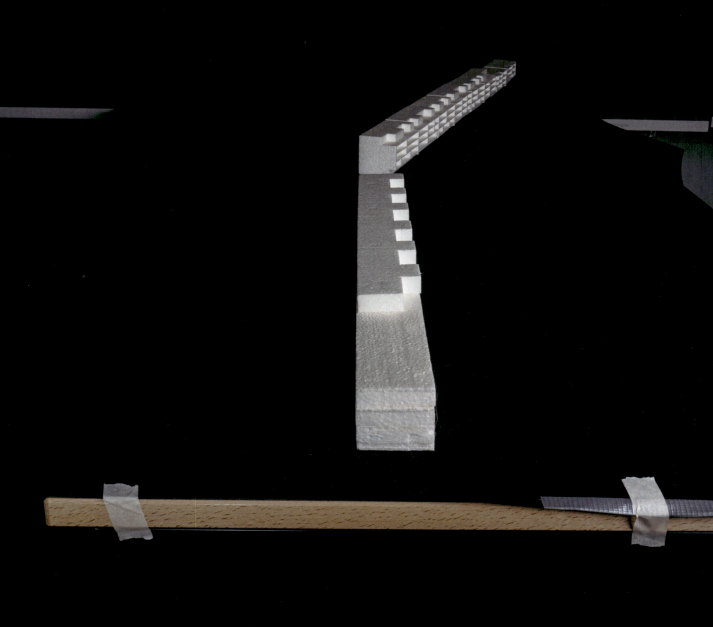

[2] View, west

[3] View, southeast

Tièchestrasse
Housing
Development

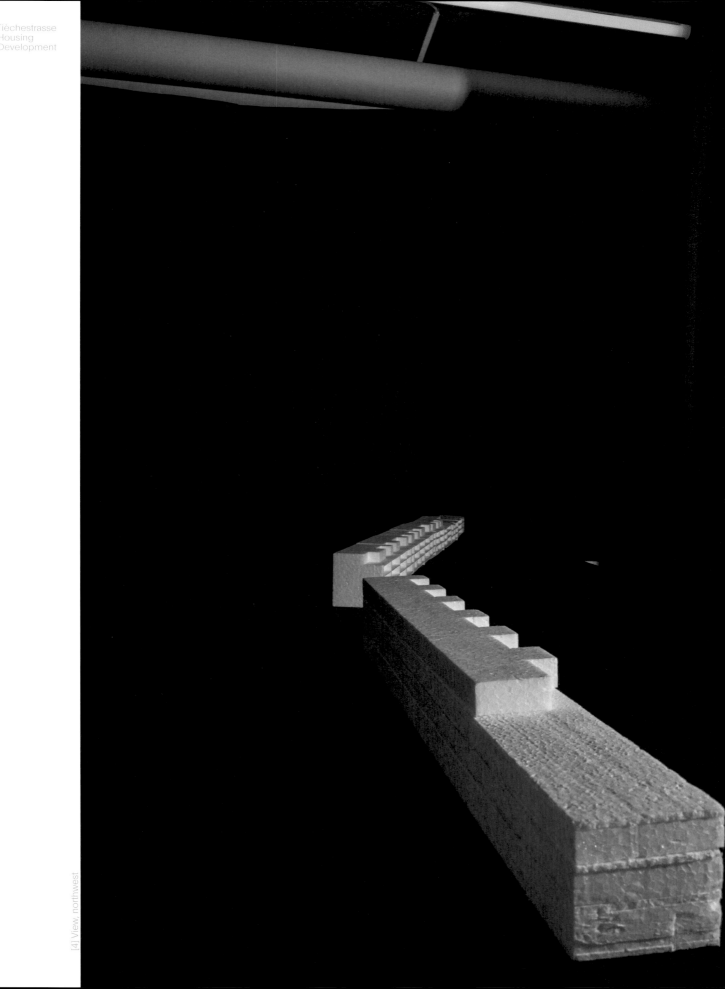

[4] View, northwest

[5] View, southwest

Tièchestrasse
Housing
Development
Selected Buildings
→ p. 217

85

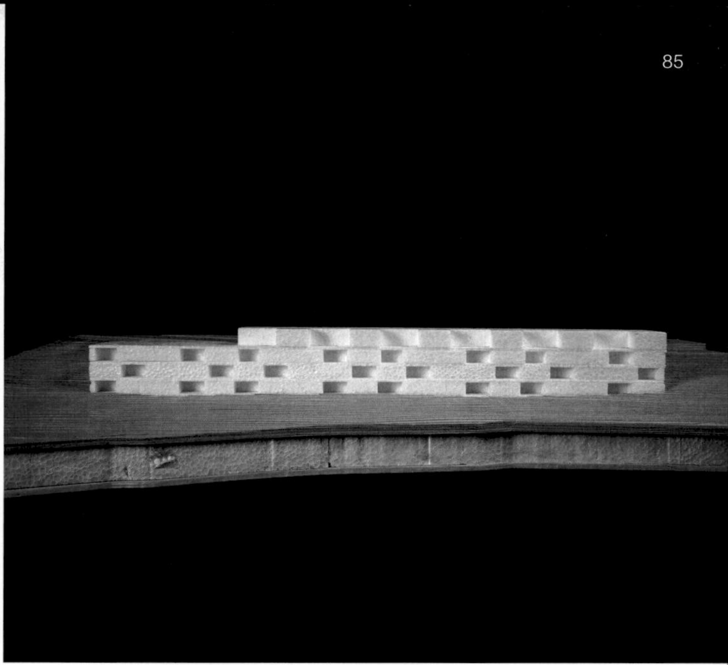

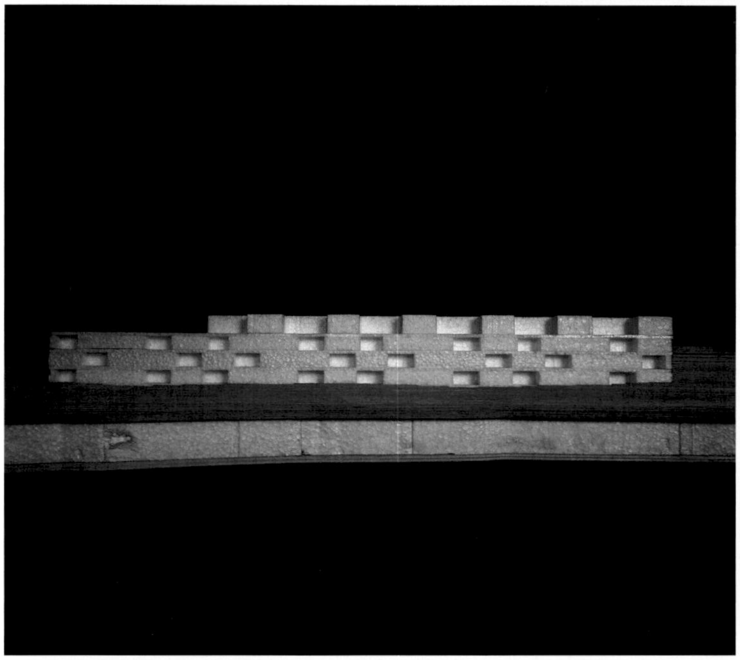

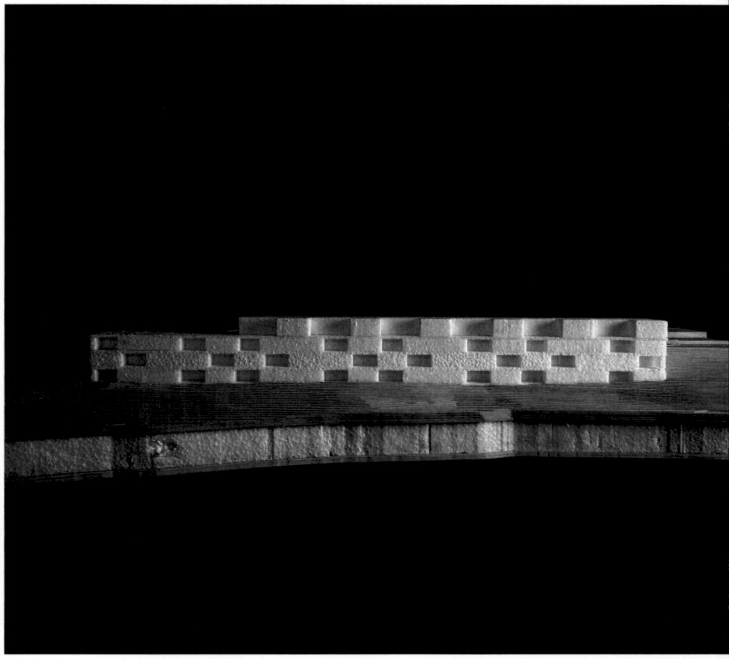

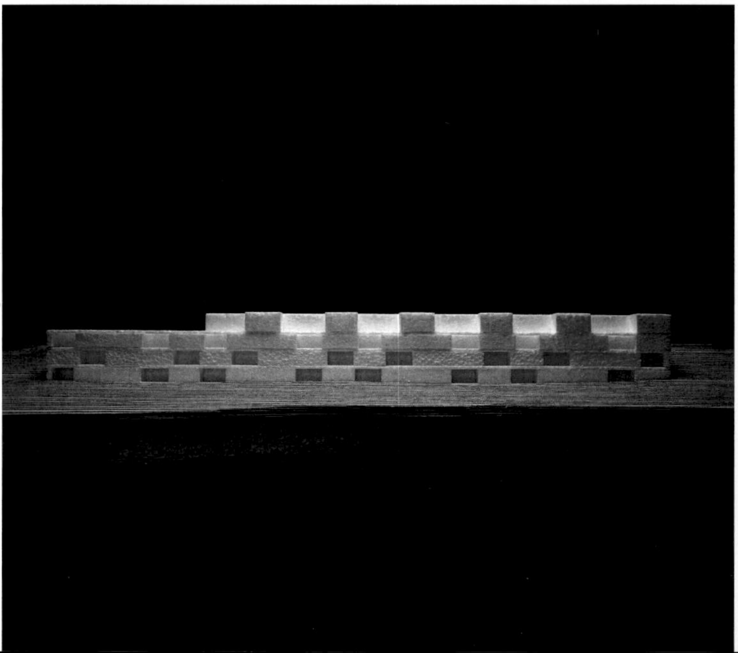

[6–11] Facade elevations, building complexes S, T, U, and V

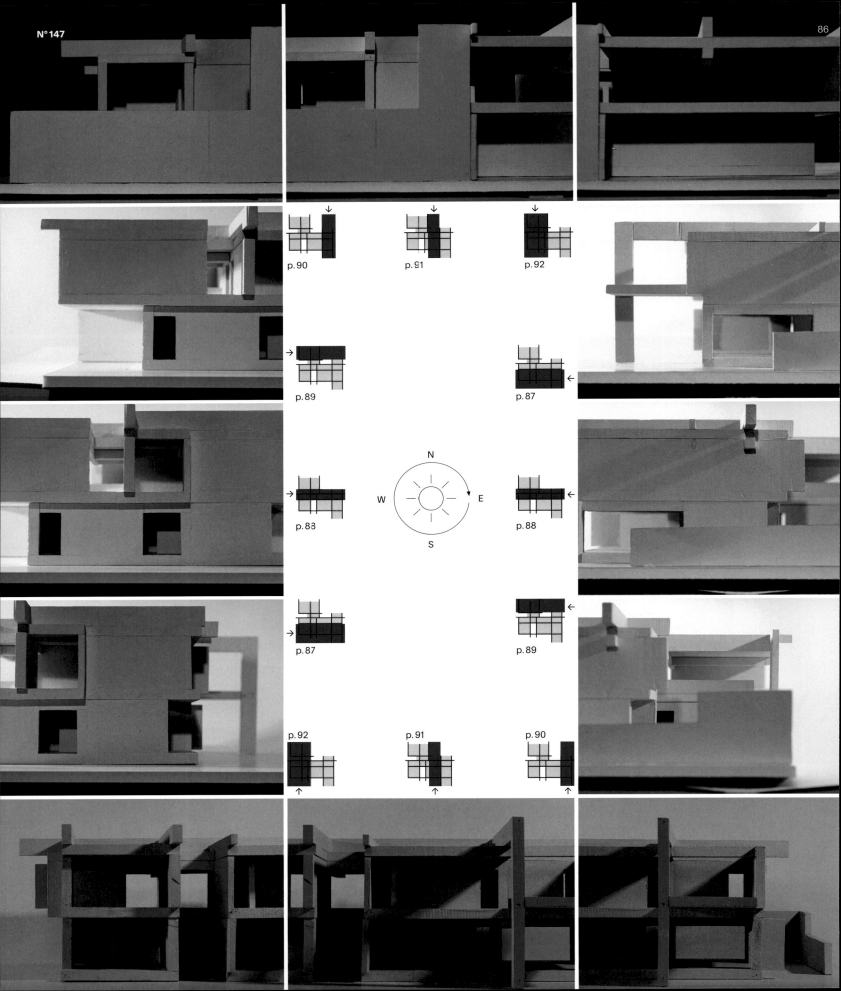

Hertenstein House

[1, 3, 5] View, east [2, 4, 6] View, west [1–12] © Ludovic Balland

Hertenstein House

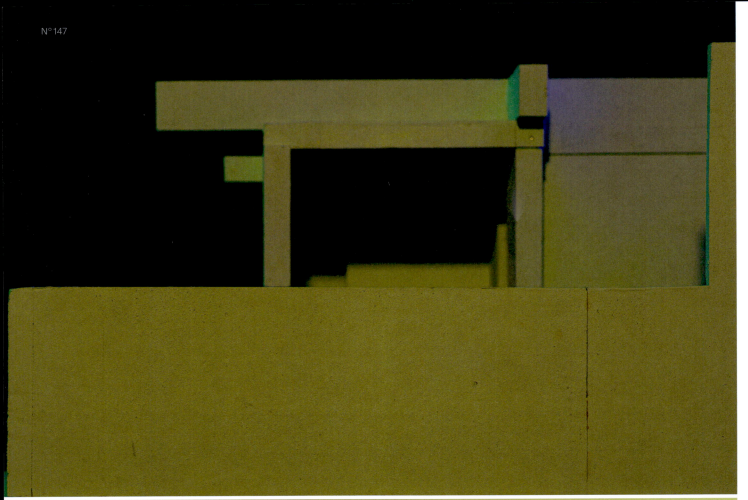

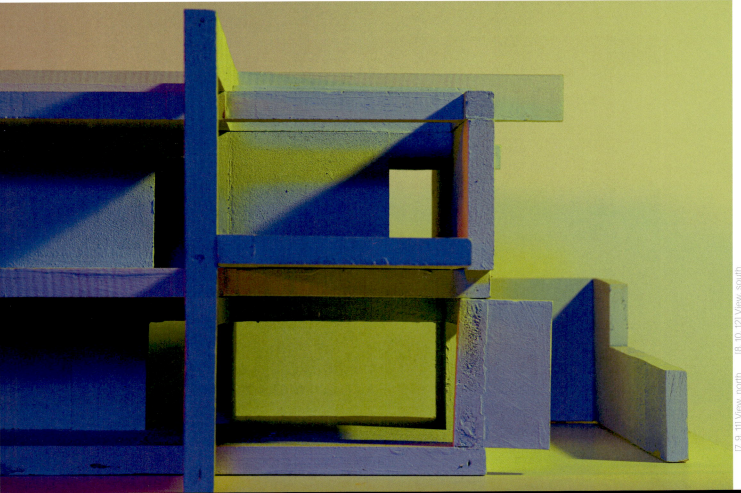

[7, 9, 11] View, north   [8, 10, 12] View, south

Hertenstein House

91

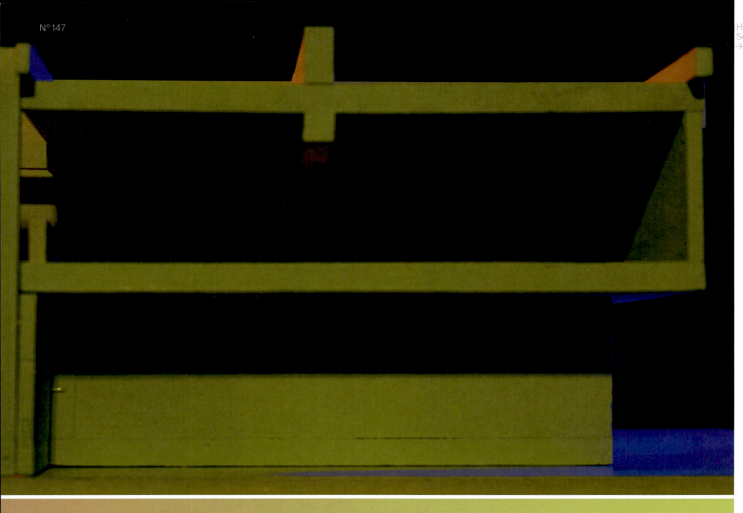
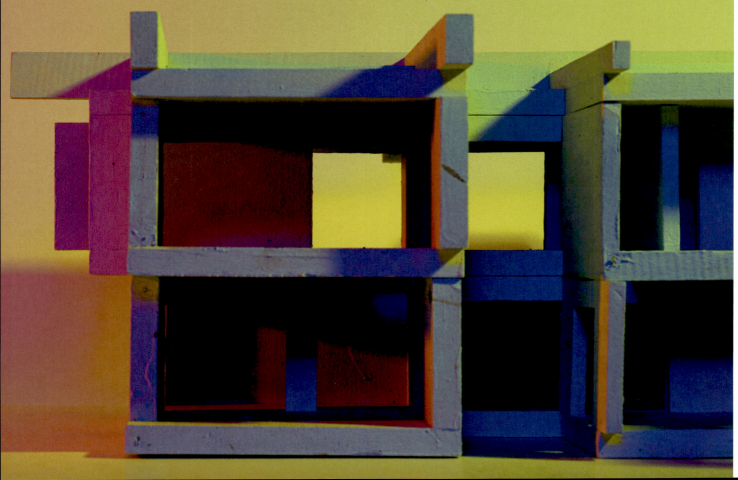

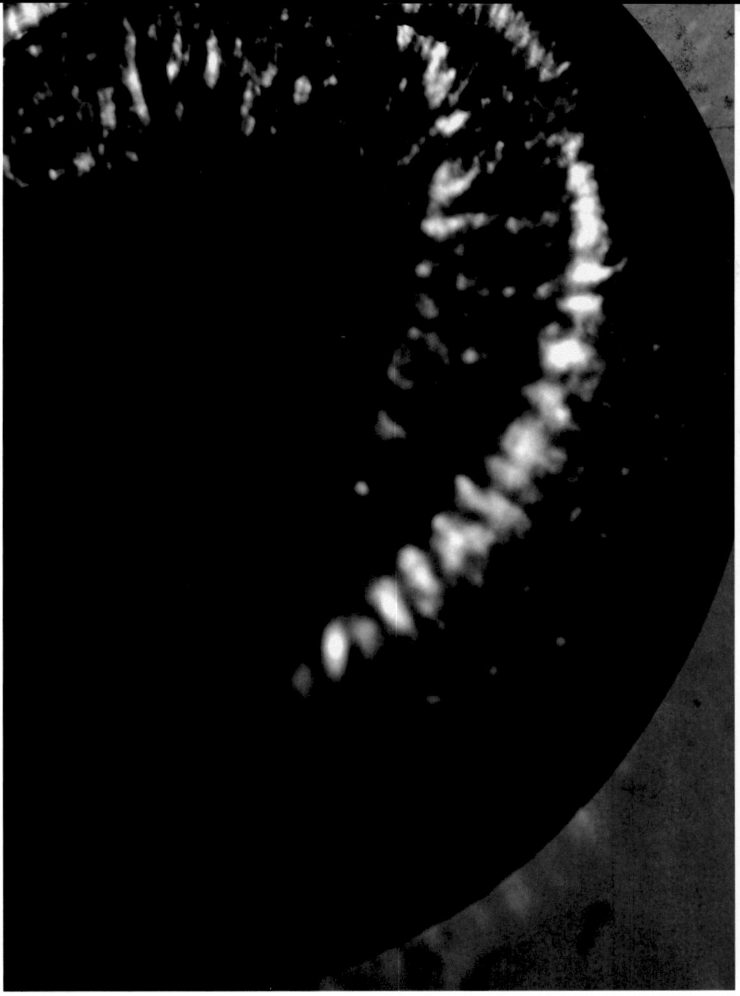

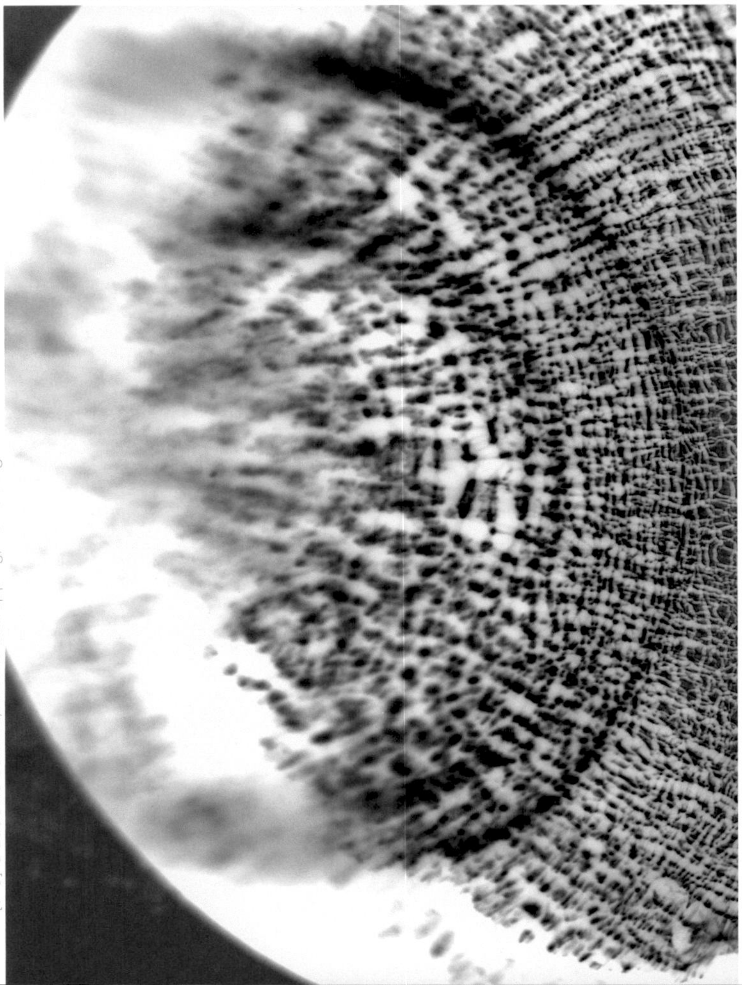

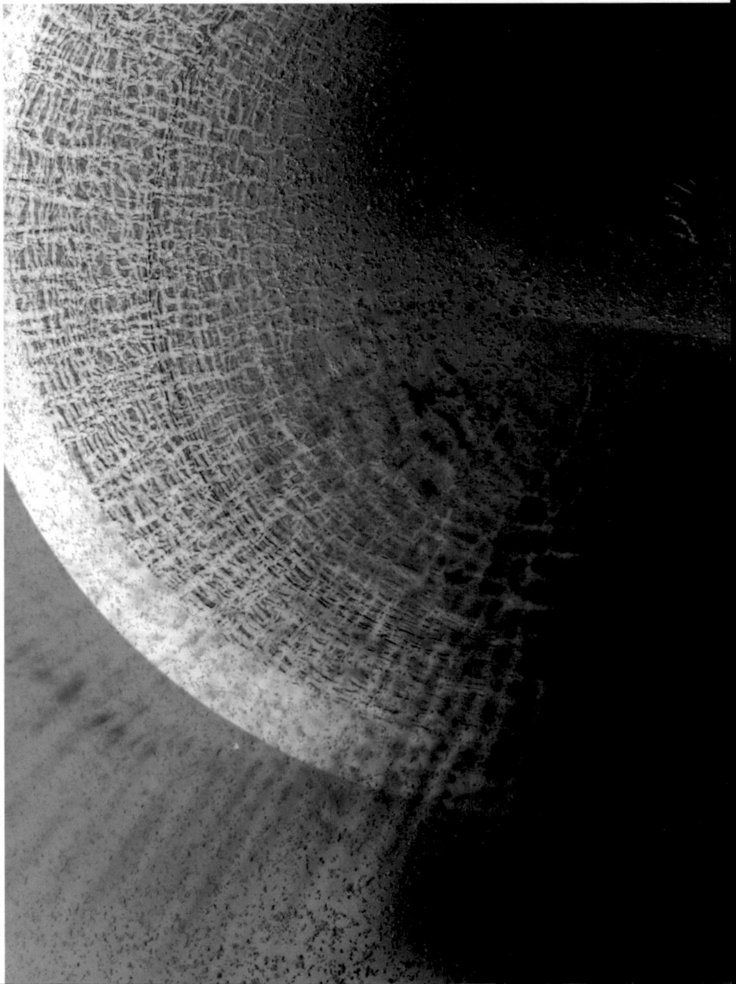

**N° 149
Credit Suisse
Place Bel-Air
Headquarters**

[1–3] Alkali glass lighting object   [4, 5] Lighting objects and sandblasted glass panel   photograms, 31.9 × 43.8 cm and 30.4 × 40.4 cm
[1–9] © Ludovic Balland, Annina Schepping, Hans-Jörg Walter

N°149

Credit Suisse
Place Bel-Air
Headquarters

95

[6.–8] Sandblasted glass panel; photograms, each 30.4 × 40.4 cm

Credit Suisse
Place Bel-Air
Headquarters
Selected Buildings
→ p. 249

[9] Lighting object and photographs of the inner courtyard; photogram, 30.4 × 40.4 cm

Amthausquai Residential and Commercial Building

99

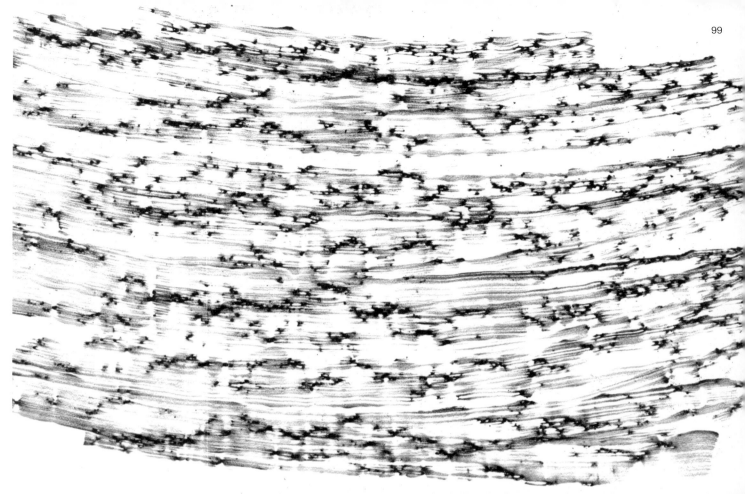

[4–6] Magistrates office, Römerstrasse 2

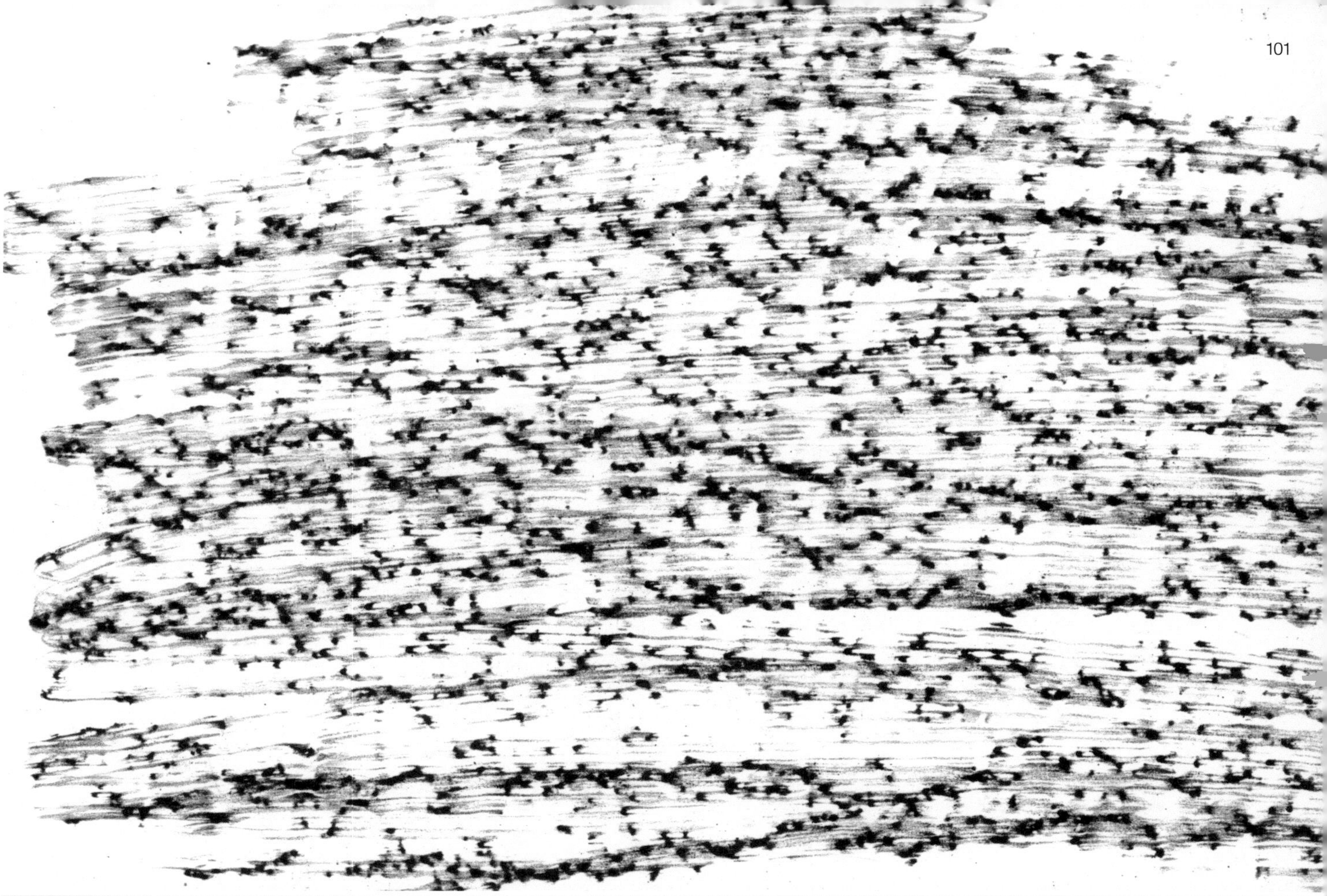

Amthausquai
Residential and
Commercial
Building

101

[10–12] Commercial premises, Jurastrasse 8

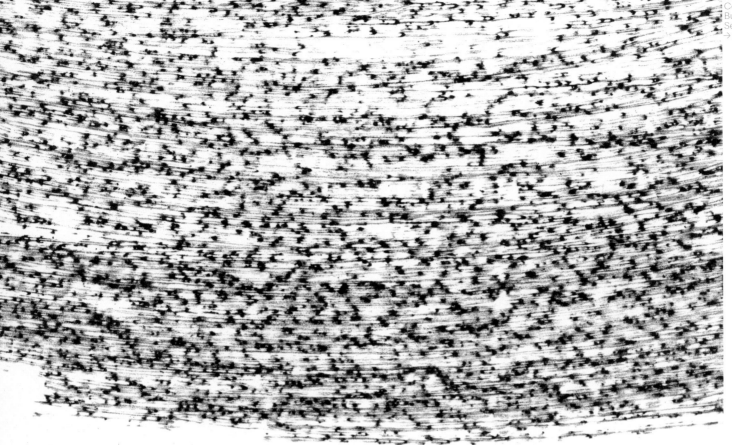

[13–15] Commercial premises, Jurastrasse 2

**N° 179
Lörrach House**

[1] Plot area   [2] Contour, outer shell   [3] Building core, inner building contour   [4] Overlay   photograms, each 30.3 × 40.2 cm   [1–9] © Annina Schepping, Hans-Jörg Walter

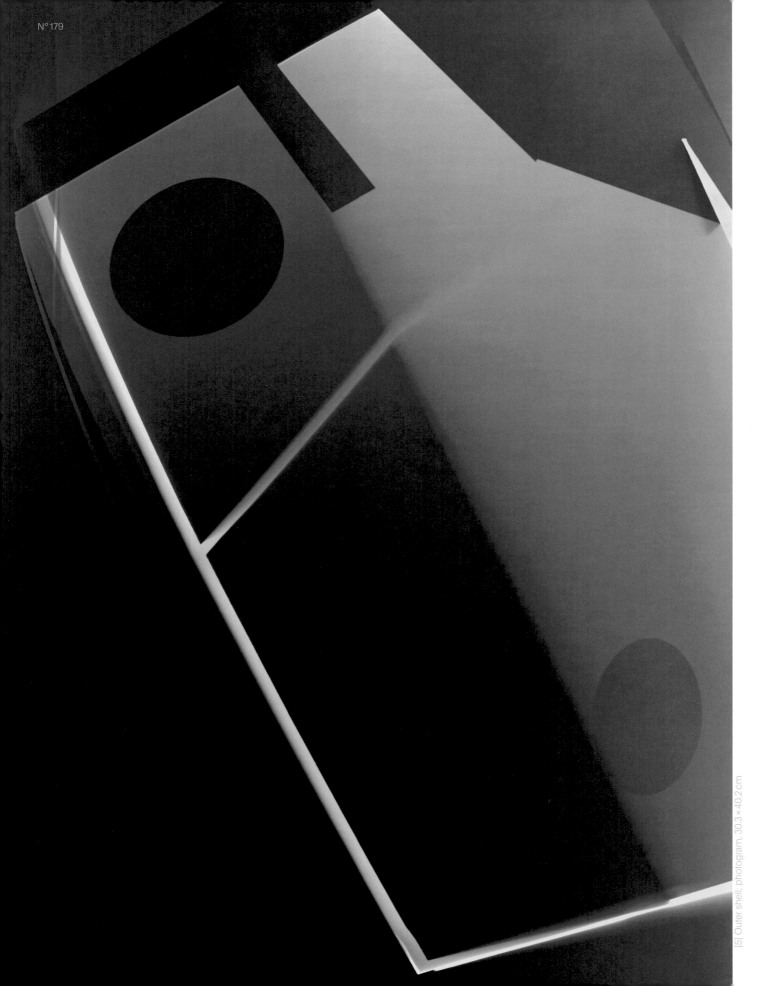

[5] Outer shell, photogram, 30.3 × 40.2 cm

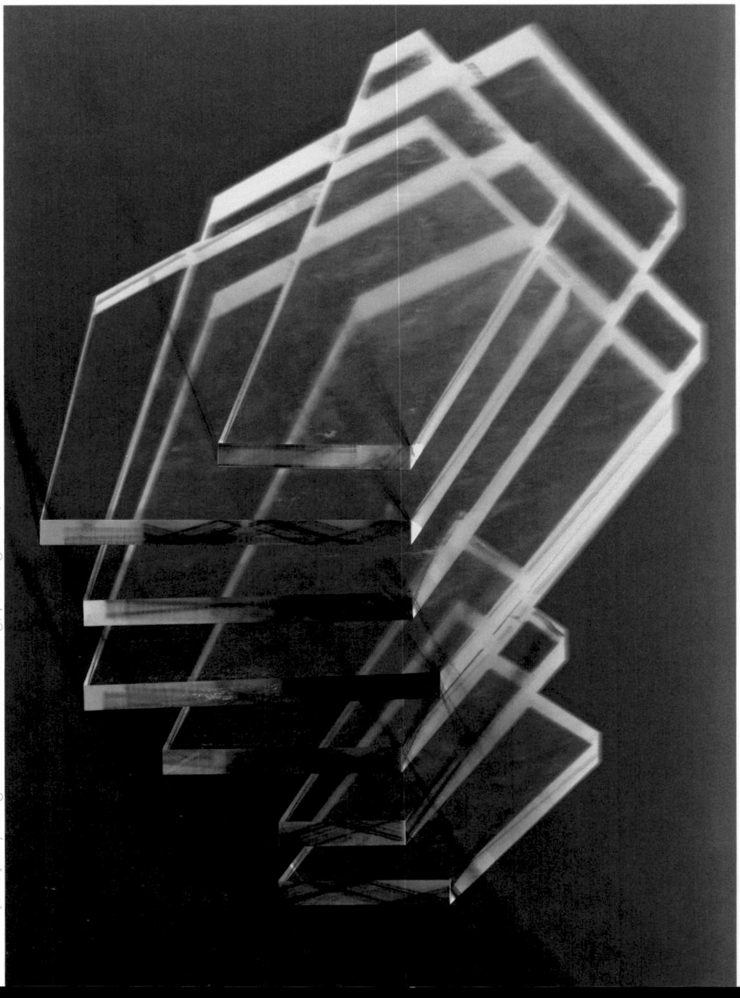

Lörrach House

105

[6–9] Layering of the inner building; photograms, each 30.3 × 40.2 cm

[1–13] Residents on the roof, between 12:00 and 16:00 in May 2019 © Ludovic Balland

Cooperative
Building Stadterle

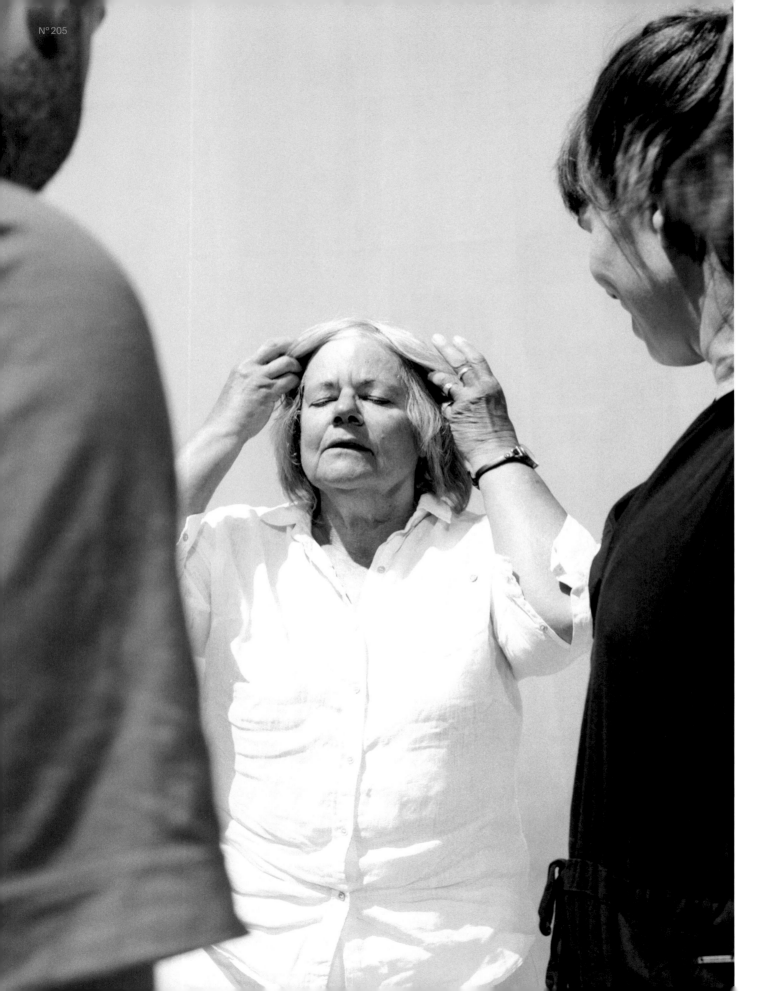

Cooperative Building Stadterle

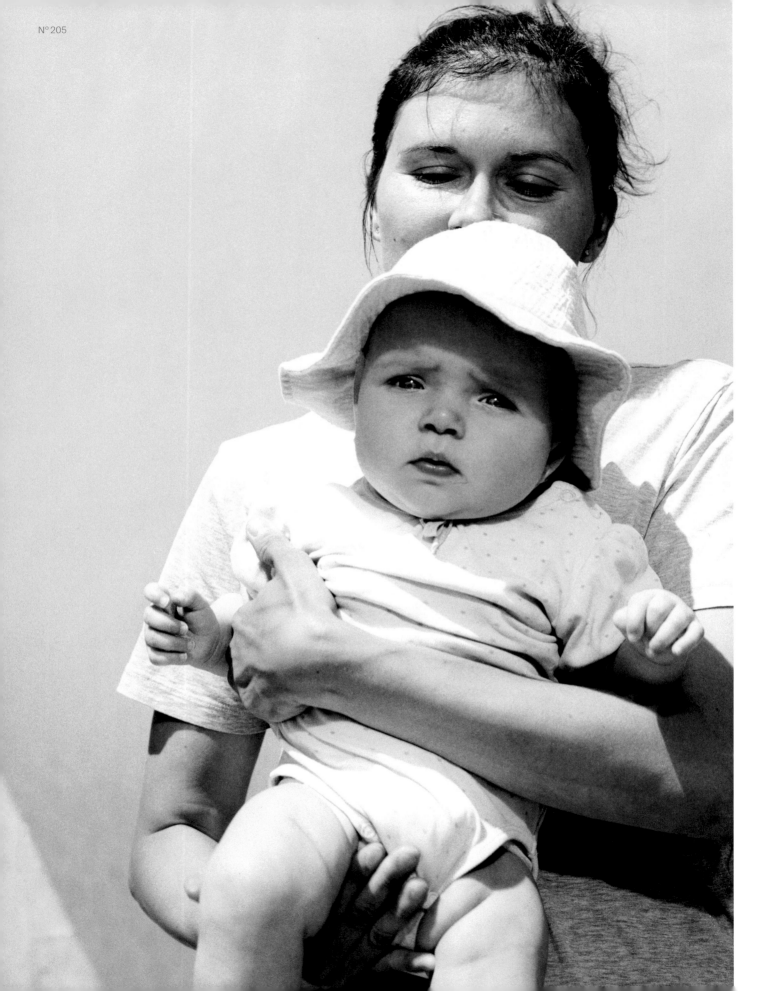

N° 205

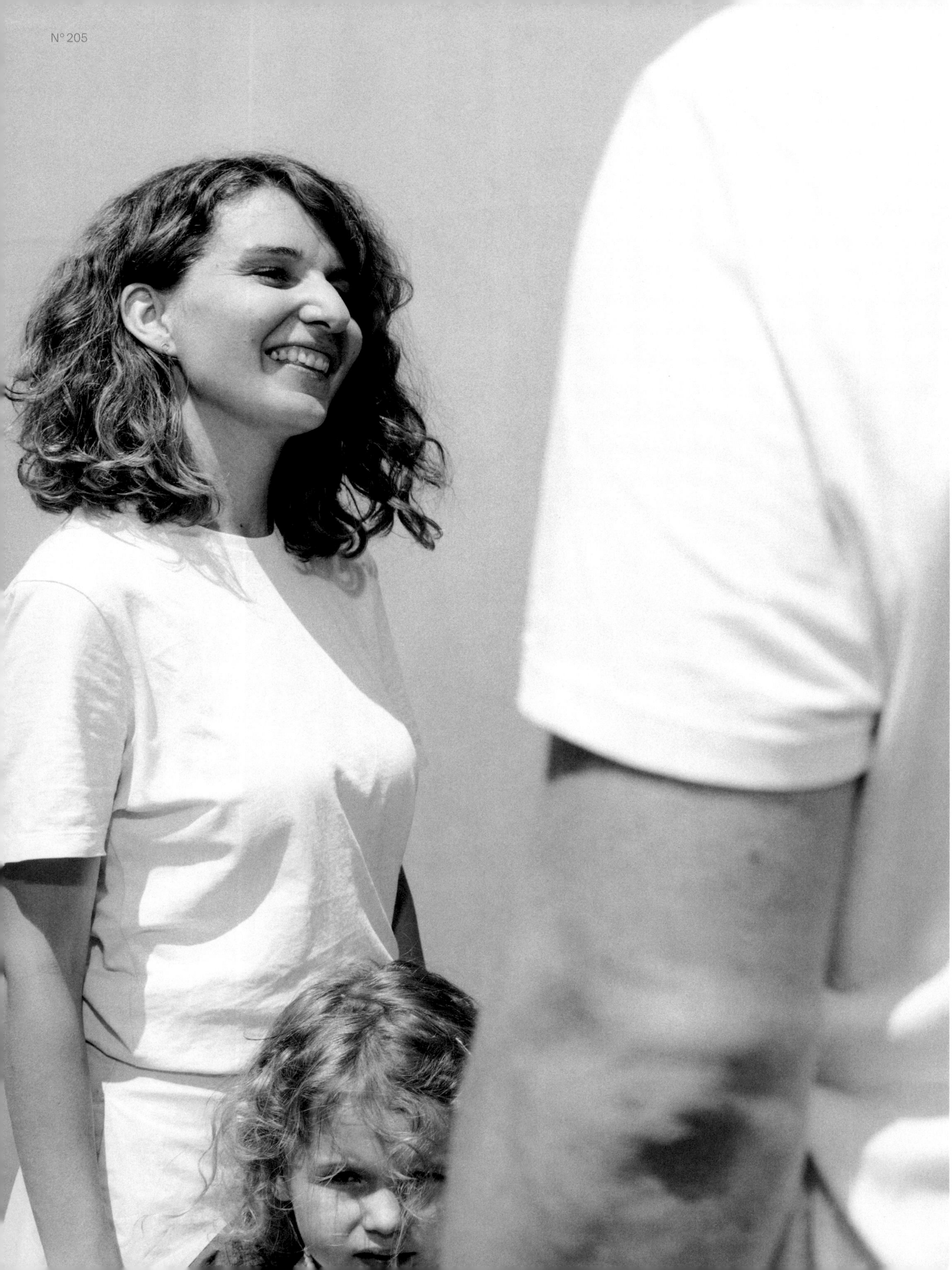

Cooperative
Building Stadterle
Selected Buildings
→ p. 297

119

Casa Mosogno

125

Casa Mosogno

127

Casa Mosogno
Selected Buildings
→ p. 313

[1–6] Buildings along Birseckstrasse © Ludovic Balland

Münchenstein
House

Kirschgarten House 138

[1–5] Deconstruction of the roof structure of the house by rearrangement © Annina Schepping

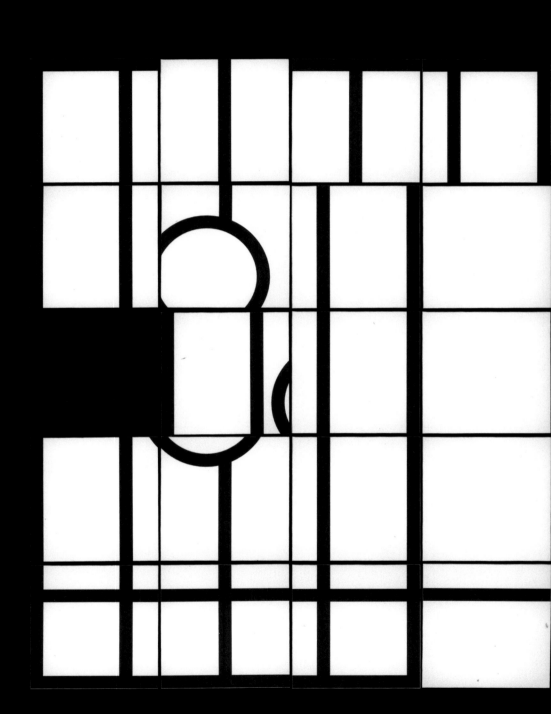

140

Kirschgarten
House

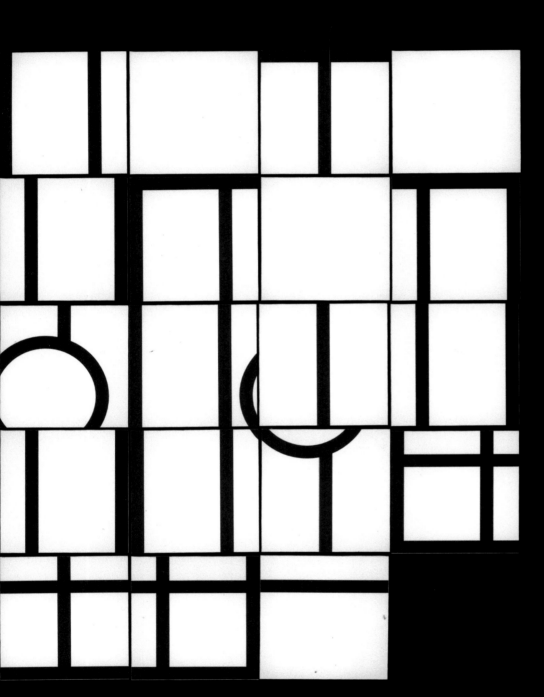

Kirschgarten
House
Selected Buildings
→ p. 343

142

**N° 249
Cherry
Storehouse
Nuglar**

[1–3, 5/6, 8/9, 11/12, 14/15] Setting up of a rudimentary model   [1–17] © Ludovic Balland

Cherry Storehouse
Nuglar

[4] Ground view, door between garage and living space

145

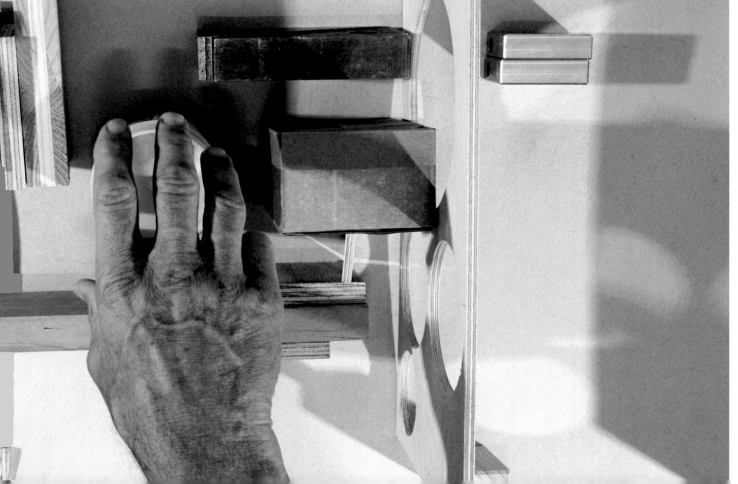

Cherry Storehouse
Nuglar

[7] Apartment entrance

Cherry Storehouse
Nuglar

[10] Ceiling view with wall end stop, studio entrance

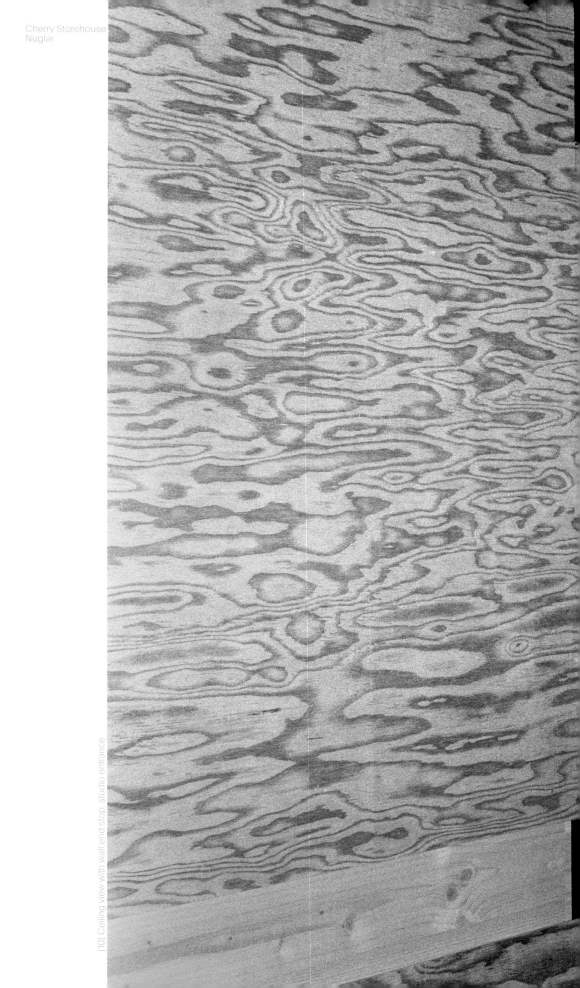

Cherry Storehouse
Nuglar

[13] Stairs leading to cellar

Cherry Storehouse
Nuglar

[16] Living room window frontage

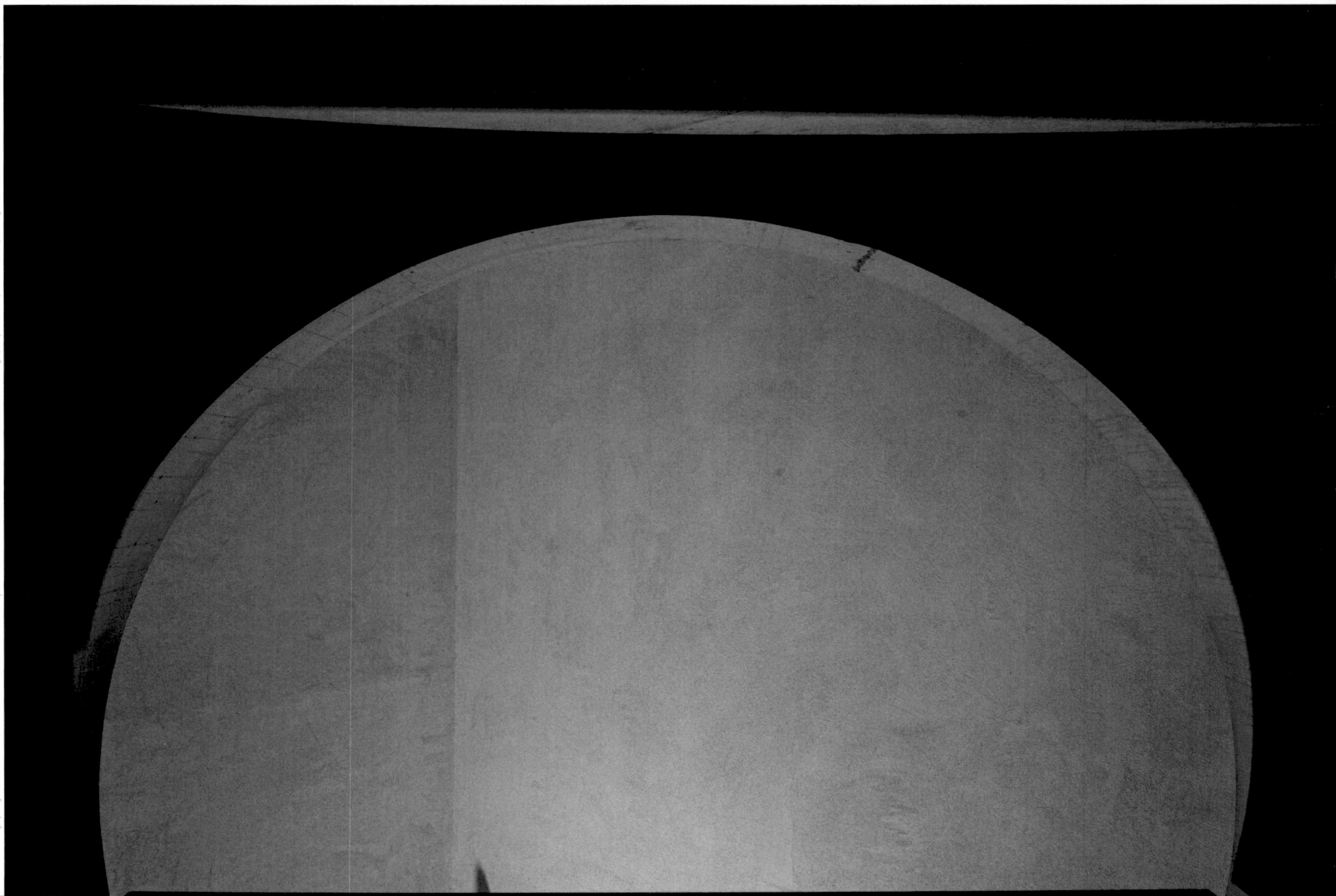

N° 260
Missionsstrasse
House

155

[1/2] View from the middle story into the southeast atrium   [1/2, 4–11, 16–24, 28] © Ludovic Balland, [3, 12–15, 25–27] © Annina Schepping, Hans-Jörg Walter

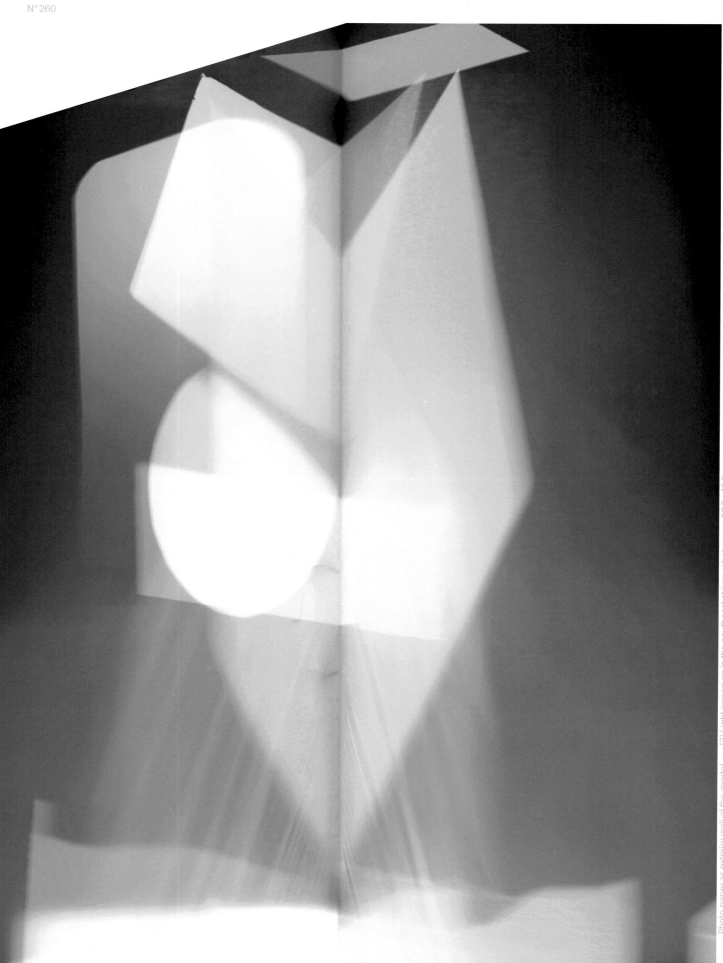

[3] Light exposure in the southeast atrium; photogram, 30.3 × 40.2 cm Photo paper as exterior wall of the model

Missionsstrasse House

157

[4/5] View from the garden-level floor up into the southeast atrium

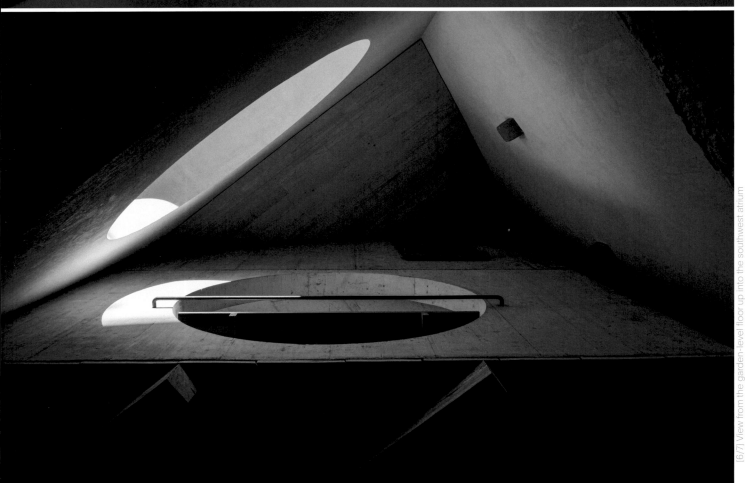

[6/7] View from the garden-level floor up into the southwest atrium

Missionsstrasse House

159

[8–11] View from the studio hall on the middle story toward the southwest atrium

[12–15], Photograms, each 30.3 × 40.2 cm

Missionsstrasse House

[16–19] View from the bathroom into the roof story in the southeast atrium

[20] View from the bathroom on the middle story toward the southeast atrium

Missionsstrasse House

[21–24] View from the stairs into the garden level and the middle story

163

[25–27] Photograms, each 30.3 × 40.2 cm

Missionsstrasse
House
Selected Buildings
→ p. 379

165

[28] View from the garden

Selected Buildings

N° 068	**Garden Tower**	169
N° 090	**Peninsula Housing Development**	185
N° 113	**Hotel Nomad**	199
N° 123	**Tièchestrasse Housing Development**	217
N° 147	**Hertenstein House**	235
N° 149	**Credit Suisse Place Bel-Air Headquarters**	249
N° 174	**Amthausquai Residential and Commercial Building**	265
N° 179	**Lörrach House**	281
N° 205	**Cooperative Building Stadterle**	297
N° 207	**Casa Mosogno**	313
N° 212	**Münchenstein House**	329
N° 224	**Kirschgarten House**	343
N° 249	**Cherry Storehouse Nuglar**	359
N° 260	**Missionsstrasse House**	379

Wabern bei Berne, Switzerland

2007–2016 **Garden Tower**

New building

N° 068 Garden Tower — New building — Selected Buildings

Location Wabern bei Berne, Switzerland **Type** New building **Status** Realized **Project phases** *Competition* 2007, 1st prize *Planning* 2010–2014 *Realization* 2014–2016 **Client** *General contractor* Priora AG Generalunternehmung, Berne *Commissioning body* Dr. Hans Widmer, Oberwil Lieli **Project data** *Lot size* 4,500 m² *Built-up area* 590 m² *Floor area* 8,200 m² (according to SIA 416) *Building volume* 26,900 m³ **Planners** *Architecture* Buchner Bründler Architekten, Basel *General management* Baumann Projektmanagement, Basel *Site management* Priora AG Generalunternehmung, Berne *Building engineering* Schnetzer Puskas Ingenieure AG, Basel *Landscape architecture* Nipkow Landschaftsarchitektur AG, Zurich *Greenery* Fritz Wassmann, Hinterkappelen bei Berne *Greenery system, planning* Forster Baugrün AG, Kerzers *Greenery system, realization* Beglinger + Bryan Landschaftsarchitektur, Zurich *Building physics and acoustics* Gartenmann Engineering AG, Basel *Building technology, planning* Bogenschütz AG, Basel *Building technology, realization* Gruneko Schweiz AG, Basel *Electrical planning* Actemium Schweiz AG, Basel *Facade planning* Christoph Etter Fassadenplanungen, Basel *Fire prevention, planning* BDS Security Design AG, Berne *Fire prevention, realization* Wälchli Architekten Partner AG, Berne **Team Buchner Bründler** *Partners* Daniel Buchner, Andreas Bründler *Associates* Bülend Yigin, Stefan Oehy *Project lead, competition* Jonas Staehelin *Project leads, planning* Achim Widjaja, Jonas Staehelin *Project leads, realization* Florian Rink, Henrik Månsson *Competition and preliminary project participants* Ewa Misiewicz, Hellade Miozzari, Felix Engelhardt *Planning participants* Stefan Herrmann, Jan Borner, Chiara Friedl, Fatima Blötzer, Reto Gasser, Michael Gunti *Realization participants* Henrik Månsson, Michael Glaser, Nadine Strasser, Jonas Virsik, Christian Käser, Carlos Unten Kanashiro **Publications** Marisol Vidal, Buchner Bründler: Concrete Turned into Atmosphere, En Blanco 16, (2014), 75–78 • José Manuel Pedreirinho, Accuracy, Quality, Functional Clarity and a Strong Formal Identity, a.mag 7 (2015), 110–17 • Ulrike Hark, Die wogenden Gärten von Wabern, SonntagsZeitung, July 17, 2016, 44 • Christian Bernhart, Langsam rankt es grün die Häuser empor, Baubio 3, Nachhaltige Baukultur (2016), 6–12 • Michaela Bossart, Garden Tower, der architekt 6 (2016), 5 • Andres Herzog, Zufall in Tranchen (Die hängenden Gärten von Wabern), Hochparterre 10 (2016), 18–27 • Marcel Hodel, Unwiderstehlich cool: Buchner Bründler Architekten—Garden Tower in Köniz, archithese 1 (2017), 78–82 • Maciej Lewandowski / Anna Zmijewska, Wiezowiec Garden Tower, Architektura murator 2 (2017), 84–95 • Daniel Kurz, Städtebau, Dissonante Kleinteiligkeit, werk, bauen + wohnen 2 (2017), 68–72 • Désirée Spoden, Garden Tower in Wabern bei Bern, AIT 3 (2017), 44–45 • Cornelia Etter, Himmelwärts, Das Ideale Heim 4 (2017), 52–60; and Atrium 3 (2017), 40–47 • Lauren Teague, The Crawling Gardens of Wabern, Mark Magazine, no. 2–3 (2017), 34–35 • Hubertus Adam, Eine Kletterpflanze als Fassadenhaut, Domus 025 (German ed., 2017), 71–81 • Country High Life, Monocle 7–8 (2017), 174 • Kirstin Klingbeil, Wohnhochhaus am Stadtrand: Garden-Tower in Wabern bei Bern, StadtBauwelt 19 (2017), 50–51 • Julia Liese, Begrünter Wohnturm bei Bern, Detail 5 (2018), 42–47

Impetus The site is an agricultural plot, onto which a mixed-form residential project is to be built, mirroring the heterogeneous surroundings. The main arterial road on which the plot is located is flanked linearly by different typologies of houses, warehouses, and settlements. The concept is based on an urban-planning strategy that deliberately adopts this collage, and that by freely sampling the proposed solutions consciously accepts the resulting frictions. In order to achieve this, the site is divided into five building segments, each of them dedicated to a typological theme with a main residential characteristic: with views, courtyards, the grove of trees, patios, and loggias. A residential tower was then developed in keeping with the allocated solutions.

Concept The choice of a residential tower design is to be understood as a typological assigment. The location's lack of an urban-spatial dialogue meant that a high-rise was not necessarily the obvious choice, therefore overarching contextualizations were looked for. Besides the spatial sequence along the main road, the cross-linkages to the landscape enabled a topographical reading of the site, leading to the design of a residential tower with an amorphous form that defies any clear typological designation. Erected on a polygonal footprint, the size and form of the tower shifts vertically. Open on all sides, it reinforces the relationship to the landscape.

The building is set back from the street and the spatial gap created indicates the new architectural sequence. Climbing plants on the outermost layer of the facade form an intense greenery that acts as a vertical garden and distinguishes the identity of the building. The apartment layouts are open-plan, determined by their all-round orientation and the theme of free circulation.

Implementation The basic frame of the building is entirely glazed. Concrete elements providing seating and as planters are incorporated into the cover slabs, which extend outward on all sides. Metal binders join the elements together, creating an architectural leitmotif. The undulating edge contours can be interpreted as the traced silhouettes of the distant mountain topography.

Via a metal net, which sheathes the stony volume, climbing plants form a vertical layer of vegetation, creating a green area in front of the apartments—a sort of garden arbor. The greenery is an integrated element in the building's structure, growing directly out of the incorporated planters. It harmonizes with the progression of the building and its orientation, additionally serving to provide shade. In autumn the building sheds its vegetative dress, exposing the glazed core to the warmth of the sun.

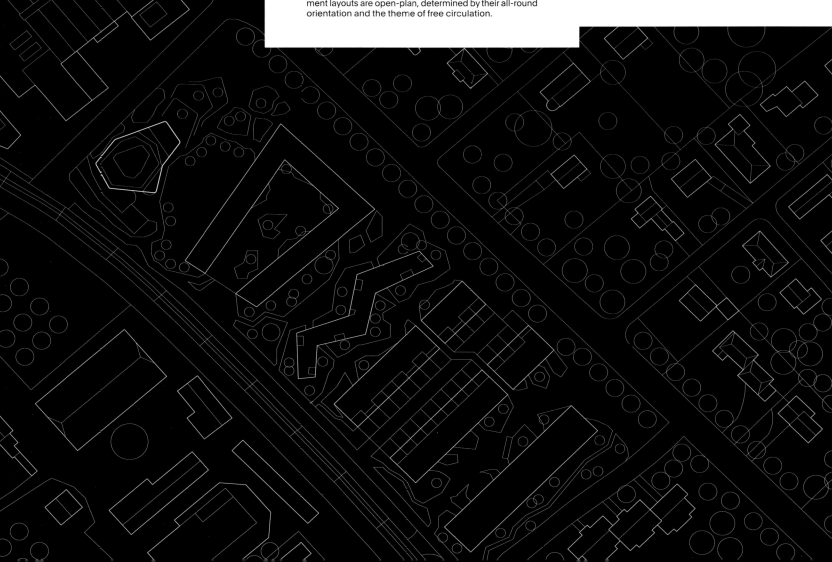

Bächtelenacker. Wabern, part of the municipality Köniz, south of Berne. "Wabern" means unstable grassland or morass. The Bächtelen area is located on a terrace between the Gurten mountain and the River Aare. First written mention 1223. At the time, the Gurten belonged to the Egerdon/Aegerten family, also the site of their ancestral castle.

R 1312, Werner and Peter von Egerdon sell the castle and mountain, with all its properties, to the Deutschordenshaus in Köniz, with the farming village now belonging to the Parish of Köniz. Following the hot summer of 1393, a spring from the Bächtelenacker area, the Zankbrunnen, supplied water for the Stockbrunnen in Berne. Wabern, standing before the gates of Berne with a view of the Alps, became a popular family seat for Berne's patricians: in the course of the 18th CENTURY, various families move to Wabern and build country houses with adjoining farms. Numerous manors appear. The estate Bächtelengut, above the Bächtelenacker, belongs to the Jenner family.

A century later: the properties are converted as institutions and welfare facilities—as a reform school for girls and boys or as a deaf-and-dumb asylum. From 1840, the Bächtelengut belongs to the Gesellschaft für das Gute und Gemeinnützige, who found a "rescue asylum for neglected, endangered boys." The Bächtelengut advances to be a model institution. **E** 1863, the first industrial firm appears in Wabern with the establishment of the Juker Brewery (later Gurten Brewery) on the Steingruben property: with the help of ox-drawn beer carts the ice is taken from the frozen Eichholz marsh. 1894, (steam-driven) tram from Berne main station to Wabern via Weissenbühl. 1899, opening of the funicular railway up the Gurten.

Around 1900, the beginnings of Wabern's development as a suburb of Berne. The settlement edges up the Gurten. 1901, opening of the Gürbetal Railroad, resulting in more building in Grosswabern. A noticeable increase in population. 1919, the first houses emerge between Grosswabern and Grünaustrasse, with intensive development after 1930. By the 1950s, the parceling up of the estates and their demolition, as well as the construction of Gurtenbühl Garden Town, the large-scale development Bondel-/Funkstrasse, is complete: Gross- and Kleinwabern merge. **P** 1994, the municipal zoning plan defines Wabern as part of the agglomeration of Berne. The federal government moves various agencies to Wabern: 1941 the Federal Office of Topography, 1966 the Federal Office of Meteorology, 2005 the Federal Office of Migration.

The municipality experiences a continuous population growth during the 20th CENTURY, from 1,186 inhabitants in 1910 to 7,997 in 2019. During all this time the Bächtelenacker along Seftigenstrasse remains vacant.

P Politics **E** Economics **C** Culture **R** Religion

The vertical garden changes its appearance through leaf-shedding climbing plants, such as wild vines. In winter, when the sun is low, the light shines deep into the apartments. In summer the plants provide shade and create a pleasant microclimate. In the distance, the views sweep across the slightly raised countryside of the Elfenau Park above the arm of the River Aare toward the Gurten, Berne's local mountain.

Set back from the main road, the building assumes a direct linkage to the heterogeneous surroundings of commercial buildings and the agricultural layouts of the Bächtelen Foundation. The free elementary form allows the apartments to be organized in multiple directions and to orientate the main living space to the south. Vertically, the floor slabs widen, while the building structure is reduced due to the lessening load application. Because of this the apartments become gradually larger the further up they are.

The continuous circulation core connects the tower structure with the 1.2-m-thick floor plates, giving a torsional rigidity, with the plates simultaneously acting as the building's flat foundation. The circumferential floor plates can be directly accessed from all the living rooms and bedrooms. The incorporated floor troughs each contain substrate for 30 m² of surface vegetation, its growth controlled by an automatically managed watering system.

The urban-planning strategy for the Bächtelen development, with five linearly arranged building sectors, is based on a sampling of various different architectural typologies, with scope for frictions.

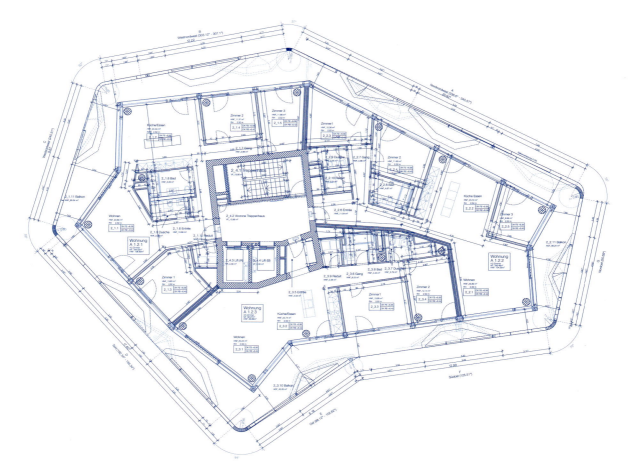

Floor plan, 2nd upper story (1:250)

Floor plan, ground story (1:250)

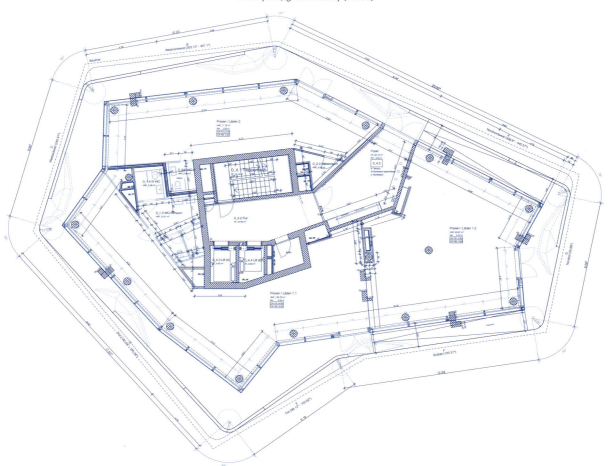

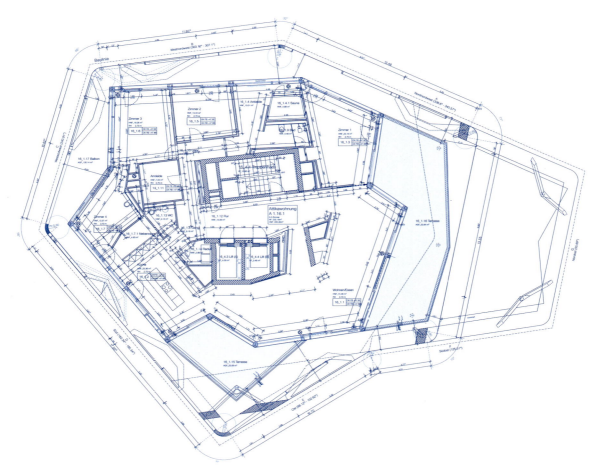

Floor plan, 16th story (1:250)

Floor plan, 14th story (1:250)

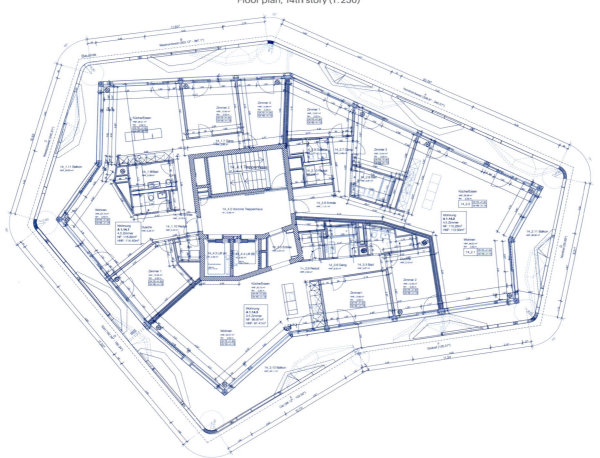

Longitudinal section (1:250)

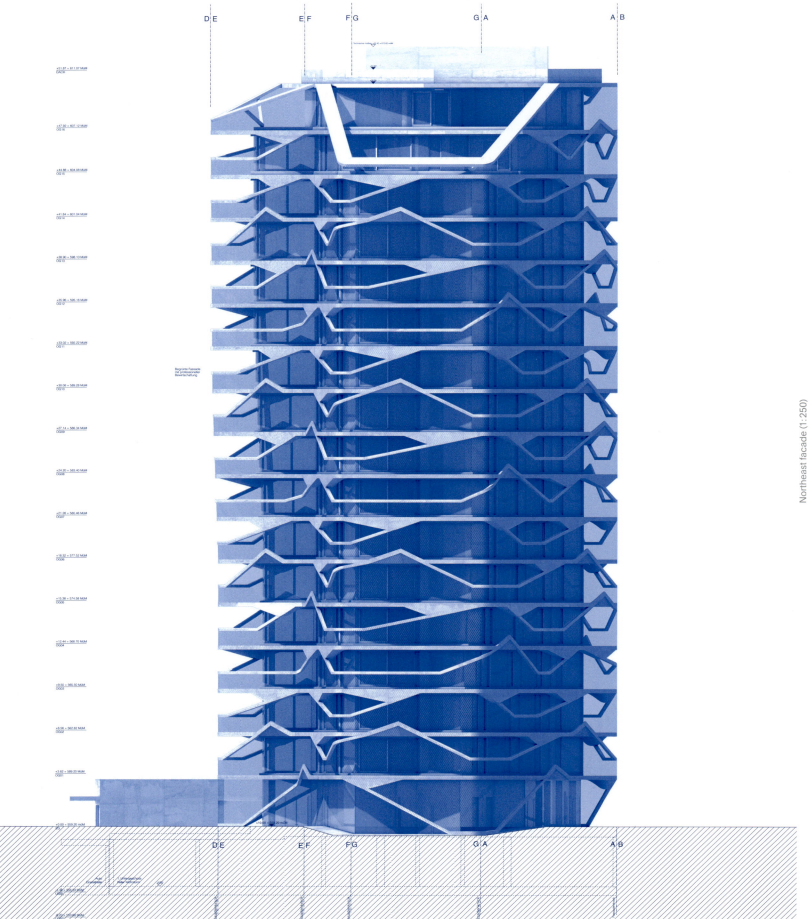

Wädenswil, Switzerland

2008–2014   **Peninsula Housing Development**

New building

N° 090 Peninsula Housing Development

Location Wädenswil, Switzerland   **Type** New building   **Status** Realized   **Project phases** *Competition* 2008, 1st prize *Planning* 2008–2011 *Realization* 2012–2014 **Client** Peach Property Group AG, Zurich *General contractor* Alfred Müller AG, Baar   **Project data** *Lot size* 13,542 m^2 *Built up area* 815 m^2 *Floor area* 8,651 m^2 (according to SIA 416) *Building volume* 145,336 m^3 **Planners** *Architecture* Buchner Bründler Architekten, Basel *Building engineering, planning* Bänziger Partner AG, Zurich *Building engineering, realization* Basler & Hofmann AG, Lucerne *Landscape architecture, planning* Berchtold.Lenzin Landschaftsarchitekten, Basel *Landscape architecture, realization* Enea Landscape Architecture, Rapperswil-Jona *Building technology* Getec Zürich AG, Zurich *Electrical planning, planning* Enerpeak Salzmann AG, Dübendorf *Electrical planning, realization* Thomas Lüem Partner AG, Baar *Building physics, planning* Michael Wichser + Partner AG, Dübendorf *Building physics, realization* Kopitsis Bauphysik AG, Wohlen *Fire prevention planning* Visiotec Technical Consulting AG, Allschwil   **Team Buchner Bründler** *Partners* Daniel Buchner, Andreas Bründler *Associate, planning and realization* Bülend Yigin *Project lead, competition* Nicole Johann *Project lead, realization* Florian Rink *Competition participants* Daniel Abraha, Ewa Misiewicz, Zahin Farhad *Planning participants* Ewa Misiewicz, Patrizia Wunderli, Florian Ueker, Maria Conen, Hellade Miozzari, Phillip Ryffel, Dominik Aegerter, Madeleine Müller, Stephanie Wamister, Martin Risch, Achim Widjaja *Realization participants* Joana Anes, Peter Beutler, Pascal Berchtold, Michael Steigmeier, Mascha Zach, Alexandra Berthold, Florian Bengert, Lorenz Marggraf   **Publications** Dorothea Gabelmann, Mit Pool verbundene Neubauten, Zürichsee Zeitung, December 8, 2008 • Maja Fueter, Schöne Aussichten am Zürichsee, NZZ Residence 2 (2016), 86–89

Impetus   As a manufacturing site, the peninsular in Wädenswil was dominated by textile production up until the 1970s. The remnants of this era on the Giessen works site include the imposing factory building, the director's villa, and numerous workers' lodgings.   The development plan involved the creation of a high-end housing area with the conversion of individual existing buildings and the new construction of large adjoining buildings. Following the study assignment, the eastern portion of the site is to be further developed.

Concept   The buildings are intended to reflect both the conglomerative qualities of the location and the spatial links to the natural surroundings. The spatial concept is shaped by the interplay of moods between the wide basin of the lake and the steep hillside topography.

The site is reconfigured by two buildings, adapted to the local geometry. By staggering and layering the volumes, they optically merge to form a porous spatial assemblage, stretching to the boat club building. The front and rear sides of the buildings are segmented with an open horizontality toward the lake and with a pronounced verticality toward the hillside. This duality marks the physical appearance of the architectural massing and shapes the living atmosphere. In a modified form, the brick facade in dark solid blocks transmits the architectural legacy of the factory building into the here and now.

Implementation   The side facing the Zimmerberg is largely formed using solid detailing. Individual expansive window openings and protruding, open atriums break the walled appearance. Facing the lake, the stony skin is reduced to encompass the horizontally projecting platforms. The horizon of the open lake surface is carried over into the building structure via a horizontal alignment. The appearance toward the lake is marked by slender vertical facade profilings. A plastically molded brick frieze mantles the form of the building and weaves the two sides together.   The meandering forms of the building allow numerous different apartment types to be realized. The wellness area housed in the central block connects the two buildings and affords all of the residents a direct visual connection to the lake. A water basin, lit from both sides, adds to the exclusivity of the complex.

Peninsula, Giessen: peninsula on the left shore of Lake Zurich in the municipality of Wädenswil around 20 km east of the City of Zurich. Giessen is first mentioned in 1468 in tax deeds, where Heiny Müller underm Giessen operated a mill, powered by water from the Giessbach. 1550, dominion of the farming village Wädenswil and the eponymous bailiwick is assumed by Zurich. **E** 1772, Wädenswil numbers 635 households: the textile cottage industry provides prosperity—a class of independent textile merchants emerges.

E In the beginning of the 19th CENTURY, industrial factories expand; Giessen peninsula develops to a manufacturing location. 1826, the wool manufacturers Rhyner und Blattmann start a red-dyeing factory. 1832 sees the founding of the wool spinning mill Rensch & Hauser, which from 1887 continues as Tuchfabrik Pfenninger & Cie. Next to the Giessbach Waterfall, the Wädenswil Brewery blasts rock cellars to store beer starting in 1858. 1875, Wädenswil is connected to the railway network; the railroad cuts the peninsula off from the rest of the town. **P** 1878, the Cantonal Zurich Parliament revises Giessen's boundaries: previously divided between the municipalities of Wädenswil and Richterswil, the peninsula and its 238 inhabitants are incorporated wholly in Wädenswil. **E** In 1897, the Tuchfabrik Pfenninger & Cie. purchases a number of properties in Giessen, becoming sole owners of the peninsula, including factory buildings, warehouses, a villa, and worker's lodgings and housing.

In the early 20th CENTURY Wädenswil experiences a boom: between 1900 and 1910 the number of inhabitants increases from 7,500 to over 9,000. **E** 1906, Pfenninger & Cie. opens a new factory building in Giessen with a high chimneystack; due to its tall halls, the industrial building was considered pioneering. 1906/07, the Lake Club Wädenswil acquires land on the eastern part of the peninsula to build a boathouse. In 1950 Wädenswil numbers 10,155 inhabitants, making it statistically a town. A majority of the residents of the peninsula are employed by Pfenninger & Cie., for instance the yarn foreman Rudolf Bachofner or the textile worker Irene Beetschen.

P 1963 onward, construction of the motorway on the left-hand side of Lake Zurich: once completed, Wädenswil is only a fifteen-minute drive from Zurich, triggering a building boom. **E** 1976, the Tuchfabrik Pfenninger & Cie. ceases production; their properties in Giessen are leased out by the newly founded real estate company Pfenninger AG. In the mid-1970s Giessen is home to numerous Italian guest workers, like the pattern weaver Orlando Gasparini or the assistant driller Arnaldo Mancini. **P** 1984, the Wädenswil authorities place a number of the industrial buildings on the Municipal Inventory of Protected Monuments. **P** 1997, the municipality of Wädenswil issues a design plan for the Giessen works site, with the aim of achieving a high concentration of buildings. In February 2002 Giessen peninsular is placed on the Inventory of Protected Townscapes of Supra-Municipal Significance.

The intact 1905 industrial building by the engineer Robert Maillart, executed with a structural steel framework and brick facade, served as the material reference for the staggered volume of the new building, deploying hand-formed clinker brick. The railway tracks and the lakeside road separate the Giessen peninsular from the village center, running adjacent to the development plot to the south. As opposed to the open side facing the lake, the design of the south facade with projecting patio structures reacts directly to the disruptive emissions it is exposed to. Dual-directionally arranged wall plates support the oversailing patio structures. Acoustically active infill panels with openly joined wooden slats absorb the noise from the surroundings.

The living and dining areas are orientated toward the basin of Lake Zurich facing north, while the private rooms open onto the patios facing south. The three-dimensional elements of the rooms with dark brick and fixtures in burnished brass contrast with the light ceilings of smooth gypsum coating and the ground-polished terrazzo floors with a scattering of marble. Rough-stone plates made of white marble are applied extensively in the bathroom areas, and smoked-glass spatial partitionings adopt the color tones of the burnished brass.

The roof penthouse level meanders all the way to the outermost facade alignment of the main architectural volume. Seen from the access lobbies, the floor-to-ceiling glazing provides views to the parking garage, which is deliberately devoid of installations.

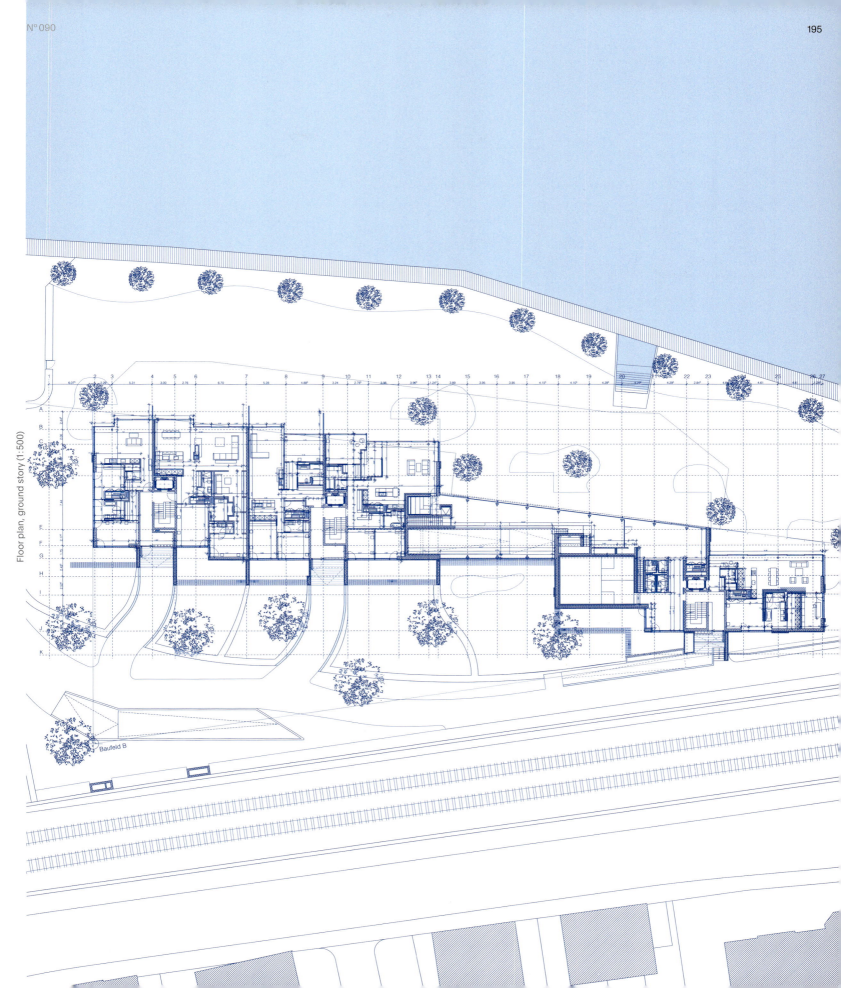

Floor plan, ground story (1:500)

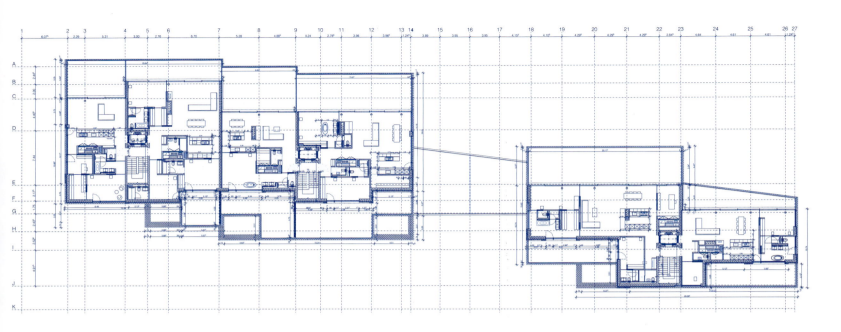

Floor plan, attic story (1:500)

Floor plan, 1st upper story (1:500)

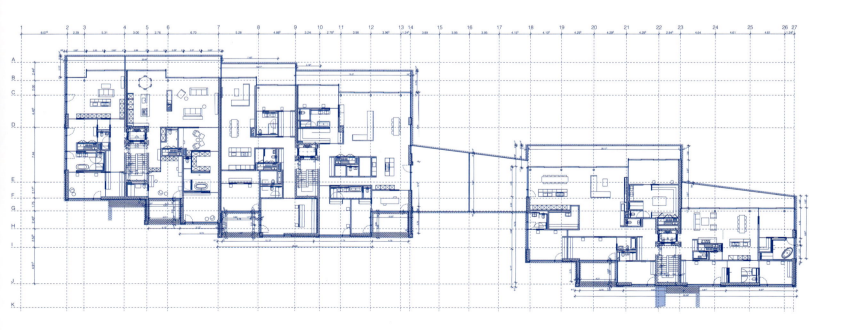

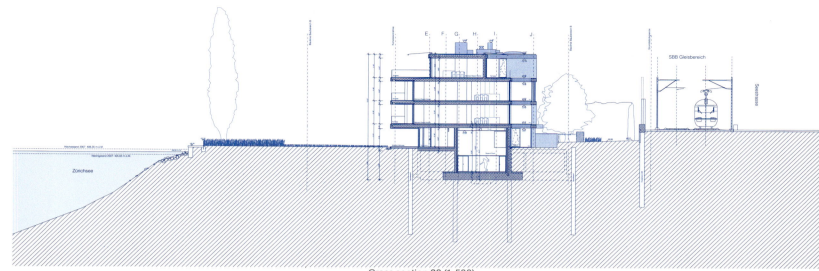
Cross section 20 (1:500)

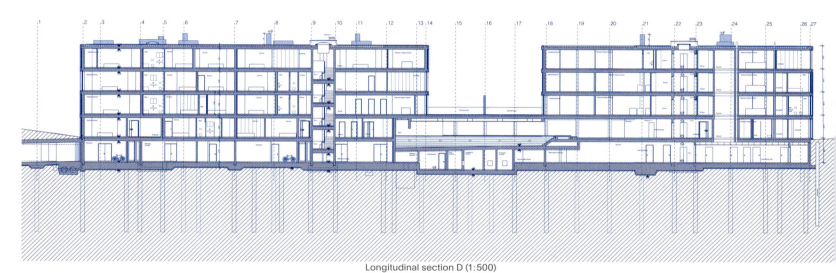
Longitudinal section D (1:500)

Cross section 17 (1:500)

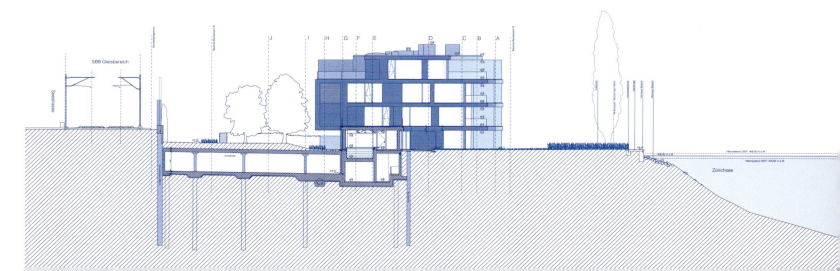

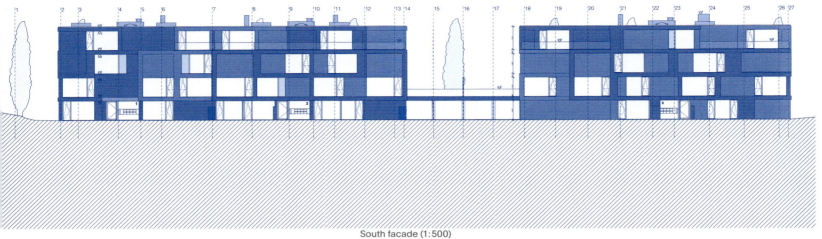
South facade (1:500)

West facade (1:500)

North facade (1:500)

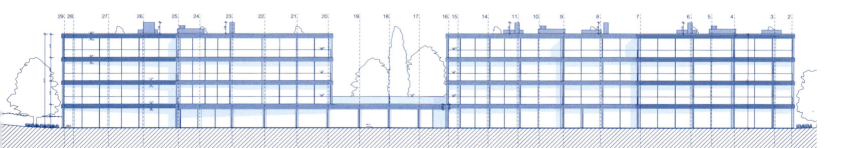

Basel, Switzerland

2009–2015 **Hotel Nomad**

Conversion and extension

N° 113 Hotel Nomad — Conversion and extension — Selected Buildings

Location Basel, Switzerland **Type** Conversion and extension **Status** Realized **Project phases** *Planning* 2009–2013 *Realization* 2014–2015 **Client** UBS Immobilienfonds Swissreal c/o UBS Fund Management (Switzerland) AG **General contractor** Losinger Marazzi AG, Basel **Tenant fit-out** Krafft Gruppe, Basel **Project data** *Lot size* 650 m² *Built up area* 520 m² *Floor area* 4,760 m² (according to SIA 416) *Building volume* 14,300 m³ **Planners** *Architecture* Buchner Bründler Architekten, Basel *Building engineering* WMM Ingenieure AG, Basel *Electrical planning* Herzog Kull Group, Pratteln *Building technology* Jobst Willers Engineering AG, Rheinfelden; Waldhauser + Hermann AG, Münchenstein *Sanitary planning* Sanplan Ingenieure AG, Liestal *Interior fittings* Jasmin Grego & Stephanie Kühnle Architektur GmbH, Zurich *Building physics* Gruner AG, Basel *Acoustics* Applied Acoustics GmbH, Gelterkinden *Facade planning* Christoph Etter Fassadenplanungen, Basel *Fire prevention planning* Visiotec Technical Consulting AG, Allschwil **Team Buchner Bründler** *Partners* Daniel Buchner, Andreas Bründler *Associate* Nick Waldmeier *Project leads, planning* Thomas Klement, Ewa Misiewicz *Project lead, realization* Dominik Aegerter *Participants* Norma Tollmann, Beda Klein, Stefan Mangold, Yvonne Grunwald, Benjamin Hofmann, Ananda Berger, Claudia Furer, Rino Buess, Henrik Månsson, Tünde König, Rebecca Borer **Publications** Jakob Schoof, Hotel Nomad in Basel, DETAIL inside 1 (2016), 38–41 • Susanne Lieber, Für Stadtreisende, Wohnrevue 02 (2016), 16 • Katharina Marschal, Home Away from Home, Modulor 2 (2016), 46–51 • Susanna Koeberle, Sinfonie der Materialien, Das Ideale Heim 4 (2016), 38–39 • Sandra Hofmeister, Nomad Hotel, Basel: Im Rhythmus der Stadt, Schweizer Baudokumentation, VISO 4 (2016), 34–41 • Lilia Glanzmann, 1001 Nacht, Hochparterre 4 (2016), 40–45 • Sylvia Steidinger, Roher Beton und weiche Teppiche, Umbauen + Renovieren 5 (2016), 110–11 • David Streiff Corti, Oase für Stadtnomaden, NZZ am Sonntag, May 8, 2016, 22–23 • Susanne Dubbert, Hotel Nomad in Basel, AIT 6 (2016), 104–109 • Franziska Laur, Von "vorbildlich" bis "meisterhaft": Heimatschutz prämiert bauliche Beispiele für innerstädtische Verdichtung, Basler Zeitung, November 8, 2016 • Jolanthe Kugler, Hotel Nomad in Basel, db—deutsche bauzeitung 12 (2016), 102–107 • Christiane Müller, Hotel Nomad in Basel: Quartiersrevitalisierung inbegriffen, Baumeister 4 (2017), 20–31 • Tobias Hilbert, Ein Hauch New York in Basel, Wohnrevue 1 (2019), 132–33

Impetus Brunngässlein is situated in the shadow of a number of busy roads in Basel city centre. The apartment house designed by Bräuning, Leu, Dürig is a protected historical monument and exhibits typical characteristics of its pedigree in the 1950s. The two-part configuration consists of a seven-story front building and a five-story rear one, joined by a shared ground floor. The building is to be converted into a city hotel.

Concept The visual recognition of the hotel as an otherwise inserted block segment is reinforced by accentuating the tripartite facade arrangement and rethinking its material components. The necessary new replacement building in the courtyard results in a differentiated conception of the various sub-sections, with the open ground floor playing a connecting role. The structurally molded ceiling surface acts as a figurative relief that legibly coalesces the parts of the building.

The organization of the rooms in the front building occurs via a spatial layering along the axis from the entrance to the point-focal casement windows. In the courtyard building the rooms follow a circular spatial sequence, which leads to the bathrooms along the spatially deep glass facade with built-in benches. Material analyses showed that the original facade had been finished in exposed concrete and had then later been painted. This discovery led to the application of concrete as a primary material in the overall concept.

Implementation The facade of the existing building was refurbished in keeping with its protected status and stripped back to its original raw concrete surfaces.

A new primary layer of attached window rectangles with raw aluminum frames forms an overlay to the plastically formed concrete surface. Large metal sliding windows on the ground floor, coupled with the slender arrangement of the top-floor extension with flat aluminum panels and extensive glazed surfaces, create a further contrast in materials to the primary tactile concrete. The courtyard building is likewise extensively glazed, extending the rooms spatially and providing them with sufficient light. In the interior the primary material palette of concrete and metal is transferred down to the furnishing elements, supplemented situationally by wooden and textile surface coverings.

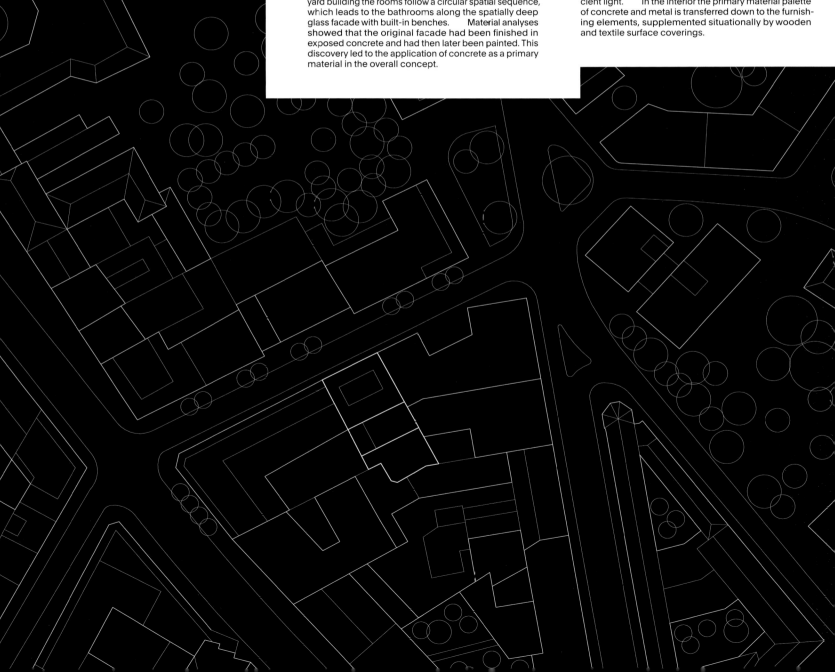

Brunngässlein no. 8, in the center of the City of Basel. Brunngässlein is 3 m wide, connecting Malzgasse and Aeschenvorstadt, the continuation of Freie Strasse. A property at no. 8 is first mentioned in the land registry in 1371. Since the end of the 14th CENTURY, within the city walls. Between the inner and outer city stands the outer Aeschentor with a forecourt and two small round towers. The outer city limits include Elisabethenstrasse (earlier Spittelschüren) and Stern- and Brunngässlein. End of the 15th CENTURY, the Aeschenvorstadt contains 65 buildings— no churches, but instead inns, numerous horse stables, and sheds for carts and goods. The residents, hand workers living off the highway traffic: wainwrights, furriers, cartsmiths, saddlers, coachmen, but also masons, potters, locksmiths, blacksmiths, rope-makers, tailors, tinsmiths, merchants, and clerks. In front of the entrance to Brunngässlein stands the Jakobsbrunnen.

Between St. Alban-Vorstadt, Aeschenvorstadt, and Elisabethenstrasse are vineyards and horticultural land. In the 18th CENTURY, two stately Baroque patrician's buildings are built at the Aeschenvorstadt—things become more genteel. In 1850 an inn appears at the start of Brunngässlein. It is the most popular tavern in the city, with a brewery, a large hall including a mirrored wall, a variety show, and a concert venue. The city expands, the railroad arrives: the city walls are demolished, the trenches filled in. The gateway disappears: in 1865 the entrance to the city is remodeled with two prestigious corner-front buildings.

1879, the Wettsteinbrücke is inaugurated as the second bridge over the Rhine, followed by the beginning of the planning of a direct link between the bridge and Aeschenplatz, threatening the "rural oasis in the middle of the city." Properties nos. 6 and 8 on Brunngässlein belong to the De Wette family, part of a larger premises: here a building with stables, storeroom, and a carriage house; a conservatory, a plant house with heating, and a glazed roof; the point marks the end of the verdant garden enclosure. 1900, Dufourstrasse pushes through to Aeschenplatz, which becomes a tram station; traffic increases. The plot's new owner plans a new building; the carriage house and storeroom are demolished in 1901. Horses and stables disappear from the alley and from the city. In the early 20th CENTURY, Vorstadt shifts to become a commercial center, with the Bankverein, Baslerhof, Aeschenhof, Coop-Haus, and Genossenschaftlicher Zentralbank. The Brunngässlein, serving "a large number of pedestrians," is to be newly widened to 10 to 14 m. 1910, complaints are raised: in the courtyard of no. 8 the proprietor of the neighboring Bären inn had established a garbage pile with ash, refuse, and kitchen slops.

1928, the carriage house and storage building is covered with two stories in masonry and sheet metal, equipped with an external cast-iron staircase, serving as motorcar parking. 1936, it becomes a garage, in 1939 including a showroom "to demonstrate particular apparatuses." The city is remodeled to accommodate automobile traffic, the streets become wider. The busiest Basel architectural office, Bräuning, Leu und Dürig, builds commercial buildings between Aeschen- and Bankenplatz, and also at Brunngässlein no. 8 in 1952: a two-part ensemble with a shared ground floor as a shop area, accompanied by a modern apartment building with small furnished units with service and communal rooms. Converted in the 1960s into office spaces. The Jakobsbrunnen has meanwhile disappeared. In 2005 the building is listed in the inventory of the Basel Office of Historic Monument Preservation as an "original representative of a style characteristic of the 1950s."

The staggered stand-alone volume of the office building on Picassoplatz by Diener & Diener Architekten is followed by the hinge-like corner building by Studio Märkli, which by means of a pivoting transmits the sequence of the commercial buildings. The original exposed-concrete composition of the facade was only established using laboratory analyses of the remaining surface coating, allowing it to be restored to its original condition. The single-story connection structure of the library area joins the two segments of the building, orientating itself along its entire width to the introverted courtyard garden.

Sliding facade elements allow the restaurant to be opened up extensively facing the street. The overlapping of existing and new load-bearing elements produces a tectonic ceiling structure. For the tables encircling the pillars, the concrete was cast directly into the brass profiles and polished to reveal its granular composition.

The scope for the use of the circulation spaces is extended by incorporating kitchenettes on each floor. The everted pyramids in the middle of the courtyard garden open up the restaurant to the sky and create a thermal effect. At night they are transformed into brightly lit lanterns in the midst of the dark green. The curtains integrated into the seating windows, made of variously thick cloth, reinforce the variability of the courtyard room.

Spatially containing volumes in oak structure the minimalist spatial shell made of raw and ground concrete. Black mosaic overlays and moveable spatial partitionings divide the openly conceived spaces into zones. Flat-woven berber carpets are crafted to fit the respective spatial masses. Floor-to-ceiling glazed elements funnel the light deep into the room.

Flat facade panels in raw aluminum reflect the evening light right to the street.

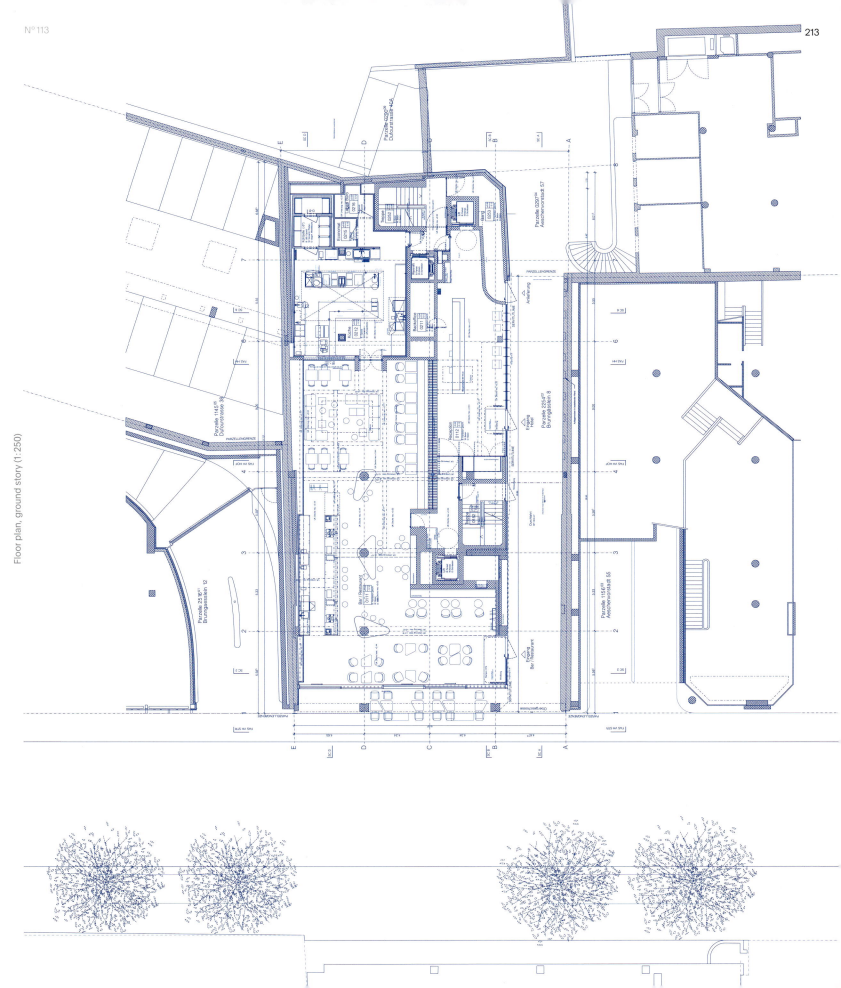

Floor plan, ground story (1:250)

Floor plan, 2nd upper story (1:250)

Longitudinal section (1:250)

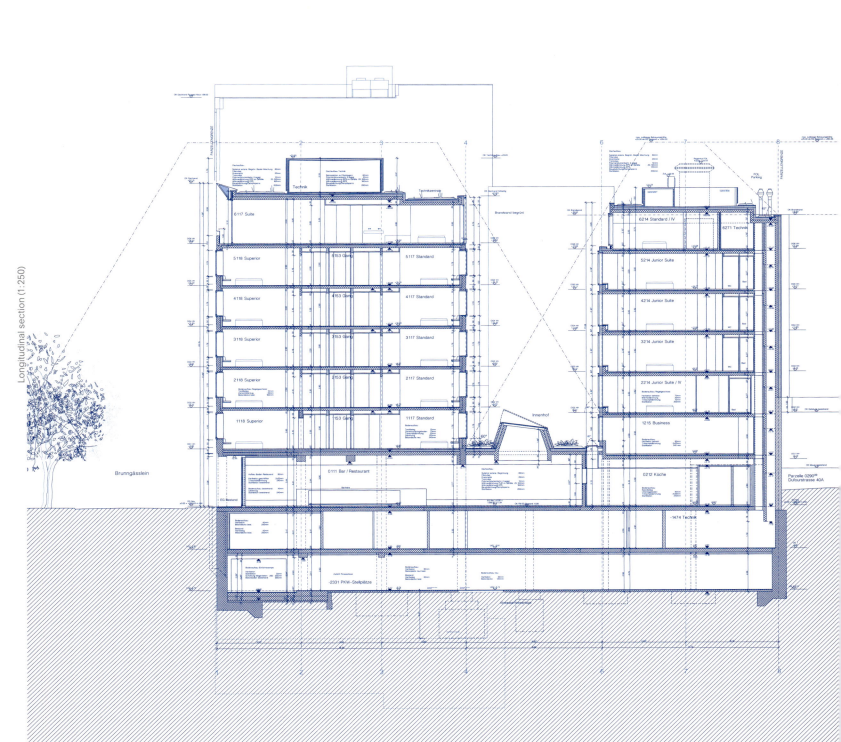

Street facade, north (1:300)

Courtyard facade, south (1:300)　　　　Courtyard facade, north (1:300)

Zurich, Switzerland

2010–2017 **Tièchestrasse Housing Development**

New building

N° 123   Tièchestrasse Housing Development

Location Zurich, Switzerland   **Type** New building   **Status** Realized   **Project phases** *Competition* 2010, 1st prize *Planning* 2010–2014 *Realization* 2014–2017   **Client** *competition* BEP Baugenossenschaft des eidgenössischen Personals, Zurich; City of Zurich, Amt für Liegenschaften, Zurich *Planning and realization* HRS Real Estate AG, Zurich   **Project data** *Lot size* 17,700 m² *Built up area* 4,076 m² *Floor area* 20,676 m² (according to SIA 416) *Building volume* 75,665 m³   **Planners** *Architecture* Buchner Bründler Architekten, Basel *Site management* HRS Real Estate AG, Zurich *Building engineering, competition* WMM Ingenieure AG, Münchenstein *Building engineering, planning and realization* Urech Bärtschi Maurer AG, Zurich *Landscape architecture* Fontana Landschaftsarchitektur, Basel *Building physics, competition* Amstein + Walthert AG, Zurich *Building physics, planning and realization* Kopitsis Bauphysik, Wohlen *Building technology, competition* Bogenschütz AG, Basel *Sanitary planning* Huustechnik Rechberger AG, Zurich *Heating and ventilation planning* Todt Gmür + Partner AG, Schlieren *Electrical planning* Herzog Kull Group Engineering AG, Baden *Facade planning* Makiol Wiederkehr AG, Beinwil am See *Fire prevention planning* HKG Consulting AG, Aarau   **Team Buchner Bründler** *Partners* Daniel Buchner, Andreas Bründler *Associate* Stefan Oehy *Project lead, competition* Nino Soppelsa *Project leads, planning and realization* Katharian Kral, Daniel Ebertshäuser, Achim Widjaja *Competition participants* Dominik Aegerter, Lukas Baumann, Rino Bless, Florian Ueker, Stephanie Wamister *Planning and realization participants* Karolina Switzer, Simone Braendle, Rebecca Borer, Michael Glaser, Stefan Mangold, Dominik Aegerter, Kim Sneyders, Florian Ueker, Benjamin Hofmann, Florian Rink, André Santos, Sebastian Arzet, Luiz Albisser, Fatima Blötzer   **Publications** Tibor Joanelly, Vorauseilender Konsens, werk, bauen + wohnen 9 (2010), 50–52 • Alexander Felix, Ersatzwohnbau Tièchestrasse, Zürich, Tec21 24 (2010), 8 • Axel Simon, Zürich wird ersatzneugebaut: Tièchestrasse in Planung, Hochparterre 9 (2011), 20–28 • Tièchestrasse: Narziss und Goldmund, in Amt für Hochbauten Zürich (ed.), *Grundrissfibel Wohnbauten: 62 Wettbewerbe im gemeinnützigen Wohnungsbau 1999–2015*, Zurich 2015, 834–35 • Isabelle Burtscher, Gegensätze ziehen sich an, Hochparterre 9 (2017), 73 • Siedlung Tièchestrasse, Wohnen: Das Magazin für Genossenschaftlichen Wohnungsbau 4 (2017), 13 • Liza Papazoglou, Im Praxistest, Wohnen: Das Magazin für Genossenschaftlichen Wohnungsbau 10 (2018), 18–21 • Wohnüberbauung Tièchestrasse, in Makiol Wiederkehr AG (ed.), *Konstruktiv mit Holz: Dokumentierte Bauprojekte 1992–2018*, Zurich 2018, 188–93

Impetus   The narrow site stretches along Tièchestrasse and forms the final conclusion of the urban fabric. To the north of the street, family gardens lead directly to the Käferberg local recreational area. Directly adjacent to the plot is the Weid Hospital complex.   The staff residencies on the site are to be replaced by a housing development. The major part of the site, which covers an area of 17,700 m², is earmarked for seventy-five cooperative apartments, while the remaining area is allocated for some thirty individual condominiums. In addition is a compensatory area of 1,500 m² for a protected grassland meadow.

Concept   The urban-planning solution approach involves on the one hand continuing the urban layout and on the other dispersing it to give greater landscape linkages.   Two lineal volumes form a defined spatial sequence along the street. The first, elongated cooperative housing complex follows the topographical gradient, splits off from the curve of the road, and spans out a greened area that ends sequentially and allows the building to emerge out of the hillside. In the concluding intermediate space, the grassland meadow forms a pivotal landscape point, providing large open-space views and guaranteeing the continuation of the green spaces of the garden settlement and the Käferberg. The second building with condominiums is set swiveled on the ridge of the terrain. Loggia and terrace cutouts perforate the compact volumes to the south.

Implementation   The form of the buildings is derived from the progression of the topography. The cooperative part is graduated parallel to the gradient of the street. The garden level is used collectively with a frontal covered encounter zone.   The interior organization is largely determined by the orientation, whereby all of the bedrooms face south and are equipped with access to the wraparound balcony layer. The four-story private-ownership part is positioned lineally on the rise of the hill and is accessed via bridgeways. A central motif is the extended heights in the living and dining areas. Facing south, the loggias elongate the continuous central space.

The buildings are erected as solid constructions and clad in dark-painted wood, whereby the rough-sawn planks are laid in alternative vertical and horizontal fields in order to generate an overall tectonic impression.

Tièchestrasse 43 and 47–61, in Zurich-Wipkingen. Traces of Roman settlment between 0 and 400 A.D in the Steimeren, southwest of Tièchestrasse. 881, first documentary mention of Wibichinga, a hamlet to the west of Zurich on the southern foot of the Käferberg, named after the numerous beetles in the forest. **R** Around 910, ownership of Wibichinga falls to the Fraumünster Monastery in Zurich. **E** Wibichinga's settlement core lies on the right-hand bank of the River Limmat; communal use of the slopes of the Käferberg in the Middle Ages for agriculture and wine-growing. Clusters of houses and single farmhouses; at the edge of the forest was most likely an infirmary. **P** 1524, the rights to Wibichinga are transferred to the City of Zurich. From the 17th CENTURY, city townspeople build country houses on the south slope of the Käferberg, including the Waid estate. **E** At the end of the 18th CENTURY, arrival of the first textile factory in the municipality of Wipkingen; a ferryboat across the Limmat connects the around 500 residents of the farming village with the left river bank. **P** 1850 to 1855, construction works within the municipal boundaries for the railway line from Zurich to Oerlikon. **E** 1871, construction of a bridge over the Limmat as a connection to the industrial district Aussersihl vis-à-vis, prompting many worker's families to move to Wipkingen, the number of inhabitants increasing to around 2,400 by 1888. **P** Wipkingen expands, but lacks rich tax payers and funds for infrastructures, leading a large majority of its citizens to vote for incorporation into the City of Zurich, taking place in 1893. 1895, Wipkingen is connected to the railway network; 1898, to the tram system. By 1900 the number of residents rises to 4,500. **E** The slopes of the Käferberg are still dominated by agriculture and wine-growing, while the Waid had become a popular day-trip destination for the city's population, the restaurant Waid—built in 1878 and still there today—acting as a popular magnet. **P** In 1904 the City of Zurich buys the forests on the Käferberg, and 1907 the Waid estate, with the aim of preserving the landscape and the view from the largely undeveloped area. The first plans for the erection of a city hospital on the Waid are formulated. 1911, the city launches an ideas competition for traffic infrastructure for the Waid, its realization delayed by the outbreak of WW I. 1915, the organization Familiengärten Wipkingen leases land on the Waid, and allotments appear on the slopes of the Käferberg. **P** 1918, the city opens an infirmary on the former Waid estate. 1932/33, downhill from today's Tièchestrasse the city builds the Waidhalde School, which is now a protected building. 1945, the authorities launch an architectural competition for the building of the Stadtspital Waid, which is erected between 1951 and 1953. Tièchestrasse is created as a connection between the hospital and the city center, named after the dermatologist Max Tièche. Between 1953 and 1957 residential buildings for the hospital staff are built at Tièchestrasse nos. 47 to 61, and at no. 43 a house for the chief physician. Between the hospital and the staff housing, an area of grassland establishes the landscape link between the city and the local Käferberg recreational area. 1976, construction of the Käferberg Thermal Baths above the Waidspital. 2000, renaturation of the formerly concreted-over course of the Wolfgrimbach between the staff housing and the hospital.

The staggered cooperative housing project follows the topographical rise along Tièchestrasse. The elongated buildings form the conclusion of the city's urban fabric, their dimensions orientated toward the buildings of the neighboring Waid hospital and the Waidhalde school, the latter built by the structural engineer Robert Maillart in the 1930s in exposed concrete and situated downhill from the adjoining group of houses. The Wolfgrimbach runs past the end of the development, flowing from a pond in the Käferberg forest to the River Limmat at the bottom of the valley. For energy-technology reasons, only 30% of the northern surface facade consists of openings.

The upper architectural volume is shifted away from the slope-stabilizing gravity wall and consists of owner-occupied apartments accessed via bridgeways. Closed balustrades made of massive steel plates form a ribbon-like conclusion facing the well of the staircase. Volumetric recesses at the attic level form triple-sided enclosed terrace spaces. Via the partial spatial heightening, the view onto the hillside is guided upward to the sky.

The attic level is situated some 90 m above the main street level. From here the viewer's gaze falls directly on the Swissmill silo tower on the Sihlquai. The cooperative apartments are equipped with a continuous layer of balconies, onto which all the living rooms and bedrooms open. The arrangement of the shared facilities and the three kindergartens on the garden level makes the frontal terrace a popular boulevard location. The wooden facade is coated in protective mineral paint. The rough-sawn planks consist of fir wood; particularly exposed elements are manufactured in more hardwearing cedar wood.

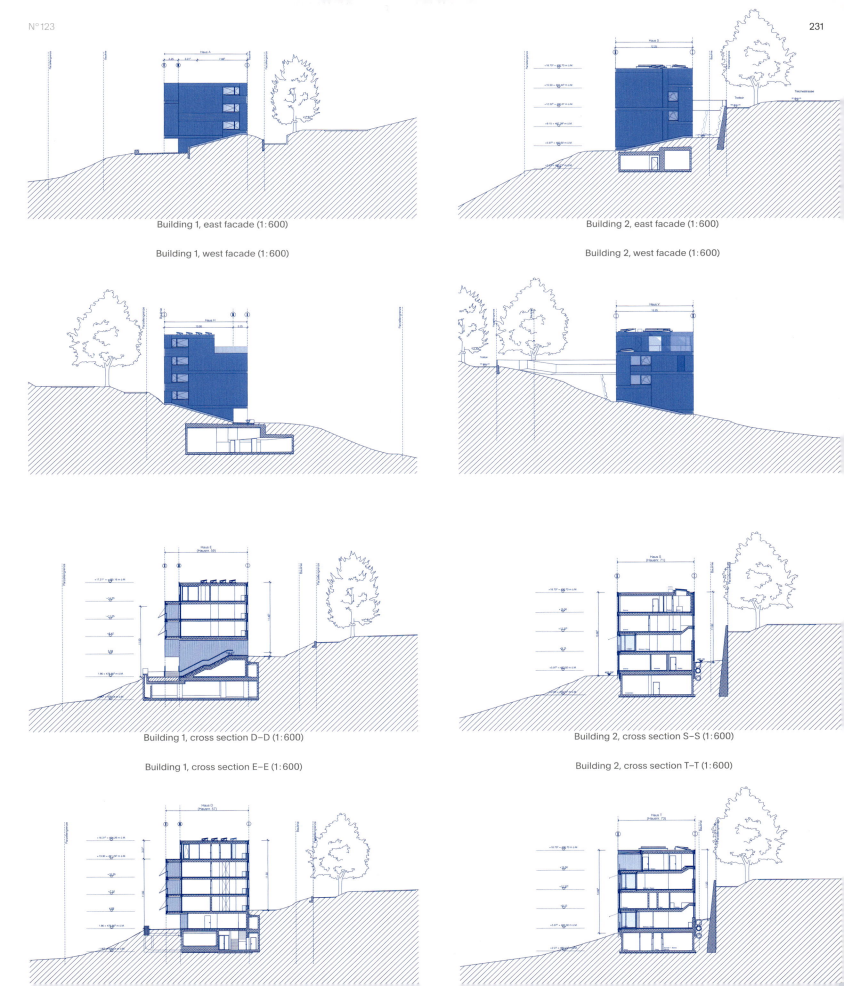

Building 1, east facade (1:600) Building 2, east facade (1:600)

Building 1, west facade (1:600) Building 2, west facade (1:600)

Building 1, cross section D–D (1:600) Building 2, cross section S–S (1:600)

Building 1, cross section E–E (1:600) Building 2, cross section T–T (1:600)

Building 1, floor plan, 2nd upper story

Building 1, floor plan, garden level

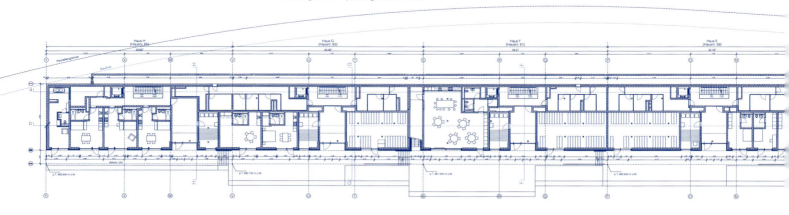

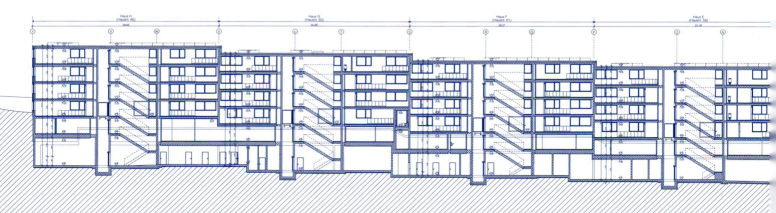

Building 1, longitudinal section E–E

Building 1, south facade

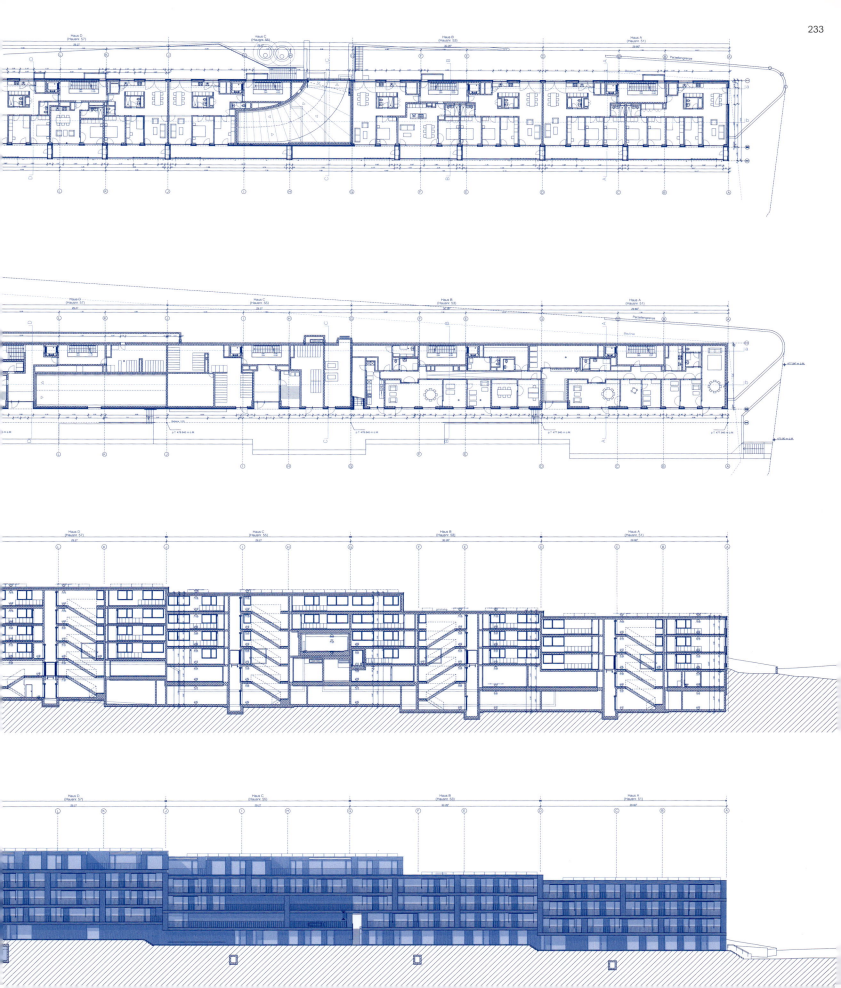

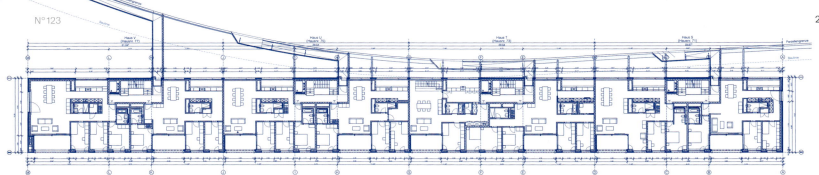

Building 2, floor plan, 2nd upper story

Building 2, floor plan, 1st upper story

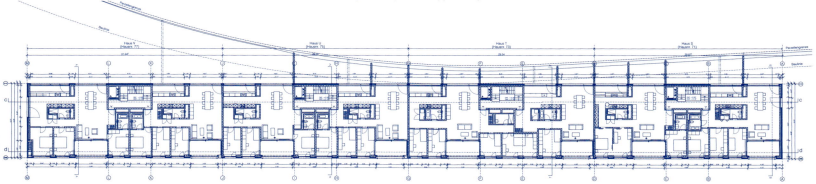

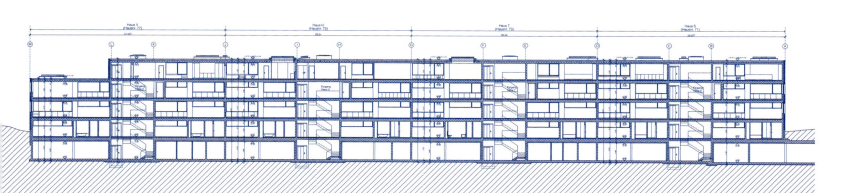

Building 2, longitudinal section C–C

Building 2, north facade

Hertenstein-Weggis, Switzerland

2010–2012   **Hertenstein House**

New building

N°147 Hertenstein House

Location Hertenstein-Weggis, Switzerland **Type** New building **Status** Realized **Project phases** *Planning* 2010–2011 *Realization* 2011–2012 **Client** Private **Project data** *Lot size* 1,500 m² *Built up area* 250 m² *Floor area* 331 m² (according to SIA 416) *Building volume* 1,370 m³ **Planners** *Architecture* Buchner Bründler Architekten, Basel *Site management* Paul Zimmermann + Partner AG, Viznau *Building engineering* Schnetzer Puskas Ingenieure AG, Basel *Building physics* Waldhauser Haustechnik AG, Münchenstein *Acoustics* Applied Acoustics GmbH, Gelterkinden *Building technology* Walter Weber AG, Gelterkinden **Team Buchner Bründler** *Partners* Daniel Buchner, Andreas Bründler *Project lead, planning* Jenny Jenisch *Project lead, realization* Achim Widjaja *Realization participants* Chiara Friedl, Florian Ueker, Rino Buess **Publications** Katharina Marchal, 3 Houses 3 Stories, Mark Magazine, no. 6–7 (2013), 170–71 • Wohnhaus Hertenstein, in Hubertus Adam / Elena Kossovskaja / S AM Swiss Architectural Museum (eds.), *S AM 10: Building Images: Photography Focusing on Swiss Architecture*, Basel 2013, 112–13 • Hubertus Adam / Wolfgang Bachmann, Wohnhaus in Weggis: Buchner Bründler Architekten, in *Häuser des Jahres: Die 50 besten Einfamilienhäuser 2013*, Munich 2013, 238–43 • Franziska Quandt, Sichtschichtung: Buchner Bründler zelebrieren Enge und Weite bei der Umsetzung eines Hauses bei Luzern, Atrium 4 (2015), 68–75

Impetus The project involved the development of a private residence for an artist couple to serve as a place of occasional retreat and regeneration. The available plot of land is situated on an exposed lip of south-facing hillside sloping down from the street. The site offers a spectacular natural panorama. Running parallel beneath the plot is the main arm of Lake Lucerne, and beyond it the Alps stretch into the intangible distance. The steep slopes of the Bürgenstock on the opposite shore are non-developable.

Concept The concept of the house focuses on these greater, overarching themes, while simultaneously adopting a connection to the immediate location. The spatial organization is anchored in the multi-sided orientation. Based on the extraordinary views, the courtyard areas are expressed as intimate, introverted spaces, providing an exciting contrast to the natural expanses around them.

The primary volume is formed as the simple addition of various rectangular solids, offset relative to one another, which in turn leads to differing spatial grains. Courtyard-like intermediate spaces give the progression of the facade a further meandering quality. The over-layering and perforation of slabs set orthogonally to each other generates a sculptural composition. On a compacted scale, the structure of the slabs reiterates the basic dynamic of shifts and overlapping.

Implementation Seen from the access road, the house appears simply as a flat elevation above the topography, only to then to present itself rising up over two stories. On entering, a view out over the lake and the mountains opens up. The living level behind extends across the projecting terrace into the garden topography. The bedrooms and a studio are housed on the upper floor. The ground floor with the lounge and guest areas is situated on the natural lip of the terrain and is slotted backward into the hillside. The longitudinal facade faces the lake, with the obverse side facing the courtyard toward the road. The building is cast in light-colored exposed concrete, the daylight and shadows falling on it emphasizing the structural framework. In the interior this spatial homogeneity is continued in the cast, smooth surface materials. The wooden frames of the large glazing units supplement the light basic color with a warm natural note. The rooms to the terrace and the courtyard can be opened up expansively via sliding doors.

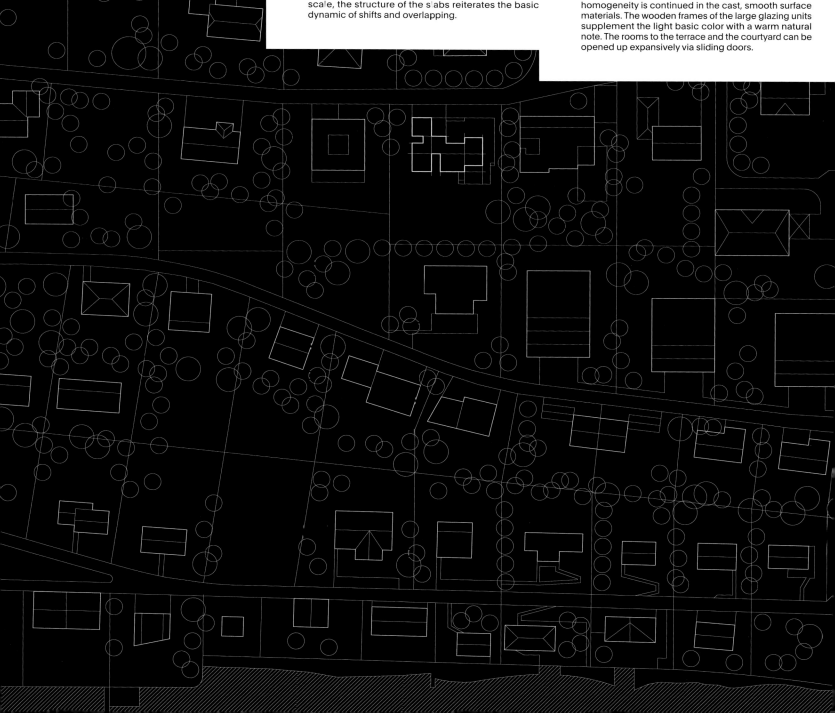

Hertenstein, location in the municipality of Weggis in Canton Lucerne. Peninsula in the Lake Lucerne, defining the lake into two basin parts: its south bank borders the Vitznau Basin, its north bank the Küssnachtersee. ▶ Named after the patrician family von Hertenstein, who administered the Weggis bailiwick from their castle. 1213, first documentary mention of the von Hertenstein family.

▶ In 1380, the bailiwick, situated strategically on the north–south trading route over the Gotthard Pass, is purchased by the City of Lucerne. 1592, Lucerne opens a customs station on the peninsula to secure customs duties from the transit trade. ▶ Fishing and agriculture (profiting from the mild climate) characterize life on Hertenstein. Sources from the 17th CENTURY report farms on which grapevines, figs, chestnuts, and almonds were cultivated. From the 15th CENTURY commercial trades developed: in the Röhrli district Lucerne patricians quarry tuff, in Zinnen is a brickyard, and at the Röhrlibach a blacksmith and armorer put down roots.

In the 17th CENTURY Lucerne patricians discover Hertenstein as a summer residence and begin to build country houses, such as the Brünnihof. At the time the parish is home to around 700 people. ▶ 1834, the municipality of Weggis builds a poorhouse and orphanage on a former patrician estate in Hertenstein, today occupied by the orphanage chapel Eggisbühl, built in 1899. ▶ The first steamer ships sail Lake Lucerne from 1837 onward, bringing tourists to Hertenstein and ushering in an era of luxury and glamour. 1864, the opening of the Pension Hertenstein, which quickly attracts illustrious guests, for instance in 1866 Queen Victoria of the United Kingdom and Ireland and King Ludwig II of Bavaria. The latter planned to build a palace in Hertenstein in the 1870s, but the project was never realized.

▶ Tourism booms: 1873/74, the Lucerne banker Friedrich Kasimir Knörr builds the Schlosshotel Hertenstein, and in 1898 a boatyard with boat rentals is erected in the bay next to Grütschelen. ▶ The open-air theater on the grounds of the Schlosshotel directed by Rudolf Lorenz produces Europe-wide headlines in 1909. ▶ 1916, the Baldegg Monastry establishes the education center Stella Matutina on the western part of the peninsula. ▶ After his dethroning as Kaiser, Karl I of Austria resides in the Schlosshotel Hertenstein for five months from MAY 1921 onward. ▶ 1930, the Russian composer Sergei Rachmaninoff buys a property on the west side of the peninsula, commissioning the building of the Villa Senar in a Bauhaus style, and where he refound his creativity after a lengthy interlude.

Due to financial difficulties, the Schlosshotel Hertenstein is demolished in 1942, leaving only an annex that has since been run as the Hotel Hertenstein. ▶ 1946, various European federalists gathered in Hertenstein to formulate a program for a united postwar Europe. 1983, listing of the peninsula in the Federal Inventory of Landscapes and Natural Monuments of National Significance.

From 1932 to 1939 the composer Sergei Rachmaninow spent the summer months each year in his villa in Hertenstein. The incised patio room indicates the division of the house into two parts, which in the interior are connected in turn via passages. By force of the lightly sunken terrace of the terrain vis-à-vis the circulation route, the visitor enters the house through the upper level. The house is provided with projecting terraces and balconies with views to the southwest to Lucerne and the Pilatus. The circumferentially encompassed courtyard is understood as a dense reverberation of the open landscape.

Hertenstein is situated on the main arm of Lake Lucerne. The opposite Bürgenstock has steep slopes and is therefore completely undeveloped. An arrangement of two parallel flights of stairs and openings on each floor allow a circular route to be taken through the two parts of the house. To the southeast, the panorama stretches along the basin of the lake to the Vitznauerstock. The exposed southern situation and the equalizing effect of the lake create a mild microclimate.

A set of side stairs leads directly from the carport on the entrance level to the back courtyard area.

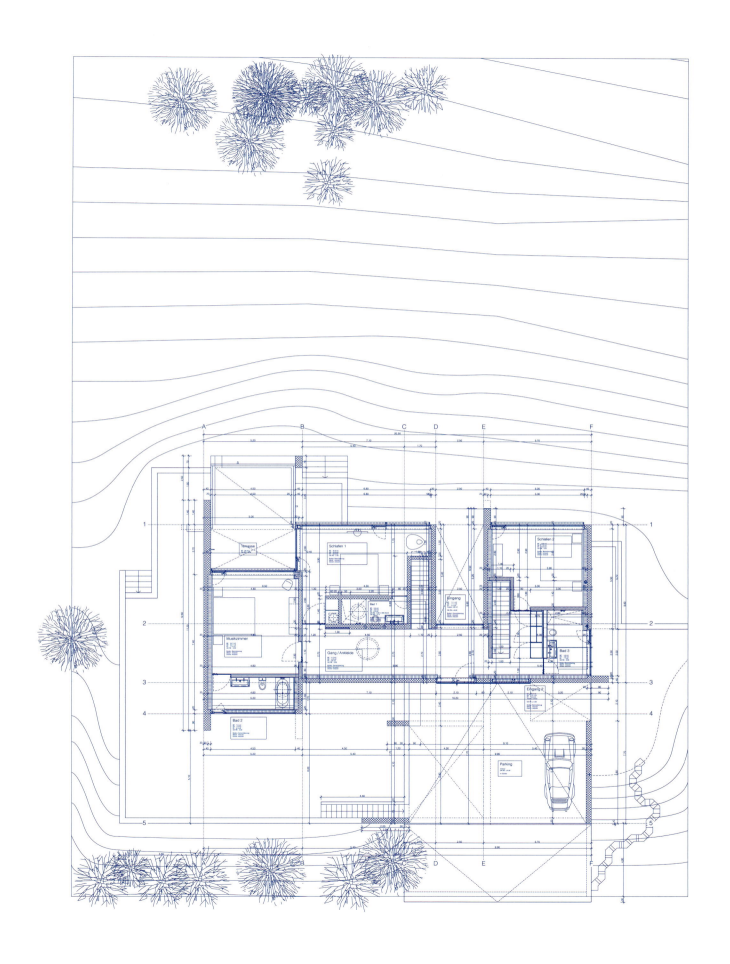

Floor plan, entrance level (1:150)

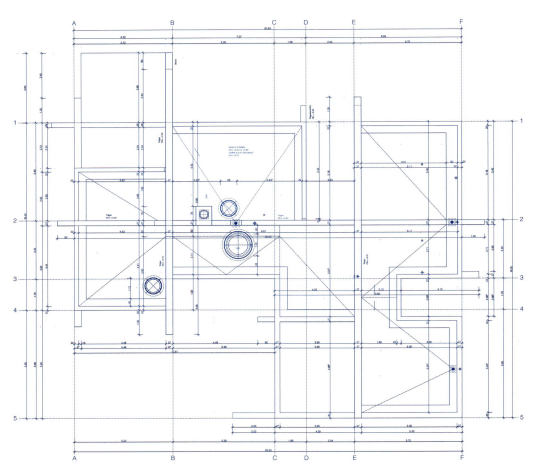

Top view, roof (1:150)

Floor plan, garden level (1:150)

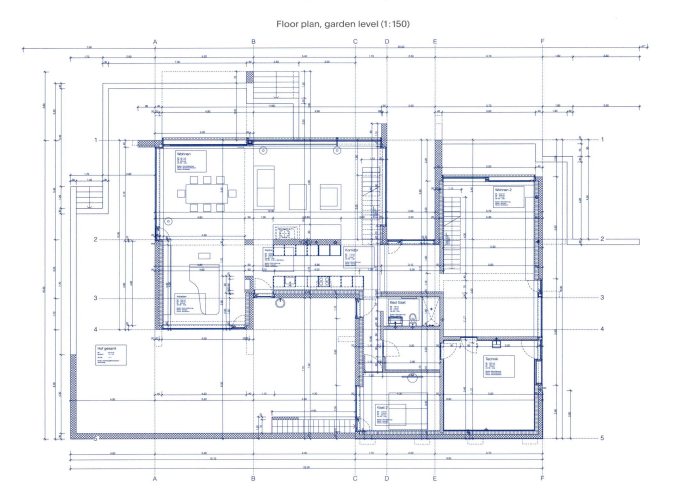

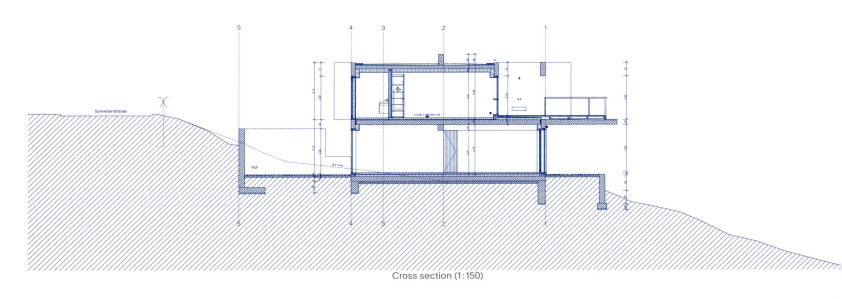
Cross section (1:150)

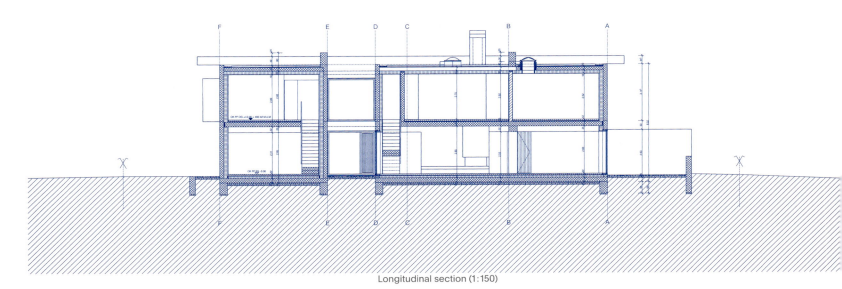
Longitudinal section (1:150)

West facade (1:150)

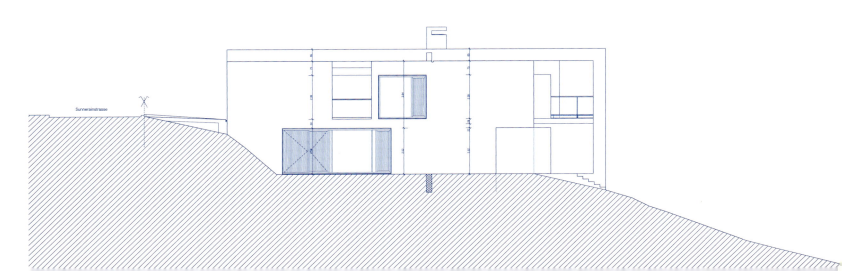

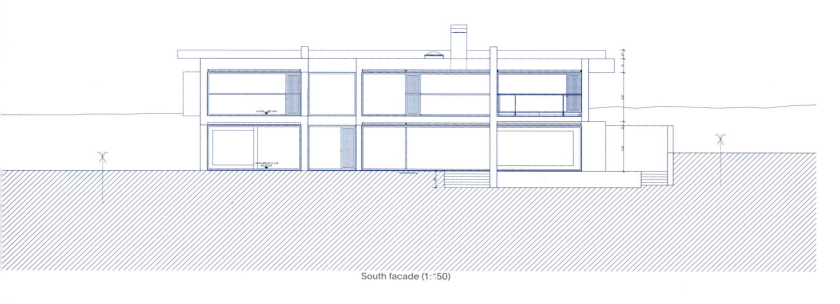

South facade (1:150)

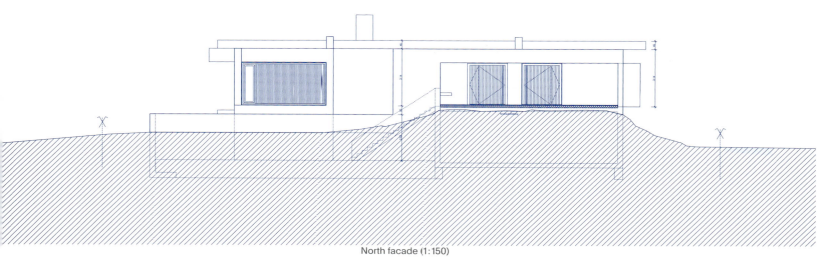

North facade (1:150)

East facade (1:150)

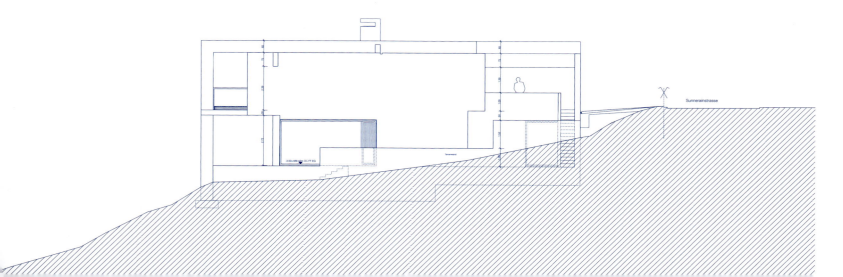

Geneva, Switzerland

2011–2014

**Credit Suisse
Place Bel-Air
Headquarters**

Conversion

N° 149   Credit Suisse Place Bel-Air Headquarters   Conversion   Selected Buildings   250

Location Geneva, Switzerland   **Type** Conversion   **Status** Realized   **Project phases** *Competition* 2011, 1st prize *Planning* 2011–2012 *Realization* 2013–2014   **Client** Credit Suisse AG Real Estate & Services, Lausanne   **Project data** *Lot size* 680 m² *Built up area* 680 m² *Floor area* 4,672 m² (according to SIA 416) *Building volume* 23,555 m³   **Planners** *Architecture* Buchner Bründler Architekten, Basel *Site management* A.S.S. Architectes associés, Le Lignon *Building engineering, competition and planning* Walther Mory Maier Bauingenieure AG, Basel *Building engineering, realization* T-Ingénierie SA, Geneva *Construction costs, planning* Ernst AG, Basel *Building physics* AAB – J. Stryjenski & H. Monti SA, Geneva *Acoustics* Applied Acoustics GmbH, Gelterkinden *Building technology* Bogenschütz AG, Basel; SB Technique SBt sa, Geneva *Electrical planning* DSSA Dumont & Schneider Ingénieurs conseils SA, Geneva *Facade planning* Christoph Etter Fassadenplanungen, Basel *Fire prevention planning* Protectas, Geneva *Light planning* Reflexion AG, Zurich *Development light filters* Glassworks Matteo Gonet GmbH, Münchenstein   **Team Buchner Bründler** *Partners* Daniel Buchner, Andreas Bründler *Associate* Bülend Yigin *Project lead* Jan Borner *Competition participants* Nicolas Hunkeler, Florian Ueker, Matthias Leschok *Planning participants* Martin Risch, Christoph Böckeler, Peter Beutler, Norma Tollmann, Stefan Herrmann, Lorraine Haussmann, Beda Klein, Mascha Zach, Anaï Becerra *Realization participants* Martin Risch, Hannah von Knobelsdorff, Patrizia Wunderli, Fabian Meury, Simon Ulfstedt   **Publications** Christian Bischoff, Une Banque à Genève: Flambant neuf, Heimatschutz / Patrimoine, Wie einst: Architektur heute 3 (2015), 28–29 • Anders Modig, Baselarkitekter 2.0, Tidskriften Rum 1 (2016), 137–49 • Credit Suisse Bel-Air Siege Principal, in SIA section romandes (ed.), A voir, 11 (2016), 70–71 • Désirée Spoden, Bankhauptsitz in Genf, AIT 12 (2016), 24 • Knut Brunier, Credit Suisse Bel-Air Hauptsitz, Geneve, in Daniel Mettler and Daniel Studer (eds.), *Made of Beton*, Basel 2018 n.p.

Impetus The bank building on the Place de Bel-Air is situated on a geographical and historical landmark site in Geneva. In 1760 the Hotel des Trois-Rois formed the first freestanding building on what is a corner plot in the historic old town. A first Credit Suisse building was realized on the same site as early as 1897, replaced by a new bank building in 1930. Despite its status as a historical monument worthy of preservation, various remodellings profoundly altered the building's appearance and obscured its sober impact. The proposal was to now convert it into a prestigious headquarters for all the bank's customer activities, as well as providing ample space for advisory services and workplaces.

Concept The potential of the significant site lead to the idea of a solitary monolith that impacts on all sides, that defines the Place de Bel-Air, and that orientates itself to the Rue de la Monnaie, a traffic-free connecting passageway. The valuable original historical substance is made newly evident by stripping away distorting elements, while the vertical emphasis of the stony structural framework invests the building with a tranquil presence.

In terms of appearance, the building is reduced to a small number of materials, reinforcing its timeless character and monumentality. In the interior the spatially liberated atrium, acting as representative main hall, radiates an expansive openness. The atrium is encircled by a grid structure cast in seamless white concrete, establishing a correlation with the exterior appearance. The clear typology creates an organizational efficiency. A cascade of crystalline-like bays thrusts out into the open space of atrium and contrasts with the minimalist stringency of the grid structure. The bays serve as informal meeting points on the various floors. By means of a typological simplification, the layout is clarified and the interior light well becomes an orientation point with a central circular gallery on each floor.

Implementation The exterior appearance is determined by a discrete tectonic combination. A circumferential architrave-like girder joins the composite supports made of concrete and sandstone together, which then form a foreground motif. Slightly recessed elements delineate the roof ends. The openings in the building have full-surface glazing, their frames hidden as insets. The forcefully articulated projecting roofs visually accentuate the heightened ground floor, the design also foregoing any additional architectural edging in the base. The original rooftop window openings remain as historical pointers to the earlier enunciation. The entrance space extends across the entire width of the building to the Passage de la Monnaie, its colossal access stairs indicating the dimensions and importance of the central space, the homogenous impact of which further reinforces the inner openness and transparency.

Place de Bel-Air, Geneva. First settlement on the lower basin of Lake Geneva in 5,000 B.C., a hill on the left bank of the River Rhone serving as a natural refuge in prehistoric times. The settlement of the hill, on which the old town is today situated, begins around 120 B.C. by the Romans. As a link to the right bank, the Pont du Rhône bridge is built in ca. 58 B.C.; in the 3rd CENTURY fortifications appear to protect the hillside settlement. ▶ In the 13th CENTURY Geneva experiences a heyday, the city markets developing to become international trading sites and to the nucleus of Geneva as a financial center. By 1377 the population grows to over 3,300 and the settlement area spreads from the hill to the Rhone, with the fortifications being expanded.

▶ In the 14th CENTURY the settlement Bourg de Palais appears, site of the later Place de Bel-Air, home to the city's houses of ill repute and the horse-carcass industries. 1424/25, the knight Pierre de Menthon builds a residence against the city walls later known as Hotel Trois-Rois: the hotel is situated on an important intersection, giving the place its name. In 1670 a fire destroys the Pont du Rhône and part of the riverside district, subsequently rebuilt, during which the Place des Trois-Rois is enlarged and renamed Place de Bel-Air. ▶ 1674, the hotelier Jean de La Combe purchases land next to Place de Bel-Air and opens a hotel. It welcomes diplomats and representatives from Europe's noble and royal dynasties, and, by virtue of its imposing facade, becomes a landmark on the left bank of the Rhone. In the 18th CENTURY Geneva ranks amongst the most powerful financial centers in Europe, along with London and Paris; in 1710 it numbers over 20,000 inhabitants. 1787, the merchant Jacob Melly takes over the Trois-Rois and converts it to an apartment building.

▶ 1846, the City of Geneva decides to demolish the fortifications and an urban planning awakening starts. ▶ The Place de Bel-Air advances to a traffic hub, especially with the introduction of tramlines in the 1860s, and meanwhile, in the mid-1800s, a watch company installs itself in the Trois-Rois building. In 1856 industrialists and politicians found the Schweizerische Kreditanstalt (SKA), which quickly rises to be the largest commercial bank in Switzerland. 1897, the SKA purchases the lot on which the Hotel Trois-Rois stands, replaced in 1906 by the Geneva architect Jacques-Elysée Goss with a representative building: on the upper floors, rental apartments; on the ground floor, the SKA runs its banking business. At this time the City of Geneva numbers over 100,000 inhabitants.

▶ Competitors open modern bank branches in the district in the early 20th CENTURY and the SKA building on the Place de Bel-Air looses its prestige. 1929, the SKA commissions the architect Maurice Turrettini and the engineer Robert Maillard to erect a new building. Popular protests try to block the project; demands for an overall building moratorium on Place de Bel-Air become loud. 1930, the SKA opens the six-story cube of reinforced concrete with a sandstone-clad facade. The new building gives the SKA a modern image and plays a pioneering role in the boom in city center office complexes that takes place post-1945. In the 1970s the SKA undertakes a renovation: the facade is given more luxury by means of marble panels and gilded brass. Following reorganization, the SKA is incorporated into the Credit Swiss in 1997.

The view into the central atrium space is transfigured by roughly blasted glass surfaces, inserted as frameless infillings in the primary concrete structure. Originally built as a bank in 1930 by the architect Maurice Turrettini and the structural engineer Robert Maillart, over the years the building has been disfigured by innumerable remodellings. With the removal of the defective parts and an interpretative extension of the original substance, the intention is to recreate the esprit of the late nineteenth century.

View from the Rue de la Corraterie to the prominently situated cornerstone building, which can be seen as the departure point of the Rue de la Confédération, the busiest shopping street in Geneva. The wide corner guides the vista to the Place Bel-Air tram stop on today's Pont de l'Ile and into the Rue du Rhône.

The existing U-shaped composite supports of concrete and natural-stone are ideally suited to be insulation-clad and to support the new load-bearing structure. At the roof parapet level are the meeting suites for talks with private clients. Nine hundred and twenty-three hand-blown glass shells, around half of them with a craquelure effect, form a cloud-like glass ceiling. A specially developed safety coating means the shells can be fixed at localized points at the height of the atrium. The circumferential circulation corridor shows people's contours without them being identifiable.

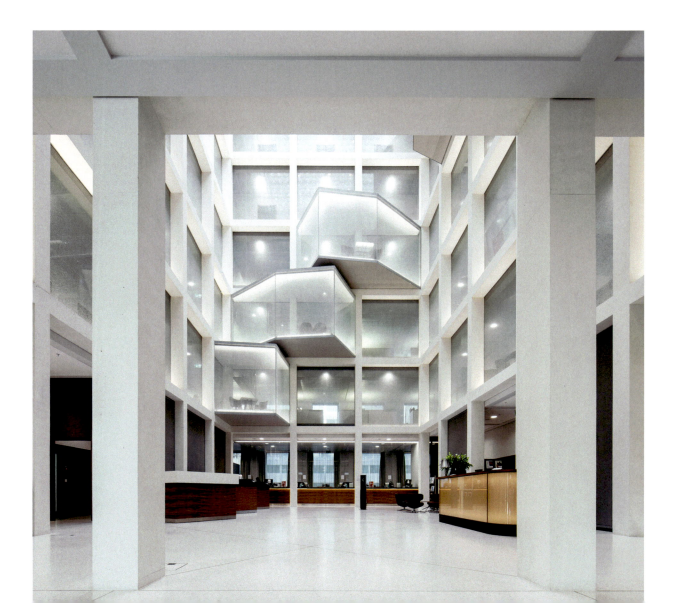

The entrance hall spans the entire width of the building along the Rue de la Monnaie. From the openly accessible counter hall, visitors can look into the work and meeting areas inside the bank. The term "Geode" was used to describe the mixed character of the interior space, enclosed by a strict grid structure with the freely cantilevered, crystalline appearance of the spatial core.

The rich effect of the composite columns of Estavayer shell limestone—a calcareous sandstone that had already been quarried by the Romans—unfolds after having been stripped back. Additional elements, such as the architrave, the individual roof ends, and the roof parapet level, are finished using cast stone and surface acid washed in order to harmonize with the porosity of the natural stone.

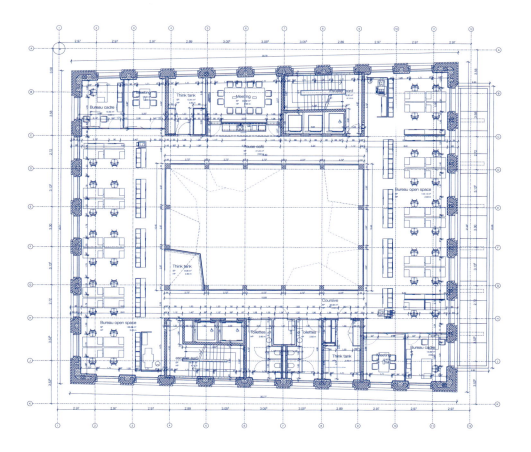

Floor plan, 1st upper story (1:300)

Floor plan, ground story (1:300)

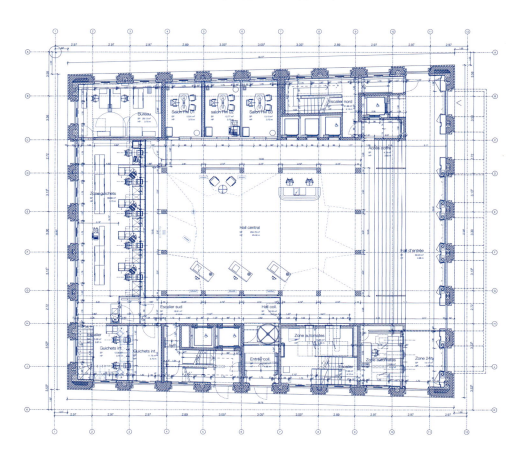

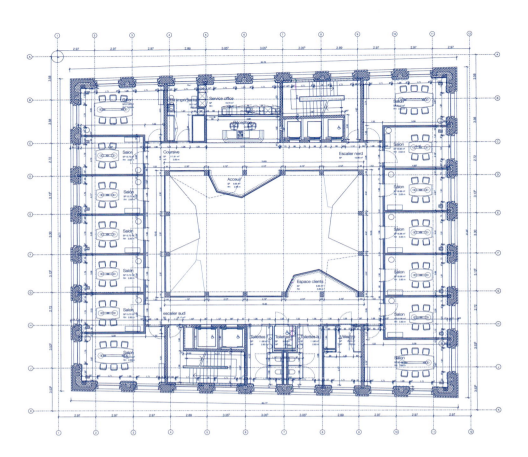

Floor plan, 5th upper story (1:300)

Floor plan, 4th upper story (1:300)

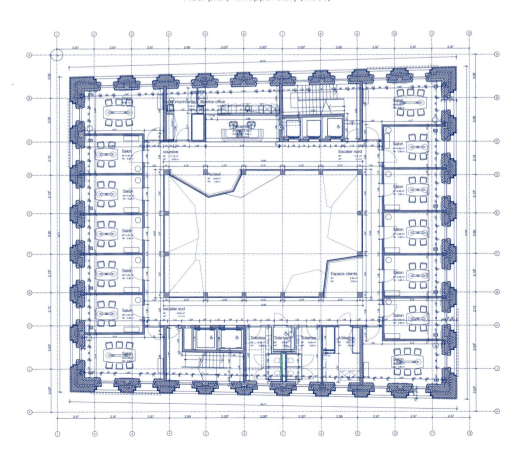

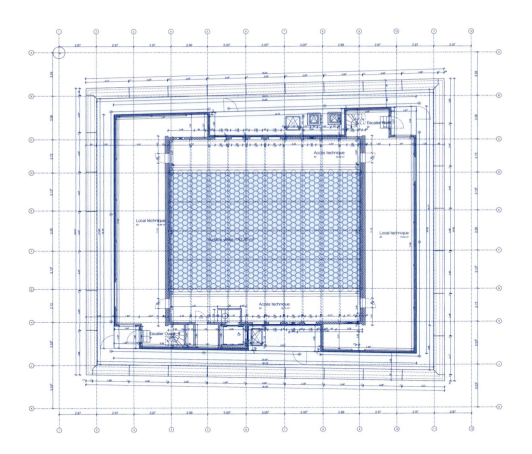

Floor plan, 7th upper story (1:300)

Cross section (1:300)

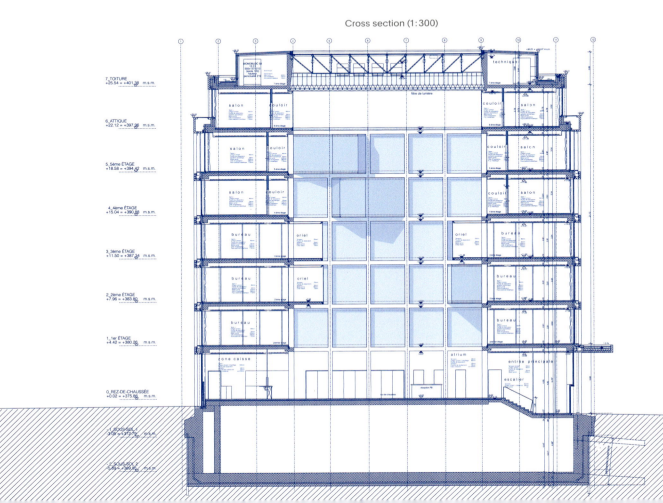

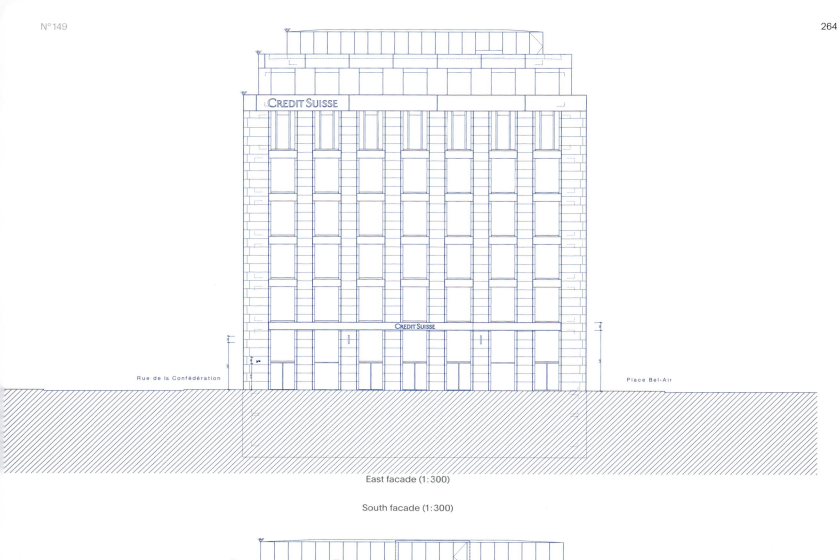

East facade (1:300)

South facade (1:300)

Olten, Switzerland

2012–2017

**Amthausquai
Residential and
Commercial Building**

New building

N° 174 Amthausquai Residential and Commercial Building — New building

Location Olten, Switzerland **Type** New building **Status** Realized **Project phases** *Competition* 2012, 1st prize *Planning* 2012–2015 *Realization* 2015–2017 **Client** PAT-BVG, Personalvorsorgestiftung der Ärzte und Tierärzte, St. Gallen *Client representatives* Walter Lüthi AG, Thun **Project data** *Lot size* 954 m² *Built up area* 655 m² *Floor area* 3,954 m² (according to SIA 416) *Building volume* 12,089 m³ **Planners** *Architecture* Buchner Bründler Architekten, Basel *General planning* ARGE GP Buchner Bründler Architekten AG, Basel; Proplaning AG, Basel *Construction management and site management* Proplaning AG, Basel *Building engineering* WMM Ingenieure AG, Münchenstein *Building physics* Bakus Bauphysik & Akustik GmbH, Zurich *Building technology* tp AG für technische Planungen, Biel *Electrical planning* Hefti. Hess. Martignoni. AG, Berne *Facade planning* Christoph Etter Fassadenplanungen, Basel *Fire protection planning* Visiotec Technical Consulting AG, Allschwil **Team Buchner Bründler** *Partners* Daniel Buchner, Andreas Bründler *Associate, competition* Raphaela Schacher *Associate, planning and realization* Nick Waldmeier *Project leads, realization* Rino Buess, Tünde König, Hannah von Knobelsdorff *Competition participants* Dominik Aegerter, Julian Oggier, Jonathan Hermann *Realization participants* Peter Beutler, Simone Braendle, Mihails Staluns **Publications** Fabian Ruppanner, Palast ohne Schnörkel: Wohnhaus Amthausquai in Olten SO von Buchner Bründler, werk, bauen + wohnen 1–2 (2019), 68–69; and Werk-Material 01.02/726

Impetus Olten's emergence as a Swiss railway hub in the 19th century was accompanied by the erection of numerous prestigious buildings, appearing either as closed perimeter block developments or as series of individual freestanding edifices. This urban-planning variety still characterizes the architectural surroundings where Bahnhofstrasse, Amthausquai, and Jurastrasse converge. Next to the Aarhof, the intention was to build a new apartment building with mixed occupancies at ground-floor level, on a par with its historical architectural context in terms of quality.

Concept An oblong volume is developed within the heterogeneous situation, on the one hand incorporating itself within the primary block structure, and on the other also detaching itself from the adjoining Aarhof toward the river in order to establish it as a corner-front building. This physical shift creates a new urban layout sequence, generating intermediate spaces and new visual connections.

The frontal facade facing the River Aare and the Amthausquai is plastically articulated. A play of symmetries, framings, and infills interprets the neighboring Aarhof facade with its inlays and textures anew. The massings of the building are clad on all sides with a coarse-grained, mineral scraped rendering, allowing a homogeneous materialization of the vertical and horizontal plaster segments with their varying depths of finish. Together, the plastic impression of depth in the outer walls, the free arrangement of the openings, and the formation of the loggias give the building a representational character.

Implementation On the ground-floor level the building has a multiple orientation, enhancing the spatially enclosed courtyard and giving it a public character.

In their typology, the apartments reflect the old town palazzo. The spatial sequence, with an entrance hallway and rooms facing in numerous directions, is arranged fluidly, opening the apartments up to the town and the river area. While the bedrooms are orientated toward the courtyard and the minor street, the living areas face the Aare and via the large loggias spatially extend out to the river. The western section of the building is similarly characterized by intimate loggias, articulating the full-depth living rooms with views to the north and sunlight to the south. The interior spaces are strictly executed in concrete, overlaid with precisely arranged openings and spatial framings with oak paneling in order to allow a refined atmosphere to emerge.

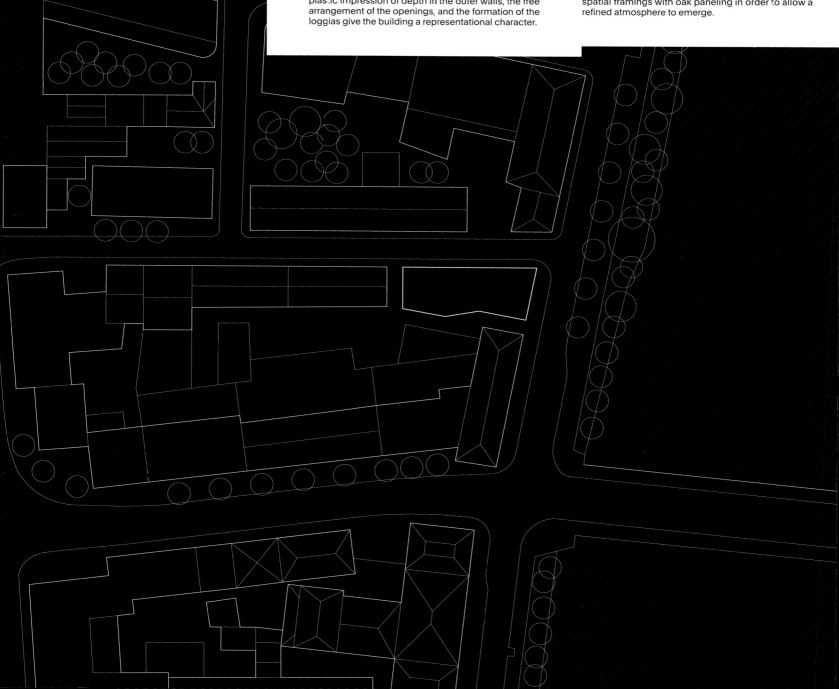

Olten, Jurastrasse no. 1. Olten, a small city situated at the foothills of the Jura mountains in a valley basin and at an angle between the River Aare and the mouth of the Dünnern. The settlement core is on the west side of the Aare; the Dünnern flows into the Aare at the northern end of the old town. A place with the name "Oltun" is first mentioned in 1201, a bridge over the Aare in 1295. The medieval town evolves on top of the foundations of a former Roman castrum—a Basel-Episcopal deed under the charter of the Counts von Frohburg, who ruled a large part of what is today northeastern Switzerland, including the Unterer Hauenstein, and with it the still fledgling Gotthard route. 1406, Olten is passed as a forfeit from an Episcopal dominion to the City of Basel. After two great town fires in 1411 and 1422, Basel loses interest in the provincial town and mortgages the seigneurial rights in 1426 to Solothurn, the purchase being agreed to in 1532. Olten's inhabitants, in 1600 numbering around 500, live from trade and transport. Under the rule of Solothurn, Olten loses numerous ancestral rights, including in 1653, as a result of the Peasant War, even its municipal charter.

Up until the MID-19th CENTURY the right bank of the Aare remains a developmental no-man's land, a situation that only changes in 1853 with the founding of the Schweizerische Centralbahn, which envisions Olten as the focus of a Swiss railroad intersection and as a site for workshops. From 1855, the workshop complexes on the right bank of the Aare rapidly develop to become a notable supplier and servicer. Together with the station, opened in 1856, the railway becomes a growth engine for the town. In the subsequent years, numerous new bridges are built, connecting the industrial area to the old town. 1883, the Bahnhof Bridge, solely financed by the Centralbahn, is built. At the end of the bridge, on the then Zielempstrasse and today's Amtshausquai, a series of imposing freestanding buildings are erected in the coming years, directly opposite the station, also lovingly known as the "Olten Acropolis."

1885, the building of the neo-baroque town palace at Jurastrasse no. 2; two years later the town palazzo housing the Ersparnisskasse Olten, the concert hall, and the Amtshaus (today courts and a theater). 1891, Olten City Parliament decides to build the quay wall, inaugurated in 1893, along with, a few months later, the meteorological column in front of the concert hall. 1895, commissioned by the ophthalmologist Felix Adolf Heim, the second town palace is erected at Jurastrasse no. 1. The architect Arnold von Arx-Munzinger designs a three-story, neo-baroque residential and surgery building clad in slate. The ground floor houses the client's surgery rooms, with a waiting room, an examination room, and an operation theater and a small ward. In the upper two stories lives the large family with two servants. From 1896 the palace serves Heim as a private eye clinic. Heim is also politically active in Olten, as a co-founder of the Social Democratic Party, as a municipal councilor, and as a "crank" and "ogre to the bourgeois," famous for his biting articles in the worker's press. Even prior to WW I, his political influence wanes; he leaves Olten in 1927 and sells the property at Jurastrasse no. 1. 1958, the Canton Solothurn acquires the town palace and installs a cantonal police station there. The building is only superficially maintained and deteriorates.

The Amtshausquai emerged in the course of Olten's advancement to an important railway node. The "0" marker stone in the railway station opposite is testimony to the fact that the entire Swiss railway network was surveyed starting from Olten. Glazed roof windows channel zenithal light into the two staircases. The spatial structure is executed in cast-in-situ concrete using panel shuttering, while the ground cement floors form a smooth surface. Room-high windows and doors in solid oak create a contrast to the mineral spatial shell. The retracted loggias have floor grates of Douglas fir.

The spatial typology of the river-facing apartments is determined by open living, dining, and kitchen areas, while in the other apartment units the combined kitchen-cum-dining room is situated facing the street and the living room facing the courtyard. The interior bathrooms are lighted linearly. The front-to-back apartments are given a meandering spatial sequence.

The homogenous structural volume is stripped back using a scraped plaster technique. Facing the River Aare a café enlivens the street space.
The entrances to the house are situated to the side on Jurastrasse.

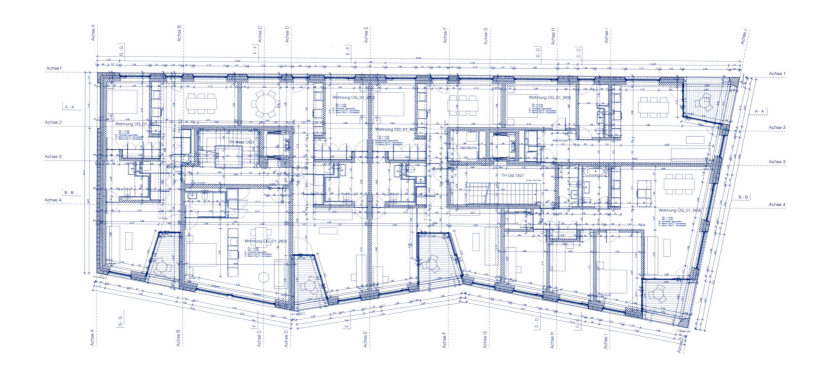

Floor plan, 1st upper story (1:250)

Floor plan, ground story (1:250)

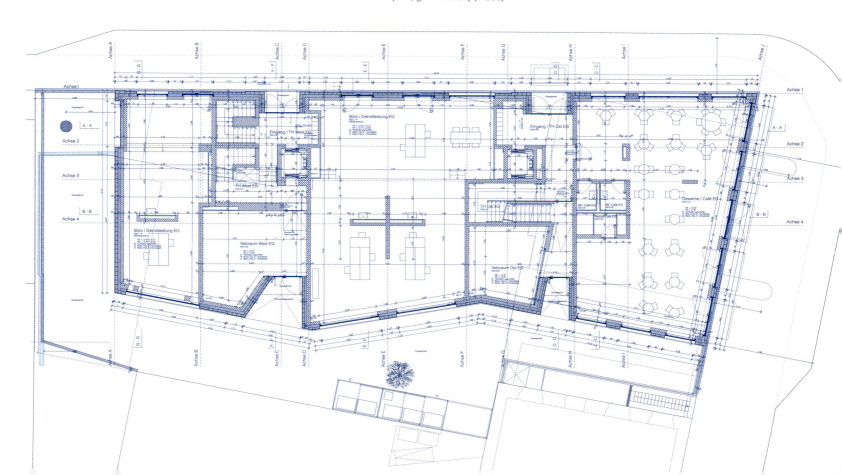

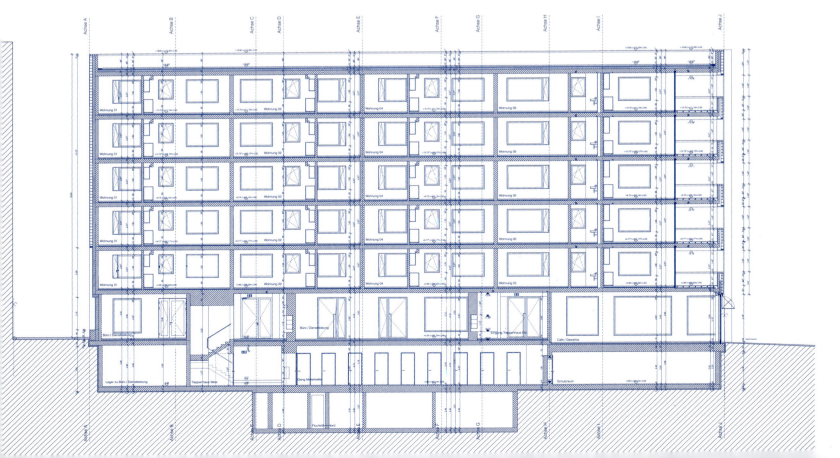

Cross section D–D (1:250)

Cross section E–E (1:250)

Longitudinal section F–F (1:250)

East facade (1:250)

North facade (1:250)

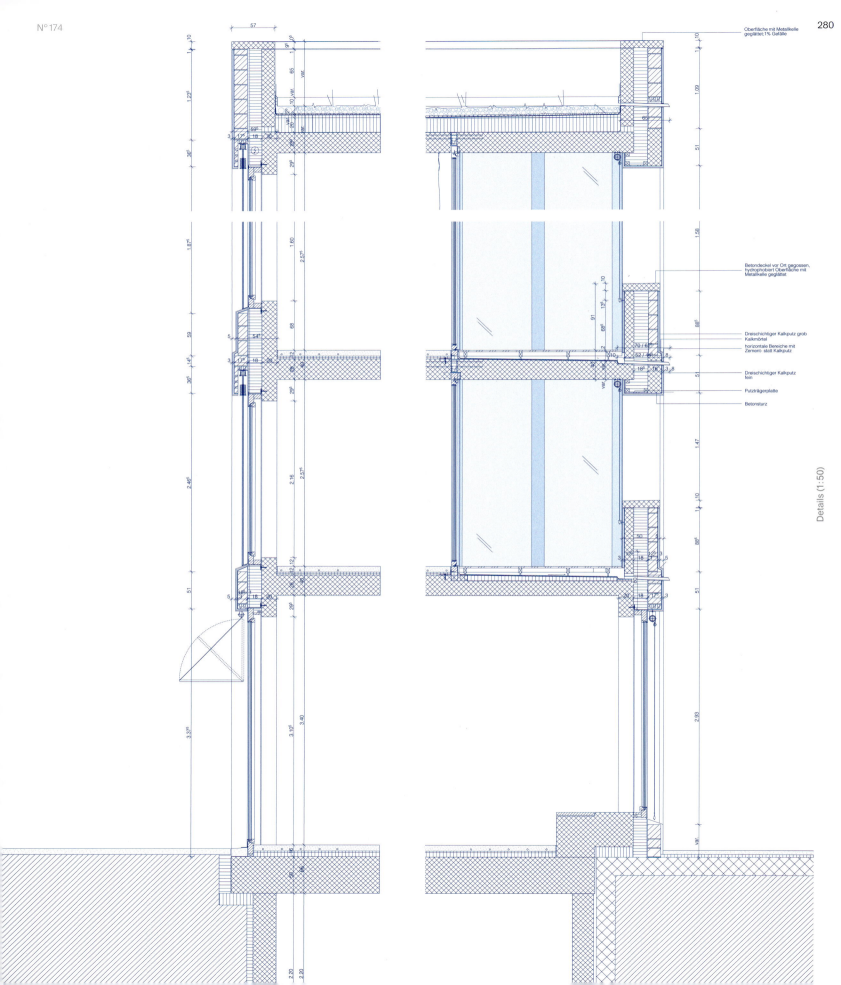

Lörrach, Germany

2012–2014   **Lörrach House**

New building

N° 179 Lörrach House

Location Lörrach, Germany **Type** New building **Status** Realized **Project phases** *Planning* 2012–2013 *Realization* 2013–2014 **Client** Private **Project data** *Lot size* 617 m² *Built up area* 232 m² *Floor area* 236 m² (according to SIA 416) *Building volume* 1,380 m³ **Planners** *Architecture and site management* Buchner Bründler Architekten, Basel *Shell construction site management and building engineering* Kevin M. Rahner, Lörrach **Team** Buchner Bründler *Partners* Daniel Buchner, Andreas Bründler *Project lead* Norma Tollmann *Participants* Fabian Meury **Publications** Michel Frei, Urhütte im Agglo-Dschungel: Buchner Bründler Architekten— Wohnhaus in Lörrach, archithese 1 (2015), 8–13 • Antonia Kühnemundt, Wohnhaus in Lörrach, AIT Wohnen / Living 1–2 (2015), 118–23 • José Manuel Pedreirinho, Accuracy, Quality, Functional Clarity and a Strong Formal Identity, a.mag 7 (2015), 101–9 • Claude Denu, Wohnhaus Lörrach D, Architektur im Licht 9 (2015), 92–93 • Wladimir Kaminer and Wolfgang Bachmann, *Häuser des Jahres: Die 50 besten Einfamilienhäuser 2015*, Munich 2015. 216–19 • Anders Modig, Baselarkitekter 2.0, Tidskriften Rum 1 (2016), 137–49 • Ulrike Hark, Eine gnadenlose Fassade, SonntagsZeitung, February 14, 2016, 54 • Susanne Vécsey, Verschattung seiner selbst: Einfamilienhaus von Buchner Bründler in Lörrach, werk, bauen + wohnen 10 (2016), 22–27

Impetus The building plot is situated on an elevated position in the middle of a densely developed single-family-house neighborhood that has sprung up over the last ten years based on a mandatory zoning plan. Despite the main planning regulation, the built surroundings are heterogeneous, with each house striving as far as possible for its own individuality. Based on the development plan, the aim was to design a two-story house for a young family.

Concept In response to the officially defined context, the design takes the form of an autonomous building, consisting of a stony enveloping volume with a wooden building core inscribed within it. Correspondingly, the outer contour traces the largest possible volume of the zoning lines, while the inner volume—separated on all sides from the envelope—assumes its own, independent spatial logic. The layering of the architectural volume generates spaces with differing characters between the surrounding casing and the inner facade, used as seating areas or an exterior hallway and serving as an extension of the interior rooms. Cutouts in the shell and large circular openings in the concrete roof provide ample light and specific visual axes. The building is entered via a narrow door on the ground-floor gable side. The wooden architectural volume is equipped with large, multipartite glazed surfaces and is divided over two levels. Surrounding the concrete-cast core are utility rooms, such as the kitchen and bathroom. The intermediate ceiling is partly divorced from the facade, creating full-building-height rooms that connect the ground and upper floors. Floor-to-ceiling doors and precisely set hatches reiterate the layering motif, allowing the inner rooms to be freely closed or open in relation to each other.

Implementation The cast-concrete architectural envelope is supported by an inner core and four peripheral columns, creating an interstice between the ground and the concrete shell. The wooden structure, monochrome dark and precisely integrated, nestles under the concrete shell and around the core, with additional interior wooden insertions structuring the rooms. The gravel surface in the covered outside areas translates as a grinded concrete floor on the ground floor. The large, multiply subdivided glazing provides good interior daylighting, as well as a visual amplification beneath the shell. When opened, the five ground-floor doors elongate the interior to spatially touch the stony shell.

Dieter-Kaltenbach-Strasse, Lörrach-Stetten. Stetten is situated in the extreme southwest of Germany at the base of the foothills of the Upper Black Forest and on the River Wiese, which turns to the south to Basel, where it flows into the Rhine. Facing east rises the wooded Leuselhardt hill, south of the Maienbühl, and through which the "Eiserne Hand" runs—a tip of territory that protrudes toward Germany but belongs to Switzerland, separating Stetten from its neighboring German parish of Inzlingen.

The village originates from the EARLY MIDDLE AGES. In a stone box grave, a reddish chin beard from the 7th or 8th CENTURY was found—the beard of an ancient Stetten inhabitant, a lanky man aged about forty; an Alemannian. A further fifty similar graves from the same period were found at the bottom of the valley.

E Stetten is a farming village, a scattered village, built on the scree of the Talbach, and as opposed to the neighboring Lörrach, which evolves along the roadway. The first mention of "Stetiheim" dates back to 763: R the St. Gallen Cloister is gifted two bonded Stetten peasants, plus farmyard, arable land, and meadows. Eleven years later, in 774, Stetten and its manorial farming estate pass to the possession of the Säckingen Cloister and advances to become an administrative center for the lower Wiesen Valley, which is presumably why Stetten also becomes a parish. The oldest evidence of a church dates from 1225. The first Church of St. Fridolin is erected around 1440; the village develops around the church. The feudal rulers switch—the lords of Stein; the knights of Grünenberg, Eptingen, Bärenfels; again and again the lords of Schönau. The cloisters Wettingen in Aargau and St. Alban in Basel also draw tithes on the land in Stetten.

R Through its connection to the Säckingen Cloister, Stetten belongs to Further Austria and hence the House of Habsburg. After the Reformation—despite a fifty-year conflict with the Margrave Karl II; despite violence, the interruption of field processions, and the arrest of Catholic priests—Stetten remains in the Church of Rome while the rest of the surroundings, the larger town of Lörrach and the parish of Riehen, convert to the new religion.

P In 1648, after the Thirty Years' War, the Peace of Westphalia results in session of the Swiss Confederation from the German Empire, with Stetten now situated on the Swiss border. In around 1700 some 150 people live in Stetten. The village is caught up in various wars of succession, with marauding and plundering soldiers repeatedly quartering themselves in it. 1682, the Rötteln Castle is destroyed; neighboring Lörrach receives a town charter. E In the 18th CENTURY, vineyards and forest around the village. Up until the 19th CENTURY its 250-m diameter is encompassed by a pasture fence with trenches, beyond which are no buildings: the circular village is bordered by wide fields and meadows. Most likely there was the first brickworks, with the clay for the bricks coming from the Eggenbuck. R P 1803, Stetten becomes part of the Land Baden, the population grows, the church is too small and is rebuilt in 1821. In SEPTEMBER 1848, the Baden Revolution; the German Republic is declared in the Rössle Inn, but the revolution fails.

P Transport networks are expanded: in 1855 the railway line from Karlsruhe to Basel is opened, in 1862 the Wiesental Railway, Stetten is given its own station. E In and around Lörrach factories appear. Tobacco processing, tool manufacturing, above all the expansion of the textile branch: spinning mills, doubling mills, weaving mills, cloth factories; silk ribbon, finishing, indienne printing, cotton processing. Numerous new companies are established by Swiss. Emanating from Basel, a prosperous, cross-border agglomeration, with Stetten as a part of it. The textile firm Koechlin Baumgartner establishes itself in Lörrach. 1856, the company commissions the first worker's apartments in Stetten for its workforce, three rows of ten houses; in less than two years Stetten has 200 extra inhabitants, around ten years later already 140 extra houses. A worker's association building and the first building of the General Worker's Cooperative.

Neustetten appears; the pasture fence is obsolete, the settlement boundary between Lörrach and Stetten disappears; Stetten has 5,000 inhabitants, Lörrach, 10,000; the two grow together. ▣▶ 1908, the village incorporates itself with Lörrach. The agrarian character fades, the district Lörrach-Stetten becoming more industrialized. ▣▶ In around 1900 a brickworks is built on the Eggenbuck, beside mixed-fruit orchards and fields and directly adjacent to the clay pit. The works are taken over by the Lange brothers, who expand it. Around 1928, a new brick factory covering three floors with walled kilns, chamber ovens for artificial drying, rooms for the metalwork shop, and an electrical installation—plus five small incorporated lodgings for members of the workforce. The ca. 7-m-high smokestack is visible from far away. On the other side of Buckweg a quarry. ▣▶ The pits and wagons on the Buck in front of the entrance are a magical attraction for children and youths, also serving as the site of the annual Shrovetide carnival bonfire. ▣▶ 1969, the brickworks ceases production; the buildings are demolished and the rubble tipped into the clay pits. Auf Eggen becomes wasteland. Lörrach-Stetten continues growing: the buildings in the valley stand closer and closer together, a first high-rise block appears, and a second Catholic church. Now settlement occupies the slopes, since the 1990s also in Stetten-Süd. ▣▶ The brownfield site is rehabilitated and zoned as a residential area, allowing detached single-family houses to be built. 2006, the new Dieter-Kaltenbach-Strasse is built, named after the long-standing director of the Kaltenbach company (a large machinery and tool factory) and the founder of a charity to foster personal development through artistic design.

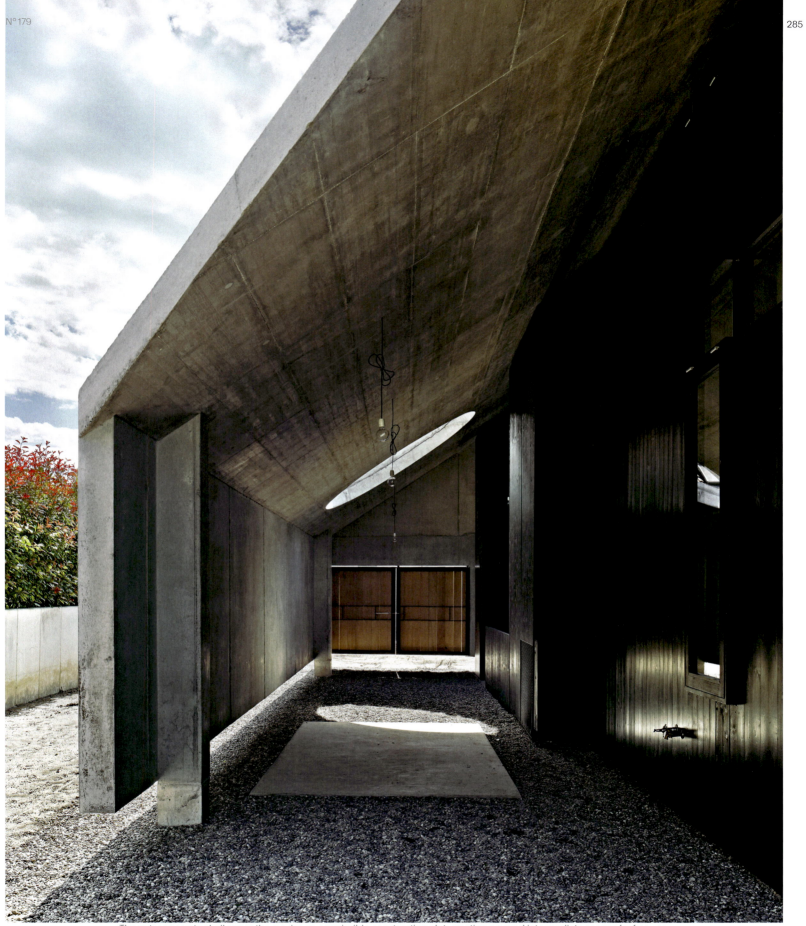
The outer concrete shell spans the maximum permissible construction plot, creating covered intermediate spaces for free use.

The inner house was only inserted once the outer concrete shell had been completed. A new entity emerges, assembled out of individual wooden elements that were subsequently painted black. The concrete shell rests on four supports that lift the shell off the ground. Tension rods were inserted in order to support the seating frames of the panorama openings. The intermediate ceiling, for its part, is detached from the wooden facade, creating double-height spatial zones of differing dimensions and proportions. The meandering core is situated centrally in relation to the roof shell and gives the structure its torsional rigidity.

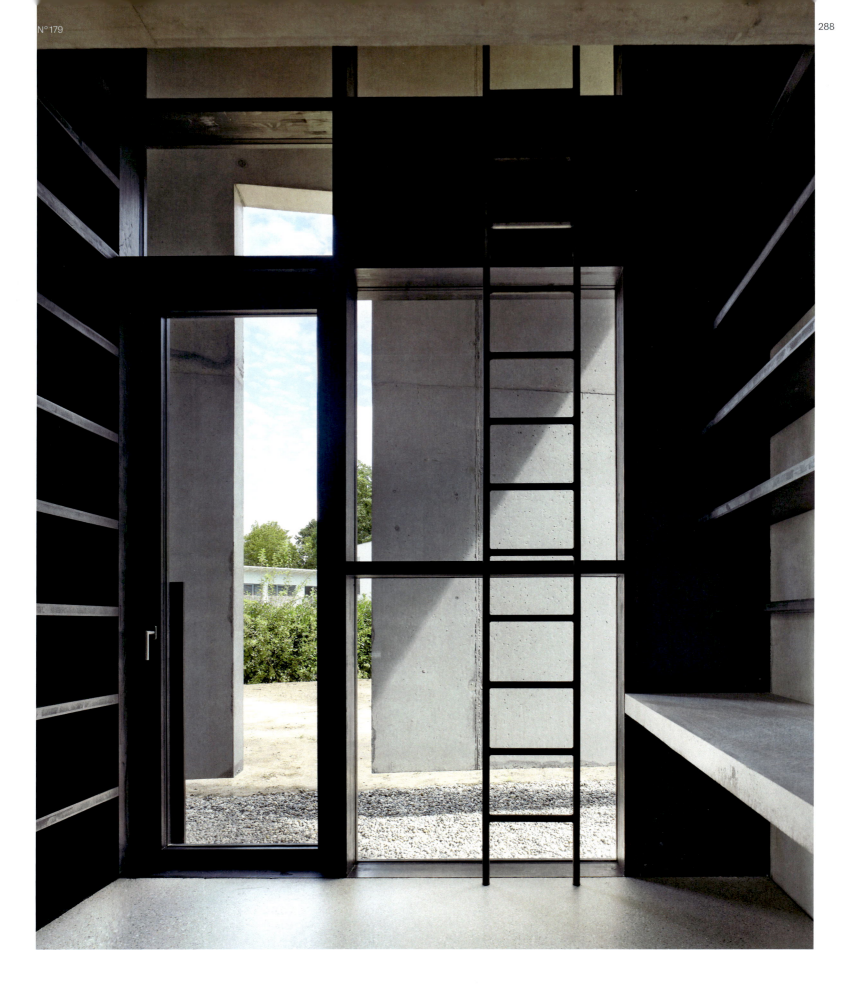

Permanently fixed bookcases reach up to under the roof. The openings in the shell provide select sight lines. At the sleeping level the interior doors are supplemented with hatches, allowing the sleeping areas to be opened to the double-height rooms. The roof chimney is enlarged to additionally serve as a light-channeling spatial expansion.

Large-format, freely placed openings have a figurative effect and transfigure the uses of the inner house. The floor joints suggest that the wooden inside bears the stony shell. The erratic block is part of a rapidly erected new single-family-house neighborhood.

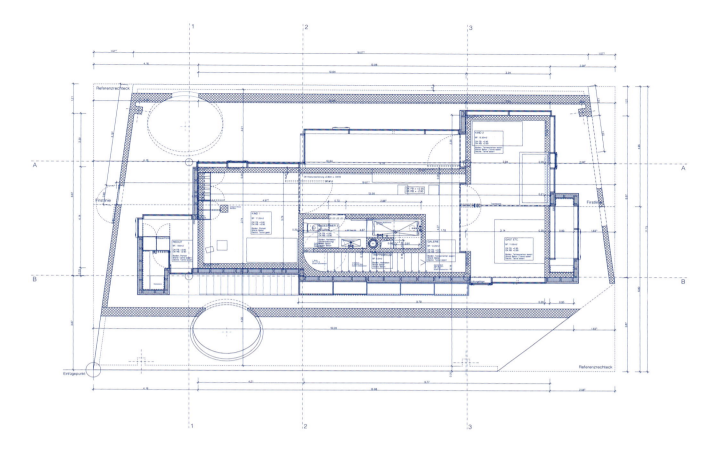

Floor plan, upper story (1:150)

Floor plan, ground story (1:150)

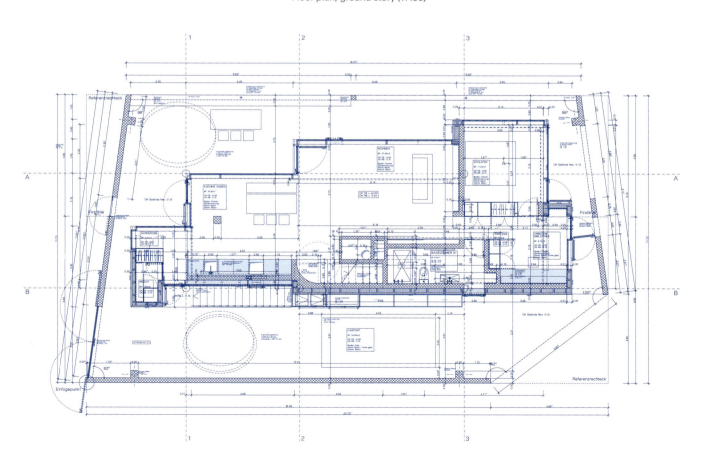

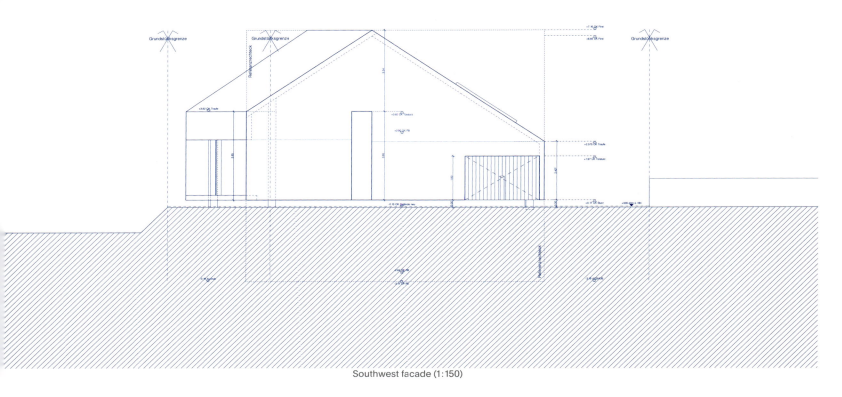

Southwest facade (1:150)

Southeast facade (1:150)

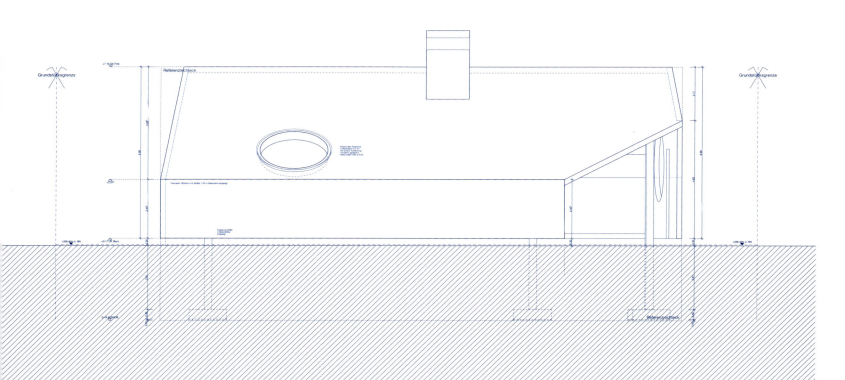

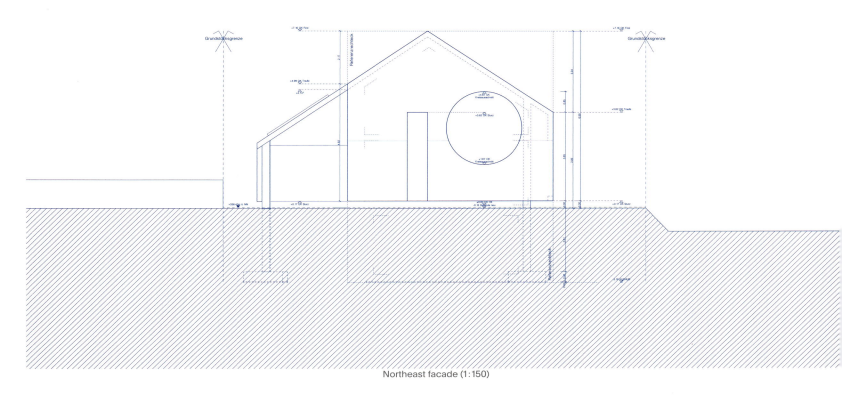

Northeast facade (1:150)

Northwest facade (1:150)

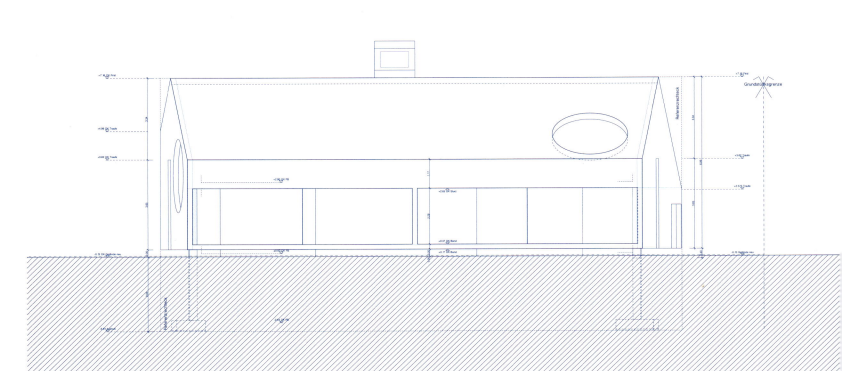

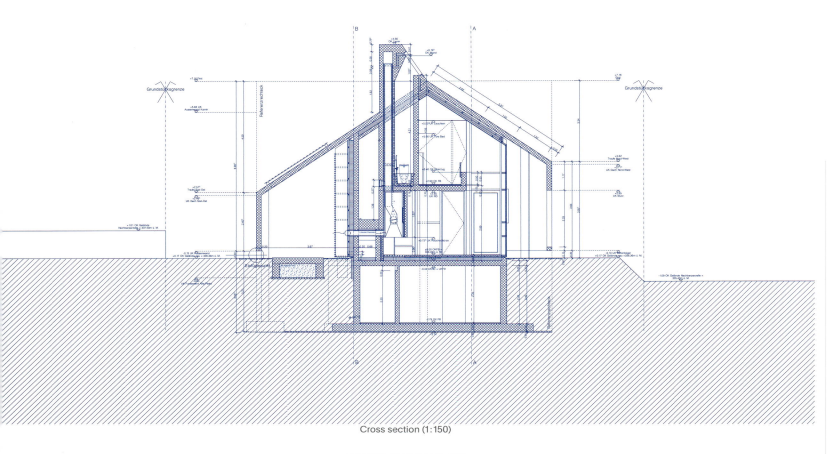

Cross section (1:150)

Longitudinal section (1:150)

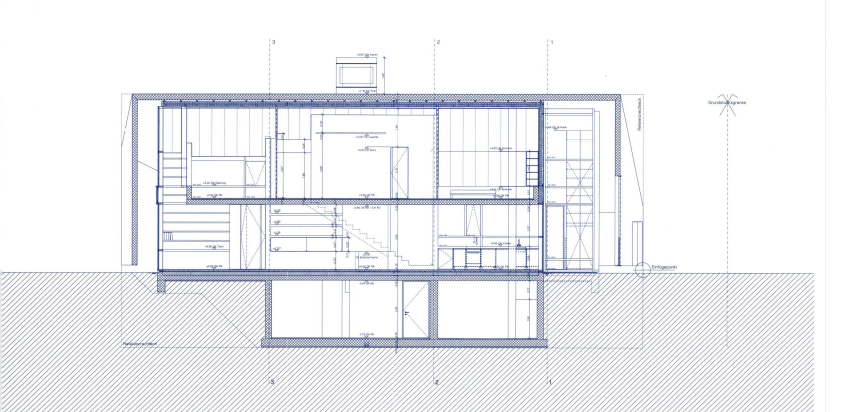

Basel, Switzerland

2014–2017 **Cooperative Building Stadterle**

New building

N° 205 Cooperative Building Stadterle

Location Basel, Switzerland **Type** New building **Status** Realized **Project phases** *Competition* 2014, 1st prize *Planning* 2014–2016 *Realization* 2016–2017 **Client** Wohngenossenschaft Zimmerfrei, Basel **Client representatives** Baumann Projektmanagement GmbH, Basel **Project data** *Lot size* 1,014 m² *Built up area* 822 m² *Floor area* 5,619 m² (according to SIA 416) *Building volume* 17,215 m³ **Planners** *Architecture* Buchner Bründler Architekten, Basel *Site management* Probau Baumanagement GmbH, Basel *Building engineering* Ulaga Partner AG, Basel *Timber construction engineering* Makiol Wiederkehr AG, Beinwil am See *Building physics* Kopitsis Bauphysik AG, Wohlen *Building technology* Zurfluh Lottenbach GmbH, Lucerne *Electrical planning* Actemium Schweiz AG, Basel *Facade planning* Christoph Etter Fassadenplanungen, Basel *Fire protection planning* Makiol Wiederkehr AG, Beinwil am See **Team Buchner Bründler** *Partners* Daniel Buchner, Andreas Bründler *Associate, competition* Raphaela Schacher *Associate, realization* Stefan Oehy *Project leads* Daniel Ebertshäuser, Norma Tollmann *Competition participants* Benjamin Hofmann, Flurin Arquint, Benedict Choquard, Marlene Sauer *Realization participants* Tünde König, Omri Levy, Henrik Månsson, Dominik Aegerter, Benedict Choquard, Pascal Berchtold, Jonas Hamberger, Jakob Rabe Petersen, Lennart Cleemann, Alexandra Galer **Publications** Alexander Felix, Neubau Mehrfamilienhaus "Stadterle", Basel: Genossenschaftlich planen, Tec21 40 (2014), 8–9 • Postindustrielle Lebensvielfalt, Arch—Architektur mit Faserzement 2 (2018) 24–27 • Stadterle: 16-Zimmer-WG und Sperrholzküche, Wohnen—Das Magazin für Genossenschaftlichen Wohnungsbau 3 (2018), 17 • Daniel Kurz, Stadt im kleinen Massstab: Quartier Erlenmatt Ost in Basel und Genossenschaftshaus Stadterle in Basel, in: werk, bauen + wohnen 6 (2018), 65–71; and in Werk-Material 01.02/714 • Energie- und Soziallabor Erlenmatt Ost, Tec21 11 (2018), 27 • Gewinner, Genossenschaftshaus Stadterle, in Schweizer Baudokumentation—Sonderausgabe Arc-Award 2018, 40–44 • Genossenschaftshaus Stadterle, in S AM – Schweizerisches Architekturmuseum and Andreas Kofler (eds.), *Dichtelust: Formen des urbanen Zusammenlebens in der Schweiz*, Basel 2018, 78–79 • Tina Cieslik, Lebendiger Beton: Genossenschaftshaus Stadterle; Andreas Bründler, Mit Beton frei über Architektur nachdenken, DBZ 2 (2019), 22–29 • Tektonisk Strøm: Interview med Nini Leimand ved Martin Keiding, Arkitekten 5 (2019), 37–43

Impetus The site of the former Deutsche Bahn railway goods yards was to be developed to become the new Erlenmatt urban district, and essentially consists of two building zones that encompass a park-like open space. In the eastern part, building rights were acquired by the Habitat housing foundation, their remit being to determine the urban structure and a specific set of rules with sustainability goals. One building block is the leasehold given to the Zimmerfrei cooperative, whose mission is to provide affordable living space in conjunction with community, sustainable, and self-sufficiency projects. The planning and construction process were undertaken in a participative scheme with the cooperative members.

Concept The corner volume is based on the existing basic urban geometry, with open-air walkways facing the courtyard, making the apartments directly accessible while simultaneously, due to their large dimensions, serving as commonly usable exterior spaces. The simple basic structure creates an efficient organizational spatial scheme. The apartments are freely conceptualized, creating a spaciousness by avoiding any circulation spaces, as well as being amply daylit by virtue of their double orientation. On the gallery side are the functional areas with a combined kitchen/dining room, and facing the park the living and sleeping areas. The living amenities are supplemented by centrally arranged shared areas, such as the lobby, the roof terrace, the workshop, laundry rooms, and guest rooms. Sustainability is writ large in the openness of circulation, the optimization of the living spaces, and the range of apartment types for various life phases and living ideas.

Implementation Constructed as a hybrid building, the materials are implemented according to their properties. The concrete structure of the floor slabs and the main dividing walls are executed with infilled prefabricated facade elements and wooden-fabricated partition walls. Industrial materials are used for cladding, all of them low-maintenance and long-lasting, their direct character a reflection of the location. Industrially raw aluminum, untreated corrugated fiber-cement panels, galvanized elements, and glass-fiber-reinforced, translucent corrugated artificial-resin sheets combine to form a tectonic composition, giving the building a vibrant appearance. Sail-shaped textile sun-shading elements and the drapes and awnings transfuse a lightness, while the two open stairwells on the front facade create a plasticity. In the interiors, maritime-pine plywood and polished and raw concrete surfaces generate a contrasting atmosphere.

Erlenmattstrasse, nos. 71–101. Basel, Erlenmatt site, on the right side of the Rhine, situated on the scree field left by the Rhine and the Wiese. First settlement traces from around 1,600 B.C. In the MIDDLE AGES, a plane known as Horburgacker with a gravel pit at the north end. Adjoining marshland, to the east the Goldbach. **P** 1225, following the building of the Rhine Bridge, the emergence of Kleinbasel; from 1270 on the town is fortified. **E** In the MID-13TH CENTURY, construction of the Kleinbasel commercial canals, with the Riehenteich, fed by the Wiese, as a central component. The waterpower from various subsidiary canals enables the settlement of various tradespeople on the right side of the Rhine. **P** 1285, King Rudolf bestows a town charter on Kleinbasel. 1392, unification with Grossbasel. The Innere Horburg, the later Erlenmatt site, is part of the so-called "Great Drainage," with numerous arms from the Riehenteich feeding into the city. **E** It remains agriculturally used grassland.

    In the MID-19th CENTURY the fortifications are torn down and Basel begins growing beyond the medieval walled cordon in all directions, including toward Horburg. The number of inhabitants in Kleinbasel increases between 1847 and 1860 from 6,000 to 10,200.

    P 1852, arrival of the railroad: signing of the state contract between the Grand Duchy of Baden and Switzerland regulating the continuation of the Baden railway line on Basel territory, which still applies today. Three years later, 1855, the railway begins operating. The site is sealed off in the east toward the city. Creation of Horburg- and Bahnhofstrasse along the first buildings of the Baden Railway Administration. Draining of the marshes of the Lange Erle and its transformation into a municipal park begins in 1861; opening of the Animal Park in 1871. 1876/1878, second re-channeling of the grassland following serious flooding: dam construction and straightening above Kleinhüningen.

    P In 1892 the German Rail Administration purchase a 19-ha area between Schwarzwaldallee and Erlenstrasse for the construction of a planned freight yard. The terrain is raised to accommodate the tracks and installations. The Güterbahnhof, a railroad terminus with tracks arranged in a fan shape, is opened on DECEMBER 15, 1905. A steel-cage-fence closes the yards site to the outside; entry is prohibited for unauthorized persons. Use as a storage yard for timber, coal, and other goods. The relocation of the railway and the new station clash with the network of commercial canals. Sale of the water rights to the canton; complete cessation of the use of the canals by 1917. 1989, the Deutsche Bahn announces the decision to abandon the Güterbahnhof in Basel. 1996, beginning of the first planning for a new urban district on the site.

    E Temporary occupancy: 1999, the k.e.i.m. association "for the development of urban sites and locations" starts negotiations with the Deutsche Bahn. Between 1996 and 2002, two urban planning ideas competitions for the site. From 2002 on the temporary uses on the entire site—now the nt/Areal, as in "non-territorial"—are organized by Fahrenheit GmbH: **C** an art space in the wagon engineering works, the Erlkönig Restaurant, the Grenzwert Sonnendeck bar, concerts, and numerous small open-air experimental projects. 2003, complete end of rail operations by the Deutsche Bahn; renaming to Erlenmatt in the same year. **E** 2005, the Deutsche Bahn's real estate company begins selling the site, parcel by parcel; 2008, all temporary uses stop.

    A remnant from the period of temporary occupancy: in 2003 the VIP association begins considering how to stage the outdoor spaces, resulting in a trend-sport facility, a children's project, the talent shed Funambolo, and a Sunday market.

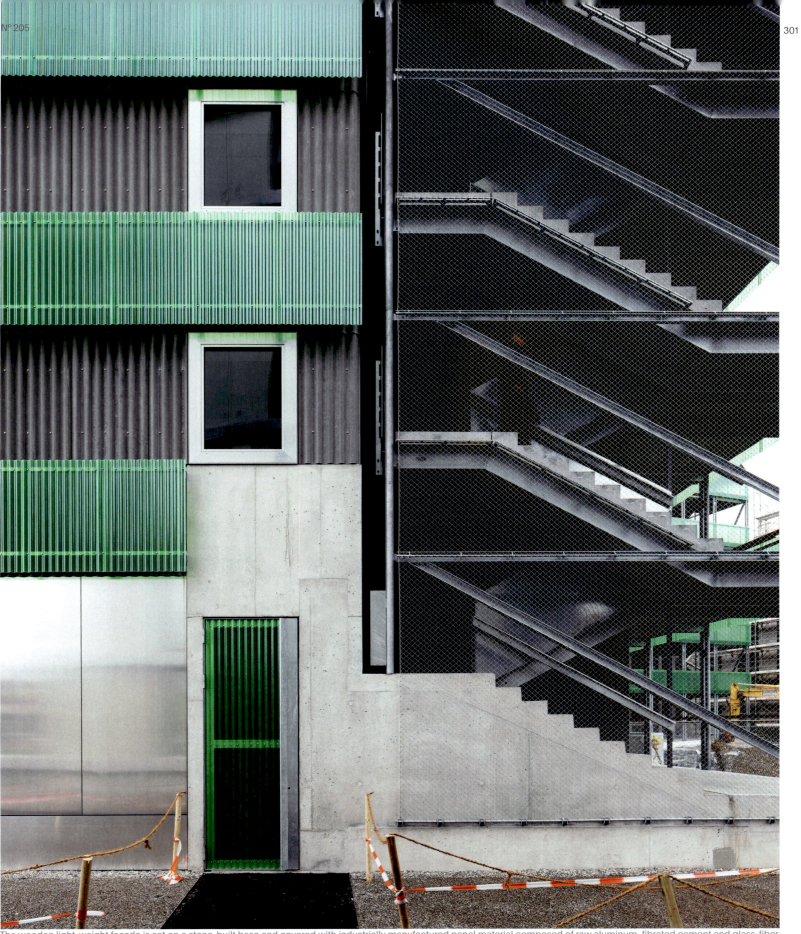

The wooden light-weight facade is set on a stone-built base and covered with industrially manufactured panel material composed of raw aluminum, fibrated cement and glass-fiber-reinforced synthetic resin. The circulation layer is constructed in galvanized steel and is framed with galvanized wire mesh at either end

The area east of the Erlenmatt Park was acquired by the housing subsidy foundation Habitat in order to transfer the leaseholds of segments of the land to young housing cooperatives. By using a collage of simple materials, a pointer is provided to the temporary occupancy of the site following the closing of the railway goods yard, during which a variety of ephemeral structures were erected. From the heightened arcade space on the upper floor, the views extend over the Erlenmatt Park, with its ruderal stretches giving it a scenic quality. The large architectural volume in Erlenmatt West is a result of the urban-planning configuration of the area for institutional investors.

All of the apartments are freely accessible from the public spaces via open-air walkways. Additionally to the staircase with lift, the sets of steps arranged on the galleries provide free scope for circulation. The community space with the large kitchen is directly accessed via the exterior lobby, as are the laundry areas.

The cluster apartments with their eight personal areas, each accommodating up to two people, are equipped with two interconnected shared kitchens. The strict orthogonal spatial system is broken only by the corner apartments. Originally conceived as a timber construction, for cost reasons the building was built in a hybrid form. The compartment-like nature of the project resulted in a concrete cross-wall construction with additional isolated supports. Non-load-bearing walls, as well as the exterior facade, are produced from wooden elements.

A roof terrace for shared use with raised plant beds for individual cultivation. By clearly demarcating the keep-clear areas for eventual escape routes, permission was granted to partially furnish the gangways.

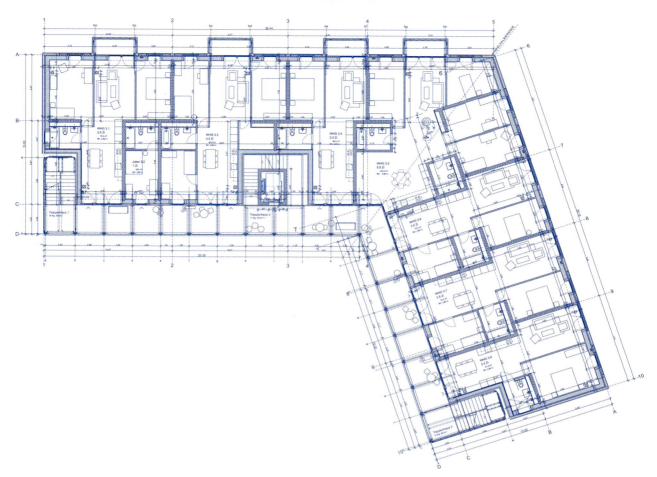

Floor plan, 3rd upper story (1:300)

Floor plan, ground story (1:300)

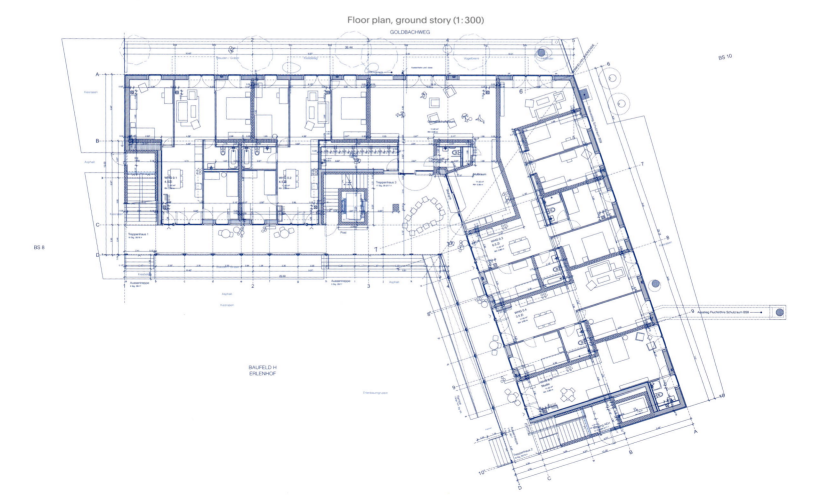

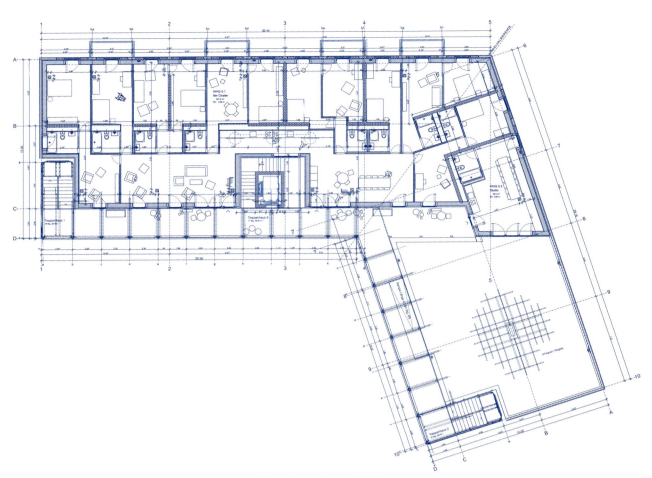

Floor plan, roof story (1:300)

Floor plan, 4th upper story (1:300)

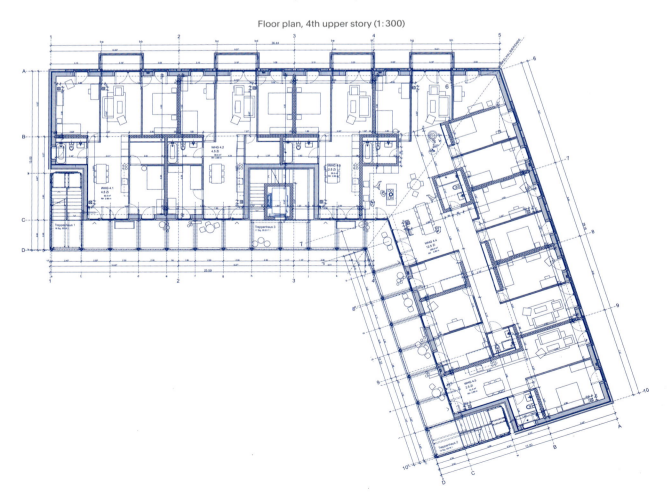

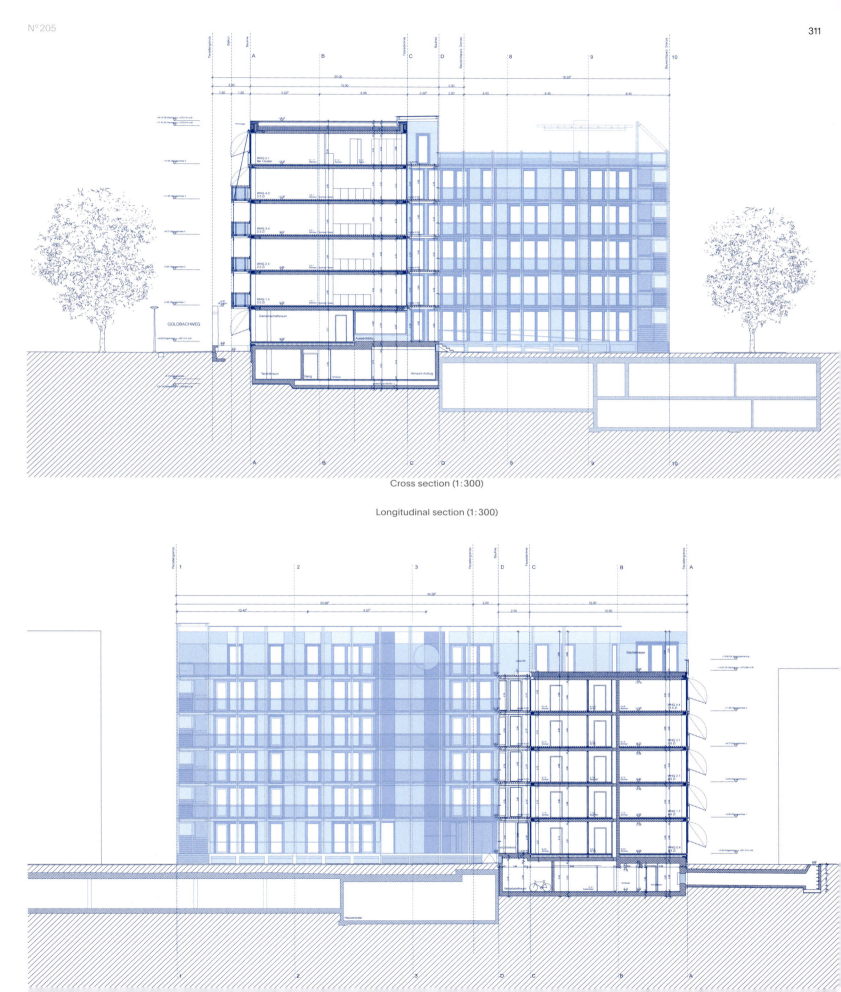

Cross section (1:300)

Longitudinal section (1:300)

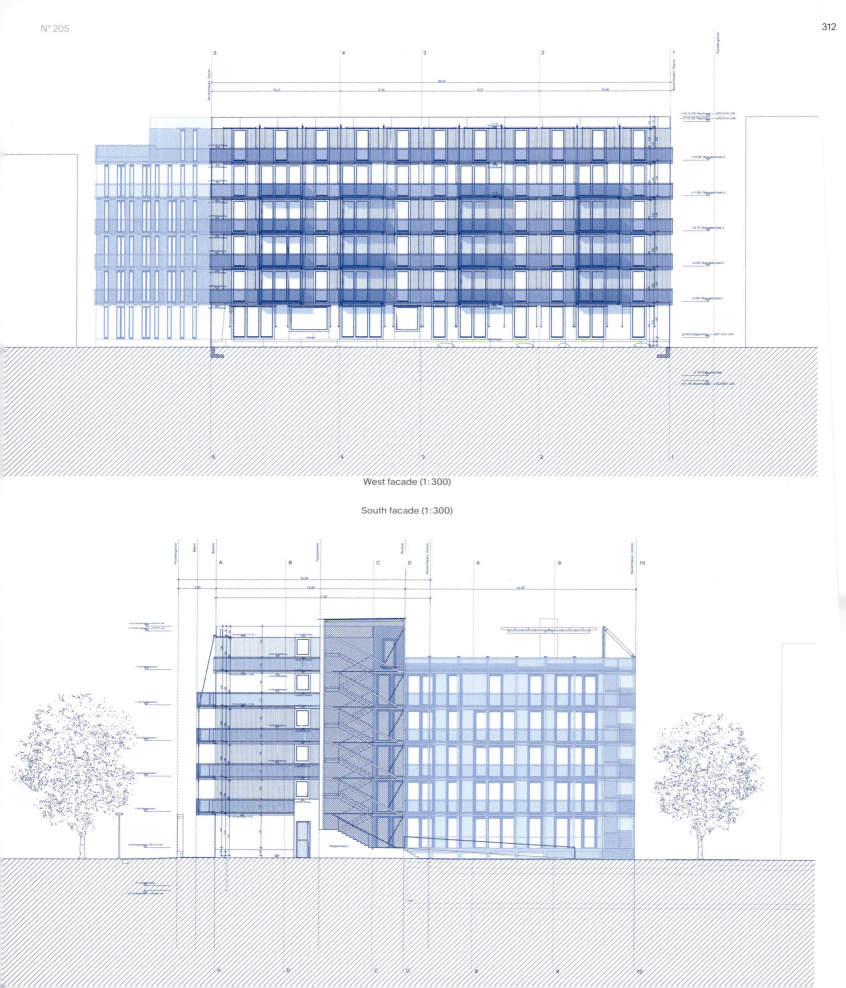

West facade (1:300)

South facade (1:300)

Mosogno Sotto, Switzerland

2014–2018   **Casa Mosogno**

Conversion

N° 207 Casa Mosogno

Location Mosogno Sotto, Switzerland **Type** Conversion **Status** Realized **Project phases** *Planning* 2014–2015 *Realization* 2015–2018 **Client** Private **Project data** *Lot size* 6,331 m² *Built up area* 116 m² *Floor area* 202 m² (according to SIA 416) *Building volume* 1,135 m³ **Planners** *Architecture and site management* Buchner Bründler Architekten, Basel *Building engineering* De Giorgi & Partners, Muralto **Team Buchner Bründler** *Partners* Daniel Buchner, Andreas Bründler *Associate* Nick Waldmeier *Project lead* Hellade Miozzari *Participants* Fabian Meury **Publications** Steffen Hägele, Schutz und Überschreitung: Die Casa Mosogno im Tessiner Onsernonetal von Buchner Bründler Architekten, Archithese 2 (2019), 28–37 • Carmen Nagel Eschrich, Minimalismus und Historie: Feriendomizil Mosogno Sotto, db—deutsche bauzeitung 3 (2019), 133 • Palle Petersen, Brutal idyllisch: Die Besten 2019, Architektur, Anerkennung für Casa Mosogno, Hochparterre 12 (2019), 37 • Katharina Köppen, Jurysieger: Was ist angemessen?, Umbauen + Renovieren 2 (2020), 30–38 • Casa Mosogno: Buchner Bründler Architekten entwickeln ein Sommerhaus mit Winterstube, AIT 3 (2020), 124–27 • Massimo Curzi, Buchner Bründler Architekten: Casa Mosogno in Canton Ticino, Casabella 3 (2020), 4–13

Impetus Situated in the Onsernone Valley on a hillside below the through road, the ensemble of stone-built houses evolved over generations but was long abandoned. Set on a ridge, it opens out to the forested valley, at the same time shielding itself from the village of Mosogno Sotto above it. The clients, themselves closely connected to the ways of living in Ticino, wanted a residential house that could be designed simply using the existing situation.

Concept The architectural assemblage, consisting of various buildings and annexes, was in various states of disrepair. Apart from the small outhouses, the timber elements—such as joists, suspended ceilings, and walls—were all dilapidated and needed crucial remediation, whereby this requirement afforded a process-focused rethinking of the overall complex. In so doing, the architectural volumes were functionally apportioned: the main building was conceived as an open summerhouse and the better preserved annex building as a winter lounge, with the small intermediate part being repurposed as a bathhouse. The former terrace, which faced to the valley, is re-established in larger dimensions, shored up by a dry masonry wall. The resulting new open space relocates the spatial interconnections and combines the individual buildings anew.

Implementation Following the dismantling, the only part of the summer house that remained was the enclosing walls. The newly created hall space is covered by a protective metal roof, while the open room of the tower-like bathhouse is similarly re-roofed with a dome of cast-in-situ concrete. Vis-à-vis, the massing of the annex building is retained. This roof is also re-covered, with an isolated wooden cube spanned into the enclosing walls, serving as a heated, all-year-round living room and bedroom. During the process-driven critical appraisal of the stone buildings, the historical significance of the main building proved to be essential in understanding the overall ensemble. This history was too rich to be hidden beneath a layer of white plaster, and instead the architectural traces of the past were correspondingly left visible and experiencable: above the plastering and the structures of the living spaces, below the naked stone of the wine cellar, and in the middle a fragment of wall with a chimney, now braced by a metal frame, which bears it and reinforces the walls of the house. A homogenous concrete floor was cast, emphasizing the overall space. Individual elements with an object-like effect signify the new importance of the open hall.

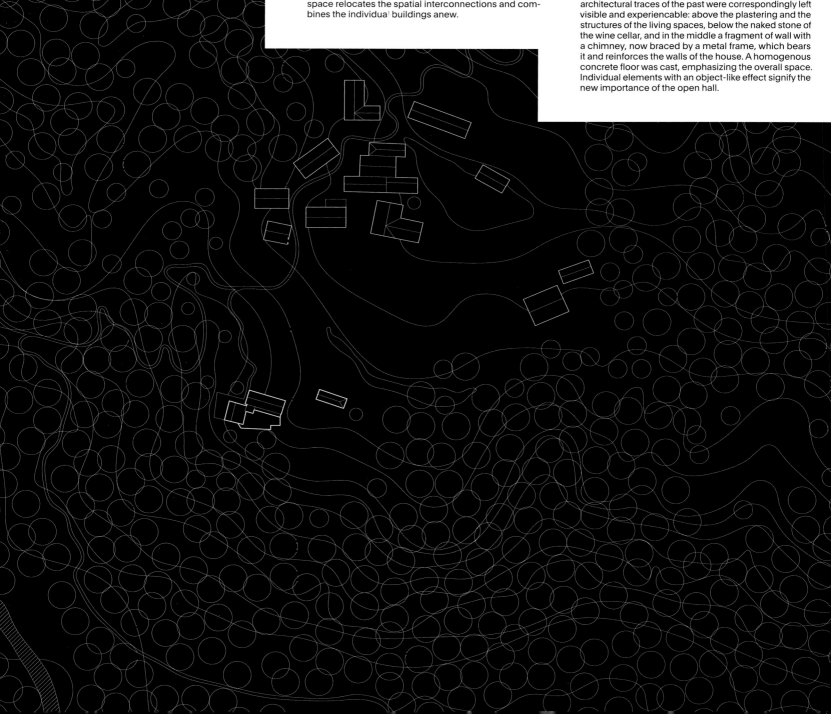

Mosogno Sotto, Raslei: the ensemble of buildings, consisting of three parts, is situated far from the road on a terrace beneath a vine yard, outside the actual settlement core of Mosogno Sotto. Mosogno is a small village in the upper Onsernone Valley between Russo and Loco in the Canton of Ticino. The ca. 20-km-long, deep V-shaped valley, stretching east–west, runs parallel to the Centovalli and the Italian Valle Vigezzo. At its base flows the Isorno, making a dogleg at Auressio to the south and flowing into the Melezza at Intragna in the Centovalli. The villages are situated halfway up the terraced southern slope on the sunny side, where the valley is forested with beeches and chestnuts.

    R In the MIDDLE AGES the valley settlements are under the tutelage of the mother church in Loco, consecrated to San Remigio. **P** In the EARLY MIDDLE AGES this communion produced a valley community, the Comun Grande. The polity, in which every village is represented by a *squadra* and has a say in decisions, regulates public affairs and is based on the local autonomy of the citizens. 1273, Barione, a part of the village of Mosogno, is first officially mentioned; Mosogno itself in 1277. The most important link route for transporting goods is the *mulattiera*, leading from Loco via Niva to Intragna, and first mentioned in the 13th CENTURY. **R** Church building in the individual villages in the valley begins in the second half of the 14th CENTURY; the parish church of San Bernardo in Mosogno is erected in the late 16th CENTURY. **C** 1607, La Vallona is founded—a group equipped with canons, firearms, whistles and drums who celebrate both religious and secular festivities, giving the whole valley a luster. At the same time the first buildings appear in Raslei. **R** 1685, Mosogno splits from the mother church in Loco to become its own parish. More chapels are erected; in 1684 in Mosogno Sotto dedicated to the Madonna Addolorata, Our Lady of Sorrows.

    E Southern-alpine, insubric climate: the vegetation is lush and diverse, but the slopes are steep and farming arduous. Cultivation mostly for self-sufficiency, above all livestock and pasture farming; little forestry, little arable farming or wine-growing. The level of self-sufficiency is low: the people of Onsernone are dependent on external supplies of foodstuffs. From the 16th CENTURY, the inhabitants begin subsiding on hay manufacture: the sale of woven rye-straw braids at the markets in Russo and Loco; woven hats and bags, also for customers outside Ticino—in Lombardy, Piedmont, at markets in Flanders, France, and French Switzerland. Straw is dried on covered timber decks.

    Some thirty so-called "Roman bridges" provide transit and connections. Bridle paths, built by the inhabitants themselves, link the villages with each other. The connecting routes to the surrounding valleys are crucial. For example the Ponte della Neveria beneath Mosogno Sotto, a transit thoroughfare to Locarnese. The same routes are used by those seeking work outside—in the immediate surroundings but also in Piedmont, in German Switzerland, sometimes in France and the Netherlands, later also overseas. **E** Their income contributes to the valley's survival. Many, above all the menfolk, emigrate seasonally to sell straw products. Some people leave the valley for longer. A small handful become rich, return home, and build imposing residences in the valley. **R** Some, far from home, donate images, churches, and chapels: 1684, the large chapel in the middle of Mosogno Sotto, 1778 the chapel to the Madonna del Carmine next to the Ponte della Neveria. At around the same time Raslei is enlarged, an inscription in a granite architrave bearing the date 1772.

    P With the formation of the Canton of Ticino in 1803, municipalities are created, likewise in Mosogno. Up until the dissolution of the Comun Grande in 1855 and its transfer into a civic community, both bodies exist in parallel. ▶ At the end of the valley is Italy: grazing rights are disputed, coupled with a lot of smuggling. Since 1768 the former bridleway between Loco and Spruga can be used by horses; 1852, the winding valley road can be driven by coaches to Russo; 1863, with the opening of the Ponte Oscuro, the upper valley is also connected. In the meantime Mosogno numbers 320 inhabitants.

▶ In 1859 the chapel next to the Ponte della Neveria is sold. The owner intends to use it as a stable, but two years later it burns down and is used to shelter goats. Mikhail Bakunin, the founder of Anarchism, is given citizenship in Mosogno 1872. 1884, the burnt-down chapel is rebuilt and serves as a sanctuary. ▶ Straw manufacturing suffers a depression; the valley's economic foundations collapse. The LATE 19th CENTURY witnesses a mass emigration. In 1900 Mosogno has 280 inhabitants, by 1950 only 141.

▶ At the beginning of the 20th CENTURY artists and intellectuals discover the Onsernone, finding peace and inspiration, and during WW II also refuge. ▶ In 1944 the intensity of the partisan warfare in the neighboring Val d'Ossola is noticeable.

▶ Despite the famous new arrivals—such as Aline Valagin, Wladimir Rosenbaum, later also Alfred and Gisela Andersch, as well as Max Frisch—the population continues to decline. 1966 sees the founding of the Museo Onsernonese. In the 1970s a number of Swiss Germans arrive in the valley, tired of consumer society and in search of a life in harmony with nature: many of them leave, but some stay. 1978, a flood destroys all the bridges in the valley, including the Ponte della Neveria. The bridges are rebuilt. The village population continues to shrink: in 1980 around half of the house are second homes, and in Mosogno Sotto only 11 people are permanent residents. In summer, this number rises to around 30. In 2000 57 people have their permanent residence in the village; the last generation of the family who had lived for around 400 years in the ensemble in Raslei leaves. Raslei remains uninhabited for over ten years, nonetheless still furnished with the utensils that bore witness to the everyday life of the former inhabitants: stable chains for the cows, for goats and pigs; candle holders, hats, footstools, pictures; empty and full drawers.

▶ Until APRIL 9, 2016, Mosogno is a separate political municipality; on APRIL 10, 2016 it merged with the municipalities Isorno, Gresso, and Vergeletto and the already existing municipalitxy of Onsernone to form the larger municipality of Onsernone.

From the street a path leads down to Mosogno Sotto and to the house, past a church, the green hinged doors of which stand open all year round. The interior space is bathed in direct light, inviting anyone to come in. The church and Sergei Polunin's dance performance *Take Me to Church* are part of the project. The house has stood empty for almost a decade, but is still full of the belongings of entire generations, with all the traces of the life stories that mark the place and the house.

The first constructional measure was to secure the terrain with a new enclosing wall. There are very few artisans who still have the skill to erect dry-stone walls. The main building is in a sorry state; all of the timber elements, such as the joists and the raised floors, are dilapidated. Therefore this part of the building was transformed into a summerhouse, the better intact annex becoming a winter lounge. The projecting roof, stretching toward the valley and separate from the porch, is a relict of the earlier open-air gallery. Beyond the dry-stone walls begins the forest and the murmur of the Isorno, scratching its way slowly through the rock deep down at the bottom of the valley.

Due to the adverse circumstances and the partly ramshackle architectural substance, the construction process lasted a number of years, marked by permanent surprises that continually transformed the project. Beneath the concrete cupola is a concrete-cast bathtub, the water for which is heated with a wood-burning stove. With the all-surface cast-concrete floor, the summer hall is transformed into a covered piazza.

The family bed stretches triangularly between the enclosing walls. Thanks to the rigorously insulated shell, the winter lounge can be heated with ease. The intricate chamber structure of the main building was removed to accommodate the open summer hall. The original occupancies are legible in the enclosing walls. The old fireplace is clasped by a steel frame. The corrugated iron is held by a rigid truss structure that widens toward the ridge of the roof to avoid discharging any additional shear forces to the exterior walls.

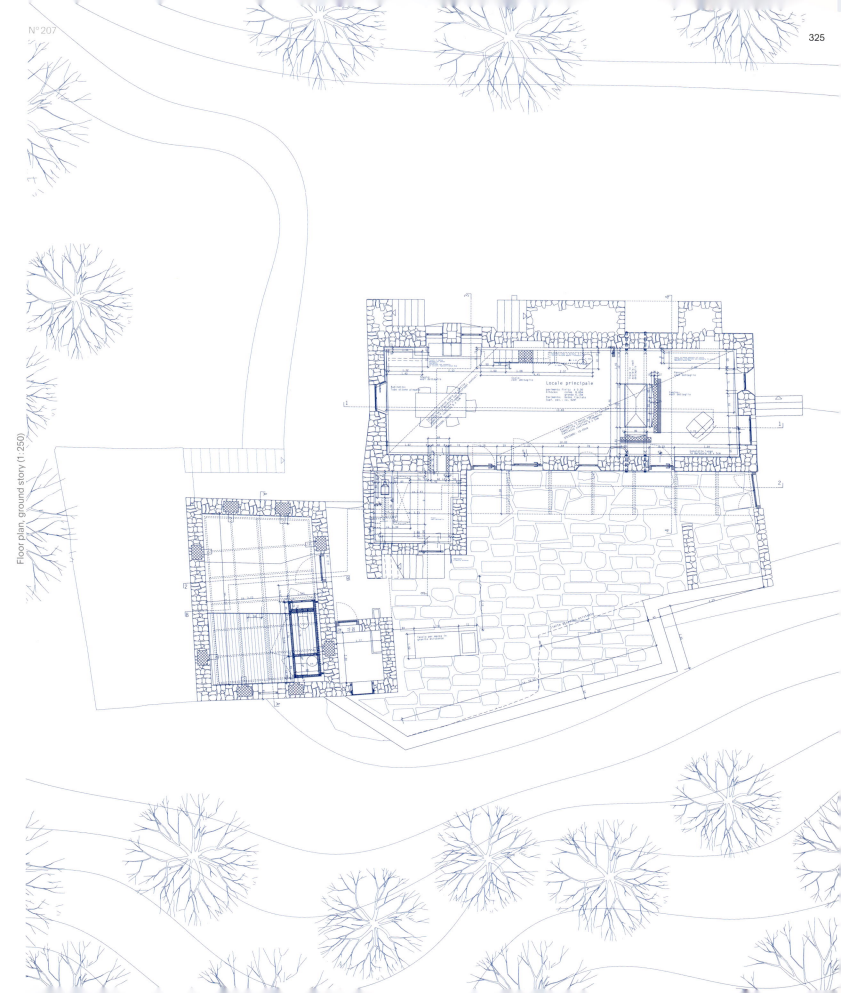

Floor plan, ground story (1:250)

Floor plan, upper story (1:250)

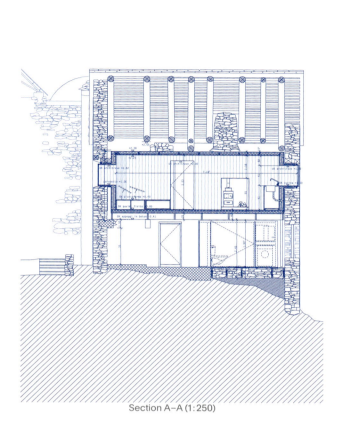

Section A-A (1:250)

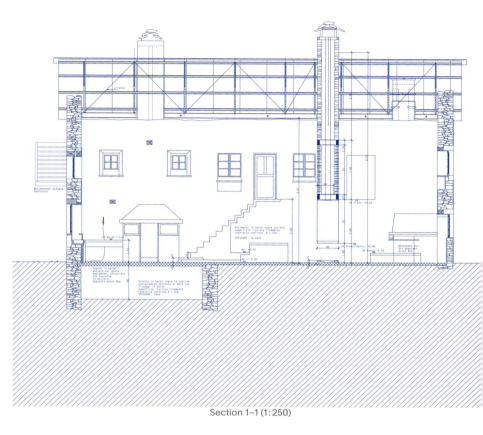

Section 1-1 (1:250)

Section 3-3 (1:250)

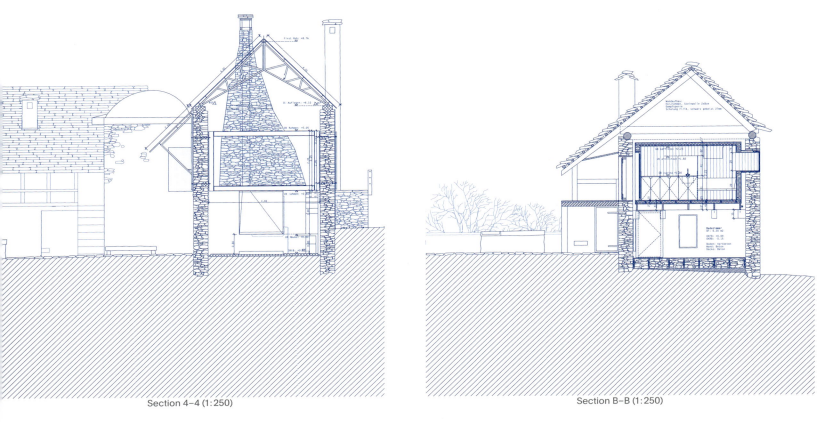

Section 4-4 (1:250)   Section B-B (1:250)

Section 2-2 (1:250)

Münchenstein, Switzerland

2014–2016   **Münchenstein House**

New building

N° 212 Münchenstein House

Location Münchenstein, Switzerland **Type** New building **Status** Realized **Project phases** *Planning* 2014–2015 *Realization* 2015–2016 **Client** Private **Project data** *Lot size* 412 m² *Built up area* 96 m² *Floor area* 231 m² (according to SIA 416) *Building volume* 743 m³ **Planners** *Architecture and site management* Buchner Bründler Architekten, Basel *Building engineering* Schnetzer Puskas Ingenieure AG, Basel *Building physics* Gartenmann Engineering AG, Basel **Team Buchner Bründler** *Partners* Daniel Buchner, Andreas Bründler *Associate* Nick Waldmeier *Project lead* Michael Glaser *Participants* Janine Bolliger, Luise Daut, Björn Wiedl **Publications** Burkhard Franke, Wohnhaus Münchenstein, DETAIL 11 (2017), 60–64 • Leina Godin, Solo Act, Mark Magazine 71, no. 12–1 (2017–2018), 36–37 • *Buchner Bründler Architekten: Münchenstein House 2016*—Photo Essay by Rory Gardiner, Rome 2019

Impetus   The existing property is situated in a quiet residential area of a suburb of Basle. The neighborhood street is arrayed with houses from the Wilhelminian era, set at regular intervals. The size and character of the houses correspond to the nearby garden-city settlement and are surrounded by green gardens that stretch to the adjoining railway embankment.   The client's house is part of a duplex structure, its gable end facing the street generating an amazing presence. In comparison, the interior spaces appeared closed and interacted little with the surroundings and the garden. It was evident that even major restructuring would add little improvement, therefore the obvious solution was to conceive a new building.

Concept   In a radical step, half of the duplex house was dismantled and a free-standing volume was set in the middle of the plot. Typologically the new building orientates itself on the secondary buildings in the environs and assumes a contrary alignment to its street-facing neighbors.   Built as a lightweight construction, the building primarily relates to the garden. The longitudinal volume, with its narrow section, stretches deep into the property, allowing the interior along its long side to be opened up expansively to the surroundings, dotted with trees, some of them fully grown.   The house is conceived using a minimal form language, with the basic geometry expressed in four walls and a flat saddle roof. The interior follows a similarly simple and logical spatial organization and is formed as a flowing, open space, structured by only a few elements.

Implementation   The simple volume is a timber construction, clad in a black bitumen skin. Starting from the roof, the slated cladding covers the entire building, giving its volume a formal precision and a material density. With its tactile quality, the overall monochrome effect reinforces the essential architectural concept of the house. At the same time the materiality references the ephemeral appearance of storage sheds and garden houses, thus avoiding having to address the street and allowing the greened area to be treated as the core spatial reference.   Large swing-arm canopies protrude outward over the volume from the sides like a second skin, expanding the simple geometry of the house. The interior is marked by a harmonious material design palette of concrete, smoothed plaster, aluminum, and wood varnished in silver grey. The windows, cut out as simple openings in the walls, pictorially frame the outside landscape.

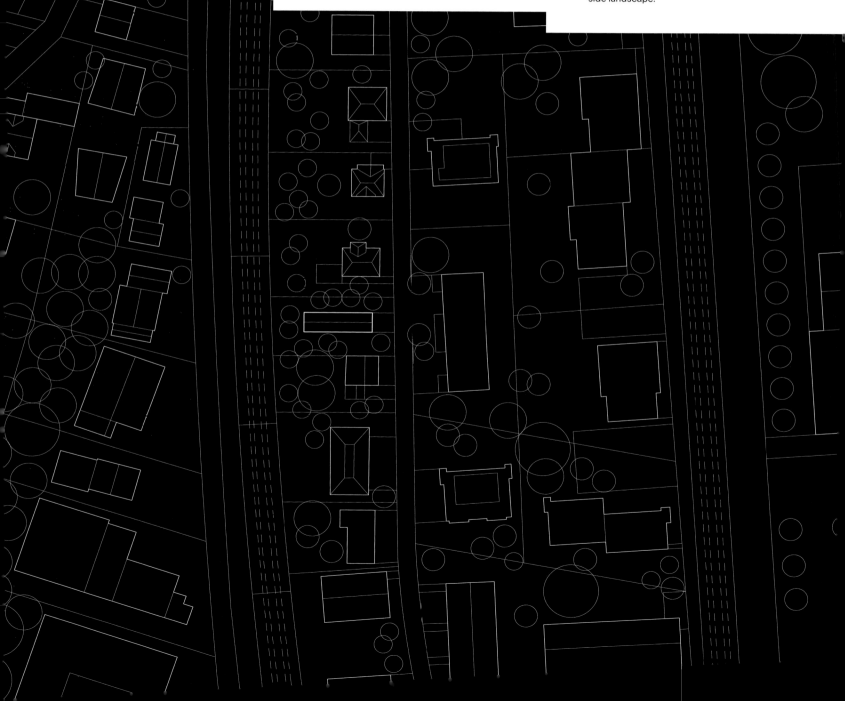

Birseckstrasse no. 28. Münchenstein, formerly Geckingen. Alemannic settlement on the narrow terrace above the Birsebene. At the lowest point in the river course, the Birs branches into innumerable arms—wild and destructive at high water. **R E** In the MID-12th CENTURY, Cluniac monks build the St.-Alban-Teich, a commercial canal, to power mills and guarantee food supplies. Water for the canal is taken from a branch of the Birs at St. Jakob. Between 1260 and 1275 the Münch family of knights builds a castle. The village, then with 30 houses, is renamed Münchenstein.

In the MID-17th CENTURY the Birs provides too little water: 1624, construction of a weir in Rütihard. The newly drained, fertile land on the Brüglinger plateau is called Neuewelt. **E** In 1661 the Basel iron merchant Ludwig Krug builds a wiredrawn hammer mill on the left-hand side of the Birs, at Schwenkenmatte. Krug and his sons acquire more and more land, it and the forge remaining in family possession until OCTOBER 1745, when Benedict and Emanuel Stähelin acquire the Schwenkenmatte and Zollweide for 10,000 pounds. Stähelin's son Balthasar establishes a silk twining plant at Neuewelt, a bleachery, stables, and a barn. Increasing industrialization along the canal.

The area around today's Birseckstrasse remains undeveloped—the area can only be safely settled following the re-channeling of the Birs in 1875. Shift in the developmental focus from the village of Münchenstein to the left bank of the Birs, toward Neuewelt. **P** 1875, opening of the Jura Railway from Basel to Delémont, the only direct rail link from Basel to France following the Franco-Prussian War. 1880, the lots between the railway embankment and Baselstrasse beneath Loogenrain are all developed save for one single house.

Ten years later, in 1890, a tramline is constructed along Baselstrasse. Up to 1900, a huge surge in development in the area between the tram lines to Reinach and Münchenstein, from Ruchfeld till Neuewelt and along the railroad embankment. Birseckstrasse first appears on maps in 1918. It forks in an L-shape from Baselstrasse and has seven houses. **E** After WW I the Neuewelt area experiences increasing industrialization: cotton mill, electrical-motor factory, cement factory, Elektra Birseck, soap factory, confectionary factory. The whole area facing the Bruderholz is consolidated and developed with standardized single-family homes. 1923, construction of the duplex at Birseckstrasse nos. 28/30; clients: Georg Ehrsam-Müller (no. 28) and Johann Nobel (no. 30). The development with semi-detached family houses is due to a restriction in the building laws—a Swiss differentiation between duplexes vertically and double-family houses horizontally, i.e. by stories. The house at Birseckstrasse nos. 28/30 is vertically divided. Prolonging of the private sphere to include access spaces such as entrances and stairwells, as opposed to double-family houses. 1933, the house is connected to the sewer system. Between 1950 and 1960, growth in the number of inhabitants from 6,033 to 10,345. In the Neuewelt and Brüglinger plateau districts, Münchenstein coalesces with the City of Basel. **C** 1980, the Brüglinger plateau hosts the "Grün 80," creating a large natural and cultural park, today the Park im Grünen.

In the process of the cooperative-initiated architectural development around Gartenstadt and in the Neuewelt, private single- and double-family houses were also to be built. One house half had to be demolished to make way for the new building. Using a prefabricated timber construction, the basic structure of the prototypical pavilion volume was erected on site in a matter of days. The center of the simple private house typology is defined by the kitchen and bathroom. The precisely set windows allow the railway embankment to appear as a greened pictorial motif.

The long, thin house seeks out the cross-references to the back gardens of the neighboring properties. The open bathing area can be closed on both sides with sliding wooden panels. Drop-arm awnings extend the basic volume into the perimeter garden space, creating a baldachin on both sides. A slated bitumen skin runs seamlessly from the ridge over the roof and the exterior walls.

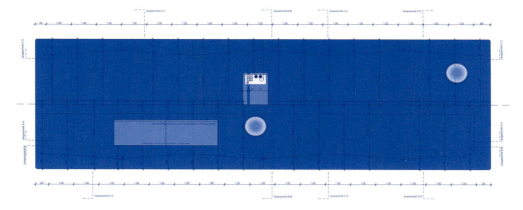

Top view, roof (1:150)

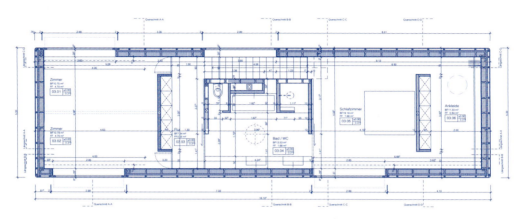

Floor plan, upper story (1:150)

Floor plan, ground story (1:150)

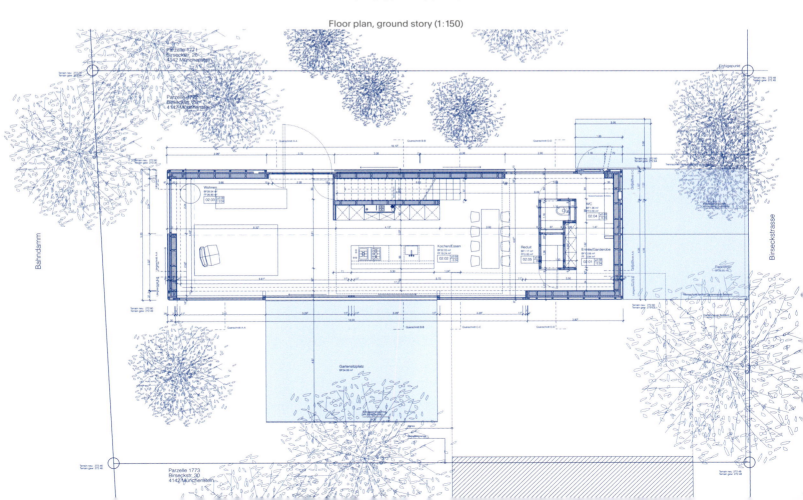

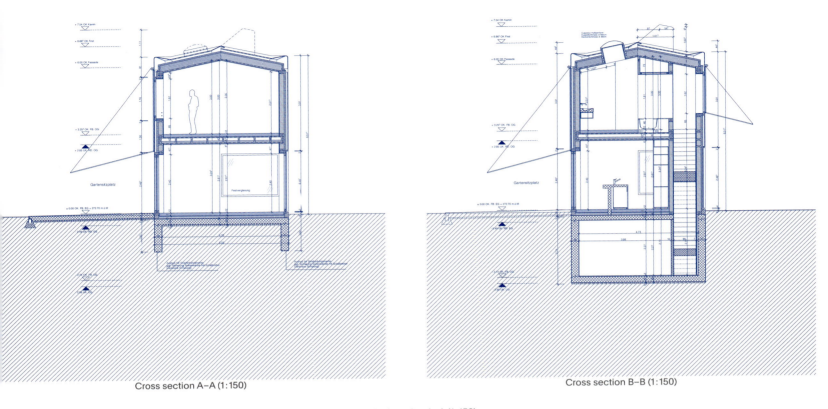

Cross section A–A (1:150)

Cross section B–B (1:150)

Longitudinal section A–A (1:150)

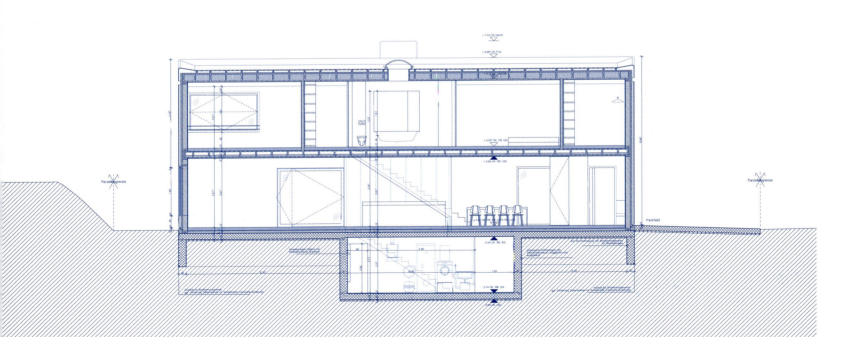

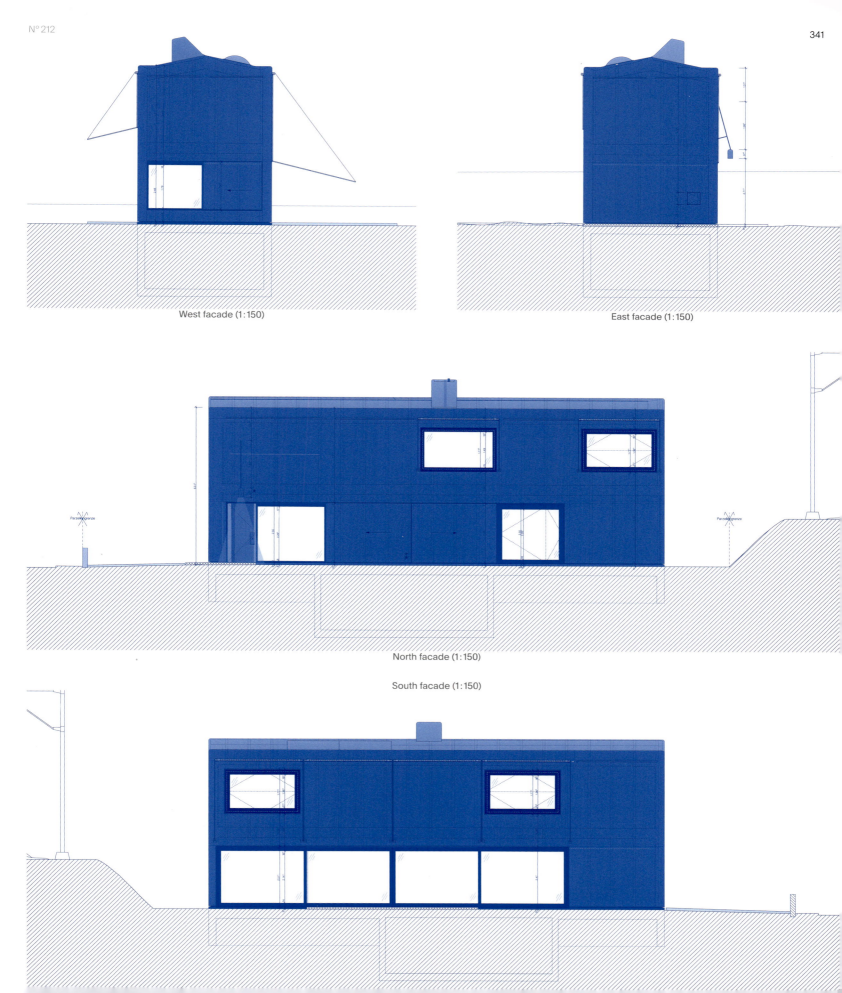

West facade (1:150)

East facade (1:150)

North facade (1:150)

South facade (1:150)

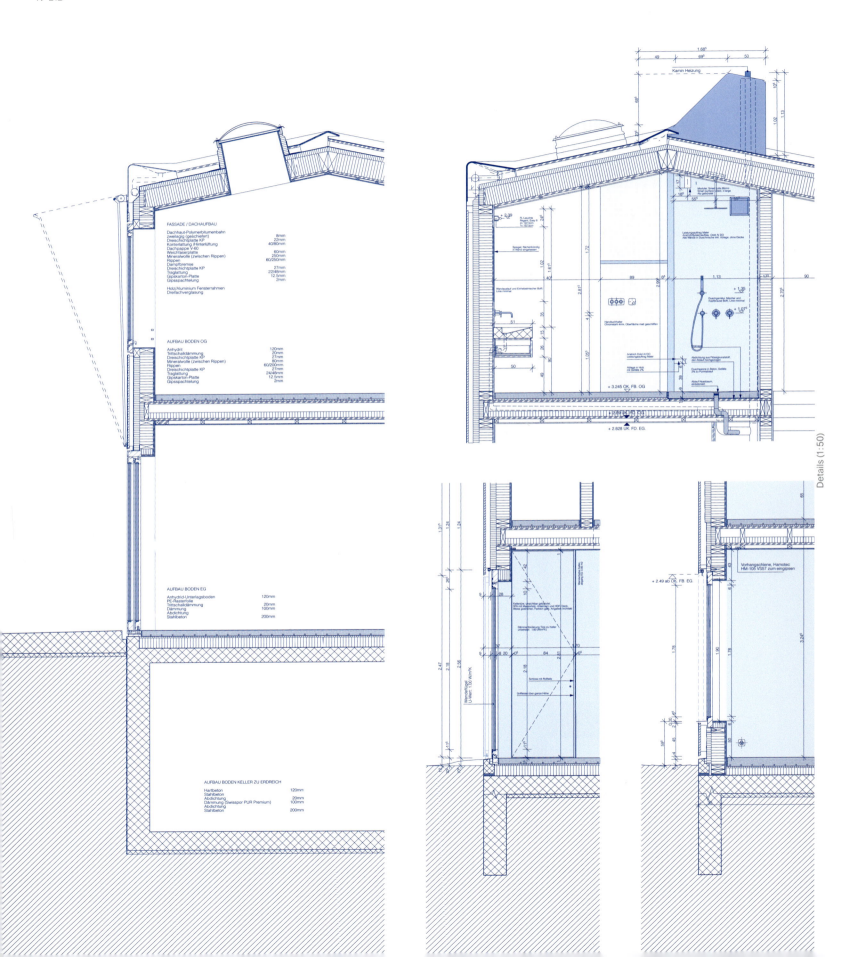

Binningen, Switzerland

2015–2018 **Kirschgarten House**

New building

N° 224 Kirschgarten House Selected Buildings 344

Location Binningen, Switzerland Type New building Status Realized Project phases *Planning* 2015–2016 *Realization* 2016–2018 Client Private Project data *Lot size* 1,054 m² *Built up area* 252 m² *Floor area* 429 m² (according to SIA 416) *Building volume* 1,530 m³ Planners *Architecture and site management* Buchner Bründler Architekten, Basel *Building engineering* Schnetzer Puskas Ingenieure AG, Basel Team Buchner Bründler *Partners* Daniel Buchner, Andreas Bründler *Associate* Nick Waldmeier *Project lead, preliminary project* Bianca Kummer *Project lead, planning and realization* Rebecca Borer *Participants* Omri Levy, Angelika Hinterbrandner Publications Hubertus Adam, Wohnhaus Kirschgarten Binningen, Domus 34 (German ed., 2018), 110–17

Impetus   The residential neighborhood is situated at the edge of the city's agglomeration belt, characterized by its richly greened scattered settlement pattern with varying grains. Directly adjacent to the Allschwiler woods, the greenery extends into the district.   The remit was to erect a house on a rectangular plot on a hillside slope, translating the features of the situation and the plot into an intimate living atmosphere distinguished by spatial qualities.

Concept   The disadvantageous north-facing slope is exploited to create a private space, allowing the house and the garden to become one. A base set in the sloping terrain terraces the topography to form a expansively sized main level, which in turn rises above the surroundings. On top of this is a single-story pavilion structure, open on all sides. A room-high wall spans the gap between the house and the street, giving the open area an additional layering.   The typological scheme is based on a continuous grid structure, within which both load-bearing and subsidiary elements are patterned. Reiteratively set concrete slabs emphasize the longitudinal relations, while the open-plan main room is additionally structured using spatial volumes in wood and brass.
  Suspended beams, arranged crosswise on the roof, allow large clear spans and an interior spatial lightness by transferring the loads to the outer elements, such as the columns and the encompassing boundary wall.
  The overlapping of the load-bearing elements in the roof construction and the enclosing wall create a flowing silhouette along the street, painted black facing the road. This graphic impact is supplemented by an additional over-layering of individual openings.

Implementation   The basic structure, together with the enclosing walls and the pergola elements, are all cast in concrete in situ. The main architectural element is the projecting roof, with the interaction between the suspender beams and binding joists assuming a spatially formative function. Wall aprons suspended from the structural framework on the end sides of the house both terminate and extend the living space, interrupting the direct sunlight and channeling it as indirect light inside. The prestressed roof structure dovetails the indoor and outdoor space. Cast-concrete pergola trellising frames the intermediary space between the house and the enclosing wall.   The homogenous surfaces, cast in paneled formwork, generate an overall tactile effect in both the exterior areas and the interior. The large openings are infilled with oak frames and extensively glazed. The material composition is further embossed with additional oiled oak surfacings.

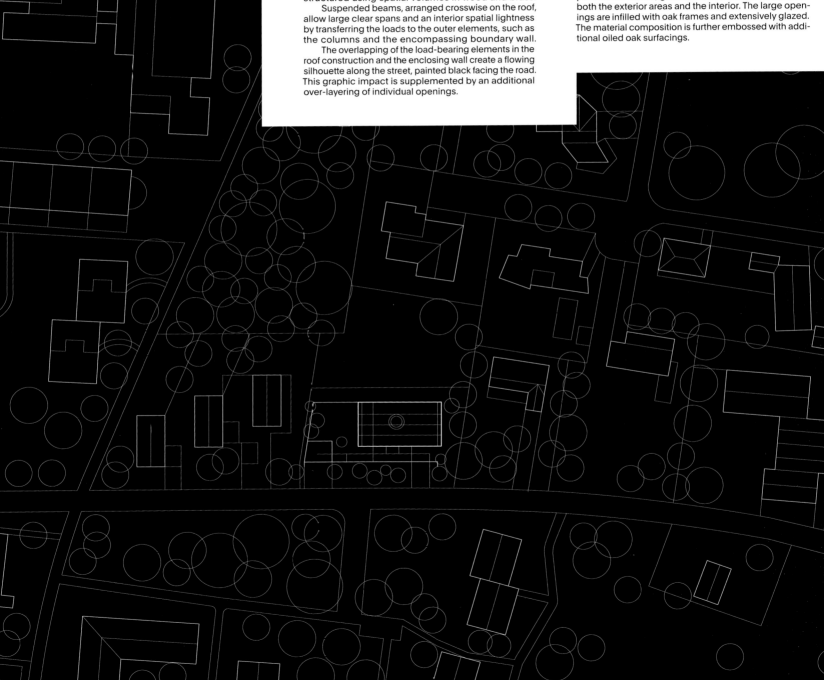

Im Kirschgarten no. 22. Binningen, a village in the Birsigebene bordering the City of Basel. Nestled between two Sundgau hills: Bruderholz on the eastern hill, Binningerhöhe with the Kirschbaumacker meadow on the western hill.

1004, charter from King Heinrich II, first written naming as "Binningun". **R** The village is a domain of the Bishop of Basel. 1299, first mention of a moated castle in the loop of the River Birsig. 1600, around 60 inhabitants; 1670, already 290. **E** 1653, agricultural farm meadow on the west hill, covered with meadow orchards, with the names Meiriacker, Hügliacker, Kirschbaumacker. 1773, 350 inhabitants, three inns, a lot of criminality, disputes, and prostitution.

P The aftershocks of the French Revolution usher in the end of bondage: 1796 and 1839, the citizens of Binningen purchase the estates on the east and west hills. **E** Additional income from fruit growing, especially cherries, with the expanding city as a reliable customer. The municipality is affected by deep poverty.

P 1882, initial registration of houses, pastures, gardens, allotments, fields, and vineyards in two value categories to tax them. Very little road infrastructure; 1887, opening of the Birsigtal Railway with a stop in Binningen. The construction of Basel Station draws numerous Italian building workers to Binningen. Poverty worsens: 1915, two thirds of the residents are entitled to emergency assistance, most of them industrial workers. The "beautiful hills on both sides of the Birsig, where rich villa owners could settle" are the hoped-for resource for the future.

Between 1923 and 1927, drawing of the parcels on the west hill. Lot 892 is created. The west hill is reserved for villas. Development begins to edge up the hill. Between 1937 and 1943 the Basel architect Fritz Rickenbacher plans the main Paradieshof airport on the west hill, which remains unrealized. From 1940 on, initial land rationalization. 1951, first zoning plan with four development zones with a projected population of 25,000 inhabitants by 2015. A particularly large zone for single-family homes. City dwellers move to the west hill. From 1957, building plots are repeatedly subtracted from lot 892 and villas are built on them. A first house stands in Im Kirschgarten. **P** 1971, a section of the west hill is specially designated as an agricultural and recreational zone. Half of the development zone is earmarked for single-family homes (villas), 100 ha for semi-detached and non-detached housing. 1977, neighboring houses are built at Im Kirschgarten nos. 24 to 28, while the lot Im Kirschgarten no. 22 stays vacant. Land prices soar from 60 centimes per m^2 in 1900 to 2,131 francs in 2016, representing the highest price for building land in Canton Basel-Landschaft.

N° 224

The house and the garden open out behind the southern encompassing wall. The intimate patio is covered by an asymmetrical pergola structure, shaped by an overlay of primary and secondary load-bearing systems. A finely framed ribbon of glazing creates spatial continuity lengthways east to west. The enfilade along the glass frontage leads to the bedroom via a bathroom area. Suspender beams arranged crosswise on the roof enable large spans.

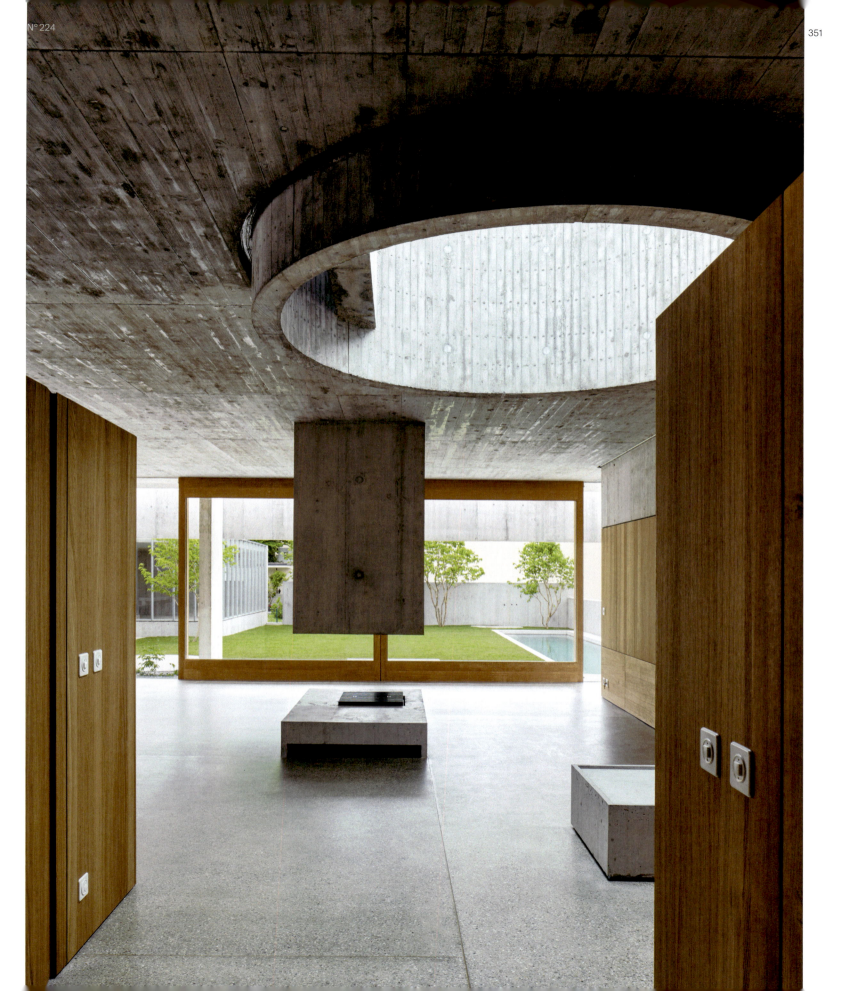

Hanging concrete aprons interrupt the direct sunlight and guide indirect light into the space. Flat inlays of oiled oak wood and a freestanding kitchen island of polished brass extend the basic mineral effect. The long, streamlined swimming pool with a jet stream is intended for training purposes.

Set on the constructed base terrace, the hall-house is orientated to assume a crowning position vis-à-vis the town and the lowland of the Upper Rhine. The hill slopes slowly down to Dorenbach and the greenery along the trench follows the descent to the town.

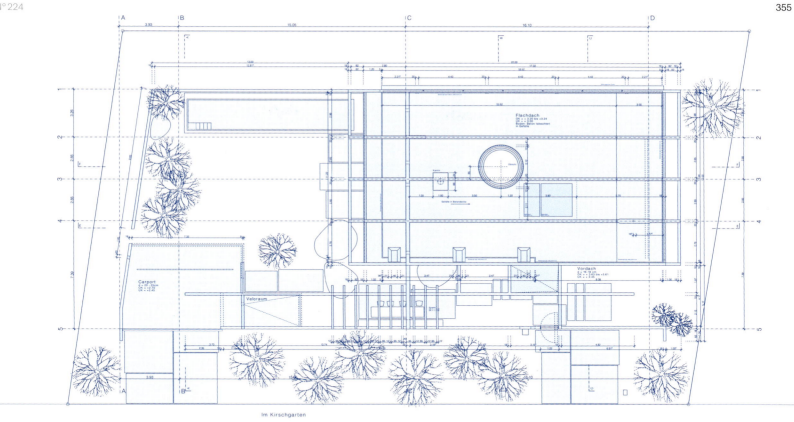

Top view, roof (1:250)

Floor plan, ground story (1:250)

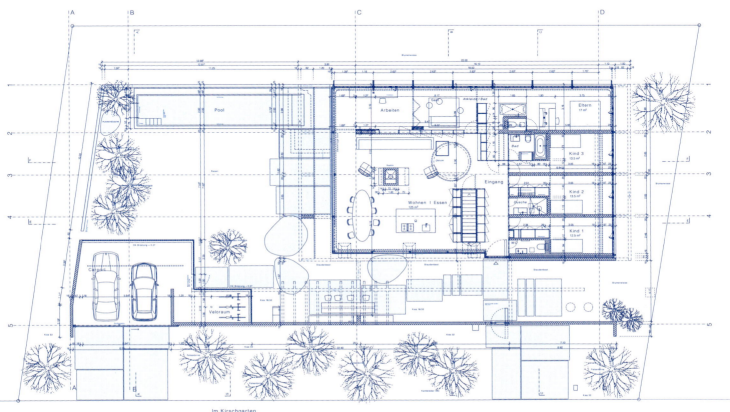

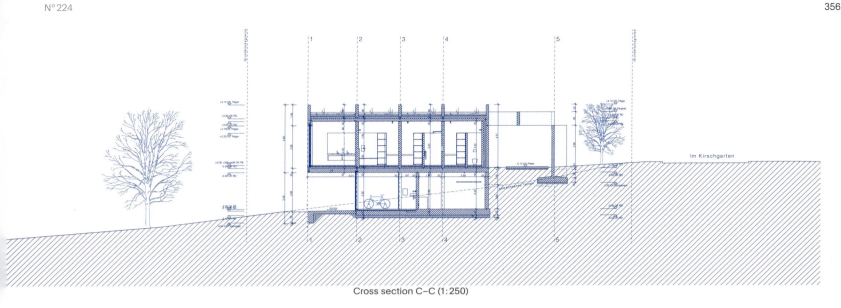

Cross section C–C (1:250)

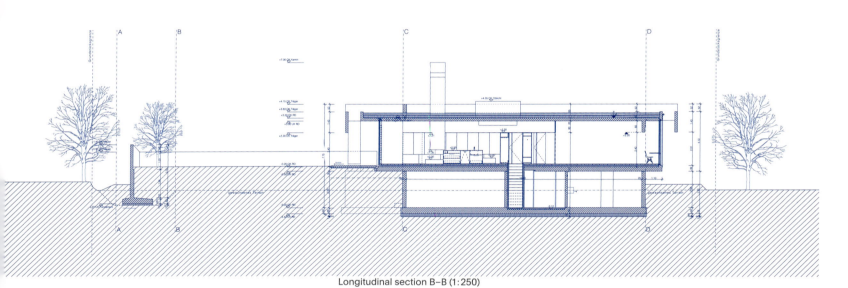

Longitudinal section B–B (1:250)

Cross section E–E (1:250)

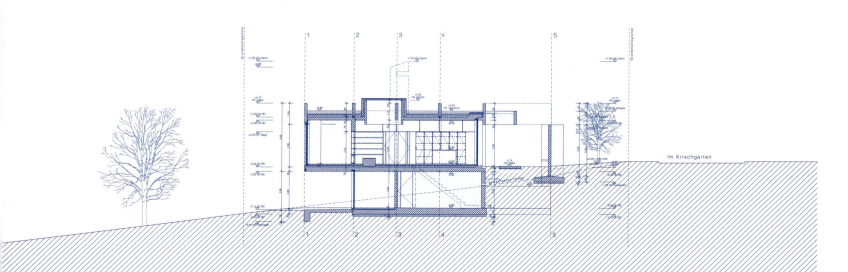

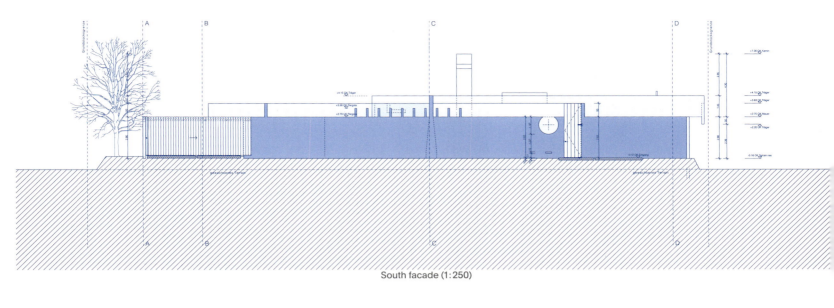

South facade (1:250)

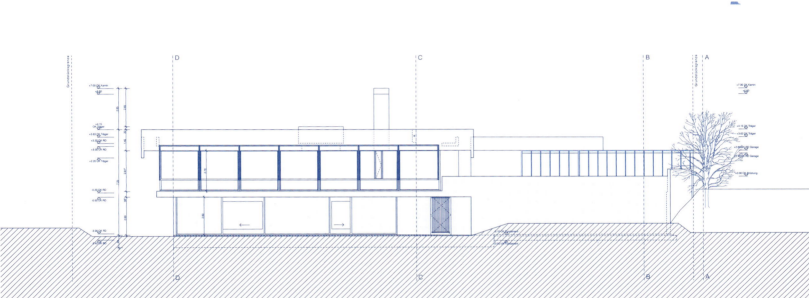

North facade (1:250)

East facade (1:250)

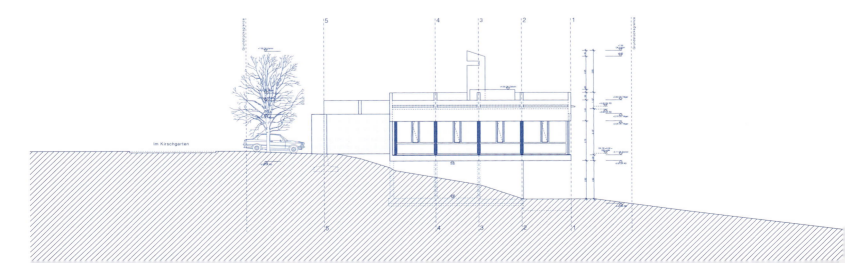

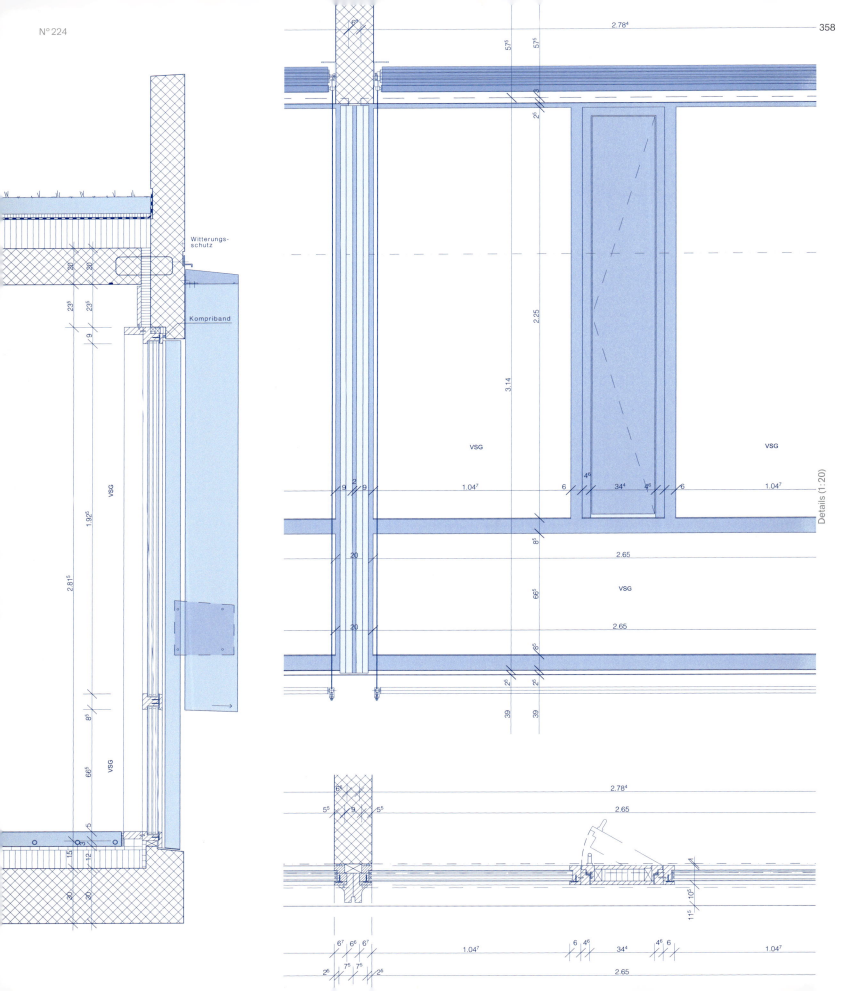

Details (1:20)

Nuglar, Switzerland

2016–2018

**Cherry Storehouse
Nuglar**

Conversion

N° 249 Cherry Storehouse Nuglar

Location Nuglar, Switzerland   **Type** Conversion   **Status** Realized   **Project phases** *Planning* 2016–2018 *Realization* 2017–2018   **Client** Private   **Project data** *Lot size* 1,212 m² *Built-up area* 430 m² *Floor area* 520 m² (according to SIA 416) *Building volume* 4,235 m³   **Planners** *Architecture* Joint partnership: lilitt bollinger studio, Nuglar; Buchner Bründler Architekten, Basel *Site management* lilitt bollinger studio, Nuglar *Building engineering* Jürg Merz, Maisprach   **Team Buchner Bründler** *Partners* Daniel Buchner, Andreas Bründler **Team lilitt bollinger studio** *Partners* Lilitt Bollinger   **Publications** Elias Baumgarten, Präzise Bastelei, archithese 1 (2019), 86–93 • Tibor Joanelly, Wohnraum statt Obstbrand: Umbau zweier Gewerbebauten in Nuglar—Lilitt Bollinger Studio und Buchner Bründler Architekten, werk, bauen + wohnen 6 (2019), 55–59 • Friederike Bienstein, Kirschlager, AIT 7–8 (2019), 132–35 • Hubertus Adam, Spaß an der Bricolage: Umbau eines Kirschlagers, Zuschnitt 6 (2019), 10 • Silvia Steidinger, Der Kirschbunker, Umbauen + Renovieren 6 (2019), 26–35 • *Buchner Bründler Architekten, Lilitt Bollinger Studio: Umbau Kirschlager Nuglar 2018*—Photo Essay by Rory Gardiner, Rome 2019

Impetus The village of Nuglar, situated on an elevated plateau on the Table Jura, is distinguished by its development along the main street. An exception to the otherwise predominant saddle-roof buildings of the village core is the flat-roofed commercial building for a local liquor distillery, built in 1968. The building consists of two separate segments: a storage space with a sales shop, and the solid-construction hall for cherry supplies. Together with the adjoining restaurant and the distillery from the 1920s, the purpose-built building forms a coherent overall complex. A decline in cherry processing meant the building long lay vacant, enabling a repurposing of the flat-roof volume for mixed living, working, and commercial occupancies.

Concept Separated by a concrete wall, the building segments are uniformly 3.80 m high, whereby the ceilings are constructed differently. The storage part is spanned by a slender wooden ceiling, its bays resting on two steel girders and one single column. The space is stepped along the contour of the adjoining buildings. The full-length steel girders mean that the delivery hall, executed with a solid concrete ceiling, is free-span. Load reserves allow a partial vertical extension. The concept is based on a harmonious dialogue between the various segments, orchestrated by the addition or subtraction of elements. Facing the valley, a continuous space spans the separation, dovetails the two sides, and forms an enclosed spatial pocket. The existing raised windows, sequenced in a band, are opened and joined to form a combined open element by means of an unbroken bench. The wall is slice open with a window box set on it to additionally layer the room toward the outside view. On the opposite side, facing the street, is a counterpart in the form of a furniture-like contained window. The spatial infilling effect enhances the flat hierarchy of walls, doors, and vehicle entrances. The plain sheer size of the production hall and its raw materiality contrast with the finely composed materials in the living and working segment, generating a playful physicality.

Implementation By removing obscuring elements and cutting open the walls, the existing wood, concrete, and steel come to light, revealing their ambient impact. These materials are largely left intact, creating a basic atmospheric feeling, and in turn supplemented by assembled parts in maritime pine, fir, and oak, free forms in poured concrete, and precise steel elements. The new formats relate to the size and proportions of the space. Individual spatial chambers create private areas.

The outer appearance is marked by the panorama window and the box-like vertical studio annex, whereby a frontal spiral staircase overlies the primary horizontal hierarchy.

Bifangstrasse no. 5, Nuglar. In terms of landscape, Nuglar and St. Pantaleon belong to the self-contained Ergolz area, but nonetheless are situated in the Canton of Solothurn. First mention in 1147 as "Nugeloro", "Nussbäumchen", or "Nussbaumwäldchen." Possible Celtic and Roman settlement, with only a few burial finds but a hoard of coins from the Roman era in Allmenhölzli. After the 6th CENTURY, gradual land seizures by the Alemanni and a comingling with the local Roman population. ▶ In possession of the Beinwil Cloister since the turn of the 11th to 12th CENTURIES. ▶ In the 15th and 16th CENTURIES, during the dissolution of the House of Homberg and the crumbling of the episcopal dominions, the region is torn into two parts. The arbitrary boundary is drawn minus any breaks in landscape features: Bretzwil, Nuglar, and St. Pantaleon fall to Solothurn.

▶ From the MIDDLE AGES to the beginning of the 19th CENTURY, Nuglar remains a farming village with fruit growing—mainly cherry and vine cultivation. The inhabitants are land-owning farmers, tenants, and day laborers. The village is characterized by large social disparities between the partially completely impoverished day laborers and a handful of very rich land-owning farmers. In 1680 Nuglar has 38 houses with 218 inhabitants; by 1739 there are 45 houses and 378 inhabitants. Around 1750 more craftsmen settle: coopers, masons, nailers, shoemakers, carpenters, and a blacksmith, with the occasional weaver, knitter, or passementerie maker. ▶ In 1842 Nuglar had to erect its first school, whereas previously children had been taught in private homes. ▶ After 1860 numerous inhabitants work in neighboring Liestal in the industrial firms; the largest employer is the schappe silk spinning works Ringwald & Bölger in the Niederschönthal. In 1871, 67 people from Nuglar and St. Pantaleon worked there, including nine girls (aged 10, 12, or 13 years old). Each day they march 1½ hours to Schönthal, work 10 to 12 hours, and then march back again in the evening.

In the early 20th CENTURY, slow emergence of infrastructure in the village: 1893, the first house is attached to the water mains; 1902, the first two telephones are installed, for which two operators had to be reachable daily between 14:00 and 18:00. 1909, street lighting is installed, as of 1910 the houses were electrified. In 1913 people in Nuglar can tune into the radio for the first time, and in 1927 the first tractor makes its appearance. ▶ In the 20th CENTURY Nuglar and St. Pantaleon remain famous for their cherry cultivation. The highest number of cherry trees is in 1971, numbering 10,792. The other major staple is wine-growing: initially only white wine, at the latest from the MID-18TH CENTURY onward red wine too.

The field name "Byfang", a piece of land enclosed by a fence, is first recorded in Nuglar in the 16th CENTURY. In 1917 Urs Saladin and his wife Rosa Saladin-Mangold build a house for their family on Bifangstrasse with a small barn for a number of goats and a cow. ▶ In 1926 they open a Liga store and a small shoe shop in their house, 1929 a wine business, to provide additional income. Saladin is employed as a factory worker in Schönthal until 1929, when a motorbike accident forces him to change trades. He sells his livestock and erects a two-story building onto the house with a wine cellar, garage, distillery, workshop, and a storage area. The building is vertically accessed via a goods lift. Saladin himself draws the plans, the work being undertaken by the local unemployed. In the 1930s the settlement pattern begins to first mushroom in the vicinity of Bifangstrasse. 1936, Saladin acquires a retail license for wine and spirits. Between 1937 and 1948 he grows wine himself and presses it. In 1937 he begins producing cherry, plumb, and damson schnapps. 1947, he modernizes the cellar with six tanks and a new still, and in 1956 a new storage hall for the bottled wines and spirits is built, along with offices under the existing building. In 1968, the erection of a larger warehouse: one half serves as a garage and a collection point for the village cherry harvest, the other is a large self-service store, the Schwarzbuebemärt. 1988 Saladin's children sell the company to Paul Schwob AG from Liestal, after which the building stands empty until 2004 when the residential part was sold and a beer brewery and a restaurant are opened up.

Situated on the eastern side of the Gempentafel, the two Schwarzbuben villages of Nuglar and St. Pantaleon have retained the appearance of an old cultural landscape with meadow orchards and thousands of standard fruit trees. The cherry storehouse was built as a utility structure to process the cherry harvest. All of the cherries gathered in the village were delivered to the garage, while the adjoining hall space served as self-service shop. The shop part is spanned by a slender wooden roof, the bay resting on two steel beams and a single support. The basic space acquired after stripping back the layers was expanded using bonded parts made of sea pine, fir, and oak; cast-concrete free-forms; and steel elements.

The cutout opening to the workshop can be closed with a large wooden door with a round compression seal. The bathroom is split up into individual functional units with prominent spatial elements. Facing the valley, the uninterrupted space spans the division between the two building parts and forms an enclosed spatial pocket.

In the west corner of the garage, between the gate and the old weighing machine, a steel spiral staircase leads to the roof studio, coated in black. From here the view stretches to the southeast to the other side of the Oris valley and the Seltisberg, and beyond that to the distant Belchenmassiv with Lauchweid, Ruchen, and Belchenflue. The turbulent topography around Nuglar was caused by a prehistoric rockslide. The village lies below the Gempenplateau, distinguished by the dominant prominence of the Chanzel.

N° 249

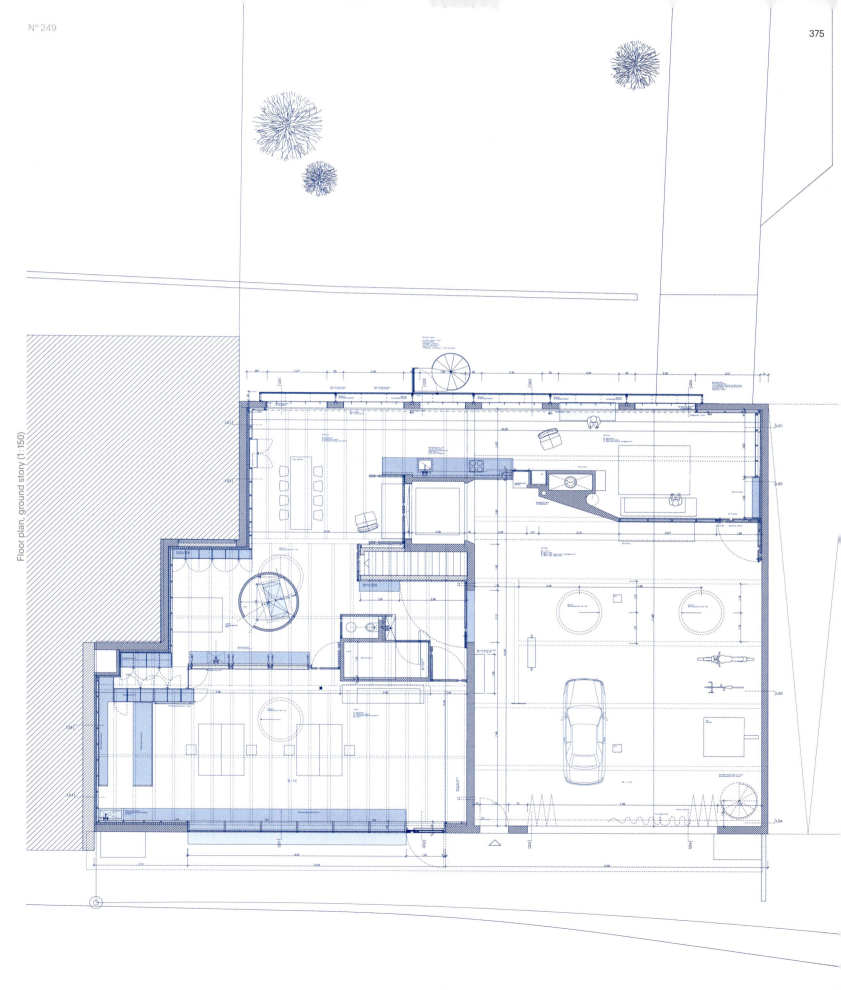

Floor plan, ground story (1:150)

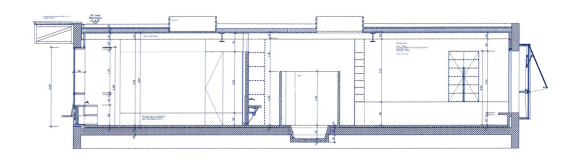

Cross section 1 (1:150)

Cross section 2 (1:150)

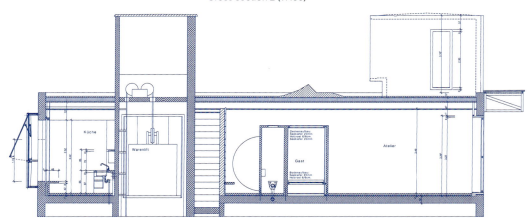

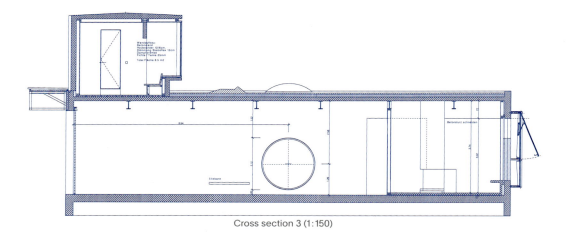

Cross section 3 (1:150)

Cross section 4 (1:150)

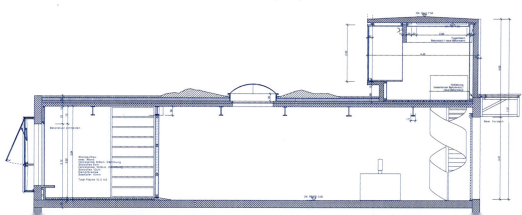

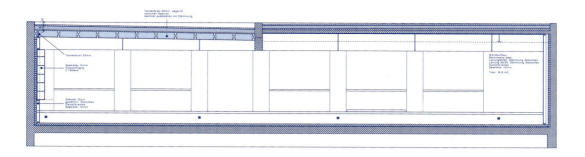

Longitudinal section 1 (1:150)

Longitudinal section 2 (1:150)

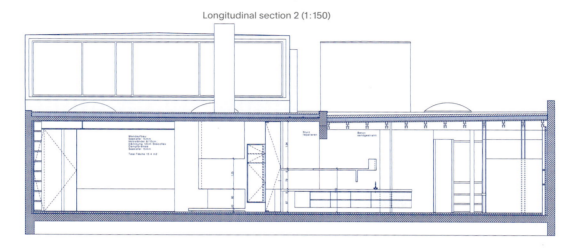

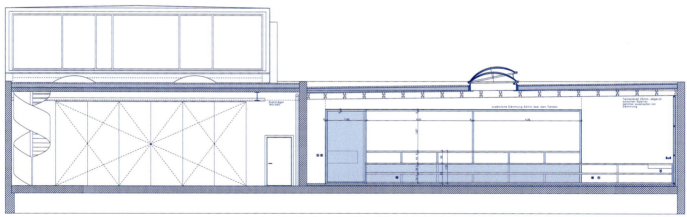

Longitudinal section 3 (1:150)

Longitudinal section 4 (1:150)

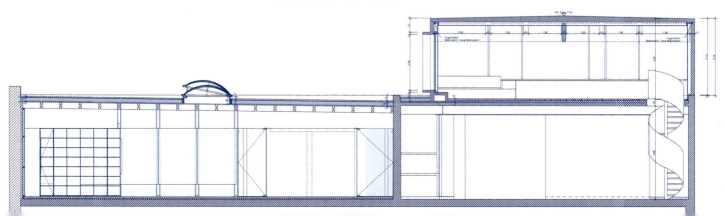

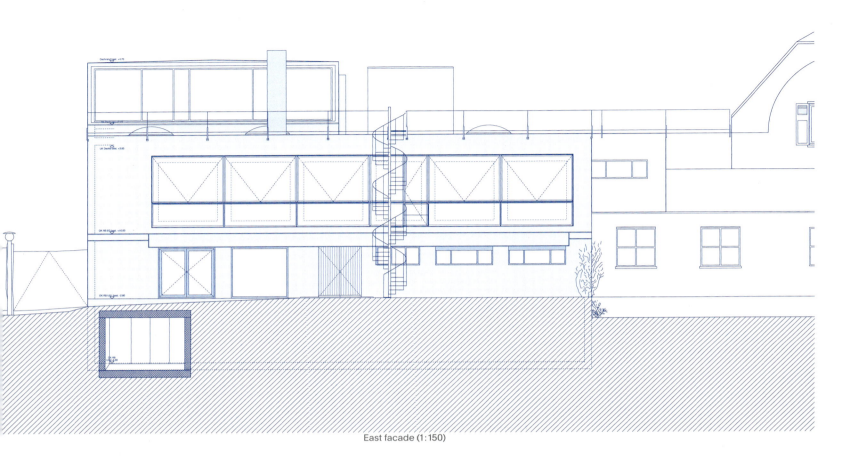

East facade (1:150)

West facade (1:150)

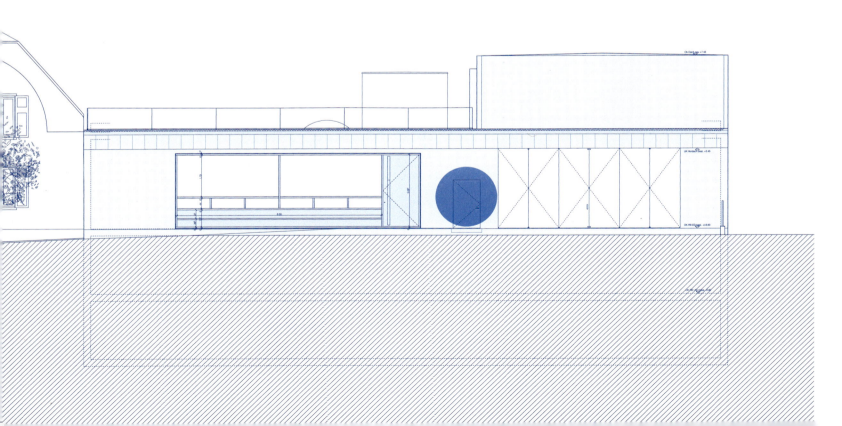

Basel, Switzerland

2018–2020 **Missionsstrasse House**

Conversion

N° 260 Missionsstrasse House

Location Basel, Switzerland **Type** Conversion **Status** Realized **Project phases** *Planning* 2018 *Realization* 2019–2020 **Client** Private **Project data** *Lot size* 446 m² *Built up area* 114 m² *Floor area* 405 m² (according to SIA 416) *Building volume* 1,190 m³ **Planners** *Architecture and site management* Buchner Bründler Architekten, Basel *Building engineering* Schnetzer Puskas Ingenieure AG, Basel **Team Buchner Bründler** *Partners* Daniel Buchner, Andreas Bründler *Project lead* Jon Garbizu Etxaide *Participants* Nina Kleber, Sharif Hasrat

Impetus The carriage house was built in around 1880 in the garden of the villa complex in front of the city walls. The building consisted of a functional section, with stables, a carriage area, and a hayloft, as well as a living area for the staff. A massive dry-stone wall separated the two, with the lodgings entered via a separate side door.

After the replacement of the villa with perimeter block developments in the early 20th century, the carriage house was successively reused. The use of the hayloft as an artist's studio in the 1950s and the subsequent use as an apartment are both documented, whereby the original basic typology remained largely intact, with only small modifications. The project involved rebuilding the carriage house into a private family residence. The garden, which still possesses trees from the Wilhelminian period, forms a rich spatial context and acts as the main determinant in reorganizing the building.

Concept A particular feature is the slightly darkened alignment of the house, caused by the garden sides facing north and the rear sides being built as closed firewalls.

The architectural concept focuses on the issue of the distribution of light and establishing an open-plan spatial composition so as to create a balanced effect. One device is the double-story circular opening cut out of the interior dividing wall, dovetailing the two building parts with each other and generating a spatial openness. The other is the insert on of a table-like skeleton structure in concrete, forming an overlay to the existing load-bearing system and acting as the main reorganizational element. Two concrete slabs diagonally connect the support structure at the garden level next to the rear firewall, allowing prism-shaped atrium spaces to emerge. These in turn open up the garden story vertically, channeling zenithal light into the garden level and the deeper interior rooms. The overlapping of the existing spatial frame with the new structural scheme generates numerous situationally formed rooms, while three large roof windows indicate the new interior hierarchy.

Implementation The external appearance of the building retains it characteristic materialization and facade tectonics, with only the solid-oak windows acting as pointers to the remodeling. The west side is opened by a double sliding door. Two round windows complement the existing vocabulary of the segmental arched windows, acting as a formal reference to the rounded verge rafters in the gable. The new concrete structure is cast in situ. The horizontal elements are prestressed in order to provide the large spans, their configuration adopting that of the existing load-bearing elements. The joisted floor and the single rafter roof remain in use and are borne by the midpoint concrete support.

Missionsstrasse no. 7a, to the west of the center of Basel. Until the beginning of the 19th CENTURY Missionsstrasse is a country road outside the town fortifications. ▣ It actually acts as the town's lifeline, linking Basel with southern Alsace, the Sundgau, Europe's wine- and bread-basket, likewise providing a route to market locations like Lyon and the seat of the Archbishop of Besançon, to which the Diocese of Basel belongs.

The Spalentor at the outer walled ring represents the entrance to the town from southern Alsace. ▣ It is the most ostentatious gateway, finished in 1398—not simply a fortification but a symbol of civic prestige. Likewise the walls: 4 km long, five gates, forty defensive towers. Fortification, entrance, landmark, and visiting card, visible from far off, covered in colorfully glazed tiles since the 15th CENTURY. Gateway and walls demonstrate the town's wealth and mark the prelude to an autonomous territorial political power—civic ambitions. Additionally, the boundary between inside and outside: inside the free craftsmen, outside the bonded serfs. Sometimes there is war; robbers and wolves or other hungry animals creep around the town, the wall offering protection. When night falls, the gate is closed; in exchange for some coins, a small side gate opens. The greater difficulty at night is to leave the town.

The old country road later acquires the name Äussere Spalenvorstadt, later again Burgfelderstrasse. The city grows. 1825, to the right of the gateway and outside the city, the Spalengottesacker is laid out, enlarged in 1845. Stately houses with gardens for rich Basel citizens appear outside the city walls. The closed gate is inconvenient; as of 1856 it stays open at night. 1859, the walls are to be torn down; 1867, the gateway is stripped of its context, standing solitary and remodeled. The Spalentor becomes a monolith. ▣ The railroad comes. The street is no longer a central transport axis; customs clearance and controls at the Spalentor cease.

▣ 1860, new building for the Basler Mission; 1861, the street is renamed Missionsstrasse. Dense development, a popular district for the upper bourgeoisie: double-story private residences with landscaped gardens, including opposite the Spalentor. In the 1850s, building of the first villa on the plot between Missionstrasse and Socinstrasse. 1868, the cemetery closes, the funeral processions to Kannenfeld lead along Missionsstrasse. 1870, Gregor Stächelin-Allgeier settles in Basel, at Missionsstrasse no. 9. ▣ ▣ He advances to become a successful builder, a member of the Cantonal Parliament, the Citizens' Council, right-wing member of the Bürger- und Gewerbepartei. Commissioned by the merchant Eduard Baerwart-Eckenstein, construction of a rear building in the courtyard of Missionsstrasse no. 7 with a stable, a carriage house, and a coachman's lodgings. Between 1885 and 1893 a row of single-family houses is erected along Missionsstrasse nos. 7 to 13: exposed brick facades with spacious front gardens and beautiful landscaped gardens. The villa from 1850 is demolished, while the building in the garden remains. The carriage house in the garden remains and is joined by a timber cottage with garden room and another rear building, which is added on as a stable.

1897, the tramline stretching from Missionsstrasse to Birsfelden is built. The carriage house remains uninhabited, the rear building is used as a shed. ▣ The carriage house then becomes an artist's studio: the sculptor and landscape painter Adolf Glatt makes plaster heads; from the 1970s he shares the studio with the artist and musician Bernhard Batschelet. Glatt dies in 1984; Batschelet remodels it, living and working in the studio. Everything merges: the hayloft becomes a rehearsal room—composing, music, science, art, sculpture, dance, entertainment, carnival, environmentalism, design and beauty combine. In the midst of the roar of the traffic, a wild jungle garden sprouts up around the carriage house.

The carriage house was built in 1879 as a utility building for a freestanding villa. It remained after the demolition of the villa at the turn of the century and was successively converted.

The floating ornamental gable with its wooden round arches prompted the development of various circular motifs. The guide rails incorporated into the projecting lintel on the northwest narrow side allow the windows to be fully opened. The outward swing radius of the gate was adopted as a general principle for all the windows. To this end, the casements are equipped with specially constructed hinges with an axis of rotation set into the jambs. A circular double-story cutout in the fire-division wall connects the previous working area—with the stables, carriage space, and hayloft—to what were the gable-facing living quarters for the servants.

The downstand beams, arranged crosswise, are pre-stressed and follow the load lines of the previously existing beams and load-carrying walls. A 14-cm-thick concrete floor was poured over the existing joist floor and merged with a beam tier and a boarded floor to form a hybrid ceiling construction. In order to compensate for the missing orientation toward the light from the south, a concrete structure was inserted, allowing two triangular atriums to be formed and to illuminate the house with zenithal daylight.

The flexibly usable central room extends up to the ridge of the roof, and by virtue of its grand situation above the garden has echoes of a piano nobile. The size and situation of the central skylight is orientated on the former atelier windows of the artist Adolf Glatt who worked in the house.

At the roof story, materials such as rough-sawn pine boards are applied; the mid-point main bearing axis expresses itself in the form of a suspender beam. The feeding troughs in what was once the stable are repurposed to washbasins.

A redwood, yews, and numerous magnolias bear testimony to the vegetative diversity of the previous villa garden. Through the open termination of the boundary development, the courtyard garden connects with the green area of the university botanical gardens opposite.

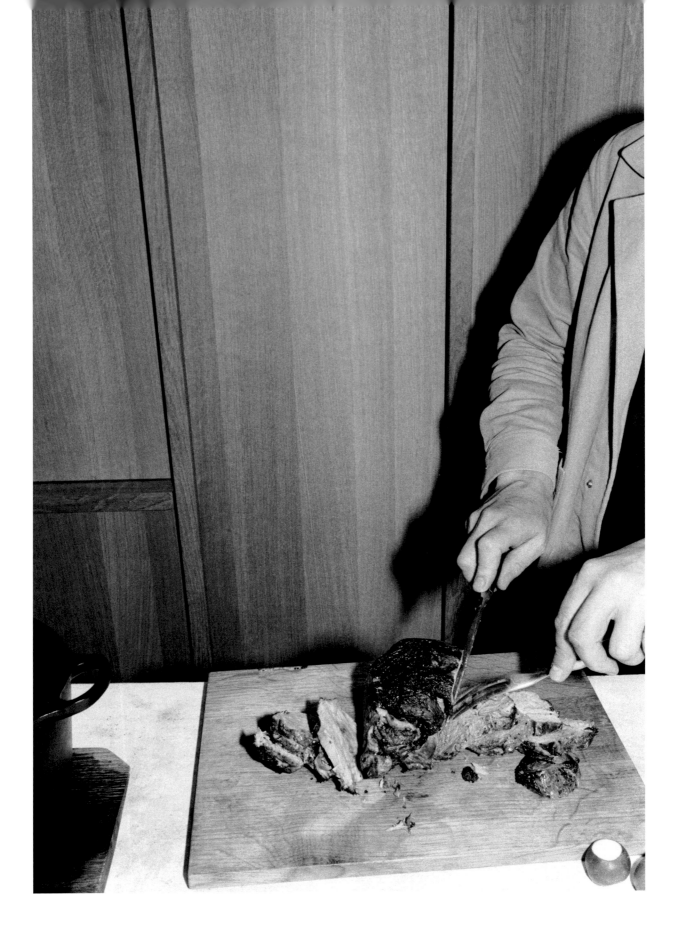

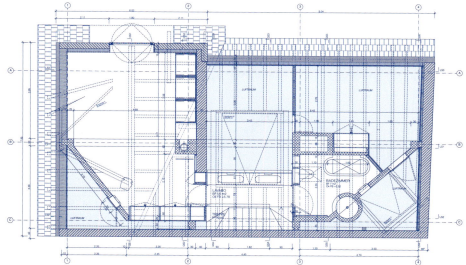

Floor plan, roof story (1:200)

Floor plan, middle story (1:200)

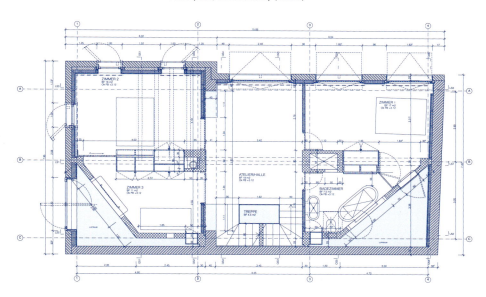

Floor plan, garden level (1:200)

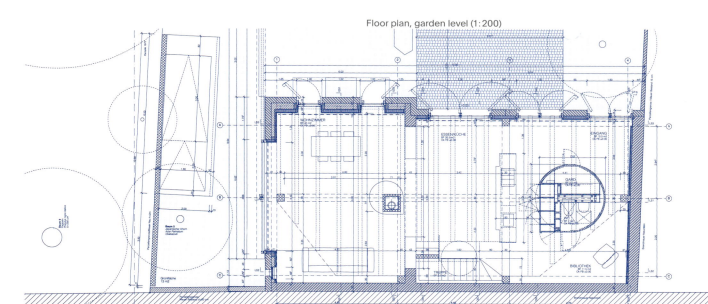

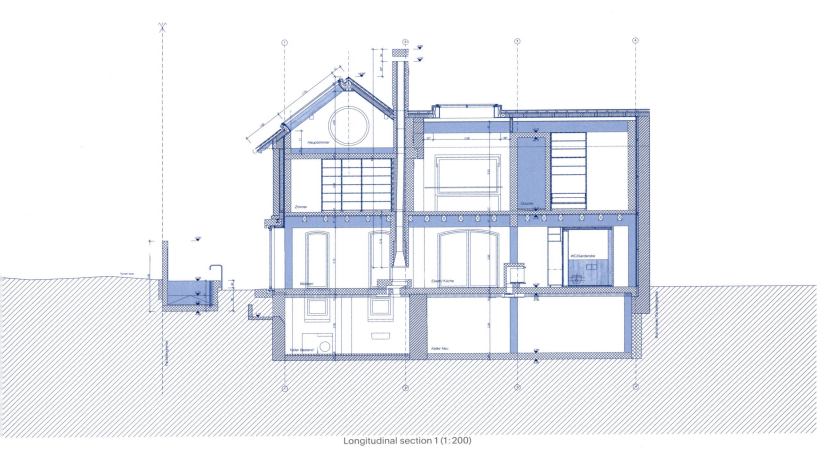

Longitudinal section 1 (1:200)

Cross section 6 (1:200)

Cross section 3 (1:200)

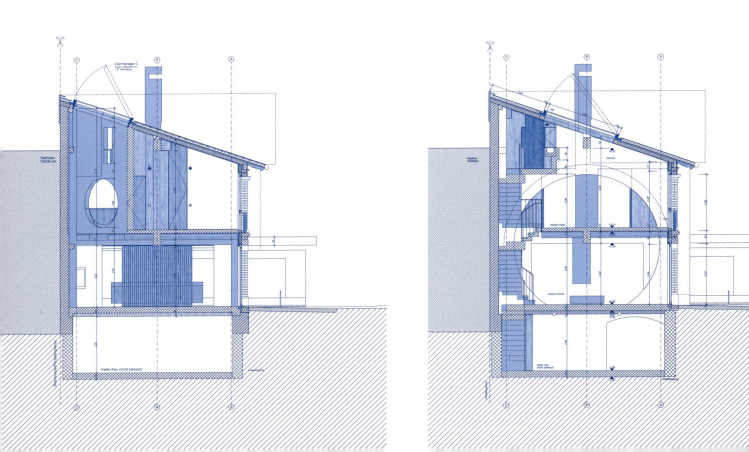

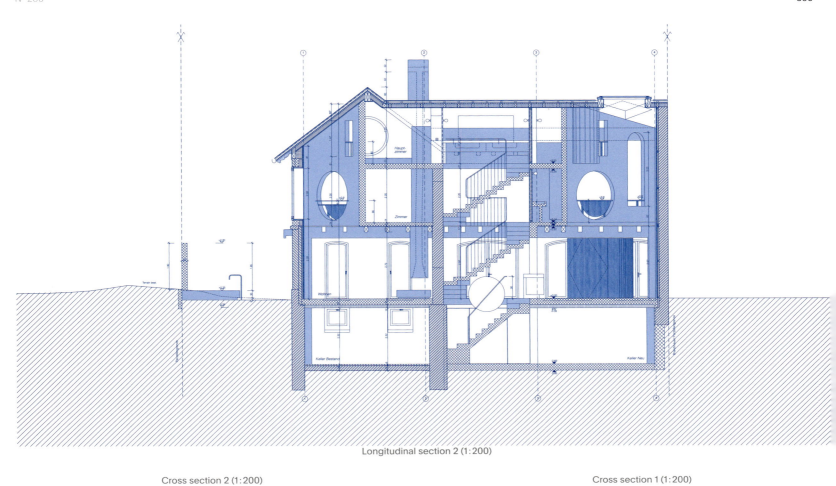

Longitudinal section 2 (1:200)

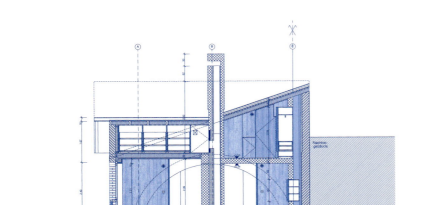

Cross section 2 (1:200)

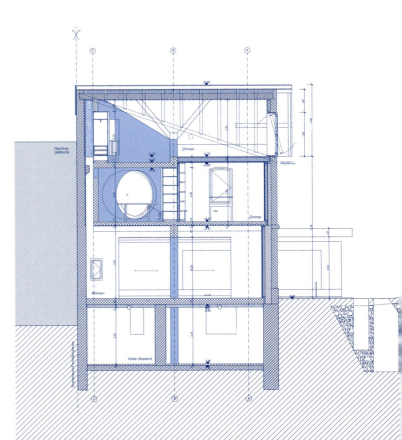

Cross section 1 (1:200)

North facade (1:200)

West facade (1:200)

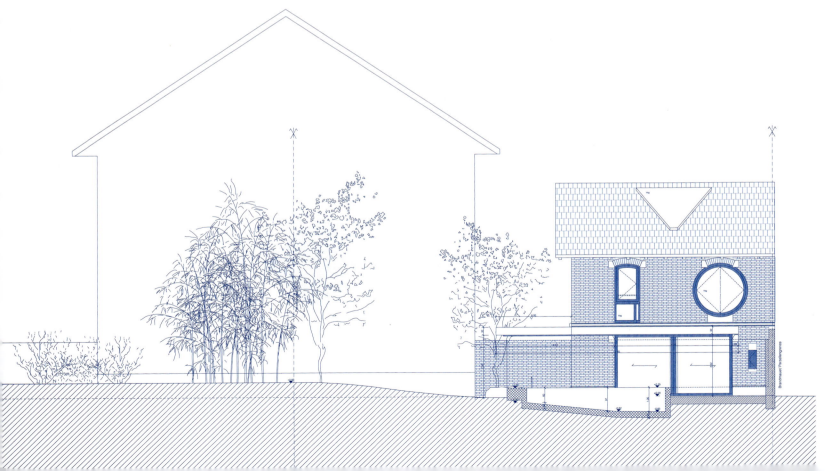

Chronology of Projects

N° 001
Loft House Basel
Basel, Switzerland
1998–2002
New building
Realized

N° 002
Blonay House
Blonay, Switzerland
2000–2002
New building
Realized

N° 003
Gelterkinden Double House
Gelterkinden, Switzerland
1997–1999
Renovation and annex
Realized

N° 004
Dumphaldenweg Houses
Pratteln, Switzerland
2000
New building
Project
In cooperation with Müller Architekten, Basel

N° 005
Oberrohrdorf Community Hall
Oberrohrdorf, Switzerland
1999
New building
Competition

N° 006
Artag Recording Studio
Zurich, Switzerland
1999
Installation
Realized

N° 007
Chrummacherweg House
Gelterkinden, Switzerland
1999–2000
Annex
Realized

N° 008
Residential and Commercial Building Sins
Sins, Switzerland
2007–2009
New building
Realized

N° 009
Häfelfingen House
Häfelfingen, Switzerland
1999–2000
Conversion
Realized

N° 010
Letz Kindergarten
Näfels, Switzerland
1999
New building
Competition

N° 011
Lupsingen House
Lupsingen, Switzerland
1999–2000
Roof extension
Realized

N° 012
Horgen Station Area
Horgen, Switzerland
2000
Town center development
Competition, 2nd prize
In cooperation with Philippe Cabane, Basel

N° 013
Spalentorweg House
Basel, Switzerland
2001
Conversion and annex
Realized

N° 014
Narrenschiff Book Store
Basel, Switzerland
2000
Conversion
Realized

N° 015
Schützenstrasse House
Bottmingen, Switzerland
2000
Conversion
Realized

N° 016
Plus Area Housing Development
Basel, Switzerland
2001
New building
Competition

N° 017
Dornacherstrasse House
Basel, Switzerland
2001
Conversion
Realized

N° 018
Büren House
Büren, Switzerland
2001–2002
New building
Realized

N° 019
Guru Nation Retail Store
Basel, Switzerland
2001–2002
Conversion
Realized

N° 020
Pantaleonstrasse House
Büren, Switzerland
2001–2003
New building
Realized

N° 022
House for Customs Officials Basel
Basel, Switzerland
2002–2003
Conversion
Realized

N° 023
House for Customs Officials Allschwil
Allschwil, Switzerland
2001
Conversion
Realized

N° 024
Restaurant Gundeldingerhof
Basel, Switzerland
2002
Conversion
Realized

N° 025
Offenburgerstrasse Roof Extension
Basel, Switzerland
2002
Conversion
Realized

N° 026
Frenkendorf Double House
Basel, Switzerland
2002–2003
New building
Project

N° 027
Frobenstrasse House
Basel, Switzerland
2003
Conversion and extension
Project

N° 028
Amselstrasse House
Allschwil, Switzerland
2003
Conversion
Realized

N° 029
Residential and Commercial Building Bahnhofstrasse
Sins, Switzerland
2004
Annex
Project

N° 030.1
Hergiswil House
Hergiswil, Switzerland
2003
New building
Competition, 3rd prize

N° 030.2
Glass Tower
Basel, Switzerland
2003
Swiss Federal Art Prize
Competition, 1st prize, (category architecture)

N° 030.3
Gotthelf Schoolhouse Extension
Basel, Switzerland
2003
New building
Competition

N° 030.4
Martin-Luther-Straße Housing Development
Wolfsburg, Germany
2003
New building
Competition
In cooperation with sabarchitekten, Basel

N° 030.5
Prognose Retail Store
Basel, Switzerland
2003
Installations
Realized

N° 030.6
Corporate Design for Small Constructions
Zurich, Switzerland
2004
New building
Competition, 3rd prize
In cooperation with Pedrocchi Meier Architekten, Basel, and Raeto Studer, Basel

N° 030.7
Automuseum Lienhard
Teufen, Switzerland
2004
New building
Competition

N° 030.8
Exhibition *Laisser Faire – Maison Verre*
Hamburg, Deutschland
2004
Exhibition design
Realized

N° 030.9
Landhof Housing Development
Basel, Switzerland
2003
New building
Competition
In cooperation with Daniel Pokora, Basel

N° 031
Merkurstrasse House
Allschwil, Switzerland
2003
Conversion
Realized

N° 032
Gartenstrasse House
Lupsingen, Switzerland
2004–2005
Conversion and extension
Realized

N° 033
UN Headquarters GA-200
New York, USA
2003–2004
Conversion
Realized
In cooperation with :mlzd Architekten, Biel, and Relax (Chiarenza & Hauser & Co.), Zurich

N° 034
Aesch House
Aesch, Switzerland
2003–2004
New building
Realized

N° 035
Grenzacherweg House
Riehen, Switzerland
2003–2004
Conversion
Realized

N° 037
Schlossburg Loft Apartment
Burg im Leimental, Switzerland
2003–2006
Conversion
Realized

N° 038
Seltisberg Community Center
Seltisberg, Switzerland
2003–2009
New building
Competition, 1st prize
Realized
In cooperation with Studer Strasser Architekten, Basel

N° 040
Manager Pavilion Jinhua
Jinhua, China
2004–2007
New building
Realized

N° 041
Bürkliplatz Mooring Platform
Zurich, Switzerland
2004
New building
Competition

N° 042
Klingnaustrasse House
Basel, Switzerland
2004–2007
Conversion
Realized

N° 046
Volta Mitte Development
Basel, Switzerland
2004
New building
Competition, 2nd prize
In cooperation with Ken Komai, Basel

N° 049
Winahouse
Gränichen, Switzerland
2006
New building
Competition, special mention

N° 050
Bachgrabenpark Housing Development
Allschwil, Switzerland
2004
New building
Competition, 1st prize
In cooperation with Raeto Studer, Basel

N° 051
Sevogelstrasse Housing Development
Basel, Switzerland
2005–2007
Conversion
Realized

N° 052
Manor Department Store
Liestal, Switzerland
2005–2013
New building
Competition, 1st prize
Realized

N° 053
Parkhotel Bellevue
Adelboden, Switzerland
2005–2006
Conversion, restaurant, bar, and rooms
Realized

N° 055
Burg House
Burg im Leimental, Switzerland
2005–2007
Conversion
Realized

N° 056
Krummacher House
Brügg, Switzerland
2006
Conversion
Project

N° 058
Latsch House
Latsch, Switzerland
2006–2010
Conversion
Realized

N° 059
Freudenberg Double House
Sins, Switzerland
2006–2011
New building
Realized

N° 060
Volta Zentrum Residential and Commercial Building
Basel, Switzerland
2005–2010
New building
Competition, 1st prize
Realized

N° 062
Raiffeisenbank Muri
Muri, Switzerland
2006
New building
Competition

N° 063
Volta Surrounding Buildings
Basel, Switzerland
2008–2009
New building
Realized

N° 064
Binningen House
Binningen, Switzerland
2006–2009
New building
Realized

N° 065
Burg House
Burg im Leimental, Switzerland
2007
Conversion
Project

N° 066
Synthes Headquarters
Zuchwil, Switzerland
2007
New building
Competition

N° 067
St. Johann Port Conversion
Basel, Switzerland
2007
Landscape development

N° 068
Garden Tower
Wabern bei Berne, Switzerland
2007–2016
New building
Competition, 1st prize
Realized
p. 66, p. 169

N° 069
Parkhotel Bellevue
Adelboden, Switzerland
2008–2009
Conversion and extension, spa area
Realized

N° 070
Freilager Dreispitz
Basel, Switzerland
2007
Site development
Competition

N° 071
Swiss Pavilion Expo 2010 Shanghai
Shanghai, China
2007–2010
New building
Competition, 1st prize
Realized
In cooperation with element, Basel

N° 072
Hollenweg House
Ettingen, Switzerland
2007–2008
Conversion
Realized

N° 074
Parkhotel Bellevue
Adelboden, Switzerland
2007
Conversion, rooms
Realized

N° 076
Aspholz Housing Development
Zurich, Switzerland
2007
New building
Competition, 2nd prize

N° 077
St. Alban Youth Hostel
Basel, Switzerland
2007–2010
Conversion and extension
Competition, 1st prize
Realized

N° 078
Swiss Embassy Moscow
Moscow, Russia
2007
Conversion and extension
Competition, 4th prize

N° 079
Warteck Area Riehenring
Basel, Switzerland
2007
New building
Competition

N° 080
SET&SEKT Fashion Store
Basel, Switzerland
2007
Conversion
Realized

N° 081
Densa Site Housing Development
Basel, Switzerland
2007
New building
Competition
In cooperation with Pedrocchi Meier Architekten, Basel

N° 082
Ettingen House
Ettingen, Switzerland
2007–2009
New building
Realized

N° 084
Hotel Seerose
Meisterschwanden, Switzerland
2007
New building and extension
Competition

N° 085
Berzona House
Berzona, Switzerland
2008–2012
New building
Project

N° 086
Wollerau House
Wollerau, Switzerland
2008
Conversion
Competition

N° 087
Villa Ordos 100
Ordos, China
2008–2009
New building
Project

N° 089
Kunsthaus Zürich
Zurich, Switzerland
2008
New building and extension
Competition
In cooperation with mazzapokora, Zurich and Raphaela Schacher, Basel

N° 090
Peninsula Housing Development
Wädenswil, Switzerland
2008–2014
New building
Competition, 1st prize
Realized
p. 71, p. 185

N° 091
Ballwil Schoolhouse
Ballwil, Switzerland
2008
New building
Competition
In cooperation with Bucher + Partner Architekten AG, Römerswil

N° 092
Hotel Neuhaus
Interlaken, Switzerland
2008
New building
Competition
In cooperation with Pedrocchi Meier Architekten, Basel

N° 093
Hochstrasse Housing Development
Basel, Switzerland
2008
New building
Competition

N° 095
Hotel Leutschenbach Tower
Zurich, Switzerland
2008
New building
Competition

N° 096
Casa d'Estate Linescio
Linescio, Switzerland
2008–2010
Conversion
Realized

N° 097
Bläsiring House
Basel, Switzerland
2009–2012
New building
Realized

N° 098
Carhartt Store Tokyo
Tokyo, Japan
2008–2009
Conversion and installations
Realized

N° 099
St. Alban Rheinweg Houses
Basel, Switzerland
2009
Conversion
Project

N° 102
Bernoulli Walkeweg Development
Basel, Switzerland
2009
New building
Competition, acquired

N° 103
Gstad Urban Development
Münchenstein, Switzerland
2009
Urban planning
Competition, 1st prize
Project phase

N° 105
Wittterswil Technology Center
Wittterswil, Switzerland
2009
New building
Project

N° 106
Opel House
Gelterkinden, Switzerland
2009
New building
Project

N° 107
Carhartt Store Munich
Munich, Germany
2009
Installations
Realized

N° 108
Schaffhauserrheinweg Housing Development
Basel, Switzerland
2009
New building
Competition

N° 109
Kunstmuseum Basel
Basel, Switzerland
2009
New building and extension
Competition

N° 110
Kahlstrasse House
Basel, Switzerland
2009–2013
New building
Realized
p. 405

N° 111
Aarenau Housing Development
Aarau, Switzerland
2009
New building
Competition

N° 112
Basel-Land Cantonal Administration
Liestal, Switzerland
2009
New building
Test planning

N° 113
Hotel Nomad
Basel, Switzerland
2009–2015
Conversion and extension
Realized
p. 74, p. 199

N° 114
Biozentrum Life Sciences Schällemätteli
Basel, Switzerland
2009
New building
Competition
In cooperation with :mlzd Architekten, Biel

N° 115
SBB Pro Volta Urban Development
Basel, Switzerland
2009
Urban development and new building
Competition, recommendation

N° 116
Werderinsel Housing Development
Bremen, Germany
2009–2015
New building
Competition, 1st prize
Realized

N° 117
Carhartt Prototype
Weil am Rhein, Germany
2009
Prototype development
Project

N° 118
Carhartt Store Rome
Rome, Italy
2009
Conversion and installations
Project

N° 121
Bernoulli House
Basel, Switzerland
2010–2011
Conversion
Realized

N° 122
Guisanplatz Administrative Center
Berne, Switzerland
2009
New building
Competition, 3rd prize

N° 123
Tièchestrasse Housing Development
Zurich, Switzerland
2010–2017
New building
Competition, 1st prize
Realized
p. 80, p. 217

N° 124
St. Moritz Sports Center
St. Moritz, Switzerland
2010
New building
Competition, 5th prize

N° 125
Kreuzlingen Alp Houses
Kreuzlingen, Switzerland
2010
New building
Study, 1st prize

N° 126
Vico Morcote House
Vico Morcote, Switzerland
2008
New building
Study

N° 127
Spalenberg Retail Store
Basel, Switzerland
2010
Conversion
Realized

N° 128
Sports Hall Liestal
Liestal, Switzerland
2010
New building
Competition

N° 129
Mattini Youth Center
Brigg, Switzerland
2010
New building and conversion
Competition

N° 131
Hubackerweg House
Reinach, Switzerland
2010–2012
New building
Realized
p. 408

N° 133
Kirchgasse House
Riehen, Switzerland
2010–2013
New building
Planning

N° 135
Visitors' Center Swiss Ornithological Institute
Sempach, Switzerland
2010
New building
Competition

N° 138
Le Hôtel Marktgasse
Zurich, Switzerland
2010
New building and conversion
Competition

N° 139
Am Strandweg House
Berne, Switzerland
2010
Conversion
Project

N° 140
Güterschuppen SBB Pro Volta
Basel, Switzerland
2011–2015
New building and conversion
Study commission

N° 141
Kreuzlingen House
Kreuzlingen, Switzerland
2010–2016
New building
Realized
p. 410

N° 142
Toblerstrasse Housing Development
Zurich, Switzerland
2009
New building
Competition

N° 143
Birsigstrasse House
Basel, Switzerland
2010–2011
Conversion
Realized

N° 144
Nachwuchs-Campus Basel
Basel, Switzerland
2010
New building
Competition

N° 145
Chienbergreben House
Gelterkinden, Switzerland
2010–2012
New building
Realized
p. 413

N° 146
Gstad Münchenstein
Münchenstein, Switzerland
2010
Urban development
Study

N° 147
Hertenstein House
Hertenstein-Weggis, Switzerland
2010–2012
New building
Realized
p. 86, p. 235

Chronology of Projects

N° 148
Exhibition Swiss Pavilion Expo 2010 Shanghai
ETH Zurich, Switzerland
2010
Installations and exhibition design
Realized
In cooperation with gta Institute, ETH Zurich

N° 149
Credit Suisse Place Bel-Air Headquarters
Geneva, Switzerland
2011–2014
Conversion
Competition, 1st prize
Realized
p. 93, p. 249

N° 150
Swatch AG Company Headquarters
Biel, Switzerland
2011
New building
Competition

N° 151
Bruderholzrain House
Basel, Switzerland
2011
New building
Project

N° 152
Maiengasse House
Basel, Switzerland
2011
New building
Competition

N° 153
Allschwiler Weiher Development
Allschwil, Switzerland
2011
New building
Test planning

N° 156
Conversion Transitlager Münchenstein
Münchenstein, Switzerland
2011
Conversion
Competition

N° 158
Innere Margarethenstrasse House
Basel, Switzerland
2011–2014
New building
Planning

N° 159
Kunstmuseum St. Gallen
St. Gallen, Switzerland
2011
Conversion
Competition, 2nd prize

N° 160
Green City Housing Development
Zurich, Switzerland
2011
New building (building lots A, B3 south and B4 south)
Competition, 2nd prize (building lot B4 south)

N° 161
Gartenstadt Münchenstein Development
Münchenstein, Switzerland
2011
Urban development
Test planning

N° 164
Swiss Chancery Nairobi
Nairobi, Kenya
2011
New building
Competition

N° 165
Reception Building Syngenta
Basel, Switzerland
2011–2014
New building
Competition, 1st prize
Not realized
p. 415

N° 167
Bündner Kunstmuseum
Chur, Switzerland
2012
Extension
Competition, 4th prize

N° 168
North Salem House
New York, USA
2011
New building
Project

N° 169
Parkhotel Bellevue
Adelboden, Switzerland
2012–2014
Conversion, entrance area and hall
Realized
p. 418

N° 170
Rhytech Area
Neuhausen, Switzerland
2011
Urban development
Competition

N° 171
Heuried Sports Center
Zurich, Switzerland
2012
New building
Competition

N° 172
Urban-Planning Study Gleisfeld Süd, Bahnhof SBB
Basel, Switzerland
2011–2012
Urban development
Test planning

N° 173
Maiengasse Site Development
Basel, Switzerland
2012
Urban development
Test planning

N° 174
Amthausquai Residential and Commercial Building
Olten, Switzerland
2012–2017
New building
Competition, 1st prize
Realized
p. 98, p. 265

N° 175
Meilen House
Meilen, Switzerland
2012–2014
Conversion and extension
Realized
p. 420

N° 176
Hotel Kurpark Engelberg
Engelberg, Switzerland
2012
New building
Competition, 3rd prize

N° 177
Bühlstrasse House
Uitikon, Switzerland
2012
New building
Study

N° 179
Lörrach House
Lörrach, Deutschland
2012–2014
New building
Realized
p. 103, p. 281

N° 180
Schoolhouse Engelberg
Engelberg, Switzerland
2012
New building
Competition, 4th prize

N° 181
Wiesental Site Development
St. Gallen, Switzerland
2012
New building
Competition

N° 182
Bürgli Area
Zurich, Switzerland
2012
New building
Competition

N° 183
Laubengarten Housing Development
Oberlunkhofen, Switzerland
2012–2017
New building
Planning

N° 185
Eisenbahnweg Housing Development
Basel, Switzerland
2012–2023
New building
Competition, 1st prize
Realization
p. 423

N° 186
Passarelle Renens
Chavannes-Près-Renens, Switzerland
2012
New building
Competition, 2nd prize

N° 187
AUE Basel
Basel, Switzerland
2013
New building
Competition, 3rd prize
p. 426

N° 188
Zahnradfabrik Rheinfelden Development
Rheinfelden, Switzerland
2013
New building
Competition, 4th prize
p. 428

N° 189
Rosentalturm Messe Basel
Basel, Switzerland
2013
New building
Test planning
p. 430

N° 190
Sekundarstufenzentrum Burghalde Baden
Baden, Switzerland
2013
New building and conversion
Competition, 3rd prize
p. 431

N° 191
Muttenz House
Muttenz, Switzerland
2013–2015
New building
Realized

N° 192
Sagi Merenschwand
Merenschwand, Switzerland
2013
New building
Study

N° 193
Migros Breitenrain
Berne, Switzerland
2013
New building
Competition

N° 194
Campus Rosental
Basel, Switzerland
2013
New building
Competition

N° 196
Maiengasse Housing Development
Basel, Switzerland
2013
New building
Competition, 4th prize

N° 197
Dufourstrasse
Basel, Switzerland
2013
Conversion
Study/potential analysis

N° 198
Lindt Chocolate Center Kilchberg
Kilchberg, Switzerland
2013–2015
New building
Competition, 2nd place
p. 432

N° 200
Kaserne Basel Main Building
Basel, Switzerland
2013
Conversion
Competition

N° 201
Das Trösch Encounter Center
Kreuzlingen, Switzerland
2013–2014
New building
Competition

N° 202
Conversion St. Alban Rheinweg
Basel, Switzerland
2014–2015
Conversion
Realized
p. 435

N° 203
Music and Vocational Training College
Lahr, Germany
2014
Conversion
Study

N° 204
Strandkai Hafencity
Hamburg, Germany
2014
New building
Competition

N° 205
Cooperative Building Stadterle
Basel, Switzerland
2014–2017
New building
Competition, 1st prize
Realized
p. 107, p. 297

N° 206
Tulière Football Stadium Lausanne
Lausanne, Switzerland
2014
New building
Competition
p. 436

N° 207
Casa Mosogno
Mosogno Sotto, Switzerland
2014–2018
Conversion
Realized
p. 120, 313

N° 208
Stapferhaus Lenzburg
Lenzburg, Switzerland
2014
New building
Competition, 4th prize
p. 438

N° 209
Natural History Museum and State Archives Basel
Basel, Switzerland
2014
New building
Competition
p. 440

N° 210
Kunsthaus Baselland
Dreispitz Münchenstein, Switzerland
2014–2022
Conversion
Competition, 1st prize
Realization
p. 442

N° 212
Münchenstein House
Münchenstein, Switzerland
2014–2016
New building
Realized
p. 132, p. 329

N° 213
WDR-Filmhaus
Cologne, Germany
2015–2024
Conversion and expansion
Competition, 1st prize
Realization
p. 445

N° 214
Bahnhofsplatz Brig
Brig, Switzerland
2015
New building
Competition

N° 215
Stedtli Site Development
Unterseen, Switzerland
2015
New building
Competition, 2nd prize
p. 448

N° 216
Campus Biel
Biel, Switzerland
2015
New building
Competition
p. 449

N° 217
Greifensee House
Greifensee, Switzerland
2015–2016
Conversion
Realized
p. 451

N° 219
Accademia di architettura
Mendrisio, Switzerland
2015–2017
New building
Competition, 1st prize
Planning
p. 453

Chronology of Projects

N° 220
Guesthouse Universität Hamburg
Hamburg, Deutschland
2016–2024
New building
Competition, 1st prize
Realization
p. 456

N° 221
Volta Ost District Enlargement
Basel, Switzerland
2016
New building
Competition

N° 222
Post Office Area Liestal
Liestal, Switzerland
2016
New building
Competition

N° 223
General Renovation Taubenhalde
Berne, Switzerland
2016
Conversion and renovation

N° 224
Kirschgarten House
Binningen, Switzerland
2015–2018
New building
Realized
p. 138, p. 343

N° 225
Pilgerstrasse House
Basel, Switzerland
2015
Conversion
Study

N° 228
Walka School Complex
Zermatt, Switzerland
2016
New building
Competition

N° 229
University Location Canton Basel-Landschaft
Allschwil; Liestal; Münchenstein; Muttenz, Switzerland
2016
Potential assessment

N° 231
SBB Pro Volta C1
Basel, Switzerland
2015–2017
New building
Study

N° 232
Wendelmatte Greppen
Greppen, Switzerland
2016
New building
Competition
p. 459

N° 233
Linde Development
Kreuzlingen, Switzerland
2016
New building
Competition

N° 234
Swiss Tropical and Public Health Institute
Allschwil, Switzerland
2016
New building
Competition
p. 460

N° 235
Life Sciences UNIL
Lausanne, Switzerland
2016
New building
Competition

N° 236
Studio Basel Bruderholz
Basel, Switzerland
2016
New building
Competition
p. 462

N° 237
Thalwil I & II Housing Development
Thalwil, Switzerland
2016–2017
New building
Competition

N° 238
Gestadeck Elementary School
Liestal, Switzerland
2016–2017
New building
Competition

N° 239
Railroad Station Building Altdorf
Altdorf, Switzerland
2016–2022
New building
Competition, 1st prize
Realization
p. 464

N° 240
Urban Development Horburg
Basel, Switzerland
2016–2024
New building
Competition, 1st prize
Planning
p. 467

N° 241
High-rise Heuwaage
Basel, Switzerland
2017
New building
Competition
p. 470

N° 242
Felix-Platter Area
Basel, Switzerland
2017
New building
Competition

N° 243
Bahnhof Nord Kloten
Kloten, Switzerland
2017
Urban development
Competition, 1st prize
p. 472

N° 244
Town Hall and Archaeology Museum Pully
Pully, Switzerland
2017
New building
Competition
p. 473

N° 245
Bubenberg Center
Berne, Switzerland
2017
New building
Competition

N° 246
Fürigen Area
Fürigen, Switzerland
2018
New building
Competition, 1st prize
p. 475

N° 247
Housing Development Rötiboden
Wädenswil, Switzerland
2016–2023
New building
Realization
p. 478

N° 248
Swiss Ambassador's Residence Algiers
Algiers, Algeria
2017
New building
Competition, 4th place, 3rd prize
p. 481

N° 249
Cherry Storehouse Nuglar
Nuglar, Switzerland
2016–2018
Conversion
Realized
Joint partnership with lilitt bollinger studio, Nuglar
p. 143, 359

N° 250
Allschwil House
Allschwil, Switzerland
2017–2019
Conversion and extension
Realized
p. 483

N° 251
Guggach III Area
Zurich, Switzerland
2017–2018
New building
Competition
In cooperation with Bache and Wagner Architekten, Basel

N° 252
Clinic Arlesheim Campus
Arlesheim, Switzerland
2018
New building
Competition
p. 486

N° 253
Papieri Area
Cham, Switzerland
2018
New building and conversion
Competition, 1st prize
(Boiler House)
p. 487

N° 254
Gruner + Jahr Development
Hamburg, Germany
2018
New building
Competition
p. 489

N° 255
Forum UZH
Zurich, Switzerland
2018
New building
Competition, 2nd prize
p. 491

N° 256
Parkweg – Gartenstrasse
Basel, Switzerland
2018
Potential assessment

N° 257
AUE Hochbergstrasse
Basel, Switzerland
2018
New building and conversion
Test planning

N° 258
Studio Rodersdorf
Rodersdorf, Switzerland
2018
New building
Study

N° 260
Missionsstrasse House
Basel, Switzerland
2018–2020
Conversion
Realized
p. 155, p. 379

N° 261
Bruderholzallee
Basel, Switzerland
2018
New building
Competition

N° 262
Pratteln Municipal Center
Pratteln, Switzerland
2018
New building
Competition
p. 494

N° 263
Heinrich Area
Zurich, Switzerland
2018
New building
Competition

N° 264
Swiss Embassy Addis Ababa
Addis Ababa, Ethiopia
2018
New building
Competition, 5th prize
p. 495

N° 265
Dielsdorf Church
Dielsdorf, Switzerland
2018
Renovation
Study

N° 266
House for Musicians
Basel, Switzerland
2018–2019
New building
Competition

N° 267
Culture Center Alpenstrasse Interlaken
Interlaken, Switzerland
2019
New building
Competition, 1st prize
p. 496

N° 268
Laurenz-Carré Cologne
Cologne, Germany
2019
New building
Competition
p. 498

N° 269
Extension Tribunal Lausanne
Lausanne, Switzerland
2019
Conversion and new building
Competition, 4th place, 3rd prize

N° 270
Banque Pictet
Geneva, Switzerland
2019
New building
Competition
p. 501

N° 271
Stiftung Blindenheim
Basel, Switzerland
2019
New building
Competition
p. 504

N° 274
National Concert Hall
Vilnius, Lithuania
2019
New building
Competition

N° 275
Reservoirstrasse Housing Development
Basel, Switzerland
2019
New building
Competition

N° 276
Grossalbis Housing Development
Zurich, Switzerland
2019
New building
Competition
p. 507

N° 277
Volta Nord
Basel, Switzerland
2019
Urban development
Study

N° 278
Webergut Zollikofen
Zollikofen, Switzerland
2019
Conversion
Competition, shortlisted
p. 508

N° 279
Spiesshöfli Site Development
Binningen, Switzerland
2019
Urban development
Test planning

N° 280
Tower at Jannowitz Bridge Berlin
Berlin, Germany
2019
New building
Competition, shortlisted
p. 510

N° 281
Streitgasse Office Building
Basel, Switzerland
2019–2020
Conversion
Study

N° 282
Baselink Office Building
Allschwil, Switzerland
2019
New building (building lot A4)
Competition

N° 283
Aurorastrasse House
Zurich, Switzerland
2019–2022
Conversion
Realization

N° 284
Maaglive Zurich
Zurich, Switzerland
2019–2020
New building
Competition

N° 285
Riqualifica dell'area ex-Macello
Lugano, Switzerland
2019–2020
New building and conversion
Competition

N° 286
Heuelstrasse House
Thalwil, Switzerland
2019
Conversion
Study

N° 287
Archäologische Bodenforschung Rittergasse
Basel, Switzerland
2020
New building
Competition

N° 288
Rütene Site
Windisch, Switzerland
2020
New building
Competition

404

N° 110 Kahlstrasse House

Location Basel, Switzerland **Type** New building **Status** Realized **Project phases** *Planning* 2009–2011 *Realization* 2011–2013 **Client** Private **Project data** *Lot size* 808 m² *Built-up area* 227 m² *Floor area* 675 m³ (according to SIA 416) *Building volume* 2,529 m³ **Planners** *Architecture* Buchner Bründler Architekten, Basel *Site management* Dominik Lingg AG, Basel *Building engineering* Schnetzer Puskas Ingenieure AG, Basel *Landscape architecture* Enea GmbH, Rapperswil-Jona **Team Buchner Bründler** *Partners* Daniel Buchner, Andreas Bründler *Project lead* Kim Sneyders *Participants* Nino Soppelsa, Lisa Schiecke **Publications** Marisol Vidal, Concrete Turned into Atmosphere, En Blanco 16 (2014), 58–63 • José Manuel Pedreirinho, Accuracy, Quality, Functional Clarity and a Strong Formal Identity, a.mag 7 (2015), 66–74

Impetus The Paulus district is characterized by grand houses built in a Historicism style or Jugendstil. Its periphery is marked by Kahlstrasse, with ribbons of more plainly expressed rowed houses set in a repetitive pattern.

A villa, connecting with the adjoining ribbon on one side, occupies the site, although its simple volume means that it hardly impacts the area. The client's wish was to establish a home to which she could retire. Studies demonstrated that the existing substance could not be adapted to accommodate the needs of the residents, resulting in the decision to replace the villa.

Concept The main design criterion is the desire to achieve a certain ostentation and privacy. The connection to the street is kept to a minimum. The volumes are detached from the existing ribbon and developed as a stand-alone structure. Through the layering of plateaus to create a sculptural form, a vertical dramaturgy emerges, giving the house an autonomy and individuality.

The abstract effect is punctuated by only a few openings. Horizontal shifts in levels allow the creation of all-round terraces that mediate between the street and the garden. The new building stops deep within the site, meaning that the many-faceted garden layout that surrounds it completes the idea of open living immersed in green. The heightened entrance hall serves as a central reference space, connecting the various levels. Via the open staircase, directly attached to the hall, the whole height of the building becomes physically tangible. Inside viewing windows generate an interior facade.

Implementation The architectural volume is formed monolithically using poured concrete. The facade layering is tectonically differentiated by varying shuttering structures. The floor slabs appear as smooth strips, the wall elements are structured by the vertical slatted shuttering. Natural-wood windows contrast finely to the concrete and act like playful infill panels. The opening sashes are executed as closed surfaces; the vertical lathing creates an affinity to the ceiling structure. The color and material palette is repeated in the interior rooms. Large wooden inlays break up the bright wall surfaces; natural-stone surfaces complement the choice of materials.

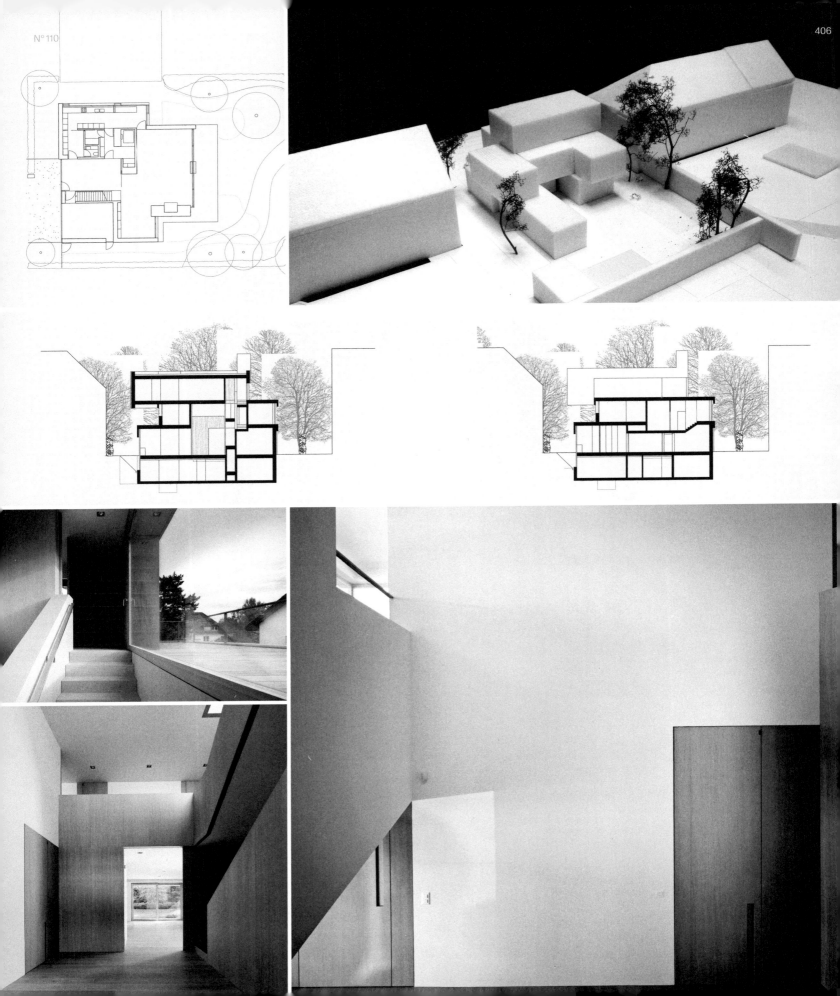

N° 131 Hubackerweg House

Location Reinach, Switzerland **Type** New building **Status** Realized **Project phases** *Planning* 2010–2011 *Realization* 2011–2012 **Client** Private **Project data** *Lot size* 1,995 m² *Built-up area* 205 m² *Floor area* 295 m² (according to SIA 416) *Building volume* 950 m³ **Planners** *Architecture and site management* Buchner Bründler Architekten, Basel **Building engineering** Studer Bauengineering GmbH, Himmelried **Timber construction planning** Hürzeler Holzbau AG, Magden **Building technology** Walter Weber AG, Gelterkinden **Electrical planning** Bracher & Schaub AG, Ormalingen **Team Buchner Bründler** *Partners* Daniel Buchner, Andreas Bründler *Project lead* Rino Buess *Participants* Stefan Mangold, Fabian Meury **Publications** Hubertus Adam and Wolfgang Bachmann, Haus in Reinach, Buchner Bründler Architekten, Anerkennung, in *Häuser des Jahres: Die 50 besten Einfamilienhäuser 2013*, Munich 2013, 54–59 • José Manuel Pedreirinho, Accuracy, Quality, Functional Clarity and a Strong Formal Identity, a.mag 7 (2015), 78–89

Impetus Situated at a slightly raised position on the edge of the building zone, the site's even slopes provide an open view over the Birstal and to the Jura foothills. At the back of the plot is an adjacent wood; the northeastern half of the site is designated a wooded area and cannot be developed. Any residential buildings erected directly on the property line would obstruct the views.

Concept The concept is determined by the situation at the edge of the hillside development and the natural area to the rear. Underneath is a minimal base, containing an entrance hall and a guest area, and on top of it a meandering, multi-sided projecting main volume, resting flush with the forest floor on the uphill side and projecting out above the neighboring roofs on the downhill side. At the outer end, facing the woods, the volume narrows in a continuous series of chamber-like rooms along the sloping terrain before ending in an open large space with multiple-sided panoramas. The sequence is interrupted by a single large incision, framing an intimate, spatially compact courtyard providing direct access from the building core to the garden. The courtyard is spanned and enclosed by a slenderly detailed wooden pergola. As a funnel-shaped incision, the loggia accentuates the viewing side while also acting as a separation space to the neighboring building. Whereas the private rooms face toward the woods, the valley-facing living areas offer spectacular views. A cantilevered terrace platform connects the bedrooms directly to the level of the forest. The platform bends slightly, allowing it to rest directly on the vegetated topography. Beneath the cantilevered building segment, a spatial zone is created, encompassed by a natural plot of terrain.

Implementation A construction of prefabricated timber elements is mounted on the solid base of poured-in-situ concrete. The cladding of the building with heavy, dark brown pinewood boards echoes the color and tactility of the forest feeling. The interior rooms are clad with white-varnished plywood panels, creating an intensive contrast to the raw outer envelope. Kitchens and fireplaces in-situ concrete emphasize the softness of the living area in wood.

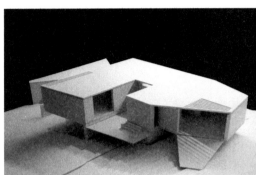

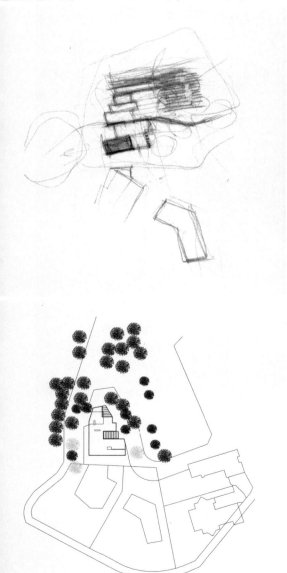

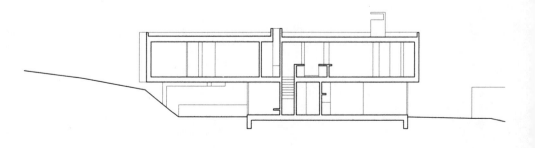

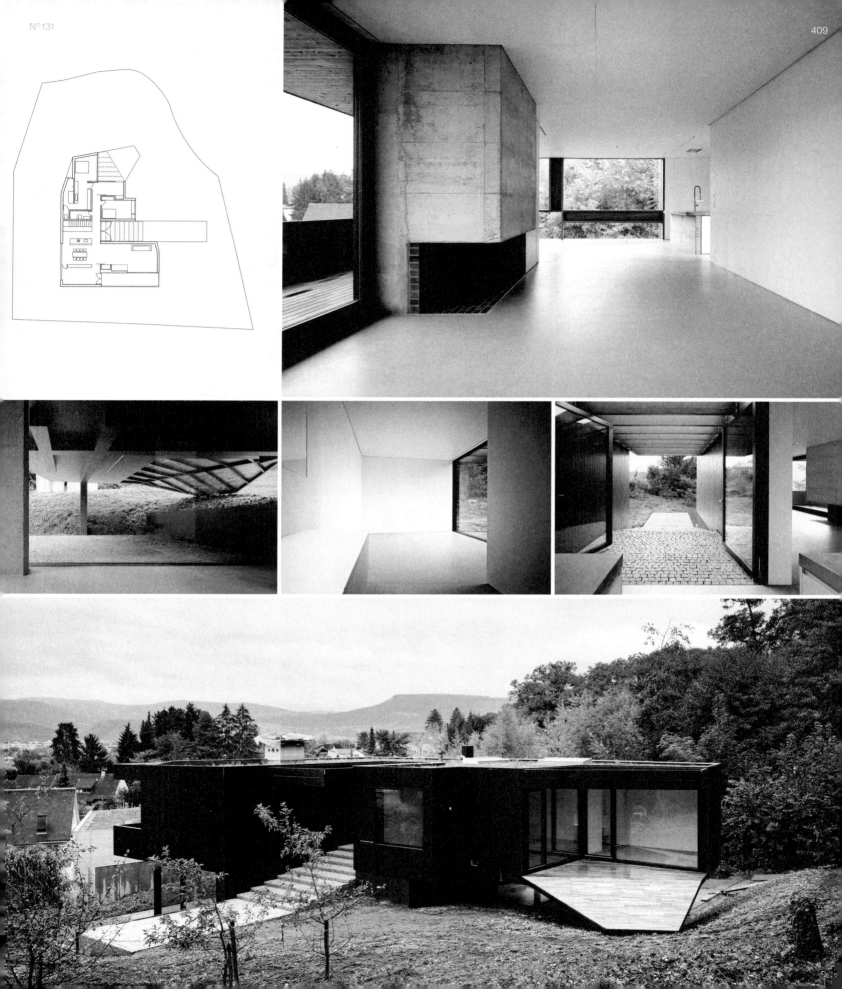

N° 141 Kreuzlingen House

New building — Further Buildings and Projects

Location Kreuzlingen, Switzerland **Type** New building **Status** Realized **Project phases** *Competition* 2010, 1st prize *Planning* 2010–2013 *Realization* 2013–2016 **Client** Private **Project data** *Lot size* 4,618 m² *Built-up area* 865 m² *Floor area* 1,200 m² (according to SIA 416) *Building volume* 3,740 m³ **Planners** *Architecture* Buchner Bründler Architekten, Basel *Site management* Forster und Burgmer Architekten und Generalunternehmer AG, Kreuzlingen *Building engineering* Schnetzer Puskas Ingenieure AG, Basel *Building physics* Michael Wichser + Partner AG, Dübendorf *Building technology* Enerop AG, St. Gallen; Tomaschett + Cioce AG, Rorschach *Electrical planning* Elektroplanung Beerli AG, Frauenfeld *Pool planning* Muchenberger AG, Bottmingen *Lighting planning* Reflexion AG, Zurich **Team** Buchner Bründler *Partners* Daniel Buchner, Andreas Bründler *Project lead, competition* Ewa Misiewicz *Project leads, planning* Raphaela Schacher, Stefan Herrmann *Project lead, realization* Stefan Herrmann *Planning participants* Lea Fahnenstich, Debora Joerin *Realization participants* Bianca Kummer, Florian Ueker, Rino Buess, Anai Becerra, Serafin Zanger-Winkler, Maša Kovač Šmajdek, Marlene Sauer

Impetus The project involves the creation of a spacious private residence on a gently sloping site with views of the town of Kreuzlingen and the bay of Lake Constance. The situation on the sweeping northern slopes requires an open building construction to facilitate sunny-side light transmission.

Concept The volumetric idea is an orthogonal addition of simple rectangular volumes, aggregated to form an overall figure using crosswalls and framework elements in light-patina concrete. By offsetting them, the rectangles are incorporated into the topography and form wide terraces. The wall slabs allow deep projections, creating sheltered areas. The shielded entrance courtyard is framed by curved walls of dark rammed concrete. The rooms are orientated toward an open atrium, connecting the three living areas and at the same time linking to the garden and the lake landscape. The hillside courtyard area is additionally articulated by a pool and an outdoor pavilion.

Implementation The high-quality material realization is defined by a wide play of colors and surfaces. The basic figure is produced on-site in white concrete with bright aggregates. Inside and out, the floor surfaces are largely covered with as-cut travertine slabs, contrasting with the dark tones of the windows in smoked oak and the walls in burnished brass and black leather. Against the background of the seamless smoothness of the concrete volume, the driveway in dark clinker brick gives a deliberately tactile nuance.

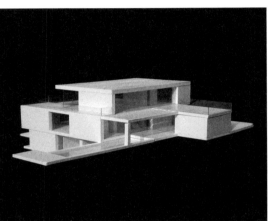

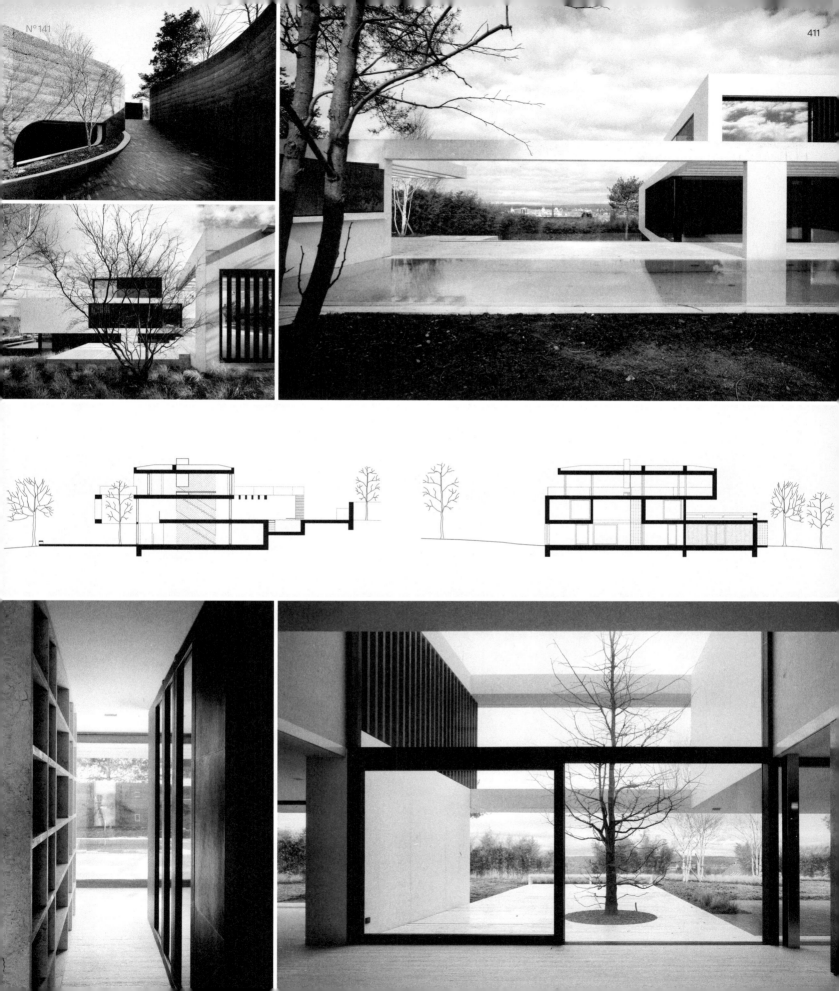

N° 145 Chienbergreben House

Location Gelterkinden, Switzerland **Type** New building **Status** Realized **Project phases** *Planning* 2010–2011 *Realization* 2011–2012 **Client** Private **Project data** *Lot size* 736 m² *Built-up area* 230 m² *Floor area* 409 m² (according to SIA 416) *Building volume* 1,255 m³ **Planners** *Architecture and site management* Buchner Bründler Architekten, Basel *Building engineering* Jürg Merz Ingenieurbüro, Maisprach *Electrical planning* Bracher & Schaub AG, Ormalingen **Team** Buchner Bründler *Partners* Daniel Buchner, Andreas Bründler *Project lead, preliminary project* Jenny Jenisch *Project lead, realization* Daniel Ebertshäuser *Participants* Stefan Mangold, Lea Fahnenstich **Publications** Katharina Marchal, 3 Houses, 3 Stories, Mark Magazine 6–7 (2013), 168–69 • Jórunn Ragnarsdóttir, Wohnhaus in Gelterkinden, in *Häuser des Jahres: Die 50 besten Einfamilienhäuser 2013*, Munich 2013, 30–35 • José Manuel Pedreirinho, Accuracy, Quality, Functional Clarity and a Strong Formal Identity, a.mag 7 (2015), 91–99 • Philip Jodidio, Chienbergreben House, in *Concrete Buildings*, vol. 1, Cologne 2015, 192–99 • Peter Chadwick, *This Brutal World*, London/New York 2016, 203

Impetus The developable plot is located adjacent to the agricultural zone on the north-facing hillside above the community center and forms the spatial boundary of the settlement area.

Concept The form of the building is shaped by the widening of the site running parallel to the hillside. The private residence is formulated as double-story whole, with the main living area on the ground floor and private rooms and a spa and wellness area on the upper level.

An entrance courtyard, fronting the building, forms the prelude to a continuous layered spatial arrangement proceeding parallel to the hillside. The spatial sequence unfolds from the compact front courtyard to the open main room, in which the functional areas are rowed linearly. A ramp-like staircase provides direct access from the entrance to the upper floor. Facing south, the house opens up via a large glass front, giving a wide panoramic viewpoint. The other facades are windowless, thereby generating a sculptural effect. The atmosphere in the rear-facing rooms is determined by zenithal light. A frontal terrace, emerging organically from the volume, extends along the entire width of the building, forming a counterpart to the windowless sides. On the upper floor the entire south side is likewise glazed from the parapet up. At this point, the terrace canopy merges into a planter that simultaneously provides visual privacy. A central, all-round-glazed interior space connects all the rooms on the upper level and opens them up to the south-facing views. Together with the spacious bathing area, with a sauna, this creates a relaxation oasis.

Implementation The architectural volume, made of concrete, has a visible horizontal shuttering pattern. Interior walls and ceilings are likewise executed in exposed concrete. The interior fittings in oak complement the raw tactility of the material, and together with the oak floors define the residential setting. Spatially overlapping forms have a connecting effect and unify the atmospheric concept.

N° 141

N° 165 Reception Building Syngenta

Location Basel, Switzerland **Type** New building **Status** Not realized **Project phases** *Competition* 2011, 1st prize *Planning* 2011–2014 **Client** Syngenta Crop Protection AG, Basel **Project data** *Lot size* 3,690 m² **Built-up area** 1,170 m² *Floor area* 6,180 m² (according to SIA 416) *Building volume* 22,960 m³ **Planners** *Architecture* Buchner Bründler Architekten, Basel *Site management* Proplaning AG, Basel *Project controlling* Drees & Sommer AG, Basel *Construction management* Proplaning AG, Basel *Building engineering* Schnetzer Puskas Ingenieure AG, Basel *Landscape architecture* Studio Vulkan Landschaftsarchitektur GmbH, Zurich; SKK Landschaftsarchitekten AG, Wettingen *Building physics* Gartenmann Engineering AG, Basel *Acoustics* Applied Acoustic GmbH, Gelterkinden *Building technology* Aicher, De Martin, Zweng AG, Lucerne; Technik im Bau AG, Lucerne *Electrical planning* Hefti. Hess. Martignoni. AG, St. Gallen *Facade planning* Christoph Etter Fassadenplanungen, Basel *Fire prevention planning* Visiotec Technical Consulting AG, Allschwil **Team Buchner Bründler** *Partners* Daniel Buchner, Andreas Bründler *Associate, competition* Raphaela Schacher *Associate, planning* Bülend Yigin *Project leads, planning* Jan Borner, Stefan Herrmann *Competition participants* Jonathan Hermann, Julian Oggier, Dominik Aegerter *Planning participants* Patrizia Wunderli, Hannah von Knobelsdorff, Jan Borner, Peter Beutler, Patrick Kurzendorfer, Yannic Schröder, Caroline Alsup, Jonas Virsik **Publications** Aaron Agnolazza, Syngenta baut neuen Hauptsitz, Basler Zeitung, Sept. 10, 2015, 12

Impetus The building complex of the Syngenta company's main headquarters on the Rosental works site is to be comprehensively modernized. Part of the measures is the idea for a new entrance and reception building on Schwarzwaldallee. The street-front arrangement is marked by adjacent buildings from the late-19th century and the early modern era. The railroad station vis-à-vis by Karl Moser, with its richly ornamented volumes and landmark high points, radiates an ascendancy over the urban surroundings.

Concept In terms of the urban-design concept, the volumes of the two new buildings with staggered contours enhance the sequence of different building types along Schwarzwaldallee. The reception building is placed opposite the main entrance to the Badischer station and defines the prestige of the open campus on Bahnhofsplatz. In a first stage, the space between the corner buildings on Rosentalstrasse/Schwarzwaldallee and the new building is filled by a square tree arrangement. In a further construction stage, the site would be occupied by a second, narrower tower. The large open space within the ensemble is preserved. The historical corner building is freed up, reinforcing its primary gateway function into the city.

Implementation The new building volumes correlate to the adjacent buildings in terms of height, proportions, and positioning. By virtue of its deep projection, the reception building accentuates a welcoming effect, in the process reflecting the open arcade structure of the Badischer station. The facade is further distinguished by a composite structure of irregularly wide, off-white concrete members that dovetail with each other. Two service cores span an open atrium space, enabling extensive glazing in the entrance area. The porosity created on the ground floor to the inside of the Rosental site, as well as to Schwarzwaldallee, naturally corresponds to what an entrance building should ideally be. The open hall, bathed in zenithal light, creates a welcoming gesture. A white spiral staircase leads up to the offices and meeting rooms on the upper three floors, which wrap completely around the open atrium.

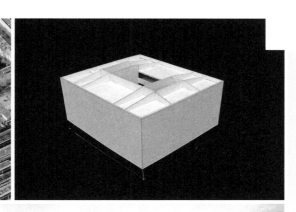
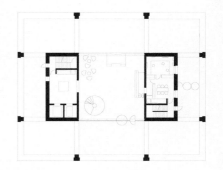

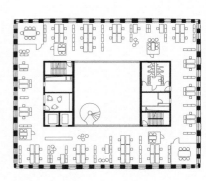

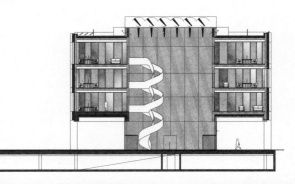

416

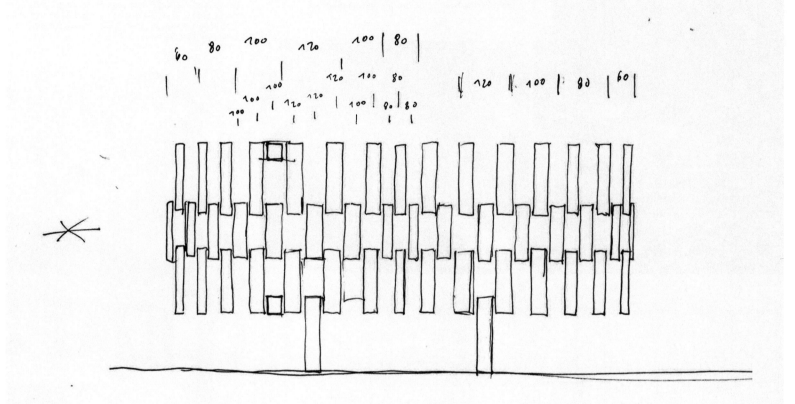

N° 169 Parkhotel Bellevue — Conversion — Further Buildings and Projects

Location Adelboden, Switzerland **Type** Conversion **Status** Realized **Project phases** *Planning* 2012–2013 *Realization* 2013–2014 **Client** Parkhotel Bellevue AG, Adelboden **Project data** *Converted floor area* 420 m² (according to SIA 416) *Converted building volume* 1,373 m³ **Planners** *Architecture* Buchner Bründler Architekten, Basel *Site management* HMS Architekten AG, Spiez *Building engineering* Ernst Bühler Bauingenieur GmbH, Thun **Team Buchner Bründler** *Partners* Daniel Buchner, Andreas Bründler *Associate* Nick Waldmeier *Project lead, planning* Claudia Furer *Project lead, realization* Rino Buess *Participants* Fatima Blötzer, Stefan Mangold, Debora Joerin, Lisa Schneider **Publications** Gemütliche Grandezza, Umbauen + Renovieren 6 (2013), 112–13 • Anita Simeon Lutz, Zu den Wurzeln, Das Ideale Heim 9 (2013), 142

Impetus The frontage base level of the hotel building by the architects Urfer & Stähli from the 1930s has undergone numerous alterations over the years that have obscured its original spatial structure and blocked entrance to the building from the driveway. Renewed interventions are intended to make the institution a recognized address again and to reestablish the spaciousness of the original hall.

Concept The removal of the fronting projection reinstates the original main access and the spaciousness of the base structure. The frontage, for its part, is experienced as an entity again and reestablishes its direct link to the main architectural volume. A covered staircase frontage accentuates the mid-height hotel entrance.   The double-sided form of the outdoor stairs is determined by the topography. Different gradients create an asymmetry, which characterize the overall front.

Spatial corrections mean that the original hotel hall is reconstituted. Spatially rich supports and mutually intersecting beams generate a vivid spatial hierarchy, making the basic structural framework manifest.

Implementation Mineral materials predominate on the outer area, reinforcing the basic character of the building. Fine plaster expanses contrast with the structured surface of the trowel coating of the plinth. The staircase frontage is executed in poured-in-situ concrete using dark limestone steps.   The prominent vertical support merges with a coffered soffit, which as a structured framework indicates the new facade arrangement with horizontal openings. New lifting sliding windows reinforce this horizontality.   The hall is marked by a restrained color scheme, while the basic structure is kept in a homogonous white. This allows sculpturally formed oak-wood fixtures to contrast with burnished brass details and dark leather. Oiled oak, herringbone patterned parquet gives the spatial intervention a restrained tactile effect.

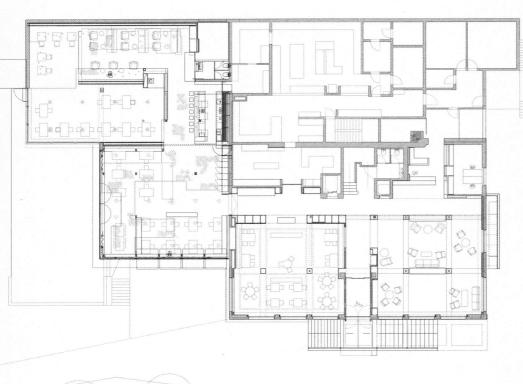

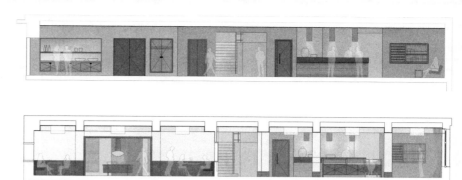

N° 175 Meilen House

Conversion and extension — Further Buildings and Projects

Location Meilen, Switzerland **Type** Conversion and extension **Status** Realized **Project phases** *Planning* 2012–2013 *Realization* 2013–2014 **Client** Private **Project data** *Lot size* 971 m² *Built-up area* 200 m² *Floor area* 508 m² (according to SIA 416) *Building volume* 1,623 m³ **Planners** *Architecture* Buchner Bründler Architekten, Basel *Site management* Dietz GmbH, Uetikon am See *Building engineering* Blöchlinger Partner AG, Küsnacht *Timber construction engineering* Makiol Wiederkehr AG, Beinwil am See *Building physics* Gartenmann Engineering AG, Basel *Electrosmog Expertise* Josef Peter, Illnau-Effretikon **Team** *Buchner Bründler Partners* Daniel Buchner, Andreas Bründler *Associate* Bülend Yigin *Project lead* Peter Beutler **Publications** Katharina Köppen, Ein Haus wächst mit, Umbauen + Renovieren 11–12 (2014), 36–44 • Daniel Ingold, Surélévation d'une habitation, Meilen, Construction bois—Habitat familial, Lignum 3 (2016), 42–43 • Katharina Matzig and Wolfgang Bachmann, Form vollendet, in *Grundrissatlas Einfamilienhaus*, Munich 2016, 98–101 • Katharina Köppen, Japanisches Badambiente, Das Ideale Heim 5 (2016), 118–19 • Katharina Köppen, Der beste Umbau, Architekturpreis, Aufstockung Einfamilienhaus, Umbauen + Renovieren 1–2 (2016), 54–59

Impetus The existing single-family home was built in 1966 and has been lived in since. The plot is situated at the end of Eichholzstrasse, directly next to the agricultural zone. Due to the raised hillside terrain, the site affords unique views over the mountains and the wide valley of Lake Zurich. The solid construction of the house incorporates the sloping typography and is stepped into the mountainside. A frontal terrace, framed by a pergola, forms the distinguishing feature of the otherwise unostentatious basic volume, which is to be extended with a roof story so as to provide the large family with more space.

Concept A pavilion-like roof construction is added on top of the basic volume, elaborating the main existing architectural motifs. In this way a spacious, faming roof extends the meandering glass top level and stretches across the basic figure of the house with its widely protruding bracket constructions, in turn providing a visual continuation of the flowing open-plan form around the corner. Solid spatial volumes, containing functional areas such as the bathroom, kitchen, and vertical access well, structure the open plan and provide a spatial-material contrast to the open lightweight construction of the roof and the facade.

Implementation The house's unpretentious appearance entails a restrained material realization of the roof extension. The constructive elements are clad in white-laminated aluminum panels, giving them the effect of coalescing with the existing solid construction. Wooden frames are kept dark. The simple outer colorfulness is juxtaposed with the interior material variety. Thus the spatial volume is executed in poured-in-situ concrete while the wooden structure on top is varnished white. Japanese hinoki wood is employed to line the "spacepieces." The bright surfacing of the poured terrazzo enters into a dialogue with the roof, signally the spatial continuum, and lends the pavilion-like roof extension an unusual spaciousness.

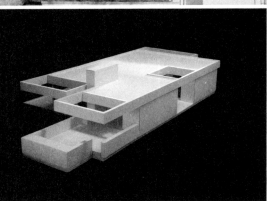

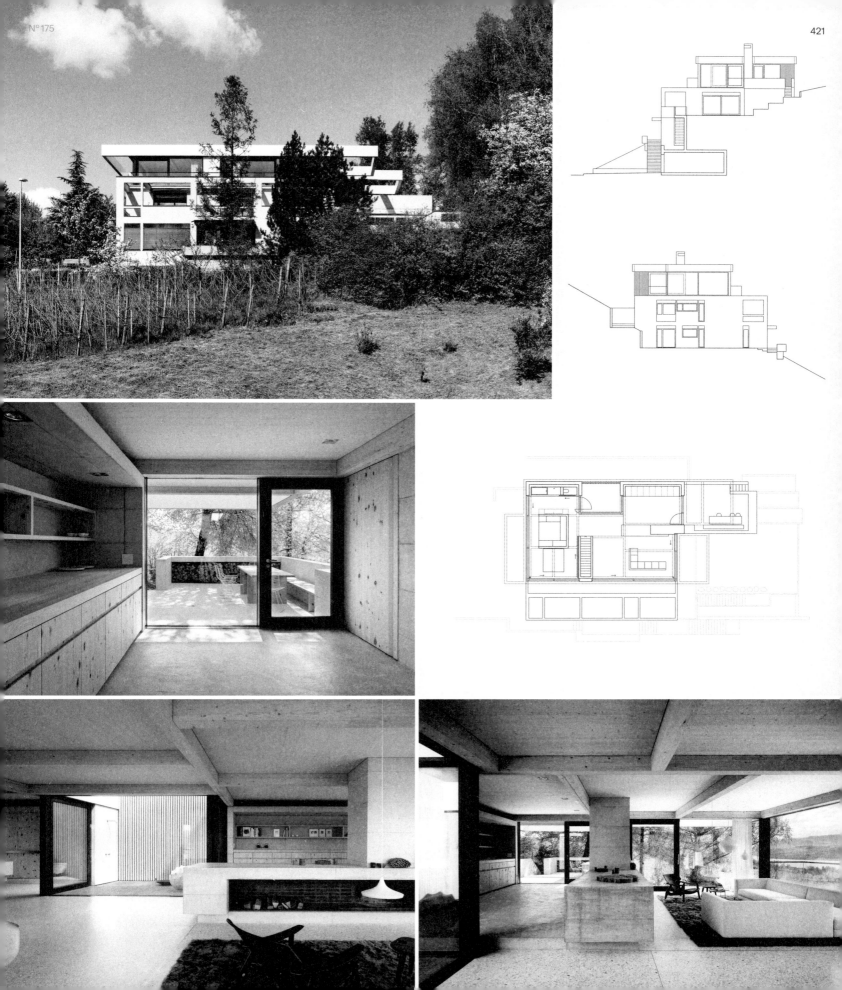

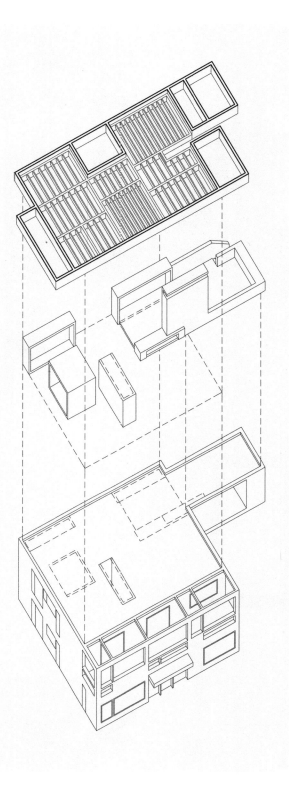

N° 185 Eisenbahnweg Housing Development — New building — Further Buildings and Projects

Location Basel, Switzerland **Type** New building **Status** Realization **Project phases** *Competition* 2012–2013, 1st prize *Planning* 2017–2021 *Realization* 2020–2023 **Client** *Competition* F. Hoffmann-La Roche AG, Basel *Planning and realization* Rapp Architekten AG, Münchenstein *Commissioning body, planning and realization* Rimmobas Anlagestiftung, Basel **Project data** *Lot size* 6,351 m², *Built-up area* 1,956 m² *Floor area* overground 16,488 m², underground 18,193 m² (according to SIA 416) *Building volume* overground 50,148 m³, underground 63,332 m³ **Planners** *Architecture* Buchner Bründler Architekten, Basel *Site management* CSG Baumanagement AG, Basel *General planning* Rapp Architekten AG, Münchenstein *Building engineering* WMM Ingenieure AG, Münchenstein *Landscape architecture, competition* Robin Winogrond Landschaftsarchitekten, Zurich *Landscape architecture, planning and realization* Studio Vulkan Landschaftsarchitektur GmbH, Zurich *Building physics, competition* Bakus Bauphysik & Akustik GmbH, Zurich *Building physics, planning and realization* Gartenmann Engineering AG, Basel *Building technology, competition* Abicht AG, Zug *Building technology, planning and realization* Kalt+Halbeisen Ingenieurbüro AG, Basel *Electrical planning* HKG Engineering AG Pratteln, Pratteln *Facade planning* Dr. Lüchinger + Meyer Bauingenieure AG, Zurich *Fire prevention planning* Visiotec Technical Consulting AG, Allschwil *Catering planning* planbar AG, Zurich *Traffic planning, competition* Stierli + Ruggli, Ingenieure + Raumplaner AG, Lausen *Traffic planning, planning and realization* Rapp Infra AG, Basel **Team Buchner Bründler** *Partner* Daniel Buchner, Andreas Bründler *Associate, competition* Raphaela Schacher *Associate, planning and realization* Stefan Oehy *Project lead, competition* Jonathan Hermann *Project lead, planning and realization* Tünde König *Competition participants* Balàzs Földvàry, Eva Körber *Planning participants* Daniel Ziółek, Sarah Simon, Jan Stiller, Georgia Papathanasiou, Vanessa Flaiban, Laura Ehme, Aude Soffer, Simone Braendle, Jon Garbizu Etxaide, Nadine Strasser, Jonathan Hermann, Norma Tollmann, Katharina Kral, Carlos Unten Kanashiro, Kaspar Zilian, Florian Marenbach, Joël Mortier, Paul Schreijäg, Nora Molari, Jonas Hamberger, Mascha Zach, Maša Kovač Šmajdek, Sharif Hasrat *Realization participants* Sarah Simon, Jan Stiller, Vanessa Flaiban, Leandro Villalba, Daniel Ziółek, Fabian Moser, Arno Bruderer, Kaspar Zilian

Impetus A set of grounds with former tennis courts on the eastern city edge is the development site for an investment project. It is situated around 2 km from Basel's city center, directly adjacent to the Schwarzwald Bridge, which with its main highway and railroad infrastructures acts as a spatial caesura. Eisenbahnweg was once the city's traffic artery along the Rhine toward Grenzach. With the building of the Solitüde Park in the early 20th century, the main route was moved to the northern side of the site, with the result that the urban fabric along the section up to the Rhine is heterogeneous and through its waterside greenery has a park-like character.

Concept In order to achieve a high-density occupancy, the project is conceived as a single slab high-rise block along the road space with an annex building facing the railway line. The slightly folded form of the slab is generated by the primary street-space geometry. The annex incorporates the deflection motif, creating a hinged effect vis-à-vis the spatial gap on the Rhine side. The form mirrors the block fragment opposite, thereby generating an enclosed courtyard area. The contrastingly arranged volumes enable a wide variety of residential typologies. The apartments profit from the meandering loggia facade facing the Rhine to the south. Additionally, the project provides a multistory parking complex for the Roche Campus.

Implementation The basic polygonal form of the building responds straightforwardly to the local noise emissions. Folds, as well as protrusions and recesses, modulate the building further. The staggered depth creates an open overall appearance with a subtle elegance. A wave-like volume emerges, presenting a distinct facade on each side and thereby allowing a differentiated perception of the building. The fluctuating Rhine-side loggia facade creates an additional spatial depth and a harmonious overall appearance in the courtyard area. The encircling architectural structure is made of greenish brick, thus conveying the colorfulness of the vegetation onto the outer building skin.

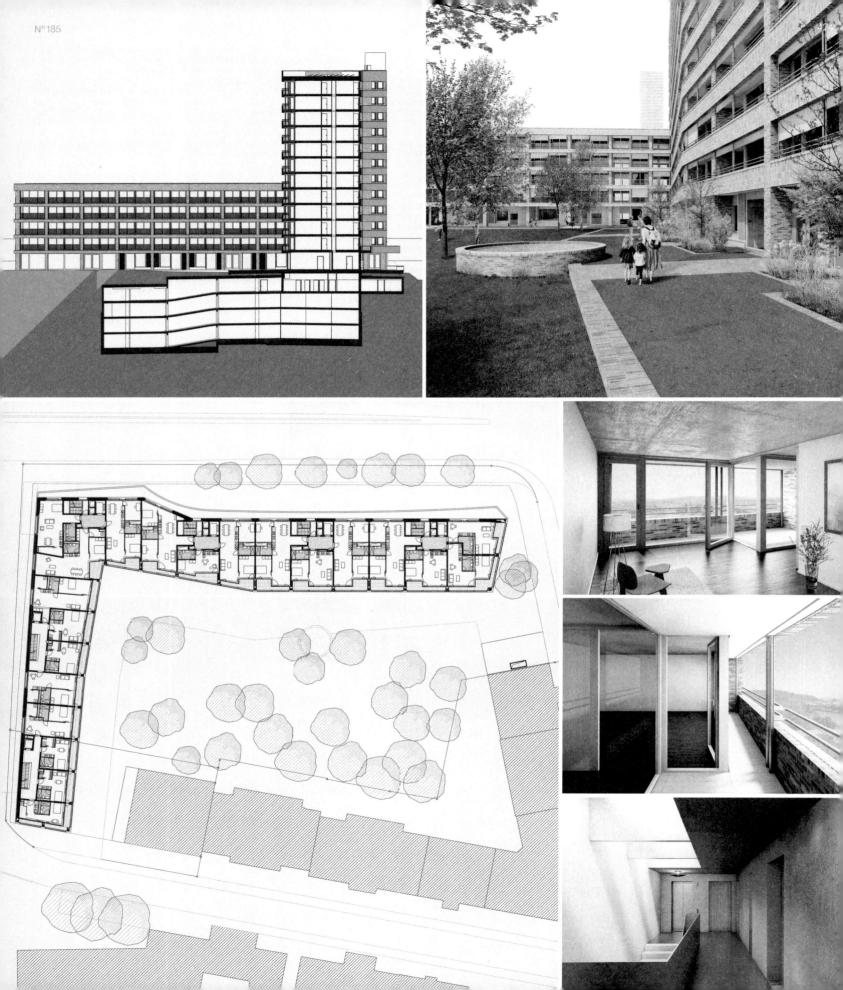

N° 187 AUE Basel

Location Basel, Switzerland **Type** New building **Status** Competition **Project phases** *Competition* 2013, 3rd prize **Client** Canton Basel-Stadt **Project data** *Lot size* 335 m² *Built-up area* 324 m² *Floor area* 2,284 m² (according to SIA 416) *Building volume* 8,191 m³ **Planners** *Architecture* Buchner Bründler Architekten, Basel *General planning and construction management* B+P Baurealisation AG, Zurich *Building engineering* Schnetzer Puskas Ingenieure AG, Basel *Building technology* Waldhauser + Hermann AG, Basel *Electrical planning* Visiotec Technical Consulting AG, Allschwil **Team Buchner Bründler** *Partners* Daniel Buchner, Andreas Bründler *Associate* Raphaela Schacher *Project lead* Carina Thurner *Participants* Baläzs Földváry, Anaï Becerra

Impetus The project involves the realization of a new building for the Basel Environmental and Energy Agency (AUE) on a prominent site in the midst of the historical city center townscape, intended to showcase sustainability and spatial organization. The currently occupied complex by the architects Rehm and Vischer & Weber is located on the intersection of two main inner-city axes, whereby an alternative site would allow a relational reorganization of the urban setting. Continuing a sequence with the Alte Börse and opposite the building by Rudolf Sandreuter, the new building reframes and redefines the Fischmarkt, embedding it in the sequence of squares along the axis up to the Totentanz.

Concept The figurative architectural volume creates a distinctive urban sequence, entering into a direct dialogue with the adjacent buildings in terms of its gradations and proportions. Deploying differentiated form and configuration motifs, it generates a specific effect within its contrasting spatial surroundings. The exterior design mirrors the building's clear structural-spatial logic. To the rear of the plot, it expresses itself as a solid circulation core, with a wooden spatial construction docking onto it, its hall-like character allowing variable uses. In material character it reflects the traditions of the other buildings in the block—an architectural continuity that is further reflected in the durable facade materials in matching colors.

Implementation The new civic institution adopts the tectonic arrangements of its neighbors and reinterprets them. The facade is horizontally staggered from floor to floor, while the window levels are slightly recessed compared to the other material levels. The axially symmetric composition and the vertical tripartite division of the facade create a distinguished effect. The facade is adorned with a ceramic-element skin with varying coloring and surfacing, giving the building a contextual anchoring. Similar to the adjacent Spiegelhof, the windows are in oak. Electric energy is generated by scaled, sloping solar-panel elements. Composite wood-cement floor panels create a corresponding mass inertia and visualize the equilibrium of the low-tech concept.

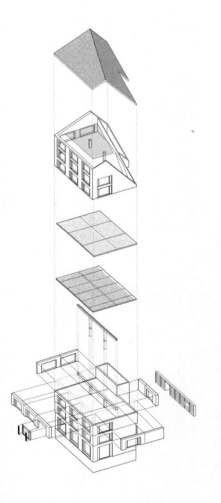

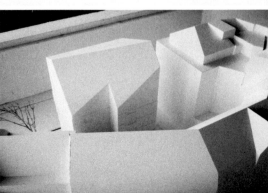

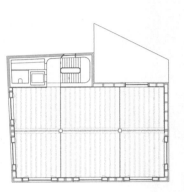

N° 188 Zahnradfabrik Rheinfelden Development New building Further Buildings and Projects 428

Location Rheinfelden, Switzerland **Type** New building **Status** Competition **Project phases** *Competition* 2013, 4th prize **Client** Anton Giess AG, Rheinfelden **Project data** **Plot size** 5,224 m² **Built-up area** 1,389 m² **Floor area** 11,740 m² (according to SIA 416) **Building volume** 35,699 m³ **Planners** *Architecture* Buchner Bründler Architekten, Basel *Building engineering* ZPF Ingenieure AG, Basel **Team Buchner Bründler** *Partners* Daniel Buchner, Andreas Bründler *Associate* Raphaela Schacher *Participants* Pascal Berchtold, Balàzs Földvàry, Alexandra Berthold

Impetus Framed by the majesty of the Rhine, which simultaneously defines its boundaries, the town of Rheinfelden is characterized by three urban patterns: the medieval old town with vivid greenery along the former moats, large-scale industry and housing, and a peppering of ostentatious town villas. The project involves the erection of a series of new buildings for the service and retail sectors, trades and housing, on the site of a former gearbox factory.

Concept The site is restaged by an open perimeter-block structure fronted by a freestanding corner-front building, creating an open configuration that blends with the heterogeneous urban surroundings. The freestanding building adopts the grain of the neighboring historical architectural conglomeration, while the block figure orientates itself to the larger scale of the riverside urban fabric. Intermediate spaces create exciting views into the site and toward the Rhine. The volumes respond to the small-scale pattern of the south-side surroundings by means of protrusions and recesses, terraces and loggias, and different vertical graduations.

Implementation The two buildings contain around forty apartments, all of which face in multiple directions. Loggias and terraces extend the living areas into the greenery and toward the Rhine. The project consists of both single-story apartments and various types of maisonettes. Directional access to the apartments takes place via the shared courtyard area. On the ground floor the volume of the block is interrupted at multiple points by passageways, thus increasing the spatial interconnectedness. The outward appearance of the building refers to the site's industrial past. Horizontally and vertically arranged metal sections structure the facade. The fine structural lattice is infilled with small-sized brickwork. Large openings provide wide views into the greenery. The window frames and the fronting balcony layer are likewise executed in metal, expanding the nuanced form vocabulary.

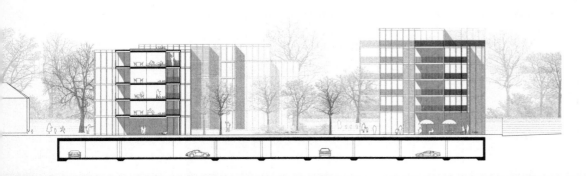

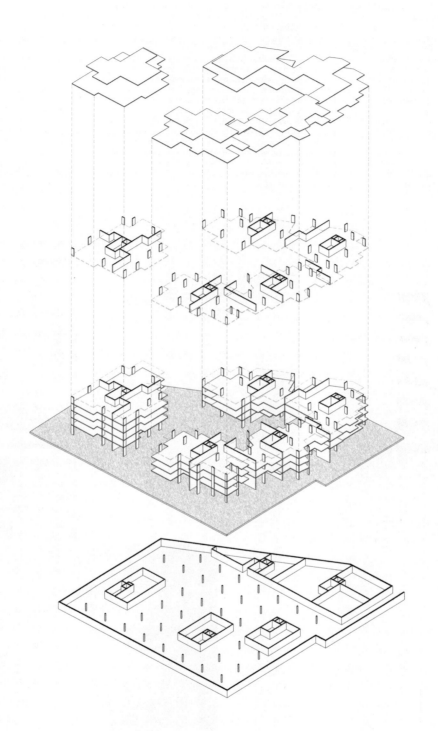

N° 189 Rosentalturm Messe Basel

Location Basel, Switzerland **Type** New building **Status** Test planning **Project phases** *Competition* 2013 **Client** MCH Messe Schweiz AG, Basel **Project data** *Lot size* 6,102 m² *Built-up area* 4,909 m² *Floor area* 83,251 m² (according to SIA 416) *Building volume* 262,402 m³ **Planners** *Architecture* Buchner Bründler Architekten, Basel *Building engineering* ZPF Ingenieure AG, Basel *Landscape architecture* Schweingruber Zulauf, Zurich *Building technology* Hans Abicht AG, Zug *Facade planning* Christoph Etter Fassadenplanungen, Basel *Fire prevention planning* Visiotec Technical Consulting AG, Allschwil *Traffic planning* Stierli + Ruggli AG, Lausen; Enz & Partner GmbH, Zurich **Team Buchner Bründler** *Partners* Daniel Buchner, Andreas Bründler *Associate* Raphaela Schacher *Project lead* Benjamin Hoffmann *Participants* Balàzs Földvàry, Bianca Kummer, Carina Thurner, Christiane Müller, Lorraine Haussmann, Michael Steigmeier, Pascal Berchtold, Lorenz Marggraf

Impetus Since the founding of the Swiss Mustermesse a century ago, the trade fair site has evolved and been enlarged in a number of building phases. Together with the conception of new halls, the current owners, MCH Messe Basel, mooted the idea to completely refurbish the parking garage on Messeplatz. Considering the development of the location, remedial work alone seems undesirable and the further occupancy potential of the parking site is to be examined with a new concept. The aim is to establish in how far an extension of the parking complex to include hospitality amenities and apartments could purposefully reinforce the Messe location and help to enhance not only the Messe site but the larger surroundings.

Concept Various potential solutions are tested and compared in a multistage dialogue procedure, involving the extension of the current structure or a new building. Different typological approaches serve to compare feasibility and assess the pros and contras. These involve simple slab-like volumetric additions and figurative variations, such as a bracketed pyramid-shaped and a stele-like freeform volume, involving an enlargement of the public space with the arrangement of an underground garage and the addition of a park to Messeplatz at the Rosental complex. The key factor in the comparisons is the spatial efficiency of the park, both in terms of spatial geometry and potential traffic flow.

Implementation The further adaptation involves a refinement of the expansion solution using slab volumes. The volume is incorporated into the basic orthogonal configuration, thereby reinforcing the urban layout of the growing site. The thin, towering high-rise volume enables a highly flexible occupancy, allowing, in a further process, a response to the Messe's short-term spatial needs. Along with the garage, the base segment primarily houses service floor space, facing the square, for the trade fair organizers. The hospitality occupancy starts at the roof space, possessing an expansive roof garden with a garden pavilion directly accessible from the street level. A twin arrangement of plates and supports reinforces the explicit structural facade appearance.

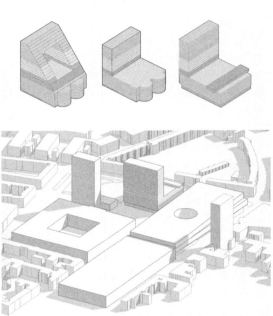

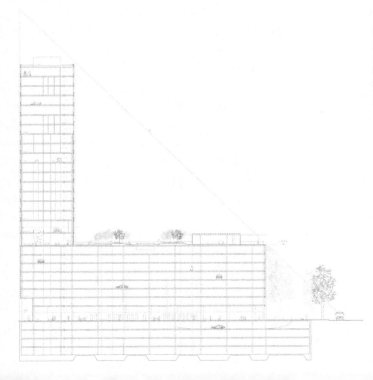

N° 190 Sekundarstufenzentrum Burghalde Baden

Location Baden, Switzerland **Type** New building and conversion **Status** Competition **Project phases** *Competition* 2013, 3rd prize **Client** Stadt Baden, Planung und Bau **Project data** *Lot size* 30,460 m² *Built-up area* 5,932 m² *Floor area* 17,387 m² (according to SIA 416) *Building volume* 76,560 m³ **Planer** *Architecture* Buchner Bründler Architekten, Basel *Building engineering* Dr. Lüchinger + Meyer Bauingenieure AG, Zurich *Landscape architecture* antón & ghiggi landschaft architektur GmbH, Zurich *General planning* Caretta + Weidmann Baumanagement AG, Basel *Building technology* Waldhauser + Hermann AG, Münchenstein *Fire prevention planning* Visiotec Technical Consulting AG, Allschwil **Team** Buchner Bründler *Partners* Daniel Buchner, Andreas Bründler *Associate* Raphaela Schacher *Participants* Jonathan Hermann, Carina Thurner, Michael Steigmeier, Alexandra Berthold, Dominik Aegerter

Impetus The Burghalde school and park complex is situated on a central site west of the core of the old town. The steeply sloping site contains the Villa Burghalde by the architects Curjel & Moser from 1904 and the municipal school building by Otto Dorer from 1930, which was successively enlarged by additional buildings up until the 1980s. The various additions almost fully obscured the original park layout to the Villa Burghalde, meaning that the outdoor space for the increasing number of students became too small and less attractive, as well as eclipsing the original architectural impact.

Concept The new concept for the complex intends to redirect attention back to the protected villa, including its pavilion and carriage house with stalls, and the historical main school building. Two new buildings replace the old extensions, positioned so as to restore the original spatial qualities and to enhance the historical garden layout by freeing the axis to the villa. The building ensemble, ranging from one to multiple stories, adopts the location's geometry, orientating itself radially. The historical garden layout is enlarged and serves as a representative circulation and amenity space for the school complex and the neighborhood. The Burghalde site is improved to become a mediating learning landscape, unifying the architecture from different eras and creating a nuanced overall appearance with a varied atmosphere.

Implementation The new west building is located south of the municipal school building, with an almost square basic form and orientated to all sides. A spatially deep facade structure with a fronting balcony layer defines the architectural volume. The free switch between group and classroom spaces creates a spatial flexibility and, combined with the large central hall, an atmospherically compact place with versatile qualities. The new east building faces the park and is equipped with an outdoor terrace, which connects the park to the entrance hall and the cafeteria behind it. Minimal architectural interventions modify the existing municipal school building, expanding it via an interior connection to the new buildings. The design elements of the existing rough stone masonry wall in the park are absorbed to form the base for the new school buildings.

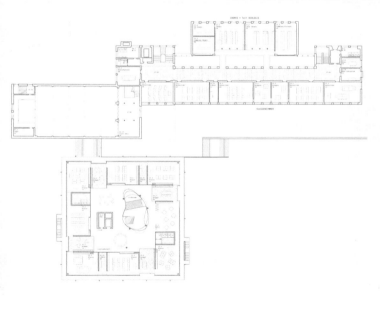

N° 198 Lindt Chocolate Center Kilchberg

Location Kilchberg, Switzerland **Type** New building **Status** Competition **Project phases** *Competition* 1st phase, 2013–2014; 2nd phase, 2014–2015, 2nd place **Client** Lindt Chocolate Competence Foundation, Kilchberg; Lindt & Sprüngli (Schweiz) AG, Kilchberg **Project data** *Lot size* 13,697 m² *Built-up area* 2,912 m² *Floor area* 21,611 m² (according to SIA 416) *Building volume* 86,404 m³ **Planners** *Architecture* Buchner Bründler Architekten, Basel *Building engineering* Schnetzer Puskas Ingenieure AG, Basel *Landscape architecture* Studio Vulkan Landschaftsarchitektur GmbH, Zurich *Service installations* Hans Abicht AG, Zug **Team** Buchner Bründler *Partners* Daniel Buchner, Andreas Bründler *Associate* Raphaela Schacher *Project lead* Bianca Kummer *Participants* Christiane Müller, Lorenz Marggraf, Simon Ulfstedt, Benjamin Hofmann, Florian Bengert, Dominik Aegerter, Sebastian Arzet, Carlos Unten Kanashiro, Christian Käser, Luise Daut, Remo Reichmuth

Impetus The Lindt factory complex has grown over the decades, creating a special spatial form within its surroundings along the shore of Lake Zurich, dominated in turn by open scattered settlements. The Competence Center extension building is intended to further consolidate the site and at the same time open it to visitors. A public pilgrimage route parallel to the lake leads through the hermetic-like factory site. Running perpendicularly to it is the historical access route, leading directly to the plot earmarked for the extension.

Concept A precisely positioned longitudinal volume complements the complex. It orientates itself on the geometry of the existing factory buildings and divides the complex into four equivalent quadrants. The structurally articulated architectural volume is layered into the hillside topography, forming a sheltered forward zone via which visitors can enter the building. The "Chocolate Factory" is treated as a metaphor and serves as the impetus for the generation of the design leitmotif of the Competence Center. This also involves the integration of a production line for new items, creating a real-world manufacturing situation that visitors can share.

Implementation Tectonic motifs in the architectural appearance facilitate an appropriate structuring of the large-scale volume. Mainly mineral materials are deployed in the constructional realization—press-finished bricks and specially formed poured-concrete elements. A boldly vertically structured roof story concludes the brick-walled primary volume, giving the building a restrained elegance. Freely set window openings with curved jambs playfully loosen the effect. In the interior, the combination of supports, ribs, and binding joists deliberately echoes the architecture of industrial sheds, creating an atmosphere balanced between lightness and weightiness.

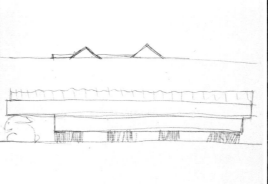

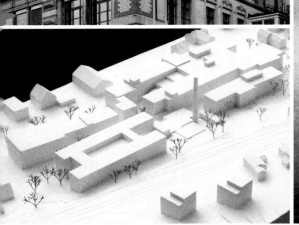

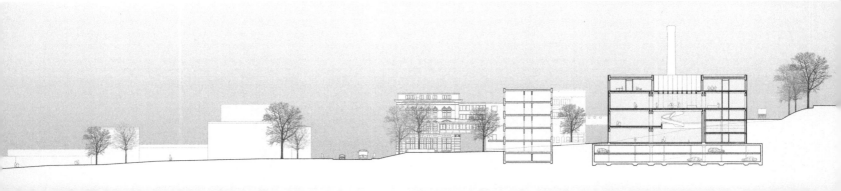

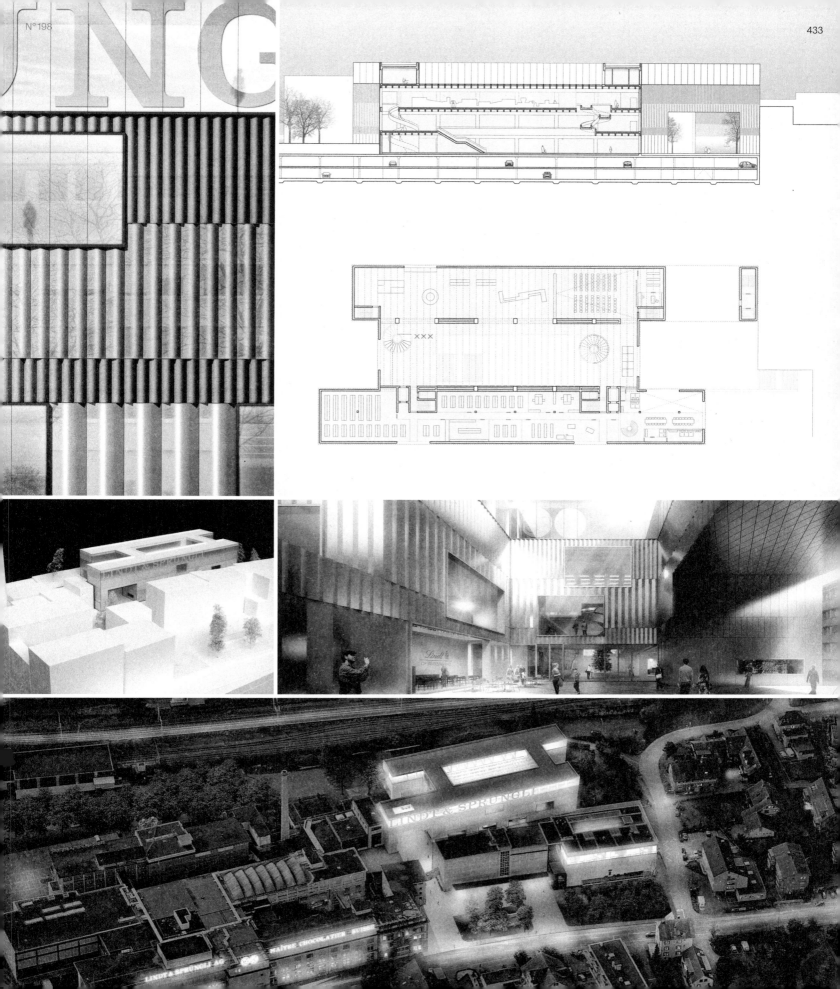

N° 202 Conversion St. Alban Rheinweg

Location Basel, Switzerland **Type** Conversion **Status** Realized **Project phases** *Planning* 2014 *Realization* 2015 **Client** Private **Project data** *Lot size* 630 m² *Built-up area* 360 m² *Floor area* 323 m² (according to SIA 416) *Building volume* ground floor 1,044 m³ **Planners** *Architecture and site management* Buchner Bründler Architekten, Basel *Building engineering* Schnetzer Puskas Ingenieure AG, Basel *Building physics* Gartenmann Engineering AG, Basel *Building technology* Sanplan Ingenieure AG, Lausen *Fire prevention planning* Visiotec Technical Consulting AG, Allschwil **Team Buchner Bründler** *Partners* Daniel Buchner, Andreas Bründler *Associate* Raphaela Schacher *Project lead* Benjamin Hofmann

Impetus The corner situation of the block, situated right next to the Rhine, is defined by two multi-story residential buildings from the 1930s and 1950s, including a single-story annex. In the inner courtyard, the building segments surround an idyllic garden. Combining the previously separated plots allows the base to be fundamentally rethought and to form a coherent garden apartment.

Concept The new overall arrangement of the building segments allows two prominent spatial axes to be defined. The main axis spans the space between the centered fireplace of the annex and the newly inset seating bay window facing the Rhine. The spatially stepped enfilade is flanked by massive concrete shelves, structurally and atmospherically molding the apartment and its open-plan spatial zones. Transversely, the bedrooms and private rooms are sequenced along the second spatial axis, defining and structuring the links to the inner courtyard garden. The joining of the individual buildings to form a whole is also obvious outside in that the new appearance of the extension and the overall ground-floor facade situation vis-à-vis the garden is visually merged. Horizontal and vertical pilaster strips echo their existing counterparts.

Implementation The openings are staggered in depth along the meandering base composition, framing newly installed floor-depth windows. A dark green-grey scraped rendering gives the base a robust character, cushioning the differing colors and surfaces and calming the overall look. The interior spaces approximate largely with the material character of the original substance. Bright walls smoothed with plaster constitute the spatial basis. Fittings and ceiling-high doors are executed in color-matched solid wood panels and the floor is covered in solid oak parquet. The spatial shelving and the bathroom fittings are made of poured-in-situ concrete with a robust shuttering pattern.

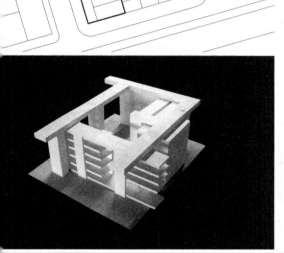

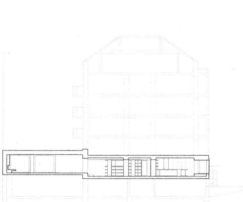

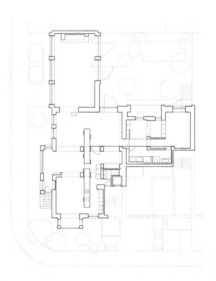

N° 206 Tuilière Football Stadium Lausanne

Location Lausanne, Switzerland **Type** New building **Status** Competition **Project phases** *Competition* 2014 **Client** Ville de Lausanne **Project data** *Lot size* 48,263 m² *Built-up area* 4373 m² *Floor area* 12,892 m² (according to SIA 416) *Building volume* 63,417 m³ **Planer** *Architecture* Buchner Bründler Architekten, Basel *Building engineering* B+G Ingenieure Bollinger und Grohmann GmbH, Frankfurt am Main *Landscape architecture* antón & ghiggi landschaft architektur GmbH, Zurich *Acoustics* Applied Acoustics GmbH, Gelterkinden *Fire prevention planning* Visiotec Technical Consulting AG, Allschwil *Building technology* Hans Abicht AG, Zug **Team Buchner Bründler** *Partners* Daniel Buchner, Andreas Bründler *Associate* Raphaela Schacher *Project lead* Bianca Kummer *Participants* Christian Käser, Remo Reichmuth, Henrik Månsson, Carlos Unten Kanashiro

Impetus The La Tuilière area, on the northern periphery of Lausanne, has been earmarked for a new football stadium for 12,000 fans. Directly adjacent, a sports center with outdoor football pitches is planned. The location forms an important hinge in the transition between the city and the countryside, and will in future be served by a subway line. To the east the terrain is bordered along its entire length by the Petit-Flon stream and its wooded banks. The site is marked by the pronounced natural presence of the stream, lined by large broad-leafed trees, and the picturesque hilly topography.

Concept The guiding idea involves a symbiosis between the stadium and the natural surroundings, achieved by deploying a specific shell form with intricate contours that adapts to the natural local geometry and allows the encircling space to flow calmly. The green belt to in the eastern section is extended, enveloping the mineral stadium volume in the form of a tree canopy. The mid axis of the symmetrically designed building relates to the center of the promenade, forming a tapered opening to the city. A convex front segment emphasizes the middle of the plaza further. Nestled in the green belt, the stadium conveys a sense of locational identity, the interaction between the building and the natural surroundings lending the complex a landmark quality.

Implementation The appearance of the architectural volume is reduced to a few forms and materials: the pitch and stands, the roof, the portico. This reduction to basic plastic and structural elements symbolizes clarity and durability, with the segments correspondingly materialized in the respective distinguishing construction designs. Concrete, steel, and glass blend coherently, creating a special elegance. The geometrical arrangement of the spectator stands are modeled on the Danish scientist Piet Hein's superellipse, allowing the corner seating to be successively swiveled toward the center of the pitch, optimizing viewing.

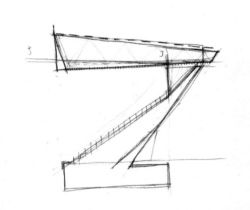

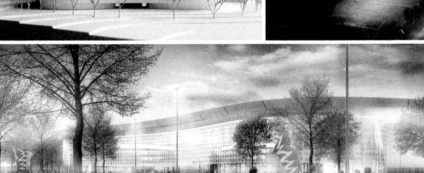
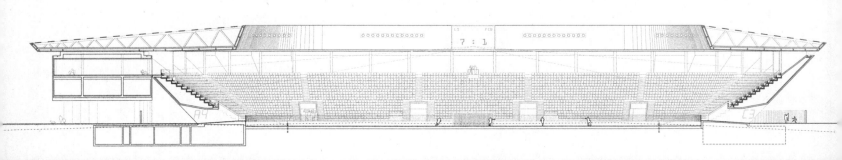

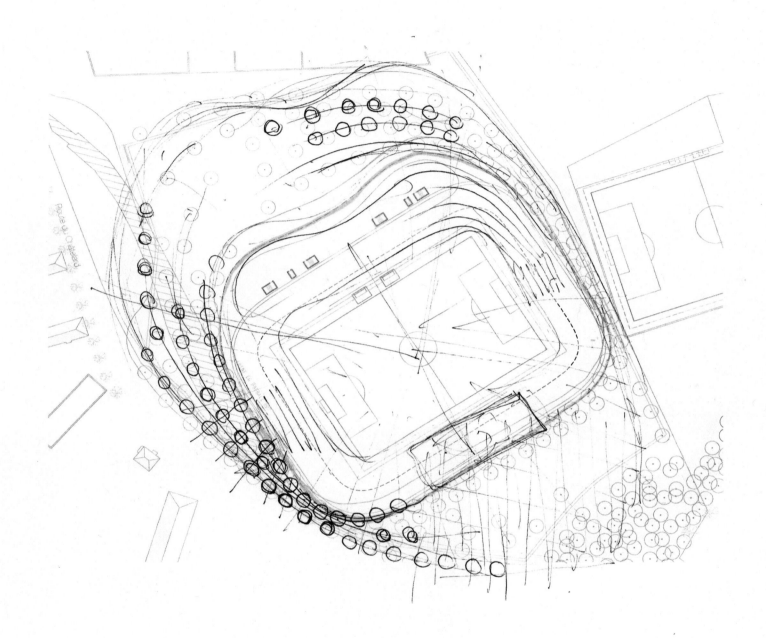

N° 208 Stapferhaus Lenzburg

Location Lenzburg, Switzerland **Type** New building **Status** Competition **Project phases** *Competition* 2014, 4th prize **Client** Stiftung Stapferhaus, Lenzburg **Project data** *Lot size* 3,773 m² *Built-up area* 1,010 m² *Floor area* 5,855 m² (according to SIA 416) *Building volume* 24,423 m³ **Planners** *Architecture* Buchner Bründler Architekten, Basel *Construction management* Dominik Lingg AG, Bauprojekte Management, Basel *Building engineering* Dr. Lüchinger + Meyer Bauingenieure AG, Zurich *Landscape architecture* antón & ghiggi landschaft architektur GmbH, Zurich *Building physics and acoustics* Bakus Bauphysik & Akustik GmbH, Zurich *Building technology* Hans Abicht AG, Zug *Facade planning* Christoph Etter Fassadenplanungen, Basel *Fire prevention planning* Makiol Wiederkehr AG, Beinwil am See **Team** *Buchner Bründler Partners* Daniel Buchner, Andreas Bründler *Associate* Raphaela Schacher *Participants* Jon Garbizu Etxaide, Romain Kündig **Publications** Ivo Bösch, Vom Schaf zum Pullover, hochparterre.wettbewerbe 2 (2015), 36–37 • Haus der Gegenwart, Stapferhaus, Lenzburg, in *Grundrissfibel Museumsbauten*, Zurich 2017, 416–17

Impetus The fame of the Stapferhaus, dedicated to current thematic socio-cultural exhibitions, extends beyond the region. The new building, situated next to Lenzburg railroad station, combines the different parts under one roof, giving the institution a more representative presence. The site is the locus of an interplay of various urban-spatial references and orientations. Bahnhofstrasse bears witness to Lenzburg's evolution and connects the old town with the industrial district at the station. The new building fits into a sequence of partly ostentatious freestanding buildings along Bahnhofstrasse.

Concept The Haus der Gegenwart is designed as a solitary volume with a systematic structure. A large forecourt affords the appropriate space to establish a representative presence vis-à-vis the station. The distinctive exterior contrasts with the modular interior, which can be flexibly organized. Demountable ceiling elements allow each exhibition to occupy its own space. The radial orientation on the ground floor is multifunctionally choreographed: as an activity space for smaller exhibitions and space-filling installations, or as an open lounge area and additional space for art education.

Implementation The three-story gable-roofed volume is designed as a timber construction with a basic grid of 8.10 meters. On the upper floors the moveable ceiling panels are held by a fixed roof wreath and can be lowered or lifted by means of permanently mounted chain hoists. Three concrete circulation cores further structure the interior. A fine, multilayered facade skin envelopes the basic volume. The outermost layer of lamellae is finished in darkly varnished cedar. Framework constructions with diagonal wind bracings form a second layer. The framework is alternatingly infilled with opaque panels or glazing. In contrast to the dark exterior skin, the interior wooden structure is varnished white.

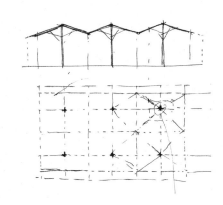

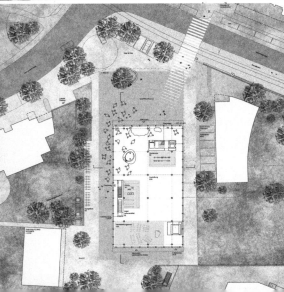
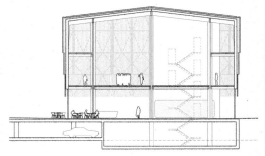

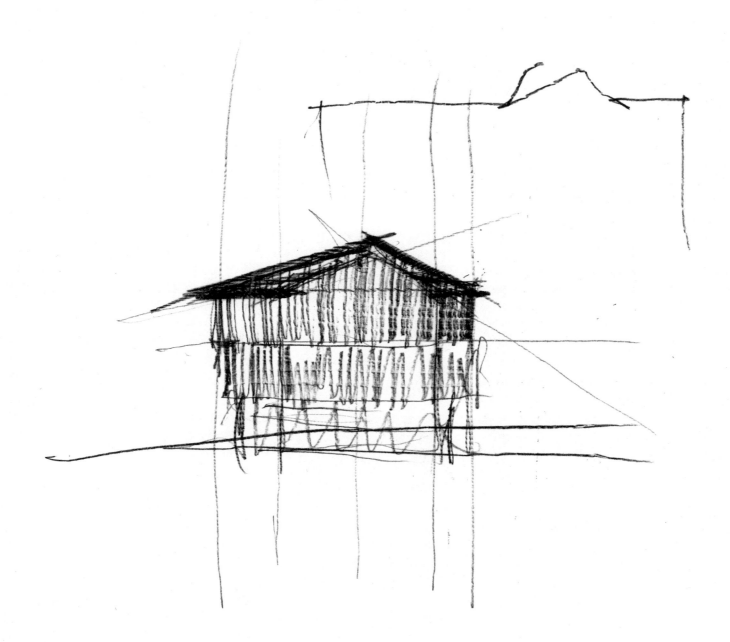

N° 209 Natural History Museum Basel — New building

Location Basel, Switzerland **Type** New building **Status** Competition **Project phases** *Competition* 2014 **Client** Canton Basel-Stadt **Project data** *Lot size* 5,120 m² *Built-up area* 4,199 m² *Floor area* 32,972 m² (according to SIA 416) *Building volume* 136,764 m³ **Planners** *Architecture* Buchner Bründler Architekten, Basel *Project management* B+P Baurealisation AG, Zurich *Building engineering* Schnetzer Puskas Ingenieure AG, Basel *Landscape architecture* antón & ghiggi landschaft architektur GmbH, Zurich *Building technology* Hans Abicht AG, Zug *Electrical planning* Herzog Kull Group, Pratteln **Team Buchner Bründler** *Partners* Daniel Buchner, Andreas Bründler *Associate* Raphaela Schacher *Project lead* Bianca Kummer *Participants* Remo Reichmuth, Luise Daut, Carlos Unten Kanashiro, Patrizia Wunderli

Impetus The municipal Natural History Museum and the State Archives are to be reorganized and merged in order to optimize operations and to provide greater public value. The new location is different to the current peripheral one, offering the potential for a diverse program in a new development area. In this sense the new building in the St.-Johann district is intended to provide an ostentatious addition on the edge of the former industrial works site.

Concept The project involves a simple volume, its physicality subtly reinforced by minimal shifts in alignment. A figurative tower soars above the longitudinal volume and marks the prelude to the Luzernerring Bridge. The urban layout of the basic figure serves to plainly clarify the identities of the two institutions. The State Archives are allocated to the tower, while the Natural History Museum is housed in the longitudinal volume.

The public uses are merged at street level, spatially connected via operational and educational rooms in the lower basement level. A freely accessible *boulevard intérieure* traverses the building horizontally, allowing the public to take part in the organizational workings.

The rooms above are earmarked for concentration and contemplation. Both the State Archives' reading room and the museum's exhibition spaces open individually onto an enclosed garden. Each courtyard is designed thematically, similar to a hortus conclusus, and mediate between the exhibition and nature.

Implementation The architectural volume is distinguished by its restrained brick materialization. Identically formatted glass blocks are used to frame the garden courtyards. The pressed structure of the glass transfigures the vegetation behind it. Large-surface glazing punctuates the stony shell, creating a light atmosphere.

The interior structural frames and ceilings are executed in in-situ concrete. Brick is similarly used for the wall bands of the tower area, in this case whitewashed in order to match the tonality of the concrete. Polished terrazzo contrasts with the porous feel of the structural materials.

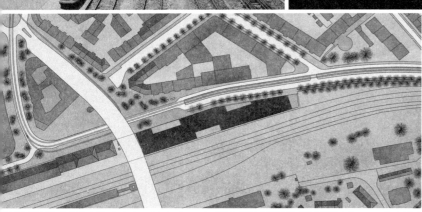

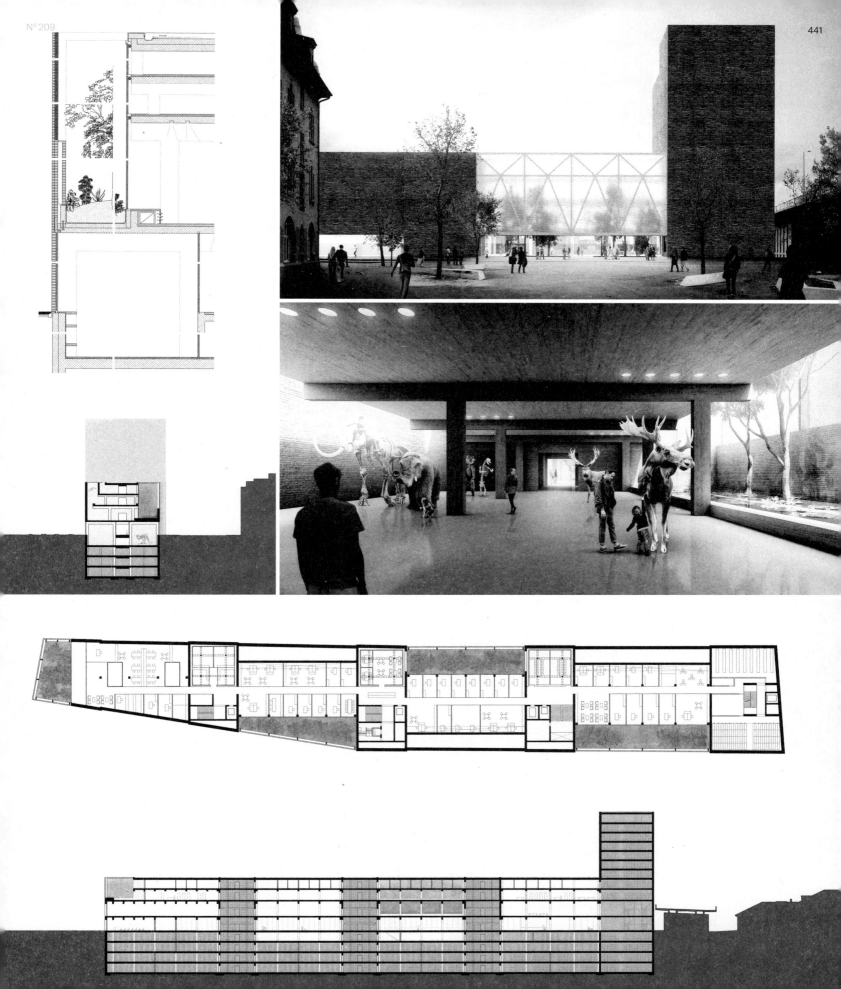

N° 210 Kunsthaus Baselland

Location Dreispitz Münchenstein, Switzerland **Type** Conversion **Status** Realization **Project phases** *Competition* 2014–2015, 1st prize *Planning* 2015, 2020 *Realization* 2021–2023
Client Stiftung Kunsthaus Baselland, Muttenz **Project data** *Lot size* 2,014 m² *Built-up area* 2,014 m² *Floor area* 2,540 m² (according to SIA 416) *Building volume* 14,000 m³
Planners *Architecture* Buchner Bründler Architekten, Basel *General planner* Joint partnership: Buchner Bründler Architekten, Basel; Proplaning AG, Basel *Building engineering* ZPF Ingenieure AG, Basel *Electrical planning* Hefti. Hess. Martignoni. AG, Basel *Building technology* Bogenschütz AG, Basel *Sanitary planning* Gemperle Kussmann GmbH, Basel *Facade planning* Christoph Etter Fassadenplanungen, Basel *Fire prevention planning* A. Aegerter & Dr. O. Bosshardt AG, Basel *Building physics* Gartenmann Engineering AG, Basel *Lighting planning* Mati AG, Adliswil **Team Buchner Bründler** *Partners* Daniel Buchner, Andreas Bründler *Associate, competition* Raphaela Schacher *Associate, planning and realization* Bülend Yigin *Project leads, planning* Daniel Ebertshäuser, Simone Braendle *Project lead, realization* Fabienne Saladin *Competition participants* Jon Garbizu Etxaide, Romain Kündig, Luise Daut, Maša Kovac Šmajdek *Planning participants* Benjamin Hofmann, Leonie Hagen, Antonia Haffner *Realization participants* Leandro Villalba **Publications** Daniel Wahl, Kunsthaus Baselland will sich sichtbar machen, Basler Zeitung, March 18, 2015, 17 • Christian Fluri, Eine Kunsthalle mit filigranen Türmen, bz, March 18, 2015, 22 • Simon Baur, Bald setzen sie das nächste Zeichen, bz Region, April 14, 2015, 18 • Thomas Dähler, Überzeugend durch die Einfachheit, Basler Zeitung, April 15, 2015, 17 • Simon Baur, Drei Spitzen für das Dreispitz, artline> Kunstmagazin 5 (2015), 4 • Jean-Pierre Wymann, Drei Lichttürme auf dem Dreispitz, Tec21 19–20 (2015), 8–9 • Stefanie Mantey, Kunsthaus Baselland, Kunstbulletin 11 (2015), 111

Impetus   The Dreispitz site is marked by its typical ribbon structure, which largely emerged from its transitory function. Long buildings for goods storage stand between access roads and railroad tracks, which in turn constitute the local macro-spatial character. The current building is situated at a midpoint in one of these typical linear buildings, subordinate to the exposed head-end area of the ribbon. The rudimentary hall is to be converted into an exhibition area for art. Its basic structure is poorly equipped to bear any greater loads, meaning demolition and replacement is an alternative.

Concept   The decision to insert a new structural volume within the largely unaltered structure of the old one leads to a specific space-within-a-space concept. The volume punctures the existing roof in the form of triangular towers, making the transformation of the institution visible from afar. The meandering exposed-concrete insertion turns the open-plan halls into a differentiated configuration of rooms with varying formats and heights. Additional curatorial scope is provided by the division into two exhibition levels.   Typical characteristic elements from the earlier warehouse, such as ramp pedestals, the infilled steel skeleton structure, and the filigree roof trusses, act as conceptual and atmospheric elements to think the site's history further and intertwine it with the new occupancy.

Implementation   The new structural volume is poured in in-situ concrete, in between the existing structure and anchored in the existing building pedestal via the three base points of the towers. The ceiling-high frame of the upper story structurally acts as a large girder in the central space, supporting and relieving the filigree truss structure. The load reserves enable a refurbishment of the roof structure.   Incisions in the vertical volumes provide natural light pulses and create manifold sight lines between the exhibition levels.

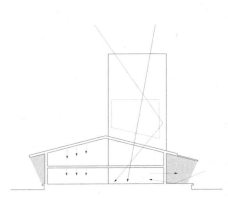
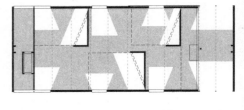
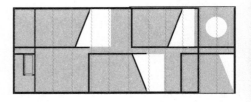

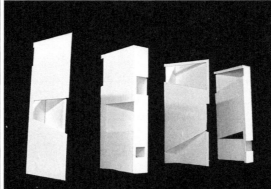
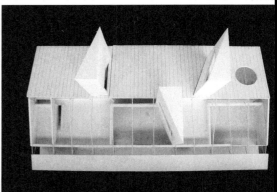

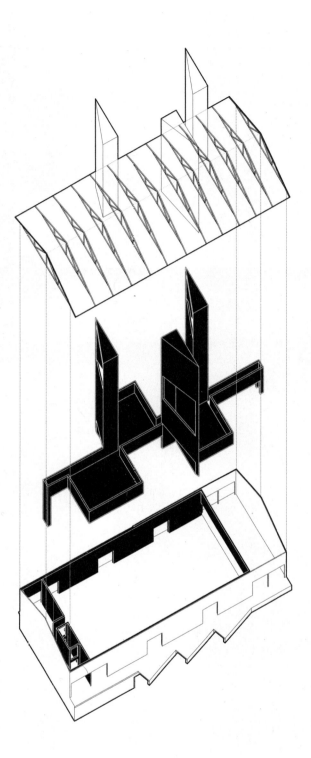

N° 213 WDR-Filmhaus — Conversion and expansion

Location Cologne, Germany **Type** Conversion and expansion **Status** Realization **Project phases** *Competition* 2015, 1st prize *Planning* 2016–2017 *Realization* 2018–2024 **Client** Westdeutscher Rundfunk, Cologne **Project data** *Plot size* 2,470 m² *Built-up area* 2,470 m² *Floor area* 25,600 m² (according to DIN 277) *Building volume* 95,900 m³ **Planners** *Architecture* Buchner Bründler Architekten, Basel *Project management* BMP Baumanagement GmbH, Cologne *Site management* Stein Architekten GmbH, Cologne *Building engineering* B+G Ingenieure Bollinger und Grohmann GmbH, Frankfurt am Main *Landscape architecture* Lill + Sparla Landschaftsarchitekten Partnerschaft mbH, Cologne *Building physics and acoustics* knp.bauphysik Ingenieurgesellschaft mbH, Cologne *Building technology* Intecplan Integrierte Technische Planung GmbH, Düsseldorf *Lighting planning* ag Licht GbR, Cologne *Facade planning* B+G Ingenieure Bollinger und Grohmann GmbH, Frankfurt am Main *Fire prevention planning* Corall Ingenieure GmbH, Meerbusch **Team Buchner Bründler** *Partners* Daniel Buchner, Andreas Bründler *Associate, competition* Raphaela Schacher *Associate, planning and realization* Bülend Yigin *Project lead, planning and realization* Dominik Aegerter *Competition participants* Bianca Kummer, Jon Garbizu Etxaide, Luise Daut, Jonas Virsik, Maša Kovač Šmajdek *Planning participants* Peter Beutler, Carlos Unten Kanashiro, Benjamin Hofmann, Elisabet Sundin, Stefan Herrmann, Jon Garbizu Etxaide, Leonie Hagen, Lea Frenz, Samuel Schubert *Realization participants* Peter Beutler, Carlos Unten Kanashiro, Simone Braendle, Miriam Stierle, Vanessa Flaiban, Roman Hauser **Publications** Ein modernes Medienhaus für Köln, Kölnische Rundschau, Nov. 18, 2015 • WDR-Filmhaus bald im neuen Look, Kölnmagazin 1 (2016), 7 • Uta Winterhager, Generalsanierung des WDR-Filmhauses, in Dezernat Stadtentwicklung, Planen, Bauen und Verkehr der Stadt Köln mit dem Haus der Architektur Köln (eds.), *Kölner Perspektiven*, Berlin 2016, 110–11 • Modernized: Zurück zu neuem Glanz, metropolis—Magazin für Urban Development, special issue 1 (2016), 6–7

Impetus The WDR Filmhaus on Appellhofplatz is situated on a historically important site in the Altstadt-Nord district of Cologne, home for over two centuries to legal proceedings. Today's law courts originate from the 19th century, dominating their immediate context via their stepped layout. The volumetry of the present film building from the early 1970s adopts this gradation in its floor plan, freely extending the motif in its section. The complex form is additionally stratified by means of freely positioned vertical additions and a curtained balcony layer. The architecture and the infrastructure of the Filmhaus are to be modified to meet the modern demands of a cross-medial and integrated editorial and production processes.

Concept The urban presence of the building is reinforced by removing its obscuring elements. The enlargement of the current basic figure creates a new facade toward Appellhofplatz, enclosing the square and providing the institution with a full-frontal address.

The new staggering creates a series of framed spatial sequences from Appellhofplatz to the Burgmauer, with the overall reorganization resulting in an interior spatial clarification. The newly designed entrance hall marks the prelude to the interior spatial hierarchy, leading to two overarching circulation axes through the building, and in turn producing organizational efficiency and a high spatial flexibility. The central element is a cascade of stairs, providing continual diagonal access to the volume and, by virtue of the sightlines, a communicative spatial character. Transparency and inner coherence conform to the idea of an open cross-medial institution.

Implementation The outer appearance is manifested through its discreet basic tectonics. Supports and slabs in white-pigmented concrete form an open structural framework, in which glazed membranes are inserted, their form shifting situationally so as to give the overall architectural volume a liveliness. The full-surface window glazing extends this spectrum in the facade depth. Floor-to-ceiling sash window casements provide specific internal ventilation. The materiality of the design adopts the mineral surfaces of the surrounding buildings, with the additional glazed layer lending it a homogenous physicality. In the interior, the original structural elements are made visible and coalesce with metal ceilings and stone and textile flooring.

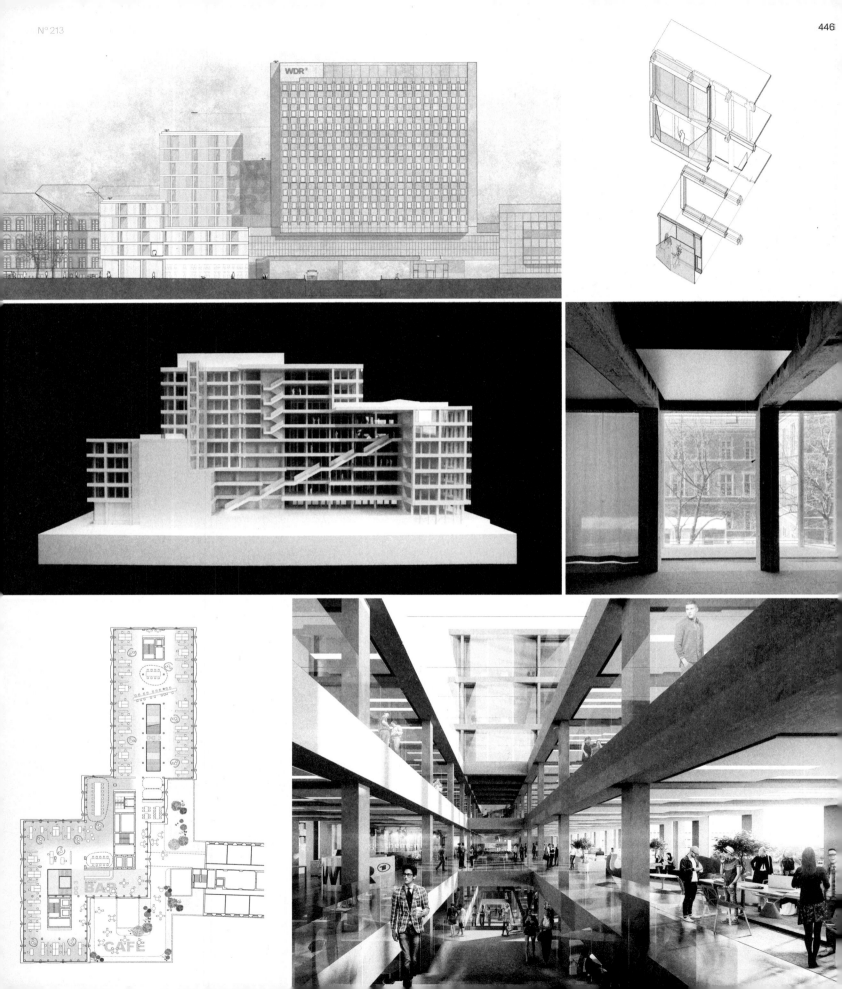

N° 215 Stedtli Site Development

Location Unterseen, Switzerland **Type** New building **Status** Competition **Project phases** *Competition* 2015, 2nd prize **Client** Einwohnergemeinde Unterseen; Ruag Real Estate AG, Berne **Project data** *Lot size* 2,348 m² *Built-up area* 1,099 m² *Floor area* 4,952 m² (according to SIA 416) *Building volume* 15,899 m³ **Planners** *Architecture* Buchner Bründler Architekten, Basel *Building engineering* WMM Ingenieure AG, Münchenstein *Building technology* Hans Abicht AG, Zug **Team** Buchner Bründler *Partners* Daniel Buchner, Andreas Bründler *Associate* Raphaela Schacher *Participants* Flurin Arquint, Benedict Choquard

Impetus The town of Unterseen lies on the River Aare on the alluvial plain between Lake Thun and Lake Brienz, framed by a majestic Alpine panorama. Historically, the town has been shaped by its lakeside situation and its function as a gateway to the Alps. Unterseen experienced a boom in the late 19th century, triggered by the building of the railroad station in Interlaken and marked by a new axis, today's Bahnhofstrasse. The Stedtli site is situated on a key location between Bahnhofstrasse and the old town, and between the smaller Aare channel and the main street. The project involves a redevelopment, allowing it to serve as a link between Interlaken station and Unterseen's old town.

Concept Two volumes are fitted precisely into the heterogeneous urban fabric. The carefully articulated volumes define the surrounding open spaces, positioning them within the primary developmental pattern.

The arrangement and height of the five-story apartment building relates to the larger free-standing buildings of the town. The double-story studio building to the east slots gently into the lower waterside urban fabric, adopting the exterior dimensions of the existing lower floor.

In terms of their spatial disposition, the apartments refer to the site's industrial past. The combination of large spans and the intricacy of classic 19th-century apartment layouts reinterprets the spatial interlinkages as a flowing articulated spatial sequence.

Implementation In appearance and grain, the buildings orientate themselves on their surroundings. An overriding structure of horizontal and vertical exposed-concrete bands fames the underlying volumetry, thus creating a reference to the site's industrial architecture.

The clear hierarchization of the concrete structure gives the building an all-sided representative look. The rigid ordering is overlaid with a subtle play of horizontal wooden bands. Large-format window surfaces and projecting loggias reinforce the residential character.

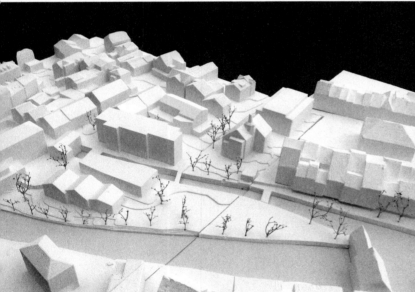

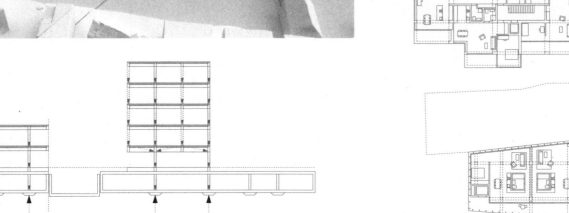
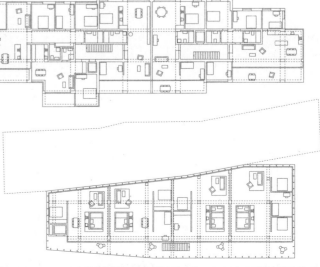

N° 216 Campus Biel

Location Biel, Switzerland   **Type** New building   **Status** Competition   **Project phases** Competition 2015   **Client** Bau-, Verkehrs- und Energiedirektion, Canton Berne   **Project data** *Lot size* 21,000 m² *Built-up area* 14,583 m² *Floor area* 59,109 m² (according to SIA 416) *Building volume* 254,302 m³   **Planners** *Architecture* Buchner Bründler Architekten, Basel *General planning* B+P Baurealisation AG, Zurich *Building engineering* Schmidt + Partner Bauingenieure AG, Basel *Timber engineering* Makiol Wiederkehr AG, Beinwil am See *Landscape architecture* antón & ghiggi landschaft architektur GmbH, Zurich *Building technology* Hans Abicht AG, Zug *Electrical planning* Herzog Kull Group, Pratteln *Facade planning* Christoph Etter Fassadenbau, Basel   **Team Buchner Bründler** *Partners* Daniel Buchner, Andreas Bründler *Associate* Raphaela Schacher *Participants* Bianca Kummer, Jon Garbizu Etxaide, Luise Daut, Maša Kovač Šmajdek

Impetus The project involves the design of a new university campus on a brownfield site between the train station and the shore of Lake Biel, providing classrooms and a publicly accessible forum and hall-sized laboratory spaces for prototype manufacturing. The plot is reachable on foot from the city center via the Bahnhofpasserelle and Robert-Walser-Platz. Adjacent to it are the former assembly halls of the GM-Autowerke company, built in the early modern era and acting as an architectural testimony to their immediate surroundings. The campus is planned to be a first-class research and development site, radiating a spirit of active inclusivity and enriching the city's public life.

Concept The project is anchored in individual timber-built volumes, which follow the form of the site and are perforated by orthogonal courtyard cutouts. All of the occupancies are united under one large roof. Its size and materiality gives the building an autonomous presence, its effect similar to that of an ark. A triangular volumetric set-back widens Marcelin-Chipot-Strasse to form a canopied front courtyard. The idea of an open building is applied consistently in the interior spatial organization. The large entrance hall and the midpoint access boulevard with wide cascades of steps, the reiteration of the courtyard areas, and the coherently linked larger library, aula and prototype areas, together create openness and an inner overview.

Implementation In architectural-constructive terms, the building is conceived as a reinterpretation of a stilt house, whereby the massive round timber columns, running linearly from the foundations to the roof edge, fill the building site in a quadratic grid. Directional hybrid roofs are spanned into the vertical structure. The appearance is distinguished by an infill of either stone or wood, alternating according to their characteristic merits, while the impact of the facade rests in the modularity of its constructive elements, molded sculpturally to give a subtle catalog of forms.

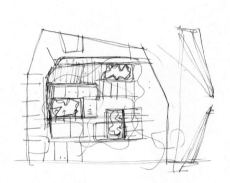
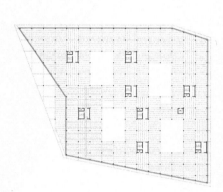

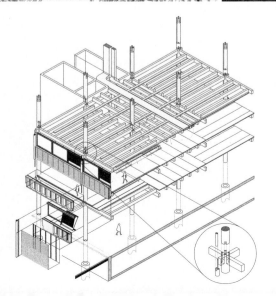

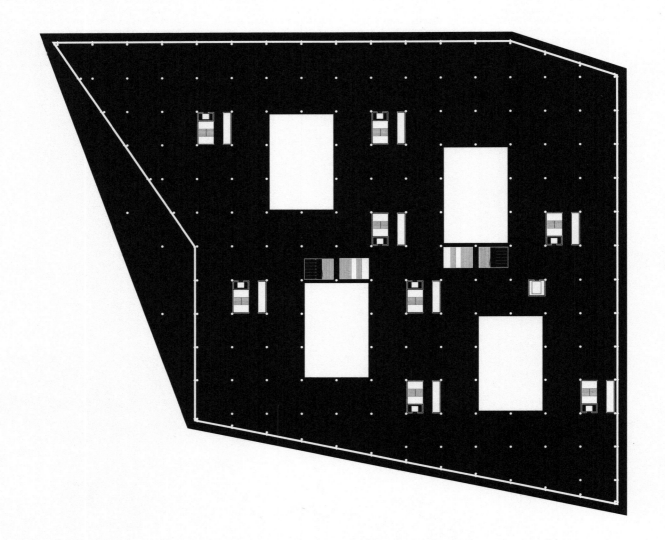

N° 217 Greifensee House

Location Greifensee, Switzerland **Type** Conversion **Status** Realized **Project phases** *Planning* 2015 *Realization* 2016 **Client** Private **Project data** *Lot size* 4,338 m² *Built-up area* 376 m² *Floor area* 516 m² (according to SIA 416) *Building volume* 1,547 m³ **Planners** *Architecture* Buchner Bründler Architekten, Basel *Site management* Linsi Delco GmbH, Uetikon am See *Building physics* Braune Roth AG, Zurich **Team Buchner Bründler** *Partners* Daniel Buchner, Andreas Bründler *Associate* Nick Waldmeier *Project lead* Bianca Kummer *Participants* Carlos Unten Kanashiro, Omri Levy, Aurelia Müggler, Jakob Rabe Petersen **Publications** Werner Huber, Respektvoll erneuert, Hochparterre 3 (2018), 57 • Hubertus Adam, Raumwunder aus den 1960er Jahren, Baumeister 8 (2018), 66–76

Impetus The house by Justus Dahinden from the late 1960s is feely situated in the landscape close to the lake on a slight rise with views. A number of massive single-pitch copper roofs tie the formally complex house together. The interior spatial character is marked by brick walls resting on a concrete base with a wooden ceiling.

The client's wish was to give the intricate spatial structure more openness and light: the kitchen and bathroom were to be remodeled and the living area modernized.

Concept In order to preserve the villa's character, the interventions are visible and independent but still in keeping with Dahinden's design. The building is shaped by a forceful materiality and the motif of combination: the walls are formed in brick, the floor in clinker surfacing, and the metal roof is composed in individual segments. This theme is elaborated in the ceramic tiles covering the entire walls of the new kitchen and bathroom. The originally subsidiary area facing the garden with the bedrooms, baths, and the kitchen is newly and spaciously opened up to the landscape by means of wall-height, non-railed glazing. This feature gives the verdant countryside to the rear, shielded from the road, a new presence.

Implementation In order to give the kitchen an open design, two rooms are combined with the new window as a large pivoted sash that can be fully opened to the outdoors. The granolithic concrete floor, which newly connects the interior with the terrace, offers a similar spatial depth. The ceramic tiles in the kitchen and bathroom respond to the brick walls: they are laid in the same bond but run vertically by virtue of their purely esthetic-covering not load-bearing function. The new feature is their color: in the kitchen a light green and in the bathroom a dark turquoise. The tones harmonize with the concrete of the floor, likewise used for the kitchen work-surface unit and the bathroom basins and bath.

The oak on the kitchen fronts adopts the same materiality as the original fixtures. In the western wing with the living area, the dark-stained, grain-polished concrete floor radiates a peacefulness, creating an antithesis to the dominating shed-like timber roof and the partly wooden, partly brick walls.

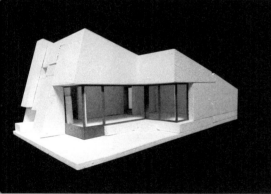

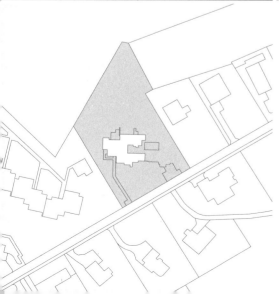

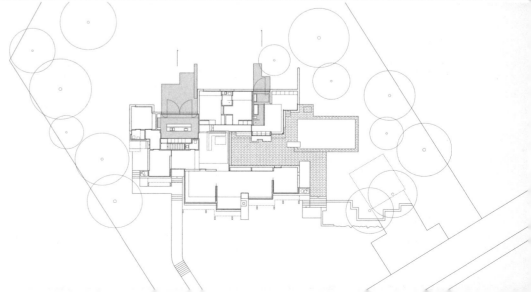

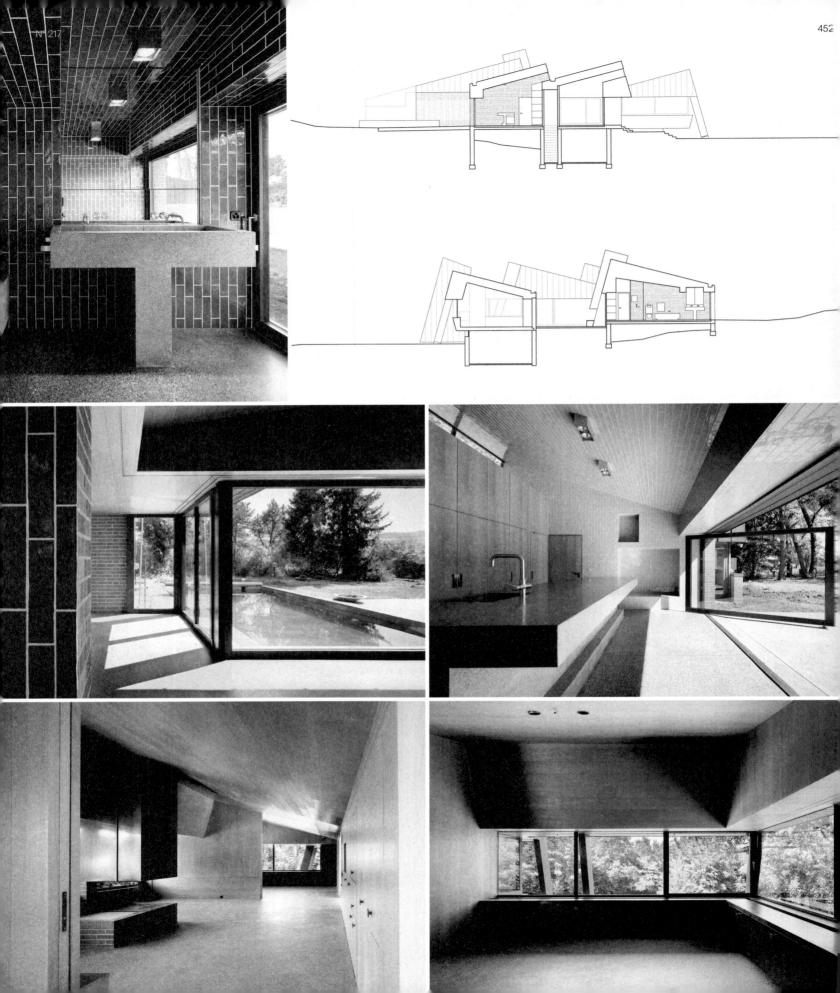

N° 219 Accademia di architettura — New building

Location Mendrisio, Switzerland **Type** New building **Status** Planning **Project phases** *Competition* 2015, 1st prize *Planning* 2016–2017 **Client** Università della Svizzera italiana (USI), Accademia di architettura, Mendrisio **Project data** *Lot size* 12,863 m² *Built-up area* 979 m² *Floor area* 2,390 m² (according to SIA 416) *Building volume* 11,104 m³ **Planners** *Architecture* Buchner Bründler Architekten, Basel *Construction management* Bondini e Colombo Sagl, Lugano *Building engineering* Schnetzer Puskas Ingenieure AG, Basel *Landscape architecture* antón & ghiggi landschaft architektur GmbH, Zurich *Building physics* IFEC Ingegneria SA, Rivera *Acoustics* Applied Acoustics GmbH, Gelterkinden *Building technology* VRT Studio d'ingegneria SA, Taverne *Electrical planning* Elettroconsulenze Solcà SA, Lugano *Facade planning* Christoph Etter Fassadenplanungen, Basel *Fire prevention planning* Elettroconsulenze Solcà SA, Lugano **Team Buchner Bründler** *Partners* Daniel Buchner, Andreas Bründler *Associate, competition* Raphaela Schacher *Associate, planning* Nick Waldmeier *Project lead, competition* Jon Garbizu Etxaide *Project leads, planning* Jon Garbizu Etxaide, Hellade Miozzari *Competition participants* Omri Levy, Mihails Staluns *Planning participants* Maria Schlüter **Publications** Felix Wettstein, Raum schaffen und Abstand halten, werk, bauen + wohnen 4 (2016), 56 • Spazi per la didattica, Accademia di architettura, Mendrisio, hochparterre.wettbewerbe 02 (2016), 45–47 • Buchner Bründler Architekten, Mendrisio, in: Andreas Ruby, Viviane Ehrensberger, Stéphanie Savio, and S AM – Schweizerisches Architekturmuseum (eds.), *Schweizweit*, Basel 2016, 52–53

Impetus The extension to the Accademia di architettura in Mendrisio makes use of a residual plot, its position determined by three buildings. The three freestanding edifices—the Chiesa dei Cappuccini from 1635, the Palazzo Turconi from 1860, and the modern Teatro dell'architettura by Mario Botta—combine to relate a cultural-historical story that the new extension expands upon. The prominent urban setting on the sloping hillside on the edge of the university campus determines a special volumetric approach.

Concept The constructive-typological choice of a hanger form as the new workplace for future architects augments the significance of the existing buildings: the teaching palazzo, the spiritual church, and the cultural rotunda. The presence and spatial density of the adjacent buildings result in a deliberate lowering of the volume to nestle in the hillside topography. This generates a primary spatial system in the form of an expansive envelope volume with an open central space, allowing the insertion of a repetitive structure in a classic square-framed timber construction. The outer contours of the stone volume follow the geometry of the site, interlocking above an expanded stair space with the volumes of the palazzo. Additionally, the hall space of the extension can be used as an open patio. The clear primary figure of the hall with the inserted lightweight construction contrasts with the geometry of the enveloping spatial skin, its apse-like spatial pockets unfolding into the hillside.

Implementation The sunken positioning gives the extension the appearance of a stepped roof landscape in relation to the upper terrace of the terrain, with the immediate surroundings shimmering in the metal surfaces. Facing the valley, the volume projects out from the terrain, tectonically ordered, and so making it autonomous. The shed hall has zenithal lighting, its introversion fostering a concentrated working atmosphere. Exterior connectivity is established by the patio and the valley-facing panorama window. The relatively simple conceptual sketch evolves into a didactic approach, resulting in the shaping of two autonomous constructional principles in concrete and wood with a clear legibility. The directness of the constructional realization generates an atmospheric density.

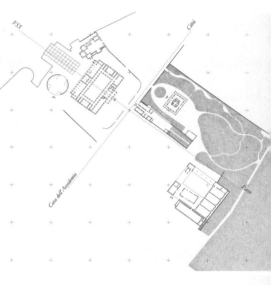

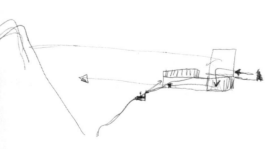
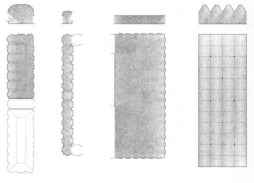

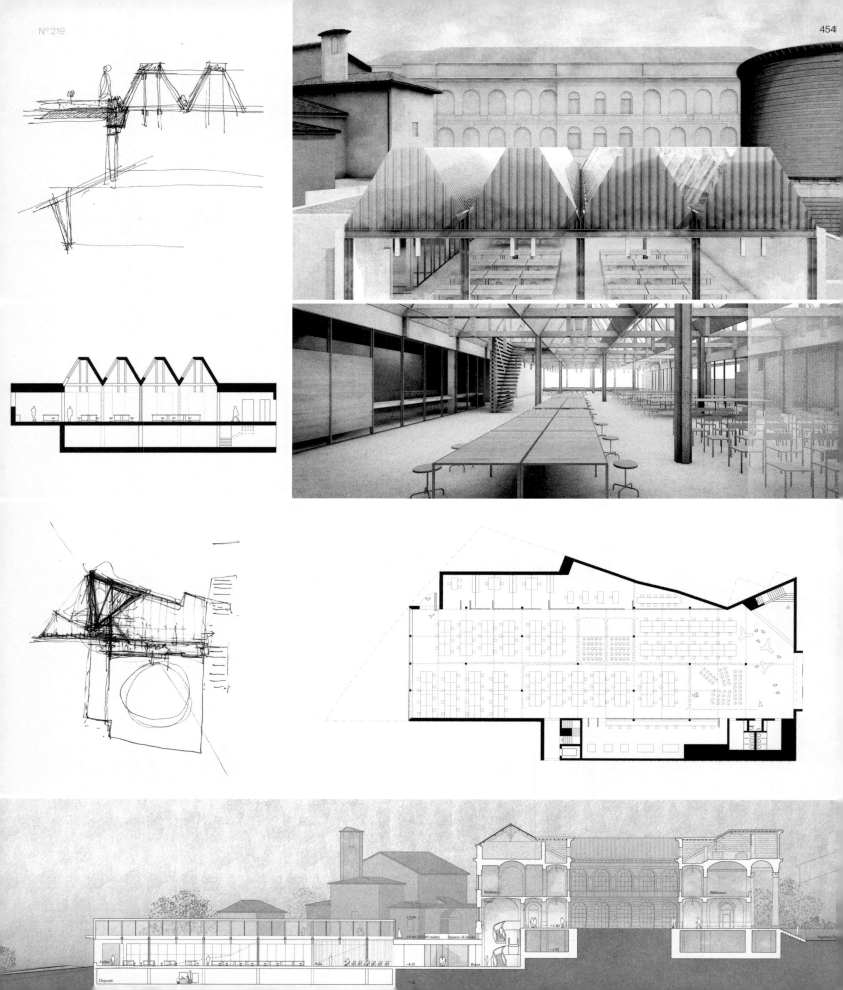

N° 220 Guesthouse Universität Hamburg

Location Hamburg, Germany **Type** New building **Status** Realization **Project phases** Competition 2016, 1st prize *Planning* 2016–2017 *Realization* 2020–2024 **Client** University of Hamburg **Project data** *Lot size* 3,706 m² *Built-up area* 470 m² *Floor area* 3,652 m² (according to DIN 277) *Building volume* 11,941 m³ **Planners** *Architecture* Buchner Bründler Architekten, Basel *Construction management* Trabitzsch Dittrich Architekten GmbH, Hamburg *Building engineering* B+G Ingenieure Bollinger und Grohmann GmbH, Berlin *Building physics* Taubert und Ruhe GmbH, Pinneberg bei Hamburg *Building technology* Reese Ingenieure GmbH & Co. KG, Hamburg *Electrical planning* Ingenieurbüro Plegge Plantener GmbH, Hamburg *Facade planning* B+G Ingenieure Bollinger und Grohmann GmbH, Frankfurt am Main *Fire prevention planning* Hahn Consult – Ingenieurgesellschaft für Baulichen Brandschutz, Hamburg **Team Buchner Bründler** *Partner* Daniel Buchner, Andreas Bründler *Associate, competition* Raphaela Schacher *Associate, planning and realization* Nick Waldmeier *Project lead* Benjamin Hofmann, Hamburg *Competition participants* Elisabet Sundin, Lennart Cleemann, Anne Kathrin Müller, Leonie Hagen *Planning participants* Laura Ehme

Impetus The project involves the erection of a guesthouse for visiting international scholars on the grounds of the University of Hamburg's sports park in the Rotherbaum district. The site on Feldbrunnenstrasse is situated directly next to the historically protected Ethnological Museum, while the opposite side of the street is a high-end residential area with protected villas and Wilhelminian town houses. The guesthouse encompasses sixty-five apartments and additional amenity spaces, and fits naturally into its surroundings.

Concept In order to preserve the quality of the park-like open space, the project develops as a compact architectural volume with a small footprint, organizing the stipulated functional program vertically. The free setting of the building and its playful formulation translates the predominant local motifs, such as freestanding positionings, symmetry and variation, and staggering and repetition. By its stepped nature, the building adopts the lines of the cornices, eaves, and roof ridges of its neighbors, interchanging with their arrangements to create a flowing contour with a sculptural flair. The autonomous typology gives the house a singular identity, while its responsive form simultaneously dovetails it with the surroundings.

Implementation The sheltered access area leads to a heightened entrance hall, which opens itself up via a roof void. The adjoining event room leads directly to the garden. The apartments are grouped around a central stairwell, opening up on each floor to a communal lounge, and thus also providing the stairwell with natural daylight. The building is conceived as a solid construction. The material composition of the reddish-tinged exposed concrete means the building assumes the colorfulness of the surrounding tile-and-brick buildings. The semi-circular motif in the openings mirrors the nearby accentuated villa architecture. The openings are backed by varyingly deep loggias, thus generating an additional play of depth.

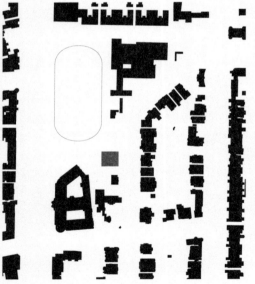

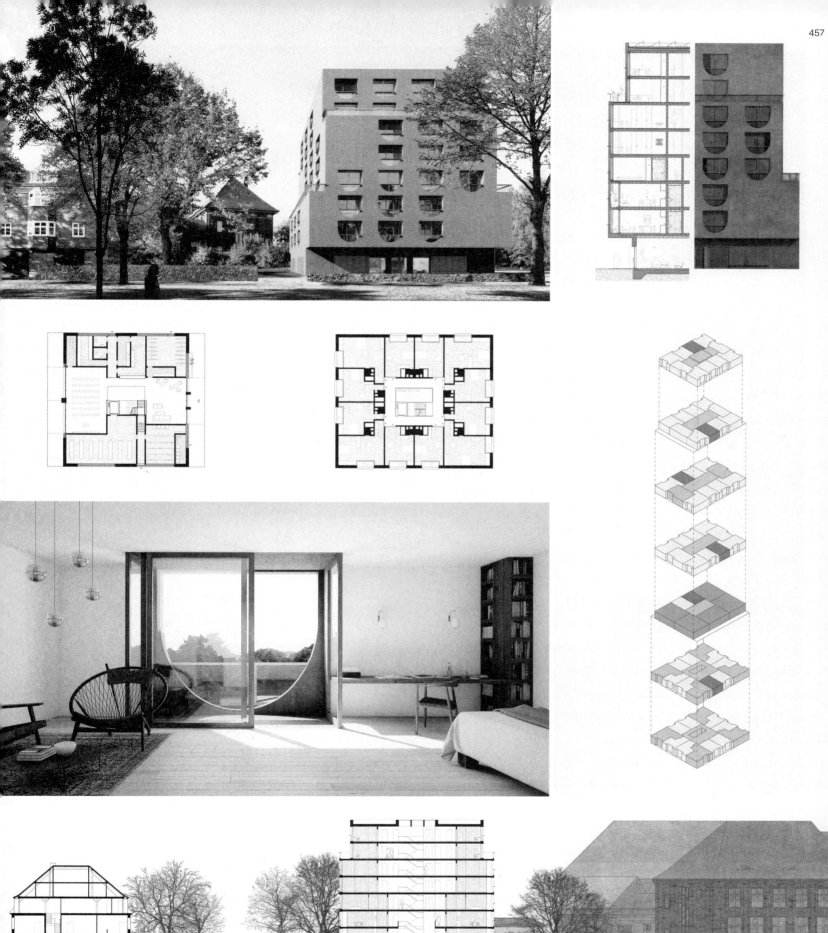

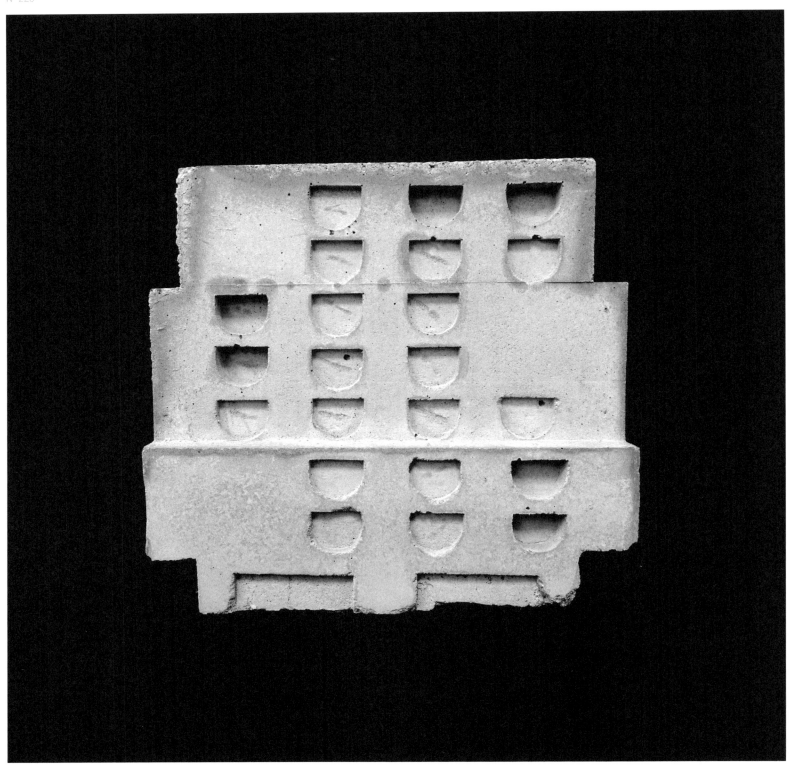

N° 232 Wendelmatte Greppen

Location Greppen, Switzerland **Type** New building **Status** Competition **Project phases** *Competition* 2016 **Client** Novoreal AG and Daniele Obino, Sursee; Merela AG, Greppen, Ruth Marty-Kaufmann, Küssnacht; Margit Kaufmann-Kopp, Greppen **Project data** *Lot size* 20,209 m² *Built-up area* 3,146 m² *Floor area* 7,808 m² (according to SIA 416) *Building volume* 37,748 m³ **Planners** *Architecture* Buchner Bründler Architekten, Basel *Landscape architecture* Fontana Landschaftsarchitektur, Basel **Team** Buchner Bründler **Partners** Daniel Buchner, Andreas Bründler *Project lead* Laura Ehme *Participants* Paula Eich, Yannic Schröder, Dimitrios Katsis, Jonas Virsik

Impetus The village of Greppen on the northern side-arm of Lake Lucerne has a historical center, reachable via from the lakeside across an open meadow, the Wendelmatte. The project involves the development of various plots on the open space. The village center consists of impressive buildings, most of them gable-ended toward the lake. An imposing inn, the St. Wendelin, is situated prominently on the axis of the historical lake route, forming a dialogue with the boathouse on the shore.

The agricultural area radiates a tranquil naturalness, while the historical development pattern and the landscape merge in a striking symbiosis.

Concept In order to preserve the local spatial and atmospheric qualities, the project focuses the volumetric positioning around the lakeside route. The proposal involves a discriminatingly formulated group of low buildings that lesser themselves to the historical architecture. The first building ensemble is situated at the lake around the existing boathouse, an accompanying longitudinal volume is set along the linear lake path, and a freestanding companion volume is erected next to the new Wendelin inn replacement building. In order to keep the area publicly freely accessible, a new, gently curving path runs along the new development through the remaining meadow to the quayside and the lake.

Implementation Typologically, the buildings relate to existing main house forms, based on a symmetrical basic structure with gently pitched saddle roofs, some of which are proportioned narrower and longer, as well as swiveled away from each other in keeping with the interrelated primary composition. The large volume on the lakeside path is an exception, referring instead to the longitudinal buildings of the sawmill on the opposite side of the inlet and echoing the topographical progression.

The proposal is to build in timber and to deploy a palpable constructional tectonic.

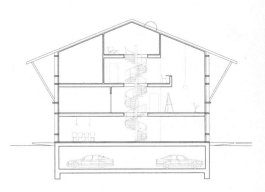

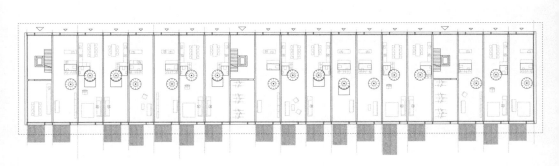

N° 234 Swiss Tropical and Public Health Institute

Location Allschwil, Switzerland **Type** New building **Status** Competition **Project phases** Competition 2016 **Client** University of Basel **Project data** Lot size 5,140 m² **Built-up area** 3,699 m² **Floor area** 19,343 m² (according to SIA 416) **Building volume** 94,380 m³ **Planners** Architecture Buchner Bründler Architekten, Basel **General management** Gruner AG, Basel **Laboratory planning** Dr. Heinekamp Labor und Institutsplanung GmbH, Basel **Team Buchner Bründler Partner** Daniel Buchner, Andreas Bründler **Project lead** Benjamin Hofmann **Participants** Aude Soffer, Tanja Schmidt

Impetus The globally active institute with its remit to improve health situations is to be expanded with a new research and learning center. The location is situated on a large parcel of wasteland, intended to become a hub for new technology companies. The new building is earmarked to communicate the institute's mandate and to demonstrate that joint learning can have a transformational impact and that knowledge can be imparted in diverse cultures and their contexts. The project is designed to express the collaboration between the institute's different fields of activity.

Concept The location is conceived as the prelude and corner-front of the progressing development, embodied in its design as a simple primary form. It translates the basic topics of gravity and tension, which distinguish the building's fundamental character, as an architectural organizational motif. In order to accentuate the entrance, the entire front facade is heightened and arranged externally via a volumetric layering. Correspondingly, in contrast the side facades are staggered backwardly toward the rim of the roof. Typologically, the design is based on themes of spatial stratification. A spacious atrium provides orientation and a central point of encounter. Its open impact merges itself with the insertion of a metallic structural grid, the slender detailing of which contrasts with the solidity of the stone form elements.

Implementation The clay and earth color of the constructional skin are understood as a synonym for primary building and thus consciously grasped as an expression for the global context of the institute's activities. The facade is coursed in small-format solid brick, the manual manufacturing of which gives the stone structural skin the appearance of having been cast in one piece. Due to the reciprocal arrangement of the layers to span the corner, the perspective impact changes while moving, allowing a nuanced interplay of solidity and transparency to emerge.

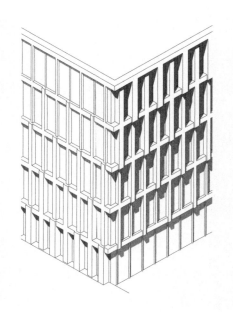

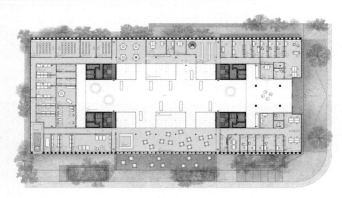

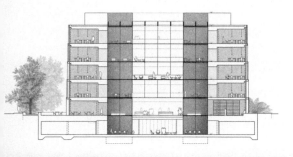
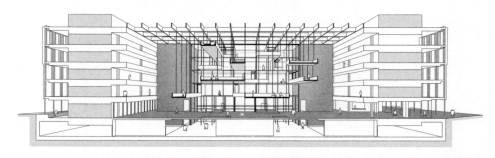

N° 236 Studio Basel Bruderholz

Location Basel, Switzerland **Type** New building **Status** Competition **Project phases** *Competition* 2016 **Client** Radio- und Fernsehgenossenschaft Basel (RFB) **Project data** *Lot size* 8,840 m² *Built-up area* 2,413 m² *Floor area* 7,236 m² (according to SIA 416) *Building volume* 25,336 m³ **Planners** *Architecture* Buchner Bründler Architekten, Basel *Landscape architecture* antón & ghiggi landschaft architektur GmbH, Zurich **Team Buchner Bründler** *Partners* Daniel Buchner, Andreas Bründler *Project lead* Peter Beutler *Competition participants* Aude Soffer, Fabio Cirronis, Luzi Speth

Impetus The development of the Bruderholz plateau stretches back to the beginning of the last century, whereby when the first Bruder studio was erected there in the late 1930s it still stood largely alone. The location was characterized by infrastructure buildings, such as the high-voltage battery and the water tower, as well as the first elements of approaching urbanization. Following WW II, the major development took place as a garden-city-like settlement interspersed with major green areas.

To the west, the openness of the plateau has been preserved, still acting today as a spatial interstice. The relocation of the radio station means that the property can be newly developed.

Concept The approach of the project is try to translate the contextual qualities into an overarching form and to match the new development with both the historical origins of radio here and the geographical beginnings of the surroundings. This intent results in a continuous large-scale form that interprets the organic structure of the radio-studio complex in a single new architectural volume, its size and specification in turn relating to the special utility structures on the Bruderholz. Volumetric offsets scale the large form to the topography and the built surroundings.

Implementation Inspired by the idea of a convent, the meandering building volume is structured additively, thus producing a high variation through an alignment of different apartment typologies. The courtyard area is entered via gateway-like openings, giving it the feel of a natural oasis with a small growing wood as its centerpiece. The planned apartment typologies adhere to a classic idea of living with separated day and nighttime areas. The core motif is a mid-set main room. In the rowed housing the functional areas are correspondingly stacked.

This stacking theme is continued in the constructional realization. Brick-built supports and slabs form the primary facade level, while wooden infills refine the material appearance.

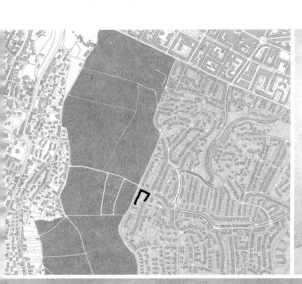

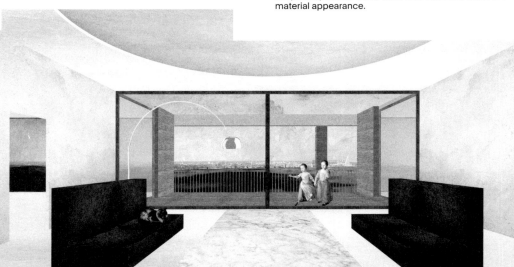

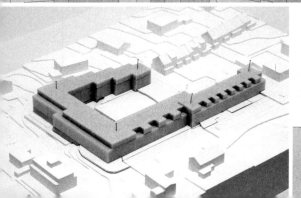

N° 239 Railroad Station Building Altdorf

Location Altdorf, Switzerland **Type** New building **Status** Realization **Project phases** *Competition* 2016–2017, 1st prize *Planning* 2017–2019 *Realization* 2020–2022 **Client** Urner Kantonalbank, Altdorf **Project data** *Lot size* 1,735 m² *Built-up area* 1,575 m² *Floor area* 10,160 m² (according to SIA 416) *Building volume* 42,665 m³ **Planners** *Architecture* Buchner Bründler Architekten, Basel *General planners* Joint partnership: Buchner Bründler Planer AG, Basel; Proplaning AG, Basel *Construction management* Proplaning AG, Basel *Site management* HTS architekten + partner AG, Altdorf *Building engineering* Dr. Lüchinger + Meyer Bauingenieure AG, Zurich *Landscape architecture* Berchtold.Lenzin Landschaftsarchitekten, Basel *Building physics and acoustics* Kopitsis Bauphysik AG, Wohlen *Building technology* Hans Abicht AG, Zug *Electrical planning* Pro Engineering AG, Basel *Facade planning* Dr. Lüchinger + Meyer Bauingenieure AG, Zurich *Fire prevention planning* Quantum Brandschutz GmbH, Basel *Traffic planning* Rapp Infra AG, Basel **Team** Buchner Bründler *Partners* Daniel Buchner, Andreas Bründler *Associate* Bülend Yigin *Project lead, competition* Georgia Papathanasiou *Project lead, planning and realization* Stefan Herrmann *Competition participants* Holger Harmeier, Nora Molari, Jon Garbizu Etxaide *Planning and realization participants* Georgia Papathanasiou, Mihails Staluns, Daniel Ziólek, Tobias Kappelhoff, Nina Kleber, Oscar Faivre **Publications** Paul Knüsel, "oder bin ich öppe-n-e Bank …?"—Projektwettbewerb Bahnhofsplatz 1. Altdorf, Tec21 01–03 (2018), 10–14 • Dienstleistungszentrum statt Bahnhof: Urnerisch urig, hochparterre.wettbewerbe 01 (2018), 45–47

Impetus The NRLA, the Alpine railway link, entails the creation of a new cantonal train station in Altdorf, connected to both the regional network and directly with the international rail system. In addition, the cantonal authorities intend to concentrate the bus routes at the new location in order to further expand the travel hub. The Urner Cantonal Bank recognizes the locational potential here and has decided to relocate their headquarters in a corresponding service center at the station. The new building constitutes the starting point for a general structural redevelopment of the Uri Valley.

Concept A precisely positioned and clearly sectioned architectural volume establishes new interplays in its immediate vicinity: Its longitudinal form spatially bundles Bahnhofplatz and the incoming axis routes. Its urban scale and geometrical hierarchy gives the building a superiority and representative look and allows a new center to emerge outside Altdorf's core zone. The building volume has a double-sided symmetrical structure and is organized around two open stairwells, producing even spatial zones that can be freely divided according to their function. The ground floor is conceived as a continuous hall of columns, transforming it into an open marketplace.

Implementation The linear and narrow train and bus arteries impact the form of the building. A structural volume is generated by the profile section, translating the progression of forces both inwardly and outwardly. The concept is anchored in a frame construction with an upper load-bearing plane. The suspended supports of the frontal facade transfer the loads of the overhangs via the connecting banded architraves to the load-bearing plane. Two rows of vertical cross supports on the ground floor, visible from all sides, transfer the loads further into the ground. The suspended supports on the facade to the square, set back from story to story, give the elevation a further plasticity. The primary structure is executed in in-situ concrete; the reiterative facade is joined using industrial-raw aluminum profiles.

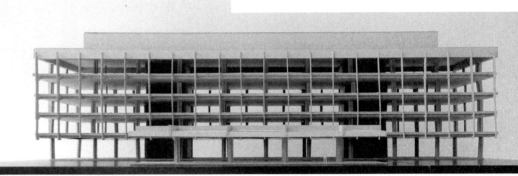
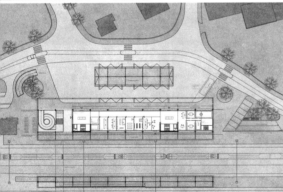
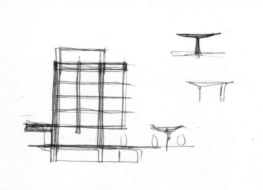
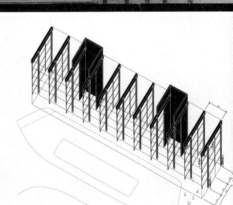

N° 240 Urban Development Horburg

Location Basel, Switzerland **Type** New building **Status** Planning **Project phases** Competition 2016–2017, 1st prize Planning 2020–2022 Realization 2022–2024 **Client** Credit Suisse Anlagestiftung Real Estate Switzerland, Zurich **Project data** Lot size 15,184 m² Built-up area 5,614 m² Floor area 13,470 m² (according to SIA 416) Building volume 42,219 m³ **Planners** *Architecture* Buchner Bründler Architekten, Basel *Construction management* Proplaning AG, Basel *Building engineering* Dr. Lüchinger + Meyer Bauingenieure AG, Zurich *Landscape architecture* Antón Landschaft GmbH, Zurich *Building physics and acoustics* Bakus Bauphysik & Akustik GmbH, Zurich *Building technology* Bogenschütz AG, Basel *Electrical planning* edeco AG, Aesch *Sanitary planning* tib Technik im Bau AG, Lucerne *Facade planning* Dr. Lüchinger + Meyer Bauingenieure AG, Zurich *Fire prevention planning* Quantum Brandschutz GmbH, Basel *Rental specialist* Smeyers AG, Münchenstein **Team Buchner Bründler** *Partners* Daniel Buchner, Andreas Bründler *Associate* Bülend Yigin *Project leads, competition* Aude Soffer, Jon Garbizu Etxaide *Project lead, planning* Peter Beutler *Competition participants* Luzi Speth, Nora Molari, Roman Hauser, Alexandra Galer *Planning participants* Holger Harmeier, Fabienne Saladin, Johanna Noell

Impetus Horburgstrasse marks the transition from a residential to an industrial district, whereby the Horburg housing scheme from the late 1940s plays an important role in deciphering the local developmental history. While the Matthäus district is dominated by Wilhelminian-era perimeter blocks, the urban morphology of adjoining Klybeck is shaped by open structures from its industrial past. With its open row developments and the six-story solid construction, the former CIBA factory housing represents an architectural and constructional innovation. Today's owners feel that the site has greater occupancy potential and have commissioned an assessment of either a renewal or a corresponding retroactive urban consolidation.

Concept Due to the particular starting point and in the belief in the city as a locus of spatial-temporal strata, the housing structure is integrally retained and only condensed by means of a single component. The volume consists of a three-story base with two rectangular-shaped vertical projections. The precise insertion in the existing settlement structure and the refinement of its architectural language creates a new overall ensemble, which sustains the singularity of the quadrangle. The loose appearance of Horburgplatz is newly framed by a corner block, with the high-rise volumes forming a presence that corresponds to the proportions of the square.

Implementation Place-specific themes such as stand-alone situations, symmetry and variation, stacking and repetition, are translated contemporaneously in the new project. The plastic design of the facades and the figurative openings create an affinity with the articulation of the factory housing. A varying vertical structure overlies the simple basic geometry. Due to the different staggering of the volumes, the two corner-front sides differ, thereby reacting to the contextual links. In their material formulation, the facades are made of light-tinted quartz stone, thus incorporating the natural colorfulness of the rough stone and plaster of its neighbours.

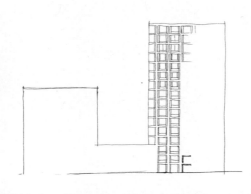

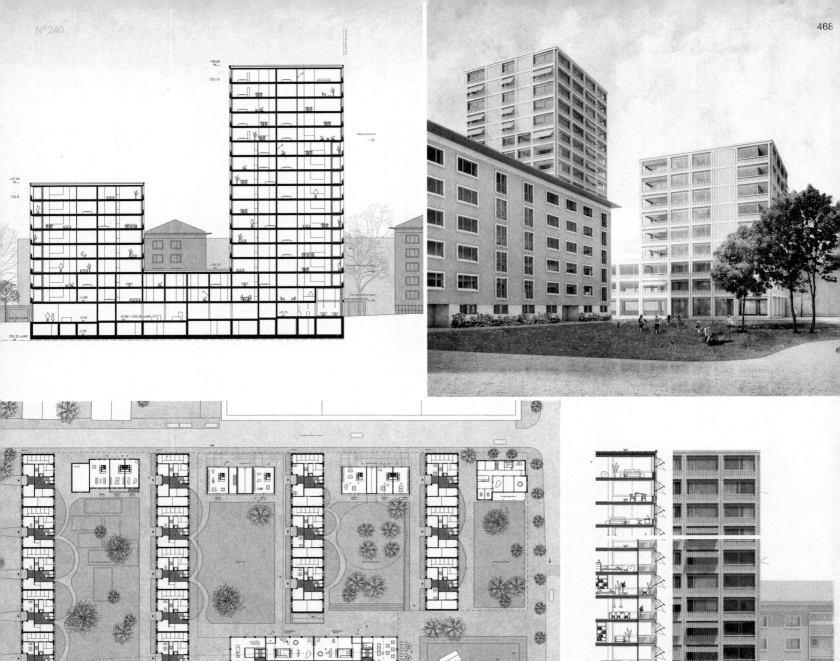
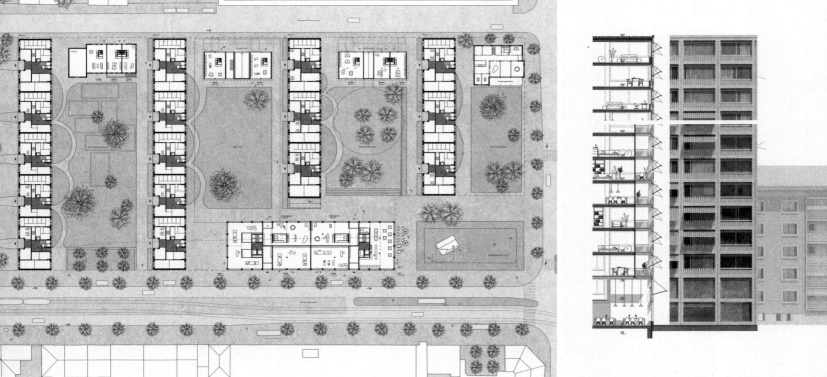
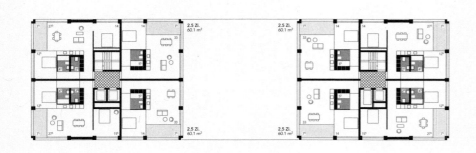

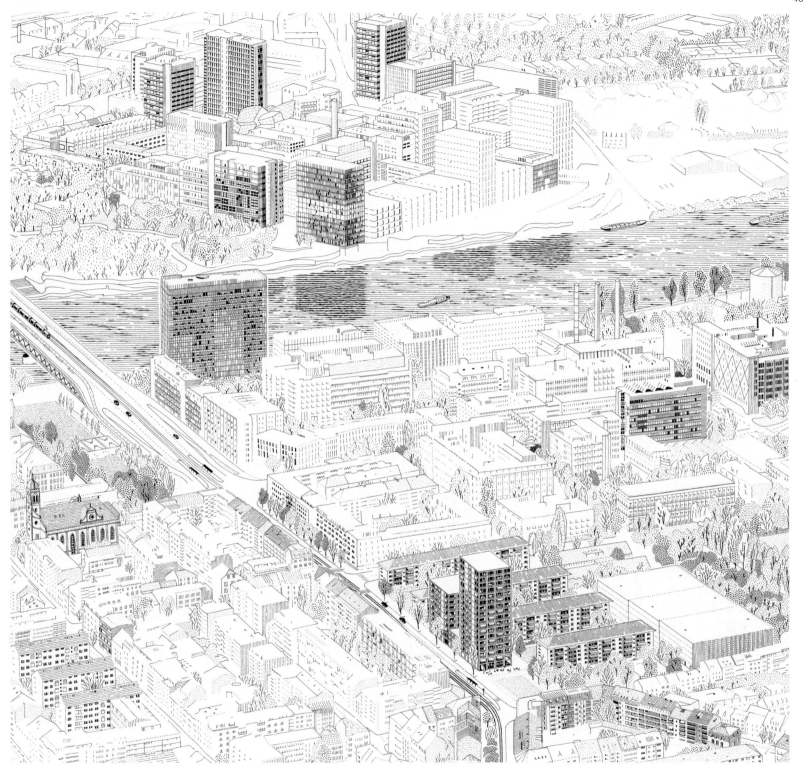

N° 241 High-rise Heuwaage

Location Basel, Switzerland **Type** New building **Status** Competition **Project phases** *Competition* 2017 **Client** Basellandschaftliche Pensionskasse, Liestal **Project data** *Lot size* 1,009 m² *Built-up area* 531 m² *Floor area* 13,942 m² (nach SIA 416) *Building volume* 37,476 m³ **Planners** *Architecture* Buchner Bründler Architekten, Basel *Building engineering* Schnetzer Puskas Ingenieure AG, Basel *Building technology* Waldhauser + Hermann AG, Münchenstein *Facade planning* Dr. Lüchinger + Meyer Bauingenieure AG, Zurich **Team** Buchner Bründler *Partners* Daniel Buchner, Andreas Bründler *Project leads* Laura Ehme, Jon Garbizu Etxaide *Participants* Aude Soffer, Jonas Schneck, Samuel Schubert

Impetus The analysis of the urban fabric clarifies the complexity of the incremental situation on Heuwaage. In order to create a continuous figure between Steinenvorstadt and Steinentorstrasse, the existing tower block and its annex enclosed the urban area inside the course of the River Birgis. The erection of the viaduct created a gateway situation, which since then has acted as a caesura, dividing Heuwaage from the urban environment.

With the renewal of the river course and the new Ozeanium building, an urban-spatial continuity is enabled, with the new high-rise building reinforcing the initial development.

Concept The realities of the site and the remit result in a slender architectural volume with an overarching role, establishing new urban spatial linkages. The basic quadratic form emphasizes the intersection between Birsigtal and Steinenring. In its geometry and proportions, the tower has a faint echo of the form of the historical Steinentor. Due to its clear stele form, the volume acts as the corner-front building of the row of buildings on Steinentor. At the connecting point to the linear development is an elevated second volume, whose open ground floor allows an urban-spatial crossing. At the termination of Steinenvorstadt is a large, spacious square, connecting Birsigparkplatz, with its dystopian feel, with the urban fabric, in turn establishing a spatial continuity toward the newly designed river area.

Implementation The constructive stratification creates an overtly structural volume, which enters into a dialogue with the surrounding elements, and with its recurrent idiom contrasts with the monolithic freestanding Ozeanium. Each side is arranged with two exterior columns with a crown of prefabricated horizontal girders spanned between them on each floor. The ribbon windows are structured by chromed, cross-shaped metal elements, which simultaneously hide the sound insulation ventilators. The mid-point positioning of the core creates a circumferential basic space, freely partitionable according to occupancy.

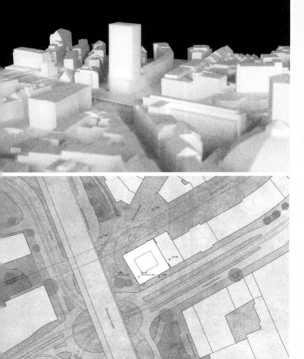

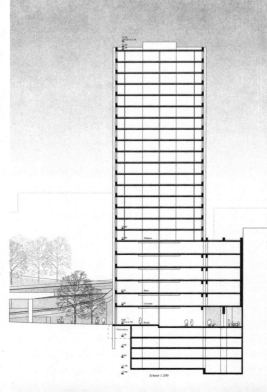

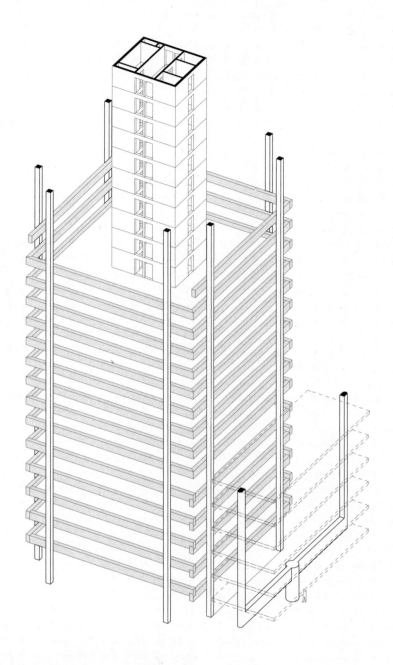

N° 243 Bahnhof Nord Kloten

Location Kloten, Switzerland **Type** Urban development **Status** Competition **Project phases** *Competition* 2017, 1st prize **Client** Stadt Kloten; SBB AG, Zurich; Pensionskasse der Zürcher Kantonalbank, Zurich; EMWE Immobilien AG, Zurich **Project data** *Lot size* 15,235 m² *Built-up area* 5,613 m² *Floor area* 52,667 m² (according to SIA 416) *Building volume* 183,731 m³ **Planners** *Architecture* Buchner Bründler Architekten, Basel *Building engineering* Dr. Lüchinger + Meyer Bauingenieure AG, Zurich *Landscape architecture* vetschpartner Landschaftsarchitekten AG, Zurich *Traffic planning* Planum Zurich, Zurich **Team Buchner Bründler** *Partners* Daniel Buchner, Andreas Bründler *Project lead* Bianca Kummer *Participants* Benjamin Hofmann, Omri Levy, Jonas Schneck

Impetus The vision for the future architectural development of the municipality of Kloten is retroactive densification. The authorities have expressed a key interest in enhancing the town center and creating attractive commercial and catering premises, as well as much-needed residential space, in the pedestrian zones. As an important arrival and departure point, Kloten railroad station is predestined to play a leading role, involving an extension of its central function by further bundling uses and services. This framework of a rethinking of the stations also encompasses examining the adjoining plots.

Concept The urban-planning concept is based on the themes of integration and cross-linkages, the newly created buildings and open spaces allowing a new center to emerge. The basic urban figure consists of a small number of landmark buildings, generating orientation and legibility and thus accentuating the importance of the station within the heterogeneous urban environment. The key open-air motif is a plaza boulevard that connects the bus station and the encounter zone to form a continuous overall expanse, also acting as a hinge between the train and bus stations and Lindenstrasse and Bahnhofstrasse. This intervention also serves to connect with the periphery developments on the Lirenächer.

Implementation The main SBB building acts simultaneously as a gateway and a bridge, the heightened entrance hall generating a welcoming gesture and creating an overview and visibility. The long, stretched volume spans the public space of the bus station, likewise anchoring the building in the urban environment. The second SBB site is occupied by a slim ribbon building that continues the themes of stacking and layering. A tripartite group of buildings results in a new overall configuration on the Lirenächer. The main bus and train building evolves in a structurally grained architectural language, variations of which can later determine the overall site. Homogenous, poured forms in in-situ concrete combine with joined elements in cast stone, brick, and glass blocks.

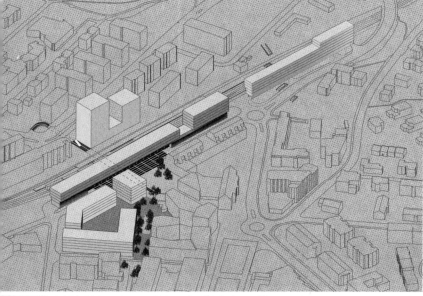

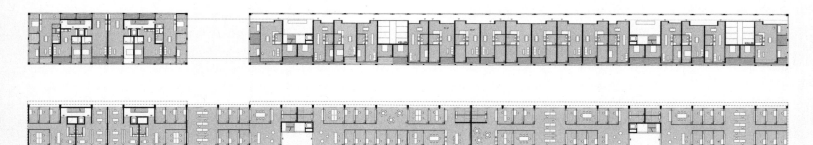

N° 244 Archaeology Museum Pully

Location Pully, Switzerland **Type** New building **Status** Competition **Project phases** *Competition* 2017 **Client** Ville de Pully **Project data** *Lot size* 12,954 m² *Built-up area* 1,516 m² *Floor area* 1,316 m² (nach SIA 416) *Building volume* 7,567 m³ **Planners** *Architecture* Buchner Bründler Architekten, Basel *Building engineering* ZPF Ingenieure AG, Basel *Landscape architecture* Maurus Schifferli Landschaftsarchitekt, Berne **Team Buchner Bründler** *Partners* Daniel Buchner, Andreas Bründler *Project leader* Aude Soffer *Participants* Jon Garbizu Etxaide, Samuel Schubert, Alexandra Galer, Tobias Kappelhoff

Impetus The site of the priory has been in continuous use for over 2,000 years now, a witness to Pully's rich history. The numerous building phases have evolved over the centuries to form a coherent architectural ensemble.

Considering its vital place in the landscape and the town's history, the authorities would like to inscribe the site with a new quality. This involves converting the priory building to serve as a town hall and the upgrading of the remains of the Roman villa and its frescos with the installation of an ArchéoLab.

Concept Taking the predominant geometric hierarchy, the design embraces the evolved town and continues and elaborates the architectural structure further. In its grain, the new ArchéoLab extends the ensemble of important public buildings. The corner of the quadrangle is architecturally defined by a landmark volume that corresponds to the size of the priory and frames the Obernai Square. The new ArchéoLab is set in front as a courtyard space, akin to a hortus conclusus. The new conception for the priory transforms the locality by directly addressing the town hall to the square. The deliberate program allows the overall complex to be publicly accessible.

Implementation In its exterior appearance, the new ArchéoLab consists of two parts: a massive ground-floor base that forms by emerging from the level of the square up toward the enclosing walls, and a tent-like roof rising above it. The low-lying roof is a pointer to the archeological excavations underneath, while its basic form acts as a reference to the hipped roofs of the key buildings around it and incorporates the institution in a row within the historical ensemble. Conceptually, the design combines the key architectural themes of protective archeological structures with the spatial complexity of purpose-made buildings. The simple form vocabulary is deliberately chosen, meaning that it can be erected in primary materials such as clay, wood, and glazed tiles, thus creating an authentic atmosphere for the historical artifacts.

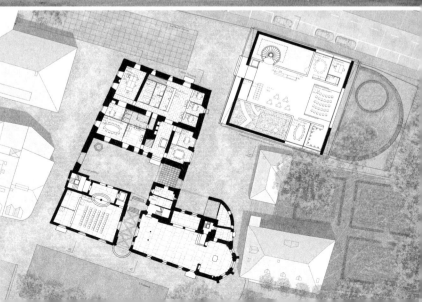

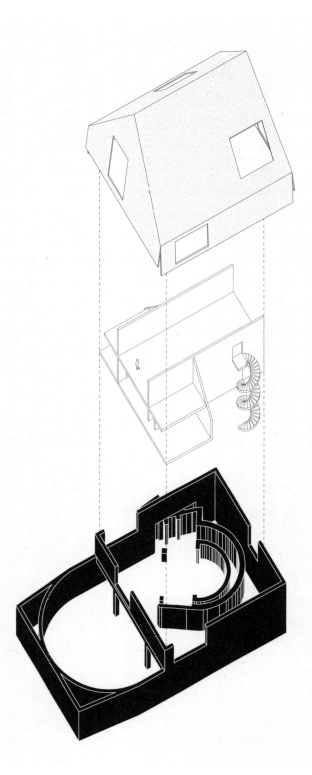

N° 246 Fürigen Area

Location Fürigen, Switzerland **Type** New building **Status** Competition **Project phases** Competition 2018, 1st prize **Client** Tellco Vorsorge AG, Baar **Project data** Lot size 15,666 m² *Built-up area* 4,630 m² *Floor area* 11,700 m² (according to SIA 416) *Building volume* 36,000 m³ **Planners** *Architecture* Buchner Bründler Architekten, Basel *Landscape architecture* August + Margrith Künzel Landschaftsarchitekten, Binningen **Team Buchner Bründler** *Partners* Daniel Buchner, Andreas Bründler *Project leads* Leonie Hagen, Jonas Virsik *Participants* Daniel Gómez Masana

Impetus Fürigen is situated on a mountain terrace above Stansstad, nestled among meadows dotted with fruit trees, forests, and the steeply looming Bürgenstock. The view over the Alpine panorama, Lake Lucerne, and into the distant landscape is breathtaking. In 1910 the Odermatt family erected an impressive hotel directly on the slope edge and closely adjacent to their own house, the hotel subsequently acting as a landmark in the predominantly agricultural surroundings. Extensions and a lido with a funicular railway connection expanded the complex. Due to a decline in tourism, the hotel was forced to close. The location is to be given a new future with a housing development in the spirit of the Wilhelminian era.

Concept Four quadratic volumes set at right angles to each other are positioned on the longitudinal mountain terrace, stretching out a field-like plot. The family house and the funicular station are preserved as witnesses to foster a sense of identity and are integrated into the new ensemble. A point building on the access road forms the prelude to the complex, while to longitudinal volumes flank the centrally situated historical farmhouse. The ensemble is concluded by a pavilion building with catering. Between the funicular and the restaurant pavilion is a large open space, providing a central access to all of the residential buildings. The apartments are individually orientated to two or three sides and are generously dimensioned. The varying gradations in height in the volume massings create a differentiated overall appearance.

Implementation In the first adaptation, the buildings were conceived as entirely timber constructions, composed using a differentiated tectonic; in the revised version they are formed as all-round structural frames in bright concrete. Meandering volumes are inscribed into the minimal-impact primary structures, activating a spatially deep intermediate layer. The recessed facade levels are built in wood, slenderly detailed and in nuanced color-contrast to the light-pigmented concrete.

N° 246

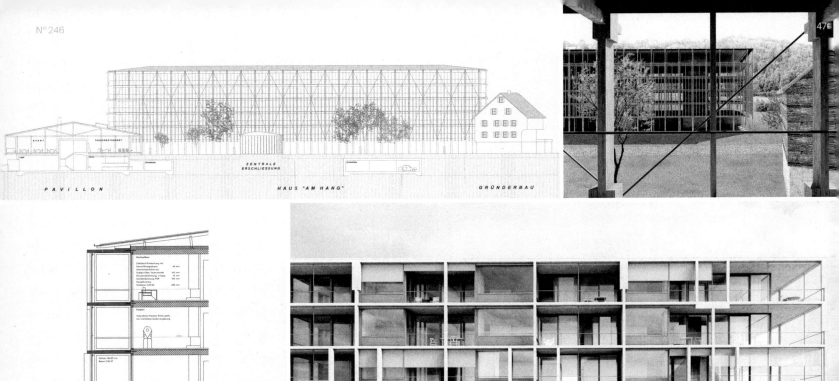

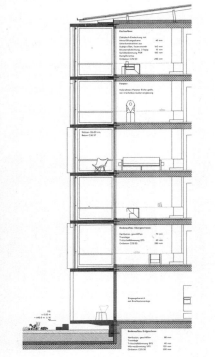

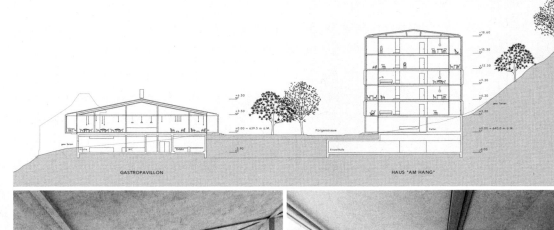

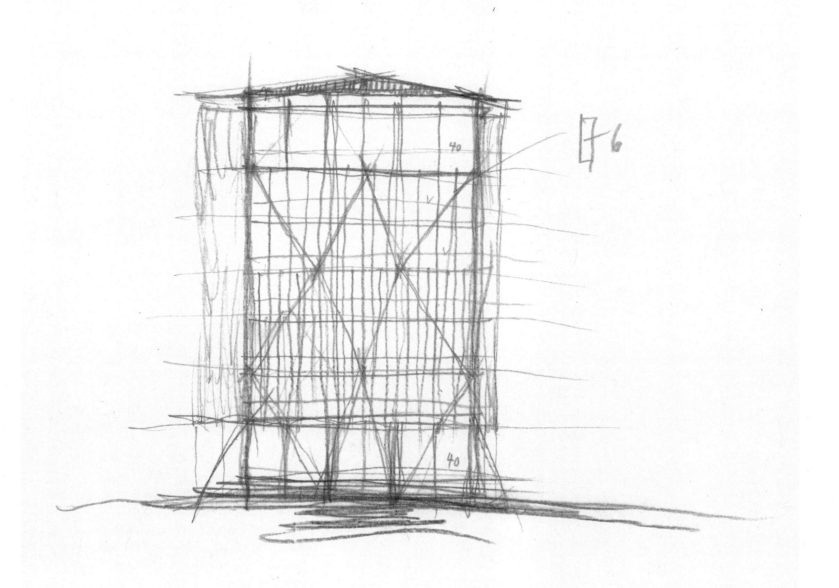

N° 247 Housing Development Rötiboden

Location Wädenswil, Switzerland **Type** New building **Status** Realization **Project phases** *Planning* 2016–2020 *Realization* 2021–2023 **Project initiator** Private **Client** BB Bauten AG, Basel **Project data** *Lot size* 2,804 m² *Built-up area* 878 m² *Floor area* 2,833 m² (according to SIA 416) *Building volume* 10,665 m³ **Planners** *Architecture* Buchner Bründler Architekten, Basel *Building engineering* Schnetzer Puskas Ingenieure AG, Basel *Building physics and acoustics* Bakus Bauphysik & Akustik GmbH, Basel *Building technology* Neukom Engineering AG, Adliswil *Electrical planning* Hans K. Schibli AG, Küsnacht *Facade planning* Christoph Etter Fassadenplanungen, Basel *Fire prevention planning* Quantum Brandschutz, Basel **Team Buchner Bründler** *Partners* Daniel Buchner, Andreas Bründler *Associate* Nick Waldmeier *Project leads* Bianca Kummer, Rebecca Borer, Andreas Widmer *Participants* Fabienne Saladin, Jon Garbizu Etxaide, Daniel Ebertshäuser, Charlotte Schwartz, Alexandra Galer, Jérémie Lysek, Lennart Cleemann

Impetus The Rötiboden is situated on a hillside terrace above Wädenswil's historical center and is mainly in agricultural use. The building for a child-support charity has marked the spot for over a century. In recent years the site has undergone extensive constructional densification, during which it has grown into a residential area.

The longitudinal free parcel of land on the edge of the hill is the site for a new housing project, focusing both on the quality of living provided by the exceptional views and on community living.

Concept Two volumes of rowed housing, slightly swiveled toward each other, are positioned along the profile of the hill, creating an expansive spatial span that forms the communal center of the complex. A retaining wall frames frontal space, slightly set back from the road, to make it a long courtyard. The two buildings consist of double-facing apartment units, organized across three floors. By deploying story-to-story offsets, the individual units dovetail together, the displacements allowing varied spatial proportions. A gradation in the ground floor slab opens the space up toward the lake.

Exterior areas, such as the roof terraces, the southerly gallery spaces, and the hillside meadow, are accessed via two large spiral staircases in the center and can be used communally. The attic-floor terraces facing the lake are for private use.

Implementation The primary structure, poured in in-situ concrete, is characterized by the pronounced cross-wall hierarchy. Heightened rooms generate a workroom character, while the spatial atmosphere is distinguished by mineral surfaces. Color-contrasting kitchen, bathroom, and stair modules stand freely, creating a forceful juxtaposition with the basic room constitutions. Facade surfaces of glazed folding doors in raw aluminum allow the rooms to be widely opened toward the terraces in front. The simple basic volumetry is enhanced by drop-arm awnings, generating a lively silhouette.

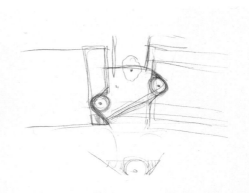

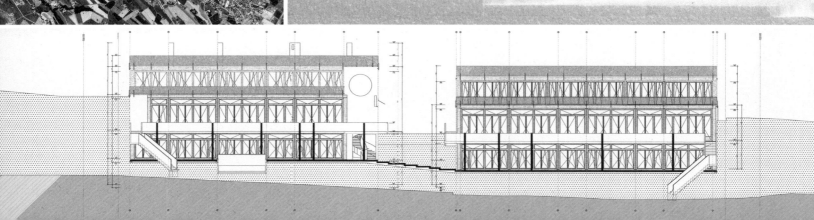

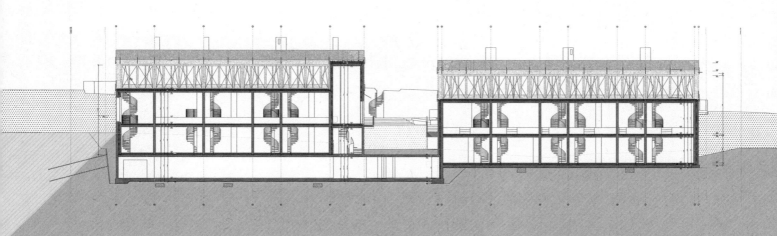
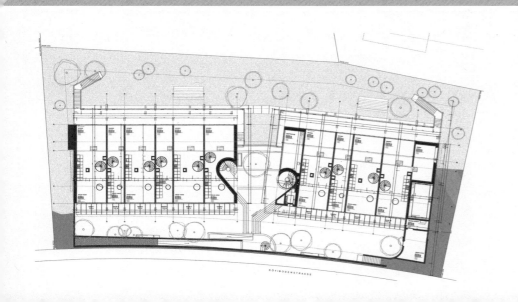

N° 248 Swiss Ambassador's Residence Algiers

Location Algiers, Algeria **Type** New building **Status** Competition **Project phases** *Competition* 2017, 4th rank, 3rd prize **Client** Bundesamt für Bauten und Logistik BBL, Berne **Project data** *Lot size* 5,313 m² *Built-up area* 267 m² *Floor area* 758 m² (according to SIA 416) *Building volume* 2,972 m³ **Planners** *Architecture* Buchner Bründler Architekten, Basel *Building engineering* Schnetzer Puskas Ingenieure AG, Basel *Building technology* Bogenschütz AG, Basel **Team Buchner Bründler** *Partners* Daniel Buchner, Andreas Bründler *Project leads* Jon Garbizu Etxaide, Aude Soffer *Participants* Tobias Kappelhoff

Impetus The Swiss Embassy in the Algerian capital is situated on a raised site in the middle of a district awash with vegetation. The grounds are stepped into the hillside topography on different levels. The park-like garden, lying behind a protective wall, provides a breathtaking view over the city out to the Mediterranean.

The somewhat outmoded ambassador's residence is to be replaced with a new building to meet growing demands and official concerns. The ambassador's chancellery was rebuilt some years ago, standing as an autonomous cube with an ornamentally structured facade deeper back in the complex.

Concept The spatial stipulations are evolved into a compact volume, representatively occupying the garden and orientated to all sides. In terms of its height progression, the volume relates to the overarching themes, simultaneously situated in balanced relation to the new chancellery. The garden can be experienced and used as a completely surrounding space. The design responds to the hermetic-looking chancellery with a typological openness that operates on all sides. The basic spatial framework is formed by a simple principle, consisting of a panel-like, rowed arrangement of identical modules. The enveloping walls are connected by primary-form openings, which also define the figurative appearance.

Implementation The stacking of the occupancies enables a clear organization—from the ostentatious rooms at garden level to the private living quarters of the residence. The insertion of the service areas into a middle story allows the unusual proportioning of the building and subdues its triple-story nature to give it a more generous impact. A hanging canopy on the main garden side creates a shaded intermediary zone, from which the garden can be explored. The newly paved paths are designed for open strolls. The verdant existing green space is restructured and extended.

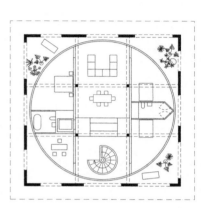

N° 250 Allschwil House

Location Allschwil, Switzerland **Type** Conversion and extension **Status** Realized **Project phases** *Planning* 2017–2018 *Realization* 2018–2019 **Client** Private **Project data** *Lot size* 925 m² *Built-up area* 195 m² *Floor area* 300 m² (according to SIA 416) *Building volume* 995 m³ **Planners** *Architecture and site management* Buchner Bründler Architekten, Basel *Building engineering* Jürg Merz Bauingenieur, Maisprach **Team** Buchner Bründler *Partners* Daniel Buchner, Andreas Bründler *Associate* Stefan Oehy *Project lead* Simone Braendle *Participants* Jon Garbizu Etxaide, Angelika Hinterbrandner

Impetus The house, built in the early 1960s, is situated in a quiet residential area in the municipality of Allschwil, within walking distance of the center. The exterior is characterized by its modest architectural volume with distinctive black single-pitch roofs and red windows. In 1968 the original building was expanded with a double-story living area, with additional annexes accompanying the conversion and extension of the garage. These interventions spatially and architecturally obscured the building volume, creating ruptures and interruptions. The modernization is intended to resolve these intersections and additionally meet the client's wish for a guest area.

Concept The additive principle is exploited to create a meandering spatial continuum that complements and concludes a further architectural element, namely the open garden annex. The interventions coalesce the various different house segments into an overall configuration without wholly ignoring the intersections.

Tall circumferential wooden panels, mounted on the existing enclosing walls, physically bind the previously unharmonious house parts together. The junction points are additionally accentuated and incorporated into the new spatial concept, while at the same time retaining their visibility as constructional fractures and architecturally non-functioning places.

Implementation The wooden paneling in dark maritime pine is a key motif in the new interventions, stretching from the living and dining area with the entrance area to the new annex, which serves as a guestroom. In the parents' wing vis-à-vis, the paneling also appears on the ceiling and floor, cocooning the entire room in homogenous wood. As a glass-and-concrete structure, the annex possesses its own appearance. In its size and arrangement it establishes a direct correlation with the existing composition of the volumes and continues them naturally. The protective envelope in cast-in-situ concrete breaks with the glazed cube form and creates a mineral spatial shell. An axially placed, circular-shaped opening generates both a focused view and a distinctive gestural form into and from the garden. The window openings are enlarged and supplemented; the once inwardly inverted living space is now orientated more pointedly to the surroundings. By freeing up a core area, with the kitchen and a bathroom, an open spatial fabric emerges. In the other room areas the boundary between the old structure and the new fixtures is similarly fluid. The spatial impact is complemented by the green-coated cement floor, which was stripped bare and added to. As a double-height main space, the living room unites the two levels. A pictorial collage of basic geometric forms, directly applied to the gallery wall, deepens the interpretive planes.

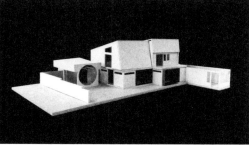

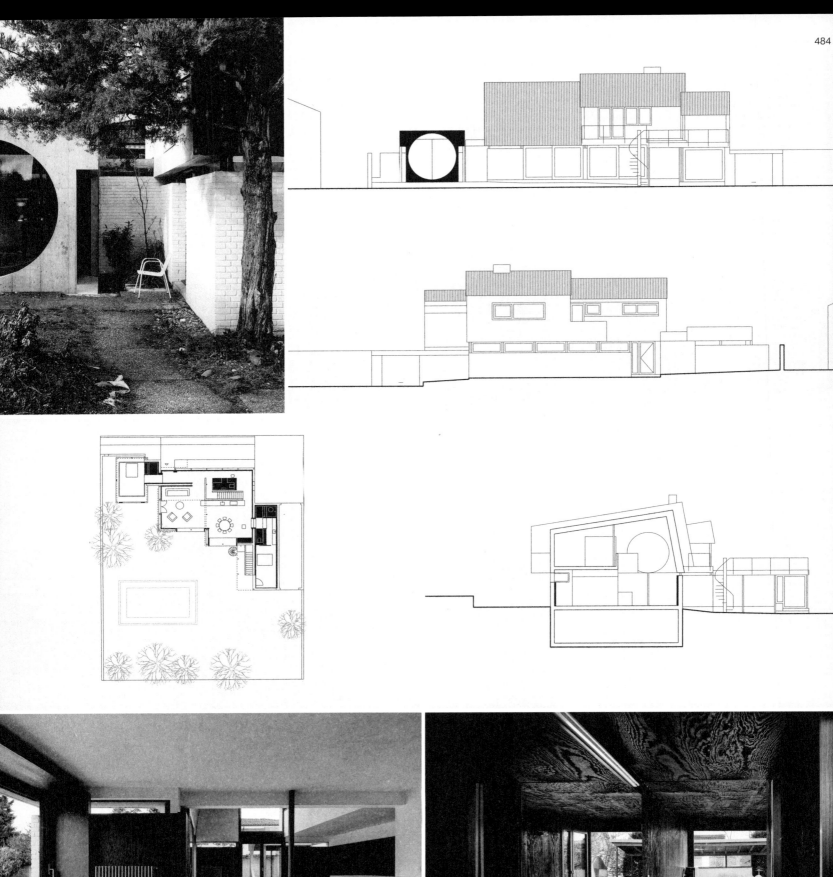

N° 252 Clinic Arlesheim Campus

New building — Further Buildings and Projects

Location Arlesheim, Switzerland **Type** New building **Status** Competition **Project phases** *Competition* 2018 **Client** Klinik Arlesheim AG, Arlesheim **Project data** *Lot size* 19,245 m² *Built-up area* 2,951 m² *Floor area* 18,474 m² (according to SIA 416) *Building volume* 72,568 m³ **Planners** *Architecture* Buchner Bründler Architekten, Basel *Building engineering* ZPF Ingenieure AG, Basel *Landscape architecture* Studio Karst GmbH, Basel *Building technology* Stokar + Partner AG, Basel *Fire prevention planning* Quantum Brandschutz GmbH, Basel *Hospital planning* PEG Planungsgesellschaft für Einrichtungen des Gesundheitswesens mbH, Karlsruhe *Building art* Till Velten, Basel **Team Buchner Bründler** *Partners* Daniel Buchner, Andreas Bründler *Project lead* Aude Soffer *Participants* Miriam Stierle, Kevin de Roeck, Florian Marenbach, Tobias Kappelhoff

Impetus The municipality of Arlesheim is situated at the foot of the Gempen. The predominantly open settlement layout allows heavily vegetated open spaces, similar in the broadest sense to a dense garden landscape. Individual prominent buildings, such as churches, castles, and palaces, as well as the Rudolf Steiner buildings in neighboring Dornach, stand out as landmarks in the scattered settlement pattern. The park-like overall complex of the Ita-Wegmann-Clinic seamlessly interweaves itself with the surroundings. A new building is designed to replace the outdated clinic building while preserving the adjacent freestanding buildings, such as Ita Wegmann's house and the therapy center, their individuality giving the future campus a special character.

Concept A building volume with an organic primary form is situated in the center of the complex, set in the main topographical thrust of the hill. The form consists of three intersecting cylindrical volumes, all of them with incised polygonal courtyards. The rounded, organic form frees the building up from its neighbors and reinforces the stand-alone effect in the center of the campus complex. At the same time, the fluid contours merge with the natural, softly formed landscape. The park surrounding the building is conceived as a web of fields of plants and organically formed paths. Architecture and landscape unite to create a holistic whole.

Implementation The curved form allows a radial orientation and gradually expands the interior spaces toward the outside. The typological segmentation creates an expansive relationship to the park, further reinforced by the ceiling-high windows. The additive basic form engenders a clearly legible arrangement and serves to allocate the various functional areas. The differing courtyards become reference spaces and create an orientation across the three main levels and beyond.

The atmosphere is distinguished by the primary materials wood and concrete, both of them enabling manual fabrication and giving a corresponding visual distinction.

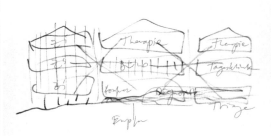

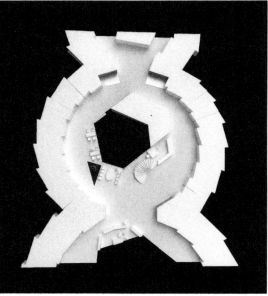
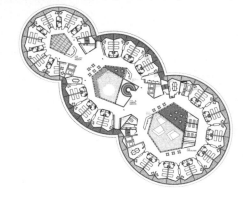

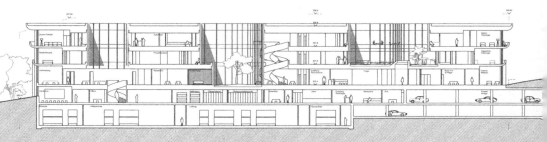

N° 253 Papieri Area — New building and conversion

Location Cham, Switzerland **Type** New building and conversion **Status** Planning **Project phases** *Competition* 2018, 1st prize Kesselhaus *Planning* 2020–2021 *Realization* 2021–2022 **Client** Cham Immobilien AG, Cham **Project data** *Lot size* 8,300 m² *Built-up area* 1,770 m² *Floor area* 14,355 m² (according to SIA 416) *Building volume* 56,677 m³ **Planners** *Architecture* Buchner Bründler Architekten, Basel *Building engineering* Schnetzer Puskas Ingenieure AG, Basel *Building technology* Hans Abicht AG, Zug *Fire prevention planning* Quantum Brandschutz GmbH, Basel **Team Buchner Bründler** *Partners* Daniel Buchner, Andreas Bründler *Associate, planning* Stefan Oehy *Project lead, competition* Magdalena Stadler *Project leads, planning* Jon Garbizu Etxaide, Stefan Herrmann *Competition participants* Holger Harmeier, Alexandra Galer, Daniel Gómez Masana *Planning participants* Markus Leixner

Impetus The closed paper factory on the northern edge of Cham is to be developed to become a new district. Since paper production began here, the works site has continually grown, with a master plan regulating the changes in urban planning. The ensemble of the boiler house, porter's lodge, locomotive shed, and the calender building remain intact as a prelude to the site, extended by a single high-rise block. The heritage-listed boiler house occupies a central position on the site and is to be restructured. By removing the kettles, the interior becomes a large, open hall-like space intended for special events and uses in the future.

Concept Based on the analysis of the existing spatial structure, the differentiated concept entails a partial reuse and spatial additions. The base of the boiler house is to be widely opened toward the square, publicly accessible as an "open salon." Via a laterally glazed roof opening, a double-story central area is created, allowing direct sightlines to the large open space above. A free-standing steel construction with intermediate levels is integrated in the former boiler room, in turn containing inserted glazed spatial volumes, accessed via open stairs in order to reinforce the zenithal light diffusion.

The atrium-like interspace communicates the spatial expansiveness and the industrial character of the historical building, simultaneously acting as an intermediate climatic zone.

Implementation The protected facade is largely preserved. New openings providing access and light, blending with the existing composition. The large factory windows are fronted with a new glazed layer, enabling the retention of the delicately subdivided frames with their original panes. The new architectural insertions foster a flexible work atmosphere, with special areas in the preserved spatial zones supplementing the amenity scope. Containers on the open-plan ground floor, which houses restaurant and retail occupancies, allow the local salon to be independently and temporarily staged.

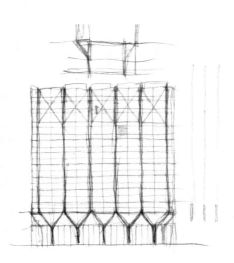

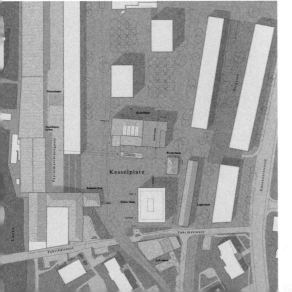

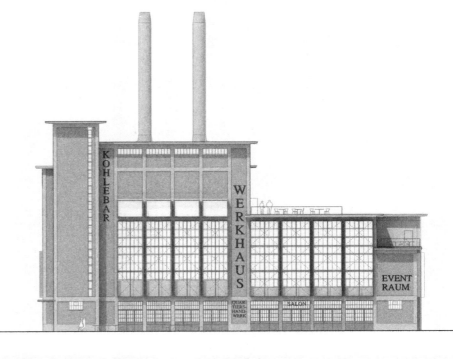

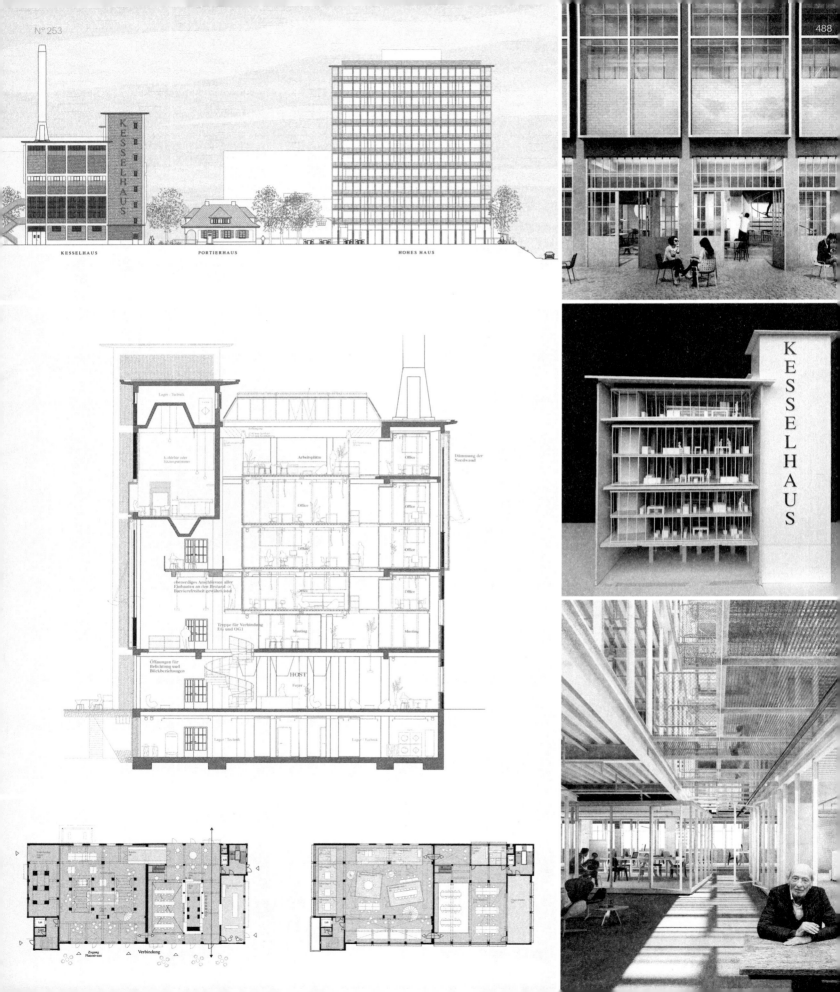

N° 254 Gruner + Jahr Development — New building — Further Buildings and Projects

Location Hamburg, Germany **Type** New building **Status** Competition **Project phases** *Competition* 2018 **Client** HIH Projektentwicklung GmbH, Hamburg **Project data** *Lot size* 15,200 m² *Built-up area* 9,031 m² *Floor area* 54,696 m² (according to DIN 277) *Building volume* 213,821 m³ **Planners** *Architecture* Buchner Bründler Architekten, Basel **Team Buchner Bründler** *Partners* Daniel Buchner, Andreas Bründler *Project lead* Jon Garbizu Etxaide *Participants* Nina Kleber, Tobias Kappelhoff

Impetus The project involves the erection of a new headquarters for the distinguished publishing company directly bordering the newly laid out Lohse Park next to the former Hannoversche railroad station. The new building is deliberated relocated in Hamburg's HafenCity to make it part of the emerging media cluster in the southeastern part of the city center and to profit from its innovational impulses. To the rear of the plot, the Oberhafen Bridge railroad embankment forms a spatial termination, meaning the building is correspondingly addressed toward the park and is to contain other public-related occupancies.

Concept The architectural concept rests on linking two basic spatial-structural principles: on the one hand, an optimized floor plan adapted to a workplace economy; and on the other, a multi-story base zone, which leads to a central, open main hall, and which, via its archetypal special form figuratively relates the wide range of uses with each other and spatially interlinks them.

The uniformly uninterrupted contour of the roof makes the building into a robust urban cornerstone, which can be understood as part of the overarching block structures, its dimensions and the exposed corner position simultaneously establishing it as independently freestanding.

Implementation In terms of appearance, the building is reduced to only a few materials, generating a calm overall effect. The outer expression is determined by a restrained tectonic composition. Supports and slabs in light-pigmented concrete appear as a basic foreground motif, forming an all-round structural framework. Inserted into it are prefabricated brick elements, each set at midpoint, creating a second material layer and organizing the facade further. With its rhombic, stepped primary geometry, the project echoes the klinker expressionist style. The interplay of the two structural levels lends the facade a plasticity and variety. The hall structure punctures the unified facade arrangement, creating a figurative entrance and an opening gesture toward the park.

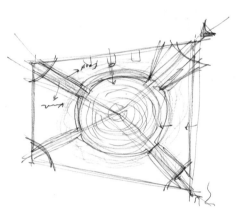
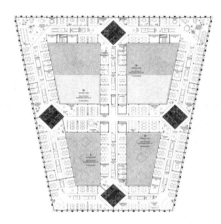

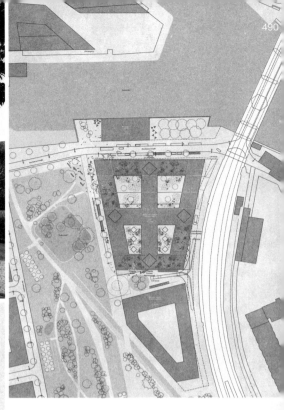
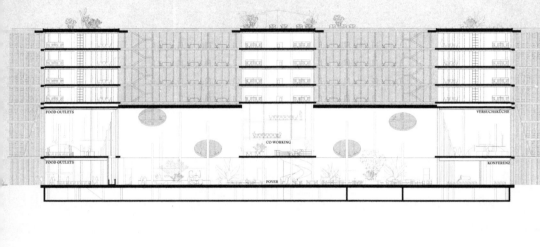

N° 255 Forum UZH

Location Zurich, Switzerland **Type** New building **Status** Competition **Project phases** *Competition* 2018, 2nd prize **Client** Bildungsdirektion des Kantons Zürich and University of Zurich **Project data** *Lot size* 22,224 m² *Built-up area* 9,617 m² *Floor area* 70,921 m² (according to SIA 416) *Building volume* 348,573 m³ **Planners** *Architecture* Buchner Bründler Architekten, Basel *General management and construction management* Rapp Architekten AG, Münchenstein *Building engineering* Schnetzer Puskas Ingenieure AG, Basel *Landscape architecture* antón & ghiggi landschaft architektur GmbH, Zurich *Building physics* Gartenmann Engineering AG, Zurich *Building technology* Hans Abicht AG, Zug *Electrical planning* HKG Engineering AG, Pratteln *Facade planning* Christoph Etter Fassadenplanungen, Basel *Fire prevention planning* Quantum Brandschutz GmbH, Basel **Team Buchner Bründler** *Partners* Daniel Buchner, Andreas Bründler *Associate* Nick Waldmeier *Project leads* Miriam Stierle, Holger Harmeier *Participants* Nina Kleber, Daniel Gómez Masana, Kevin de Roeck, Tobias Kappelhoff, Florian Marenbach, Roman Hauser **Publications** Forum UZH Zürich Zentrum, hochparterre.wettbewerbe 01 (2019), 36–37 • Andreas Kohne, Frappierende Platzidee, Tec21 7–8 (2019), 8–10

Impetus Together with ETH Zurich and the University Hospital, the University of Zurich forms the City Campus university site. Embedded between the hospital park, a small-scale residential and business area, and the "cultural mile" along Rämistrasse with the collegiate building by Curiel and Moser and the main ETH building by Gottfried Semper, the plan is to erect an internationally attractive learning and research center on the prominent corner site. Students, researchers, and the city's population are to be offered inspiring surroundings with great atmospheric qualities, fostering exchange and interaction.

Concept A prominent plastic volume adopts the form of the Wilhelminian-era university buildings, at the same time developing a differentiated local proportionality through steppings and stackings. The building's basic height corresponds to that of its neighbors, elevated at points by volumetric additions. The graduation concept mirrors the functional and spatial organization of the building. In its proportions and figurative nature, the building assumes a visual ascendancy, establishing new correlations in the immediate urban environment. Its dissolved volumetry and fine materiality establishes a dialogue with the park. The facade surfaces are glazed with panes in different formats and embossings to create a tactile form and a harmonious colorfulness.

Implementation Various spatial typologies, orientated on the allocations and organization set in the program, are stacked in a legible clarity. As an open, radially accessible central space, the Forum allows a direct interaction with the main uses. The auditoriums and the arched-like circulation area in between are directly reachable via four round exits. Next to the circular atrium are two levels with a learning landscape and a library, extended via an encompassing intermediate climatic zone. Above it, the sports area starts, also accessible from outside via two sets of spiral stairs. The sports halls are contained in the vertical additions, possessing a direct connection to the roof garden. The research floor spaces are vertically organized to the rear of the complex.

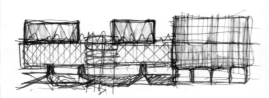

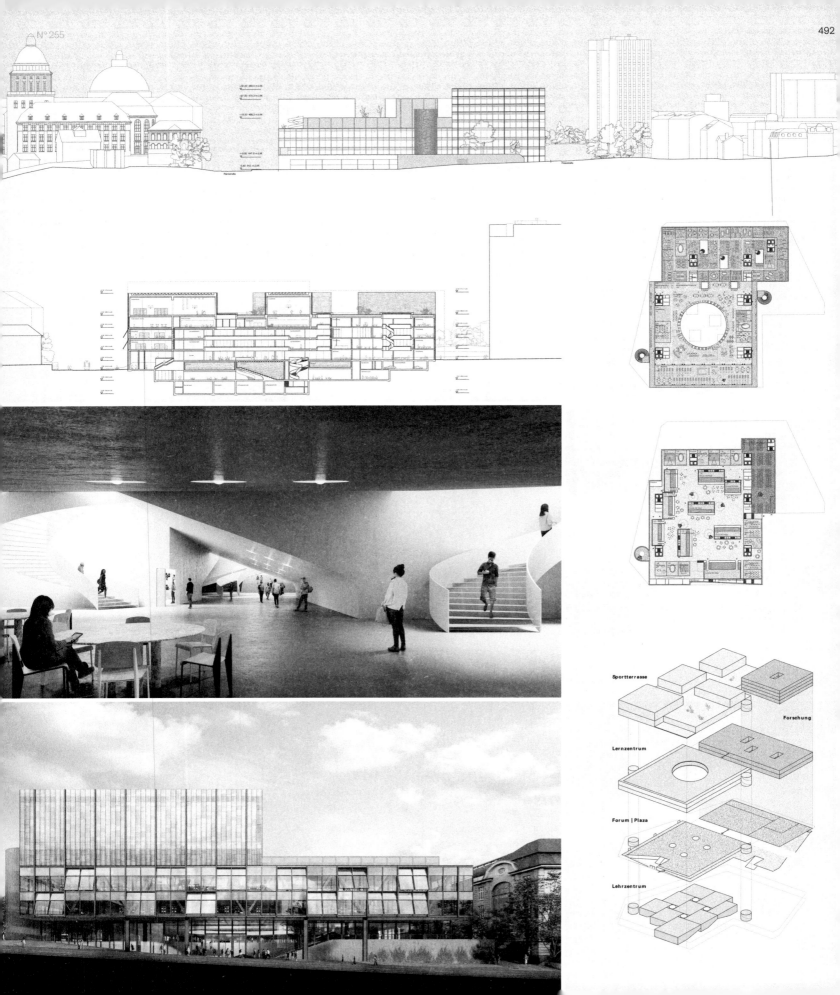

N° 262 Pratteln Municipal Center

Location Pratteln, Switzerland **Type** New building **Status** Competition **Project phases** *Competition* 2018 **Client** Einwohnergemeinde Pratteln **Project data** *Lot size* 4,048 m² *Built-up area* 1,480 m² *Floor area* 8,925 m² (according to SIA 416) *Building volume* 30,246 m³ **Planners** *Architecture* Buchner Bründler Architekten, Basel *Building engineering* Schnetzer Puskas Ingenieure AG, Basel *Landscape architecture* vetschpartner Landschaftsarchitekten AG, Zurich **Team** Buchner Bründler *Partners* Daniel Buchner, Andreas Bründler *Project lead* Miriam Stierle *Participants* Raphaël Kadid, Gerson Egerter, Jérémie Lysek

Impetus   The municipal administration's building complex, which is to be replaced, is situated on a developed field-like level of terrain between the historical village center and the railroad area. Directly adjacent is the Grossmatt school, an imposing testimony to architectural Historicism, which dominates the quadrangle between Burggartenstrasse and Schlossstrasse with its freestanding nature and classic arrangement with a prominent hipped roof. The school area is enclosed by rows of trees along the street. Other prominent buildings, such as the medieval castle and the old gym hall, occupy central stage in the basic pattern. The fragment of a Wilheminian era linear development creates an atmospheric unity with the school.

Concept   Deploying a single volume, its size and proportions relating to the school, generates a spatial clasping effect between the two link roads. Together with the historical school building, a spatial sequence is created, making the new volume appear naturally incorporated in its heterogeneous surroundings.   The displacement of the two volumetric segments, the administration and the library, generates an independent locational identity. A story-by-story backward staggering creates a prominent pyramid form, giving the civic building a unique impact. The continuation of the bordering vegetation accentuates the quadrangular square.

Implementation   The structural volume translates the organizational spatial hierarchy. The constructional concept is based on a frame construction with distribution levels on top. The visible divisional supports in the long facade dissipate the loads in respective structural fields. The access floor and the mezzanine are integrated into a heightened base, while the other floors step back, story by story. Copper-sheet-covered facade elements appear as horizontal bands, in turn transferring a plastic depth graduation into the overall pyramidal form, with the bands interconnected to form a fine lattice structure by means of guide rails for the exterior shading devices.

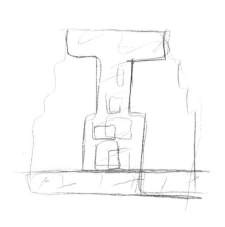

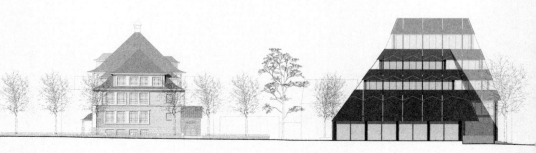

N° 264 Swiss Embassy Addis Ababa

Location Addis Ababa, Ethiopia **Type** New building **Status** Competition **Project phases** *Competition* 2018, 5th prize **Client** Bundesamt für Bauten und Logistik BBL, Berne **Project data** *Lot size* 5,668 m² *Built-up area* 987 m² *Floor area* 2,051 m² (according to SIA 416) *Building volume* 8,065 m³ **Planners** *Architecture* Buchner Bründler Architekten, Basel **Team** Buchner Bründler *Partners* Daniel Buchner, Andreas Bründler *Project lead* Magdalena Stadler *Participants* Luzi Speth **Publications** Neubau Schweizerische Botschaft, Addis Abeba, hochparterre.wettbewerbe 02 (2019), 86–87

Impetus The outmoded Swiss embassy in Addis Abada is to be replaced, simultaneously allowing an optimal reorganization of the structures and operations of the Swiss delegation.   Access to the site in the western part of the Ethiopian capital is via Jimma Road. The sloping terrain necessitates a clear allocation of the occupancies at the different levels.

Concept The residency and the chancellery are set in the sloping topography as two simple volumes, slightly swiveled away from each other. Complementarily materialized, recurring elements simultaneously create a dialogue. The filigree construction of the residency, built out of sustainably grown timber, serves as a counterweight to the heaviness of the chancellery's clay walls.

The ensemble of the two main buildings is inspired by traditional Ethiopian building methods, with a main accent on the local materials clay and wood. Overlapping awnings, verandas, and roofed galleries protect against the rain and provide shade. Large window openings allow the outdoor and indoor spaces to freely flow into each other.   The compact volume design allows the surrounding garden to be experienced as a large, continuous space, divided into different functional areas.

Implementation The embassy grounds are entered via a small lockable forecourt. A ponderous ring of clay walls with large openings houses the offices and at the same time defines the security zone. The open galleries, in a lightweight wooden construction, act as access and create informal locations for exchanges.   The residency intersects with the chancellery at the same elevation, whereby with the sloping terrain the building rises from the ground more and more, gradually elevating the viewer to an eyelevel with the dense encompassing greenery.   The skeleton construction out of local juniper wood accommodates the private and ceremonial rooms. Circumferential opening doors and windows, an inner courtyard, and the frontal veranda layer create strong connections with the outdoor space.

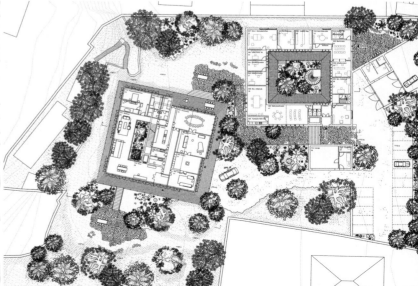

N° 267 Culture Center Alpenstrasse Interlaken

Location Interlaken, Switzerland **Type** New building **Status** Competition **Project phases** Competition 2019, 1st prize **Client** Gemeinde Interlaken **Project data** Lot size 19,831 m² *Built-up area* 1,305 m² *Floor area* 6,448 m² (according to SIA 416) *Building volume* 18,543 m³ **Planners** *Architecture* Buchner Bründler Architekten, Basel *Building engineering* Schnetzer Puskas Ingenieure AG, Basel *Landscape architecture* Antón Landschaft, Zurich *Building technology* Bogenschütz AG, Basel *Fire prevention planning* Quantum Brandschutz GmbH, Basel **Team Buchner Bründler** *Partners* Daniel Buchner, Andreas Bründler *Project lead* Magdalena Stadler *Participants* Holger Harmeier, Signe Veinberga, Gerson Egerter, Daniel Gómez Masana, Oscar Faivre

Impetus Since the foudning of the Interlacus Cloister, the Höhenmatte has played an important role in the history of the Bödeli. The preservation of the grassland in its original form mirrors its historical importance. Despite the continual developmental densification around it, individual buildings rising above the green belt continue to define its appearance. Both the hotels and the spa hall, as well as the palace complex, are all architectural structures that have grown over the years. The school complex, designed in 1962 by Hans Andres, has a similar incremental compositional appearance. The freestanding aula is to be extended or replaced by a new building with additional uses.

Concept The existing building ensemble of the school complex is treated as a starting point for a new compositional interpretation. The aula acts as a frontage building, to which two sub-buildings are added as expansions and additions. Their form evolves from the spatial and formal circumstances: on the one hand, the triangular volume of the library is integrated carefully into the landscape with its protected tree canopy; on the other, an intermediate building boasts a triangular roof volume that only linearly tangents with the adjacent buildings.

This arrangement means that the solitaire effect of the aula remains intact. In their vertical divisions, the sub-segments converge, creating a continuous overall form at ground level.

Implementation The meandering complex produces an entrance courtyard, encompassed on three sides, providing it with an appropriate locational identity and serving as a shielded outdoor area. The central building is conceived as an open hall and acts as a foyer providing access to the individual sub-segments. The essential formulation of the main space of the aula is largely preserved. The rooms for the library, adult-education, and special classes are arranged floorwise in the triangular volume. In terms of materialization, the palette of concrete, cast-stone, and large-format oak-veneer panels is continued and supplemented.

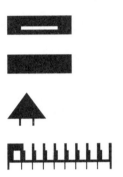

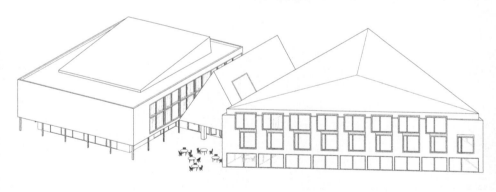
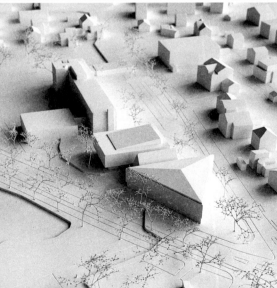
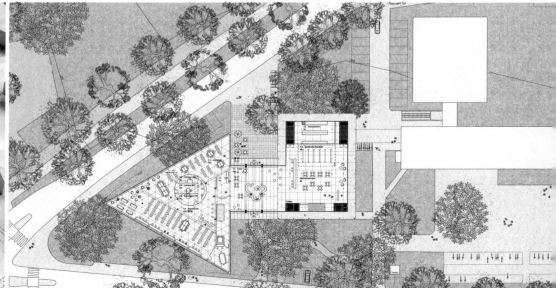

N° 268 Laurenz-Carré Cologne

New building — Further Buildings and Projects

Location Cologne, Germany **Type** New building **Status** Competition **Project phases** *Competition* 2019 **Client** Gerchgroup AG, Düsseldorf **Project data** *Lot size* 3,054 m² *Built-up area* 2,868 m² *Floor area* 17,954 m² (according to DIN 277) *Building volume* 72,752 m³ **Planners** *Architecture* Buchner Bründler Architekten, Basel **Team Buchner Bründler Partners** Daniel Buchner, Andreas Bründler *Project lead* Holger Harmeier *Participants* Raphaël Kadid, Florian Marenbach, Fabian Moser

Impetus The Laurenz-Carré is situated in the middle of Cologne's historical old town and is to be developed to become an urban and mixed-occupancy district. With its northern end adjoining Am Hof street, it forms part of the Roncalli-Platzwand vis-à-vis the south facade of Cologne Cathedral. Additionally, its location at the north end of Unter Goldschmied street means that the area lies at the gateway to the Via Culturalis, the cultural district running north–south between the cathedral and the St. Maria im Kapitol church.

Concept Modulated on the primary urban structure, a precise counterpart consisting of two sub-buildings is evolved, which act situationally. The grain and proportions of the architectural volume create a direct dialogue with the surrounding block buildings, nevertheless generating an independent urban-spatial sequence in relation to Roncalliplatz and the Via Culturalis. By means of its tectonic structural motifs, the building refers to its historical neighbors. The building segment orientated to Roncalliplatz is understood as a counterpart to the Domhotel and the newly emerging Kurienhaus. To the south, on Grossen Budengasse, the Senatshotel is taken as the key reference point. The building runs along the perimeter lines, redefining the townscape and creating clear spatial edges.

Implementation The arrangement of the six-story main volume is determined by a mineral primary structure. The floors are set in pairs in a giant order, the over-sized formation creating a reduced visual story arrangement.

A sculpturally tinged form element serves as a key motif in the facade composition, varying in width and concave filleting, thus creating a lesena-to-pilaster-like effect. The overlaying of the recurrent primary constellation with the variable concave form creates an animated appearance. In the south-facing building segment, the employment of the same form logic creates jams arranged room-for-room. Opaque window vents in different positions expand the basic variation.

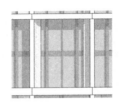
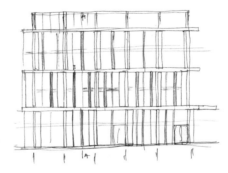

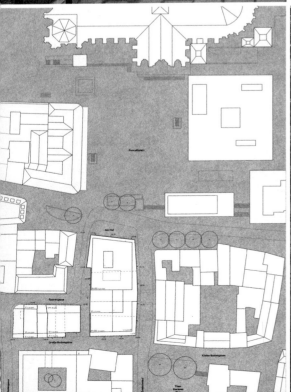

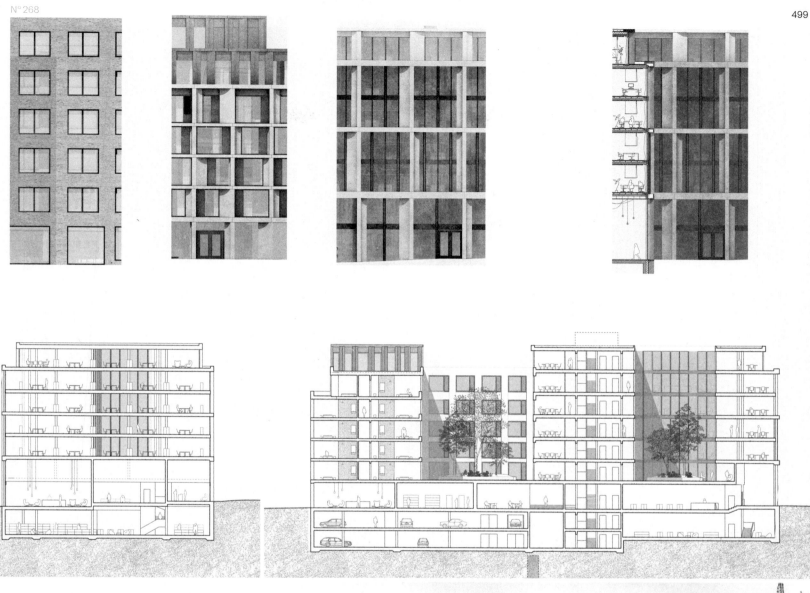
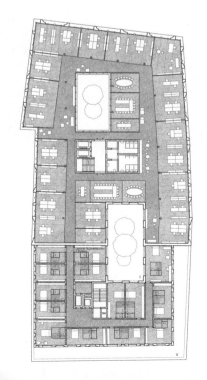

N° 270 Banque Pictet

Location Geneva, Switzerland **Type** New building **Status** Competition **Project phases** *Competition* 2019 **Client** Banque Pictet & Cie SA, Geneva **Project data** *Lot size* 29,201 m² *Built-up area* 4,834 m² *Floor area* 79,237 m² (according to SIA 416) *Building volume* 306,229 m³ **Planners** *Architecture* Buchner Bründler Architekten, Basel *Building engineering* Schnetzer Puskas Ingenieure AG, Basel **Team Buchner Bründler** *Partners* Daniel Buchner, Andreas Bründler *Project lead* Raphaël Kadid *Participants* Benjamin Olschner, Aude Soffer, Gerson Egerter, Luzi Speth

Impetus The urban-planning dimensions aimed for in the transformation site Praille – Acacias – Vernets (PAV) to the west of the core of Geneva are manifested in the scheduled large-scale high-rises in the Pont-Rouge zone. Further projected developmental stages involve a cluster of towers along the Route des Jeunes. Based on a zoning plan, a large volume is to be built for the Pictet Bank to give the institution—which prides itself on long-term values—a representative address and make it more widely visible.

Concept The overall architectural volume of the project, with a base segment and a vertical volume, is adjusted in ratio to its two parts, meaning that the base and high-rise elements proportionally correspond. A double-story arcade generates a facade layering facing the Route des Acacias and accentuates the main entrance.

A structural framework with a reiterative hierarchy divides the facades on all sides. The landmark character is defined by continuous, vertical, conical circular columns. Materialized in rammed clay, they create an archaic effect, whereby the building still appears open and transparent thanks to the floor-to-ceiling glazing. This idea of an open bank is also consistently realized in the interior spatial organization, facilitated by the free arrangement of the circulation cores, in turn producing a overall spatially integrative effect—a basic base-and-tower typology that generates an uninterrupted spatial-sequence flow.

Implementation The exterior appearance is defined by the distinctive tectonic construction. Laced columns in concrete with shell-like cladding elements in rammed clay are a focal motif, tied together by wraparound cornices in dark-patina concrete. Differently recessed elements serve to distinguish the tectonic division further.

The openings are equipped with full-surface glazing, while the light-metal frames are predominantly masked by insets. Along with the greened courtyard area is a verdantly planted garden area on the roof level of the base segment for staff and visitors.

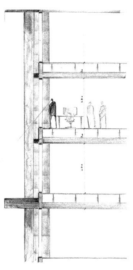

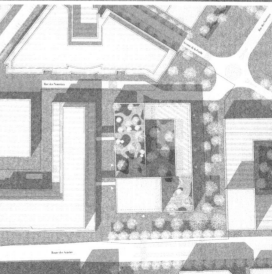

N° 271 Stiftung Blindenheim — New building — Further Buildings and Projects

Location Basel, Switzerland **Type** New building **Status** Competition **Project phases** Competition 2019 **Client** Stiftung Blindenheim Basel **Project data** *Lot size* 2,392 m² *Built-up area* 1,395 m² *Floor area* 9,029 m² (according to SIA 416) *Building volume* 32.406 m³ **Planners** *Architecture* Buchner Bründler Architekten, Basel *Landscape architecture* Berchtold.Lenzin Landschaftsarchitekten, Basel *Fire prevention planning* Quantum Brandschutz GmbH, Basel **Team Buchner Bründler** *Partners* Daniel Buchner, Andreas Bründler *Project lead* Magdalena Stadler *Participants* Signe Veinberga

Impetus   The Stiftung Blindenheim, founded in 1896, is housed on Kohlenberggasse. In the past situated on the edge of the city, the Kohlenberg district has become particularly established as an educational quarter. The local landmarks are the Leonhard High School and the vocational college by Hans Bernoulli from 1916, which is directly adjacent to the home for the blind. The urban-planning pattern is heterogeneous, starting as a sparsely settled hill location with a lot of greenery, and evolving to sections of perimeter block developments interspersed with freestanding school buildings. The main building of the home for the blind from the 1970s is to be replaced with a new one to enable reorganization.

Concept   A polygonal volume is set parallel to the adjoining building lines, acting as a contextual counterpart. Due to the compact organization of the program over five full and two stepped stories, both the home for the blind and the vocational college are given an individual status.   The detachment from the neighboring Bernoulli building allows the porosity of the former development to be reestablished, while the urban setting interlocks with the school's green area on the courtyard side. The site spanned out between the buildings becomes a public square—an arbiter between the school gardens and the city, the home for the blind and the public.

Implementation   The building is conceived as a concrete skeleton construction with flat plate floors and a solid core. The spatially dividing walls and facade elements are executed in a lightweight construction technique, guaranteeing high flexibility and to respond specifically to the changing requirements of the home.
   The interior-situated, compact detached core produces a stringent organization of the surrounding circulation spaces, with short distances and direct lateral connections. The ring of facade-side rooms opens periodically to create amenity zones with views of the surroundings. The clear room layout and a rich range of color contrasts provide easy orientation.

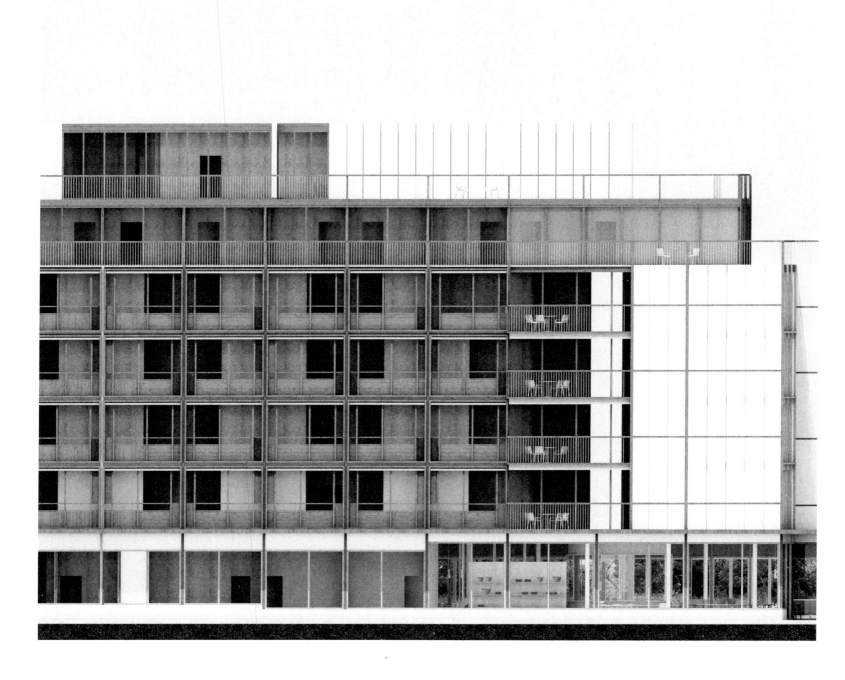

N° 276 Grossalbis Housing Development

Location Zurich, Switzerland **Type** New building **Status** Competition **Project phases** *Competition* 2019 **Client** FGZ, Familienheim Genossenschaft Zürich **Project data** *Lot size* 14,581 m² *Built-up area* 3,062 m² *Floor area* 16,786 m² (according to SIA 416) *Building volume* 50,689 m³ **Planners** *Architecture* Buchner Bründler Architekten, Basel *Landscape architecture* August + Margrith Künzel Landschaftsarchitekten, Binningen **Team Buchner Bründler** *Partners* Daniel Buchner, Andreas Bründler *Project lead* Holger Harmeier *Participants* Moritz Schmidlin

Impetus The district with the Grossalbis housing project at the foot of the Uetliberg, run by the Familienheim-Genossenschaft Zürich, was developed in the 1930s. The positioning in the urban layout was defined by the later cantonal architect Heinrich Peter, whose primary concept drew on the original parceling of what was then farmland. Beside the erection of compact family apartments, the concern was to approximate to an ideal of family-friendly living through the design of amenity spaces and the incorporation of greenery. For many years the project had a model character. The modernization plans, made necessary by age, revealed that a transformation is impossible, resulting a decision to retroactively densify the development with new replacement buildings.

Concept The new urban constellation translates the former rows of ribbon housing into six four-story blocks. The layered layout of paths, front gardens, houses, terraces, and gardens running parallel to the terrain is modified in order to provide barrier-free movement and realize the ideal of community living. The continuity of the green spaces throughout the development remains tangible, understood as a shared garden commons. At the center of the settlement is the communal square with a directly adjacent community space. The houses are accessed via the paths in the settlement and open garden galleries, providing a wide range of different multifloor apartments and maisonettes, with each apartment facing in two directions.

Implementation The buildings are erected as hybrid constructions with efficient, solid primary structures, with the reinforced construction acting as thermal energy storage. The facades are fabricated as timber-element constructions, with both sides in wood planking. The wood is protected with a coating of mineral-pigmented falu red. The dividing room walls consist of timber posts and beams with wood paneling. The flooring is made of hard concrete, while the concrete apartment ceilings are varnished white. Overall, the aim is to create a tactile and harmonious atmosphere.

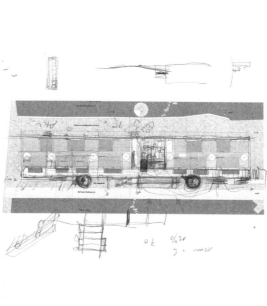

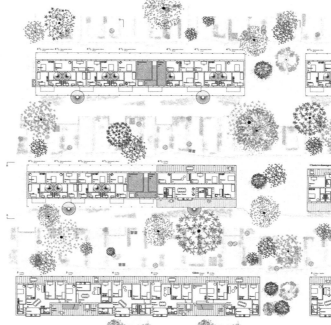
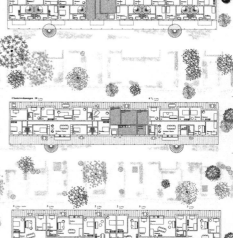

N° 278 Webergut Zollikofen

Location Zollikofen, Switzerland *Type* Conversion *Status* Competition *Project phases* *Competition* 2019, shortlisted *Client* Stiftung Abendrot, Basel *Project data Lot size* 4,235 m² *Built-up area* 2,488 m² *Floor area* 16,478 m² (according to SIA 416) *Building volume* 53,495 m³ *Planners Architecture* Buchner Bründler Architekten, Basel *Building engineering* Schnetzer Puskas Ingenieure AG, Basel *Fire prevention planning* Quantum Brandschutz GmbH, Basel *Team Buchner Bründler Partners* Daniel Buchner, Andreas Bründler *Project lead* Magdalena Stadler *Participants* Sarah Silbernagel, Daniel Gómez Masana

Impetus The Webergut business park in the suburban municipality of Zollikofen outside Berne has been re-designated as a central zone, allowing, in terms of economical ground-space management, the site to also be used for housing. An investment foundation has acquired the real estate with commercial building no. 5, with the aim of transforming it into a mixed living and working location. The building consists of two cuboids set close together, positioned on a continuous base floor and connected via a central circulation core. The main volumes have a three-bay column-slab structure and are clad in a light-colored, corrugated sheet-metal facade.

Concept The overall coherent effect is exploited to evolve a large-scale, block-like form, lending the building a pronounced individuality. In the process, the two main segments are volumetrically supplemented and the core area is re-dimensioned. The inner facade layer is inset in order to generate an expansive central courtyard area. Accessed via an aerial walkway and wide stairs, the base becomes an open precinct space and serves as an expansive arrival and amenity zone. On the other floors, ring-like platforms are arranged along the open courtyard, which serve as direct open spaces and as access to the apartments.

Implementation The structural alterations allow a versatile usability. The base continues to accommodate commercial occupancies. Individual apartments, as well as community areas and a daycare center and a café, are arranged around the central courtyard square. With the re-profiling of the volume, the apartments can be orientated toward both sides, whereby the apt depth provides good daylighting. For the exterior design, the project demonstrates the potential of a new facade skin in wood. A free logia layout blends with the monolithic appearance of the large-scale block, enabling wide views from the apartments and to reinforce their residential character.

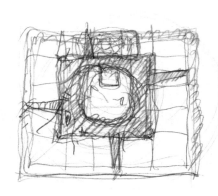

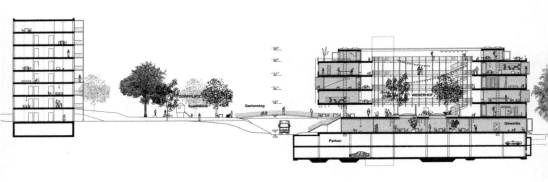

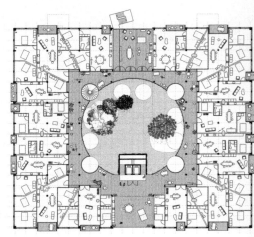

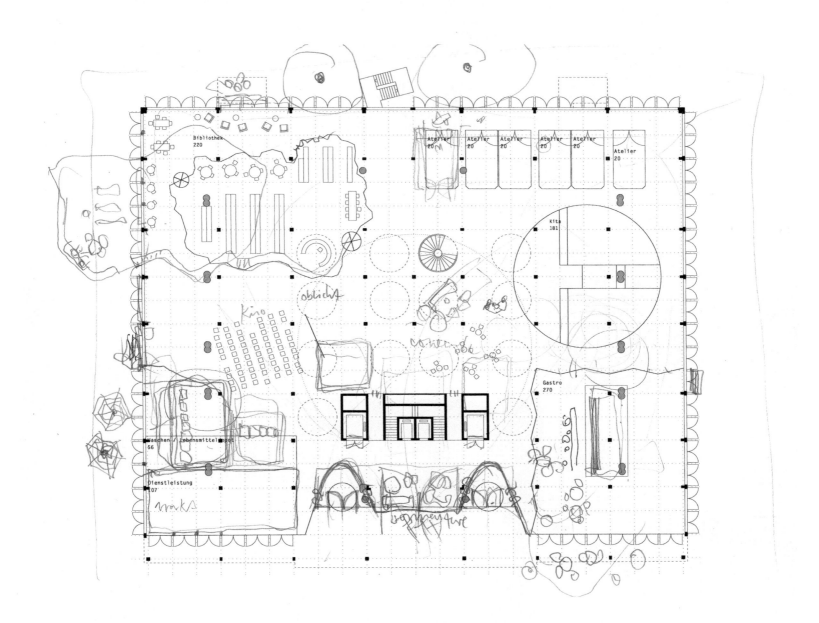

N° 280 Tower at Jannowitz Bridge Berlin

Location Berlin, Germany **Type** New building **Status** Competition **Project phases** *Competition* 2019, shortlisted **Client** Alexanderstraße Projektentwicklungs GmbH, Berlin
Project data *Lot size* 1,979 m² *Built-up area* 898 m² *Floor area* 37,841 m² (according to DIN 277) *Building volume* 142,081 m³ **Planners** *Architecture* Buchner Bründler Architekten, Basel *Building engineering* Schnetzer Puskas Ingenieure AG, Basel *Facade planning* Dr. Lüchinger + Meyer Bauingenieure AG, Zurich *Fire prevention planning* Corall Ingenieure GmbH, Meerbusch
Team Buchner Bründler *Partners* Daniel Buchner, Andreas Bründler *Project lead* Raphaël Kadid *Participants* Moritz Schmidlin, Luzi Speth, Johanna Noell

Impetus In terms of townscape and traffic, the Jannowitz Bridge occupies a neuralgic point. Situated just outside the historical core city, the site served as an early river crossing. Immediately after the bridge, the river basin of the Spree widens into the Spree Canal, the water congestion creating an almost stationary water surface.

During the industrial era, the upper city railroad and a subway line were built, making the Jannowitz Bridge into a transitory site. With post-WW II reconstruction, the later architectural development took on a socialist character. Long after reunification, the development of the buffer zones to the Spree stagnated, but is now experiencing a vigorous impulse on Holzmarkt.

Concept The transition between the historical core town to an open urban-planning pattern is imposingly signposted by a landmark tower. The building volume, with its multifaceted legibility, takes on an ascendency at the same time as entering into a dialogue with the context of the Jannowitz Bridge. The height progression of the building relates to the realities of the urban pattern, as well as the broadened Spree Basin. Similar vertical structures are planned on Alexanderstraße, establishing a direct townscape correlation with the new tower. The architectural volume is formed subtractively from simple cuboids and exhibits a flowing contour with vertical divisions. Higher ranking, facing the Spreeinsel, the slanted facade surface creates a figurative gesture.

Implementation The vertical primary concrete structure conforms to the free-plan exterior form, with hybrid floors spanned into it. The scaled skin of polygonal structural elements in glass and metal overlays the simple figure. Its slat-based forms with delicate glazing also serve to produce solar energy. In the base segment, the shell extends to form a protective awning. The free basic form allows the geometry of the square to be widened along the viaduct arches, which are to be given a stronger presence and opened up in order to free a connection to the Spree.

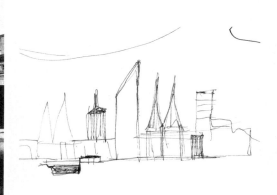

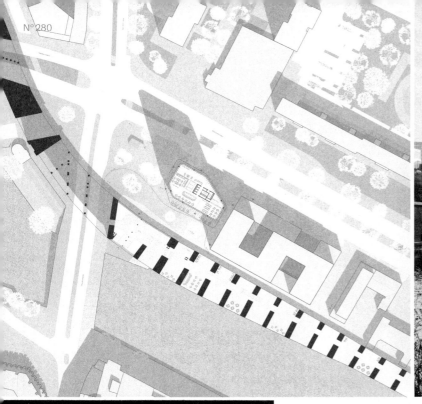

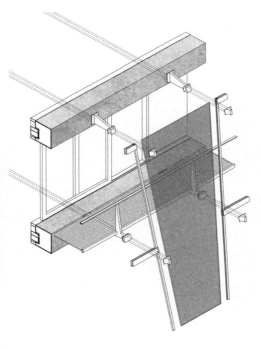
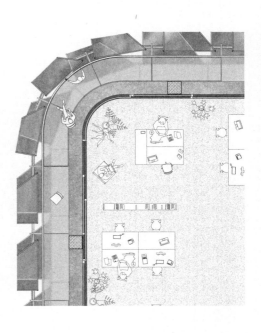
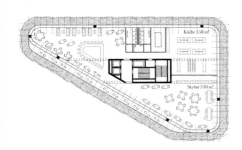
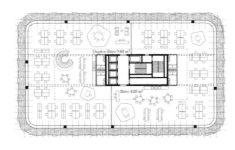
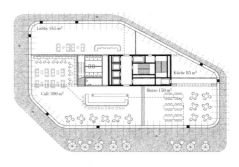

Appendix

513

Partner

Daniel Buchner (b.1967) 1984–1987, Daniel Buchner completed training as a building construction draughtsman in Berneck. 1988–1989 he studied architecture at the Ingenieurschule St. Gallen, and 1989–1993 at the Ingenieurschule beider Basel. Following a position at Morger & Degelo Architekten, 1994–1997, in Basel, in 1997 he co-founded the office Buchner Bründler Architekten, together with Andreas Bründler. 2003 he was accepted as a member of the Federation of Swiss Architects (FSA), and 2013 as a member of the Swiss Society of Engineers and Architects (SIA). He served as a visiting professor at Swiss Federal Institute of Technology in Lausanne (EPFL), 2008–2009, and 2010–2012 as a visiting lecturer in architectural design at Swiss Federal Institute of Technology Zurich (ETHZ).

Andreas Bründler (b.1967) 1984–1987, Andreas Bründler completed training as a building construction draughtsman in Zug. 1989–1993 he studied architecture at the Ingenieurschule beider Basel. Following a position at Miller & Maranta, 1994–1997, in Basel, in 1997 he co-founded the office Buchner Bründler Architekten, together with Daniel Buchner. 2003 he was accepted as a member of the Federation of Swiss Architects (FSA), and 2013 as a member of the Swiss Society of Engineers and Architects (SIA). He served as a visiting professor at Swiss Federal Institute of Technology in Lausanne (EPFL), 2008–2009, and 2010–2012 as a visiting lecturer in architectural design at Swiss Federal Institute of Technology Zurich (ETHZ). This was followed 2020 and 2021 by a visiting professorship in the master's program in architecture at the University of Applied Sciences and Arts Northwest Switzerland (FHNW). Since 2019 he has served as a member of the commission "Städtebau für Basel 2050."

Associates

Stefan Oehy (b.1977) 1993–1997, Stefan Oehy completed training as a building construction draughtsman in Widnau. 1998–2003 he studied architecture at the Zürcher Hochschule Winterthur (ZHW). He has worked for Buchner Bründler Architekten since 2004, and since 2010 has been an associate and a member of the company management. He has supervised projects such as the Swiss Pavilion at the Expo 2010 in Shanghai, the Tièchestrasse Housing Development in Zurich, the Cooperative Building Stadterle in Basel, and the house in Allschwil. He is currently in charge of the projects for the Eisenbahnweg Housing Development in Basel and the Papieri-Area in Cham.

Natalie Zeitz (b.1972) 1992–1995, Natalie Zeitz completed training as an interior decorator in Freiburg im Breisgau. 1996–2001 she studied interior architecture at the Trier University of Applied Science and at the Danish Design School (DKDS) in Copenhagen. Following positions with Steinmann Schmid Architekten, 2001–2003 in Basel, and in the Basel office of Pedrocchi Meier, 2005–2008, she has worked for Buchner Bründler Architekten since 2008. Two years after joining, she became an associate and a member of the company management. She is in charge of office operations and is responsible for publicity work and human resources.

Nick Waldmeier (b.1975) 1991–1995, Nick Waldmeier completed training as a building construction draughtsman in Stein (Aargau). 1998–2002 he studied architecture at the Fachhochschule beider Basel. Following a position with Brandenberger Kloter Architekten, 2003–2005 in Basel, he has worked for Buchner Bründler Architekten. Accompanying this, 2007–2011 he was an assistant at Annette Spiro's Chair of Architecture and Construction at Swiss Federal Institute of Technology Zurich (ETHZ). He became an associate in 2011, and since 2018 is a member of the company management. He has supervised numerous single-family houses, for instance those in Münchenstein and Binningen. In addition he was in charge of the remodeling of the Hotel Nomad in Basel, the Casa Mosogno, as well as the construction of the Amthausquai Residential and Commercial Building in Olten. He is currently responsible for the extension to the Academy of Architecture (USI) in Mendrisio, the new Universität Hamburg Guesthouse, and the Housing Development Rötiboden in Wädenswil.

Bülend Yigin (b.1976) 1998–2007, Bülend Yigin studied architecture at the Technical University Kaiserslautern. He began working for Buchner Bründler Architekten in 2007, became an associate in 2011, and since 2018 is a member of the company management. He supervised the Peninsula Housing Development in Wädenswil, the Garden Tower in Wabern bei Berne, and the conversion of Credit Suisse Place Bel-Air Headquarters in Geneva. He is currently in charge of work on the Kunsthaus Baselland, the conversion of the WDR-Filmhaus in Cologne, the Urban Development Horburg in Basel, as well as the Railway Station Building in Altdorf.

Staff

Peter Beutler, Dominik Aegerter, Stefan Herrmann, Bianca Kummer, Tünde König, Rebecca Borer, Carlos Unten Kanashiro, Aude Soffer, Georgia Papathanasiou, Holger Harmeier, Jan Stiller, Sarah Simon, Sharif Hasrat (trainee), Fabienne Saladin, Signe Veinberga, Leandro Villalba, Bosco Ferreira, Michèle Gartenmann (administration), Andreas Widmer, Camille Paragon, Markus Leixner, Jonas Schöpfer, Estelle Ayer, David Formaz, Alexandra Galer

Interns Marlene Koßmann, Livia Nowak, Alea Ebnöther, Tim Stettler, Antoine Liechti, Anna-Lena Wallner, Nele Ziegler

Former Staff Beat Meier, Doro Herbst, Stephanie Hirschvogel, Isabel Heyden, Katja Ritz, Eline Sieber, Thorsten Haack, Raul Mera, Petra Jossen, Zahin Farhad, Sabine Beer, Benedikt Ramser, Gabriella Bertozzi, Matthias Kleiber, David Merz, Daniel Abraha, Xu Zhang, Magdalena Falska, Benjamin Wiederock, Daniel Dratz, Alexander Schmiedel, Lukas Baumann, Sebastian Pitz, Nicole Johann, Jonas Staehelin, Yvonne Grunwald, Jenny Jenisch, Nino Soppelsa, Maria Conen, Christoph Böckeler, Thomas Klement, Chiara Friedl, Beda Klein (trainee), Caroline Alsup, Sandra Bründler, Friederike Kluge, Kim Sneyders, Daniela Valentini (public relations), Stefan Mangold, Carina Thurner, Joana Anes, Jonathan Hermann, Martin Risch, Ewa Misiewicz, Lilitt Bollinger, Nadine Strasser, Claudia Furer, Rino Buess, Achim Widjaja, Jan Borner, Karolina Switzer, Fabian Meury (trainee), Florian Rink, Florian Ueker, Pascal Berchtold, Patrizia Wunderli, Raphaela Schacher (associate), Renate Dornier Pernes (administration), Elisabet Sundin, Hannah von Knobelsdorff, Henrik Månsson, Katharina Kral, Michael Glaser, Janine Bolliger, Omri Levy, Annina Zimmermann (administration), Laura Ehme, Benjamin Hofmann, Norma Tollmann, Daniel Ebertshäuser, Miriam Stierle, Benjamin Olschner, Leonie Hagen, Vanessa Flaiban, Daniel Ziółek, Jon Garbizu Etxaide, Sylwia Chomentowska (public relations), Gisela Stöckli, Hellade Miozzari, Magdalena Stadler, Mihails Staluns, Simone Braendle, Raphaël Kadid

Former Interns Gabriele Schell-Steven, Birgit Stephan, Moritz Marti, Sabrina Dinkel, Hans-Jörg Sauter, Nicole Winteler, Victoria Easton, Berit Seidel, Nadine Reif, Leonie Hoffmann, Olivia Frei, Sonja Christen, Anna Dreykluft, Caesar Zumthor, Corinne Doutaz, Felix Engelhardt, Sandra Gonon, Julian Trachsel, Max Koch, Benedikt Bertoli-Sülzenfuss, Christoph Hiestand, Jaswant Stoecklin, Mathilde Sigismondi, Annika Stoetzel, Felix Moos, Philipp Ryffel, Frank Schwenk, Patrick Jaeger, Konstantin König, Dimitris Kardaras, Oliver Teiml, Stephanie Wamister, Dano Gloor, Daniel Pflaum, Nathalie Geibel, Didier Balissat, Luiz Albisser, Boris Koch, Madeleine Müller, Nicolas Hunkeler, Michael Gunti, Reto Gasser, Lea Fahnenstich, Liesa Schiecke, Zhang Chen, Matthias Leschok, Ananda Berger, Christoph Wendland, Lorraine Haussmann, Julian Oggier, Debora Joerin, Mascha Zach, Lisa Schneider, Eva Körber, Fatima Blötzer, Anaï Beccera, Bàlazs Földvàry, Michael Steigmeier, André Santos, Serafin Zanger-Winkler, Alexandra Berthold, Christiane Müller, Simon Ulfstedt, Lorenz Marggraf, Florian Bengert, Christian Käser, Marlene Sauer, Sebastian Arzet, Remo Reichmuth, Romain Kündig, Benedict Choquard, Maša Kovač Šmajdek, Aurelia Müggler, Luise Daut, Elin Näf, Flurin Arquint, Patrick Kurzendorfer, Anne-Kathrin Müller, Jonas Virsik, Mihails Staluns, Jonas Hamberger, Björn Wiedl, Jakob Rabe Petersen, Lennart Cleemann, Leonie Hagen, Yannic Schröder, Roman Hauser, Fabio Cirronis, Dimitrios Katsis, Maria Schlüter, Tanja Schmidt, Paula Eich, Luzi Speth, Nora Molari, Paul Schreijäg, Jonas Schneck, Lea Frenz, Angelika Hinterbrandner, Samuel Schubert, Joël Mortier, Alexandra Galer, Tobias Kappelhoff, Kevin De Roeck, Florian Marenbach, Daniel Gómez Masana, Nina Kleber, Jérémie Lysek, Kaspar Zilian, Gerson Egerter, Signe Veinberga, Oscar Faivre, Sarah Silbernagel, Charlotte Schwartz, Moritz Schmidlin, Johanna Noell, Dominik Hesse, Lorenz Gujer, Pauline Rohländer, Arno Bruderer, Clara Alsedà Rodríguez, Sophia Fahl, Antonia Haffner, Mariano Managò, Moritz Schmidt, Lion Rust, Sophia Frischmuth, Emmanuel Gnagne.

Die Besten 2020 (award ceremony and exhibition), December 2, 2020–January 10, 2021, Museum für Gestaltung, Zurich

Modern Living – Einfamilienhäuser in Basel und Umgebung, 1945–1975, June 10, 2020–March 14, 2021, Museum Kleines Klingental, Basel

Constellations – Correlations: Buchner Bründler Architekten (solo exhibition), February 15–March 17, 2019, House of Art České Budějovice

Dichtelust – Forms of Urban Coexistence in Switzerland, November 24, 2018–May 5, 2019, S AM – Swiss Architecture Museum, Basel

Toulouse 2030, October 11–14, 2018, Place du Capitole, Toulouse

Building Stories, July 10–August 14, 2018, Centro Cultural de Belém, Lisbon

Swiss Sensibility – The Culture of Architecture in Switzerland, June 7–30, 2018, Silver Building, Docklands, London

Grün am Bau, May 16, 2018–March 31, 2019, Stadtgärtnerei Zürich, Zentrum für Pflanzen und Bildung, Sukkulenten-Sammlung, Zurich

Ausstellung Auszeichnung guter Bauten 2018, October 31–November 12, 2018, Theaterplatz, Basel

Luftseilbahn Glück, film by iArt, Münchenstein, November 17, 2017–October 28, 2018, Heimatschutzzentrum in der Villa Patumbah, Zurich

Schweizweit – Recent Architecture in Switzerland, November 19, 2016–May 7, 2017, S AM / Swiss Architecture Museum, Basel

Constructing Film – Swiss Architecture in the Moving Image, film by Katja Loher, New York City, October 31, 2015–February 28, 2016, S AM / Swiss Architecture Museum, Basel

Ausstellung Auszeichnung guter Bauten 2013, November 12– 23, 2013, Museum Baselland; December 12, 2013–January 14, 2014, Bau- und Verkehrsdepartement Basel-Stadt

Buchner Brundler – Bauten (solo exhibition), October 5–November 1, 2012, ETH Zurich

AIT Award 2012 (award ceremony and exhibition), April 19, 2012, during the Light + Building trade fair 2012, Frankfurt am Main

Swiss Positions – 33 Takes on Sustainable Approaches to Building (touring exhibition), April 13–27, 2012, Carnegie Mellon University, School of Architecture, Pittsburgh; April 2012, University of Cambridge, Department of Architecture, Cambridge; June–July 2012, University College, London; June 23–September 16, 2012, Archipel Centre De Culture Urbaine, Lyon; September 24–October 24, 2012, Polis University, Tirana; November 12, 2012–January 10, 2013, Yuchengco Museum, Manila; March 8–April 14, 2013, Galerie Jaroslava Fragnera, Prague; September 12–October 17, 2013, Architectural Institute of British Columbia Gallery, Vancouver; September 4–26, 2014, Kunstgalerie Xcelsio, Riga; October 1–November 15, 2014, Im Adambräu, Innsbruck

Swiss Contemporary Architecture, December 16, 2010–January 30, 2011, El Colegio de Arquitectos de Cádiz

Schweizer Pavillon Expo 2010 Shanghai – Buchner Brundler Architekten und element Design (solo exhibition), September 22–November 4, 2010, ETH Zurich

Ordos 100 – The inevitable cultural negotiations when building a city in the 21st Century, June 10–14, 2009, E-Halle Basel

Ausstellung Auszeichnung guter Bauten 2008, October 1–31, 2008, Bau- und Verkehrsdepartement Basel-Stadt; November 5–16, 2008, Kantonsbibliothek Basel-Landschaft

In heikler Mission – Geschichten zur Schweizer Diplomatie, May 16–September 16, 2007, Swiss National Museum, Zurich

Vivre [L']ensemble, October 2006, Maison de L'Architecture Rhone-Alpes, Lyon

Stand der Dinge – Aktuelle Wohnbauten in Basel, July 1, 2004, Markthalle Basel

Laisser Faire – Maison Verre (solo exhibition), April 1–May 5, 2004, Salon Blauraum, Hamburg

Ausstellung Eidgenossischer Kunstpreis 2003, June 16–23, 2003, Messe Basel

Uno Hauptsitz GA-200, New York City (Swiss accession gift to the United Nations), June 15–21, 2003, Architekturforum am Neumarkt, Zurich

Wanderausstellung Bauwelt Preis 2003, January 13–19, 2003, during the Bau 2003 trade fair, Munich

Awards and Prizes

Die Besten 2020, Hase in Bronze, category Architecture, Allschwil House, organizer: *Hochparterre*
AIT Award 2020, 1st prize, category Social Design/Participative Architecture, Cooperative Building Stadterle, Basel, organizer: AIT-Dialog
AIT Award 2020, award, category Single Family Living, Casa Mosogno, organizer: AIT-Dialog
Premio SIA Ticino, edizione 2020, Menzione, Casa Mosogno, organizer: SIA, Sezione Ticino
Der beste Umbau 2020, jury prize, Casa Mosogno, organizer: *Umbauen + Renovieren*
Premio Europeo di Architettura Matilde Baffa Ugo Rivolta 2019, Menzione, Cooperative Building Stadterle, Basel, organizer: Ordine Architetti P.P.C. della Provincia di Milano
The Best of 2019, recognition, category Architecture, Casa Mosogno, organizer: *Hochparterre*
Auszeichnung guter Bauten 2018, award, Cooperative Building Stadterle, Basel; Hotel Nomad, Basel, organizer: Canton Basel-Stadt, Canton Basel-Landschaft
ARC-Award 2018, 1st prize, category Residential Buildings, Cooperative Building Stadterle, Basel, organizer: Schweizer Baudokumentation
RIBA International Prize 2018, longlist, Garden Tower, Wabern near Berne, organizer: The Royal Institute of British Architects
Fritz Höger Preis 2017, special mention, Peninsula Housing Development, Wädenswil, organizer: Initiative Bauen mit Backstein
Hugo Häring Auszeichnung 2017, award, Lörrach House, organizer: Association of German Architects (BDA), Regional Association Baden-Württemberg
db Preis: Bauen im Bestand 2016, Respekt und Perspektive, 1st prize, Hotel Nomad, Basel, organizer: *Deutsche Bauzeitung*
Bautenprämierung 2016, special mention, Hotel Nomad, Basel, organizer: Heimatschutz Basel
AIT Award 2014, 2nd prize, category Living/Housing, Bläsiring House, Basel, organizer: AIT-Dialog
Best Book Design from all over the World 2014, gold medal, Monograph *Buchner Bründler Bauten*, organizer: Stiftung Buchkunst
Auszeichnung Guter Bauten 2013, award, Volta Zentrum Residential and Commercial Building, Basel; Bläsiring House, Basel; St. Alban Youth Hostel, Basel; Manor Department Store, Liestal; Binningen House; Seltisberg Community Center, organizer: Canton Basel-Stadt, Canton Basel-Landschaft
Die 50 besten Einfamilienhäuser 2013, award, Chienbergreben House, Gelterkinden; Hubackerweg House, Reinach, organizer: Callwey Verlag
Architecture Prize Beton 13, winner, Casa d'Estate Linescio; Private Residence Bläsiring, Basel, organizer: Betonsuisse
D&AD Awards 2013, winner Book Design, Monograph *Buchner Bründler Bauten*, organizer: D&AD
AIT-Award, Global Award for the Very Best in Interior and Architecture 2012, 1st prize, category Living, Interior, Casa d'Estate Linescio, organizer: AIT-Dialog
Bautenprämierung 2010, Volta Zentrum Residential and Commercial Building, Basel, organizer: Heimatschutz Basel
Die Besten 2010, recognition, St. Alban Youth Hostel Basel, organizer: *Hochparterre*
Bautenprämierung 2008, Sevogelstrasse Housing Development, Basel, organizer: Heimatschutz Basel
Auszeichnung Guter Bauten 2008, award, Aesch House, organizer: Canton Basel-Stadt, Canton Basel-Landschaft
Der beste Umbau 2008, jury prize, Sevogelstrasse Housing Development, Basel, organizer: *Umbauen + Renovieren*
Swiss Federal Art Prize 2003, 1st prize, category Architecture, Glass Tower, organizer: Federal Office of Culture
Bauwelt Preis 2003, 1st prize, category Residential Architecture, Loft House Basel, organizer: *Bauwelt*
Auszeichnung guter Bauten 2002, award, Loft House Basel, organizer: Canton Basel-Stadt, Canton Basel-Landschaft
Auszeichnung guter Bauten 2002, special award, Lupsingen House, organizer: Canton Basel-Stadt, Canton Basel-Landschaft

Image Credits

Despite best efforts, we have not been able to identify the holders of copyright and printing rights for all the illustrations. Copyright holders not mentioned in the credits are asked to substantiate their claims, and recompense will be made according to standard practice.

If not mentioned otherwise, all photographs, drawings, plans, model images, and visualizations are intellectual property of Buchner Bründler Architekten.

Georg Aerni, Zurich 47, 51→, 319, 320, 322/323, 347–354
Mathilde Agius, Berlin 244
Yves André, Vaumarcus 258↓
Ludovic Balland, Basel 6–8, 12–14, 16/17, 37, 39, 80–85, 86–92, 107–119, 120–131, 132–137, 143–154, 155, 157–159, 161–163, 165, 253, 254, 255↓, 256↓, 317, 318, 394–396
Ludovic Balland, Annina Schepping, Hans-Jörg Walter, Basel 4, 9, 35, 66/67, 69, 70, 93–97
Ludovic Balland, Basel, Alexander Rosenkranz, Berlin front endpapers, 513–522, back endpapers
Michael Blaser, Berne 173, 176, 179↘, 180, 222–225, 226↑↙, 229
Basile Bornand, Basel 48←, 212, 302↓, 304/305
Daniela Droz & Tonatiuh Ambroselli, Penthalaz 174/175, 177, 178, 179↙, 255↑, 257↓, 258↑, 259, 260
Luca Fascini, Geneva 257↑
Rory Gardiner, London 43, 50↓→, 202, 205–207, 208↙↘, 269–273, 274↑, 276, 301, 302↑, 303, 306/307, 332–336, 363, 369↓, 370↑, 371, 374, 384↑, 388/389, 391–393
Bruno Helbling, Zurich 240↓
Daisuke Hirabayashi, Basel 308
Maris Mezulis, Basel 383, 384↓, 385–387, 390
Mark Niedermann, Riehen 204, 364–368, 369↑, 370↓, 372/373
Michel Pretterklieber, St. Gallen 338
Alexander Rosenkranz, Berlin 74–79
Annina Schepping, Basel 5, 10, 15, 98–102↑, 138–142
Annina Schepping, Basel, Frederik Sutter, Hechingen 71–73
Annina Schepping, Hans-Jörg Walter, Basel 11, 36, 103–106, 156, 160, 164
Hans-Jörg Walter, Basel 98–102↙↘
Ruedi Walti, Basel 48→, 50←, 51←, 179↑, 189–194, 203, 208↑, 210/211, 221, 226↘, 227, 228, 230, 239, 240↑, 241–243, 274↓, 275, 285, 286↙↘, 287–289, 292, 337

29↑ © ELEMENTAL / Tadeuz Jalocha
29↓ © ELEMENTAL and Estudio Palma / Cristobal Palma
32 © Kurt Caviezel
33↑ Keystone / AP Photo / Emilio Morenatti
33→ Courtesy Library of Congress, Prints & Photographs Division, FSA/OWI Collection, LC-USF34-061577-D (b&w film neg.)
33↓ Courtesy National Archives (106-WB-602)

Further Buildings and Projects pp. 405–512
Unless otherwise stated in the thumbnail images, all photographs, sketches, plans, model images, and visualizations come from Buchner Bründler Architekten.
405–414 Ruedi Walti, Basel
415 A © Google Maps B maaars architektur visualisierungen, Zurich
418 A/D Ruedi Walti, Basel B Andrea Diglas, Zurich C Christian Aeberhard, Basel
419 A Parkhotel Bellevue Archive, Adelboden B/C Ruedi Walti, Basel D Christian Aeberhard, Basel
420/421 Ruedi Walti, Basel
428 Bildbau, Zurich
430 loomn architekturkommunikation, Gütersloh
431 Hans Schmidt, *Entwurf Nr. 33: «BSB» – Ansicht aus Süden*, in: *Schweizerische Bauzeitung* (ed.), 03, 1927, p. 33.
432 A Walter Mittelholzer, *Kilchberg (ZH), Lindt & Sprüngli Schokoladenfabrik*, photograph, 13 × 18 cm, June 26, 1924, in: Image Archive ETH Library Zurich / Stiftung Luftbild Schweiz
B/C loomn architekturkommunikation, Gütersloh
433 loomn architekturkommunikation, Gütersloh
435 Ruedi Walti, Basel
436 loomn architekturkommunikation, Gütersloh
438 Bildbau, Zurich
440 A Hiroshi Sugimoto, *Dioramas*, photograph, 1992; © 2021 Goodman Gallery, New York
B/C bloomimages GmbH, Hamburg
441 bloomimages GmbH, Hamburg
442 Gordon Matta-Clark, *Days End Pier 52.3* (documentation of the action "Day's End" made in 1975 in New York, United States), film still, 1977; © 2021 ProLitteris, Zurich
443 CYAAN, Zurich
445 A © Google Maps B/C bloomimages GmbH, Hamburg
446–467 bloomimages GmbH, Hamburg
448 Bildbau, Zurich
449 CYAAN, Zurich
451 A Country home on Greifensee, Switzerland, Dr. Dahinden J., Zurich, in: *Detail* 05/1971, p. 1012
B Ruedi Walti, Basel
452 Ruedi Walti, Basel
453 A © BAK B Giorgio de Chirico, *Piazza d'Italia*, oil on lithograph, 50 × 70 cm, 1913; © 2021 ProLitteris, Zurich C © BAK / image: Bruno Pellandini
456 © Google Maps
457 bloomimages GmbH, Hamburg
459 Swissair Photo AG, *Greppen*, photograph, 10 × 12 cm, 1978, in: Image Archive ETH Library Zurich / Stiftung Luftbild Schweiz
460 A © Google Maps B/C bloomimages GmbH, Hamburg
467 A CIBA Wohngebäude A.G.: Horburgstrasse – Müllheimerstrasse – Wiesenschanze development, in: Arnold Gfeller, *Rückblick auf meine Arbeit und meine Liebhabereien*, Basel 1962, n. p. B © Google Maps
469 Éva Le Roi, Brussels
470 A Johann Friedrich Mähly, detail *St. Margarethen, Birsig, Steinen*, colored steel engraving, 1847, in: Staatsarchiv Basel-Stadt, Bild 1, 835.
B bloomimages GmbH, Hamburg
473 A © Google Maps B Bernard Grenfell and Arthur Hunt excavating at Oxyrhynchus in 1897, in: *Biblical Archaeology Review*, vol. 02 2011, p. 63; © Egypt Exploration Society
475 A Author unknown B Werner Friedli, *Fürigen, Hotel Fürigen*, photograph, 13 × 18 cm, June 11, 1948, in: Image Archive ETH Library Zurich / Stiftung Luftbild Schweiz
478 © Google Maps
481 Archiv Bakker & Blanc architectes, Lausanne
483–484 Daisuke Hirabayashi, Basel
486 Otto Rietmann, wood carvers working on the arching between the columns of the interior wall, 1915, in: Rudolf Steiner Verlag (ed.), *Rudolf Steiner Gesamtausgabe, Vorträge*, Dornach 1985, p. 86
487 Comet Photo AG, *Papierfabrik, Cham ZG*, photograph, 13 × 18 cm, 1964, in: Image Archive ETH Library Zurich
489 Cigarette factory Reemtsma, Hamburg-Wandsbek, 1926–29, perspective view of the side wing, contemporary photograph, in: Piergiacomo Bucciarelli, *Fritz Höger – Hanseatischer Baumeister 1877–1949*, Berlin 1992, p. 29
490 bloomimages GmbH, Hamburg
491 A © 2021 UZH Zürich / image: Ursula Meisser B bloomimages GmbH, Hamburg
492–493 bloomimages GmbH, Hamburg
494 Emanuel Büchel, *Blick vom Erli nach Westen zum Dorf und Schloss Pratteln*, gouache, 1735, in: Staatsarchiv Basel-Landschaft, Liestal; © Gemeinde Pratteln
495 Walter Mittelholzer, *Strassenszene in Addis Abeba*, photograph, 6 × 6 cm, 1934, in: Image Archive ETH Library Zurich
496 A © Google Maps B Filippo Bolognese Images, Milan
497–499 Filippo Bolognese Images, Milan
501 Constantin Brancusi, *The Endless Column*, sculpture, 1937; © Succession Brancusi – all rights reserved / 2021 ProLitteris, Zurich
504 A Women's Domestic Science School, Kohlenberg, Basel, in: Karl and Maya Nägelin-Gschwind, *Hans Bernoulli: Das architektonische Gesamtwerk*, Basel 1993, p. 169
B Comet Photo AG, *Nationalstrasse N2/Autobahn A2, Baustelle bei Basel-Heuwaage*. photograph, 13 × 18 cm, 1969, in: Image Archive ETH Library Zurich
507 © CNES, Spot Image, swisstopo, NPOC, swisstopo
510 A Friedrich Albert Schwartz, *Jannowitzbrücke – Dampferpavillon – bzw. – Anlegestelle*. photograph, 28.1 × 36.6 cm, 1885, in: Landesarchiv Berlin; © Landesarchiv Berlin B ArtefactoryLab, Paris
C Michael Dean, *Yes* (working title), concrete sculpture, 175 × 65 × 9 cm, 2011; © 2021 Herald St., London / Supportico Lopez, Berlin / Michael Dean
511 ArtefactoryLab, Paris

Cover
Annina Schepping, Hans-Jörg Walter, Basel **front**
Alexander Rosenkranz, Berlin **back**↑
Ludovic Balland, Basel **back**↓

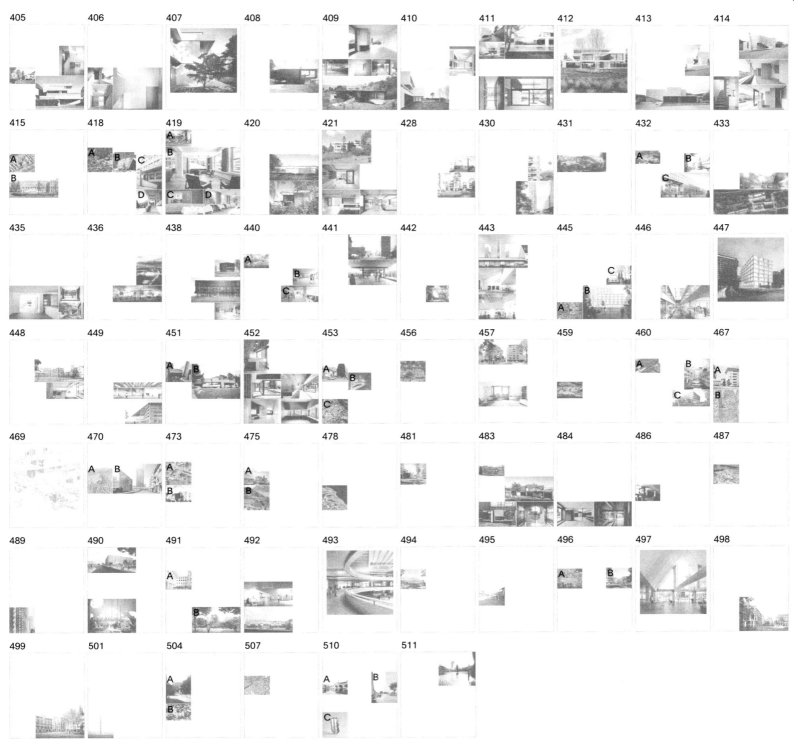

Contributors

Tibor Joanelly (b.1967) Tibor Joanelly is an architect, journalist, and university teacher. He completed his studies at Swiss Federal Institute of Technology Zurich (ETHZ) and has worked in renowned Swiss architecture and design offices. Besides his freelance work, he has chaired studio discourses with creative Swiss architects such as Christian Kerez, Valerio Olgiati, Livio Vacchini, Peter Märkli, and Flora Ruchat-Roncati. He has published essays and critiques in international architectural journals. He is currently giving a course of lectures on architectural criticism at the Zurich University of Applied Sciences (ZHAW) and is a writer for the Swiss architectural journal werk, bauen + wohnen. He is a researcher and lecturer and works on publication and exhibition projects, including his book Shinoharistics: An Essay About a House, which appeared in 2020.

Urs Stahel (b.1953) Urs Stahel studied German, history, and philosophy. After completing his studies he worked as a writer for Der Alltag and du, as an art critic for Die Weltwoche and for ART in Hamburg, as well as a freelance journalist and curator. In cooperation with the publisher Walter Keller and the sponsor George Reinhart, he founded the Fotomuseum Winterthur, where he worked as a curator and director for twenty years. Since 2013 he has worked freelance as a curator, author, lecturer, and consultant, mainly for the MAST Foundation, the new institution for industrial culture in Bologna. He has curated numerous exhibitions and is the author/editor of innumerable books.

Ludovic Balland (b.1973) Ludovic Balland has been active in graphic design, typography, book design, and photography since 2003. In 2006 he founded his own office, Typography Cabinet, in Basel, with its main emphasis on editorial projects, primarily in the fields of architecture, art, and science. In 2016 the Swiss Federal Office of Culture awarded him the Jan-Tschichold Prize for his outstanding achievements in book design. Ludovic Balland has gathered a wide range of teaching experience in Switzerland, Europe, and America, as well as delivering numerous talks. He is also the editor and author of the book American Readers at Home (2017), a project that was exhibited at the Museum im Bellpark, Kriens, in summer 2020.

Annina Schepping (b.1993) Annina Schepping works as a graphic designer in Basel, focusing on editorial design. Following an education in communication design at University of Applied Sciences (HTWG) in Konstanz and a six-month internship at the ZEITMagazin in Berlin, she has worked for Ludovic Balland's Typography Cabinet since 2018.

Isabel Koellreuter (b.1974) Isabel Koellreuter, lic. phil. I, studied history, cultural studies, and national economy. Following her studies she worked as a freelance historian, and in 2010, together with the cultural scholar Franziska Schürch, she founded the office Schürch & Koellreuter, Kulturwissenschaft und Geschichte, specialized in exploring historical and cultural content and mediated in the form of texts, exhibitions, films, audio stations, and online projects.

Oliver Schneider (b.1982) Oliver Schneider, M.A., studied history and politics at the University of Fribourg (Switzerland) and the Graduate Institute in Geneva. Following his studies he worked as a producer for the ARD-Hörfunkstudio Switzerland in Geneva and Zurich for many years. Since 2016 Oliver Schneider works as a freelance historian. As an author and academic assistant, he has since then been involved in numerous publications and exhibitions. His research focus is in social and economic history.

Franziska Schürch (b.1972) Franziska Schürch, Dr. phil. I, studied theater studies, cultural studies and music studies. She subsequently undertook teaching and research work, as well as the scholarly leadership of the inventory of the Kulinarisches Erbe der Schweiz. In 2010, together with cultural scholar Isabel Koellreuter, she founded the office Schürch & Koellreuter, specialized in exploring historical and cultural content and mediated in the form of texts, exhibitions, films, audio stations, and online projects.

Acknowledgements

We are very pleased to be able to showcase our buildings and projects in this second monograph. At this point we would like to thank the publisher Park Books for this unique opportunity, in particular Thomas Kramer for the openness and trust that he extended to us in this process, as well as Lisa Schons and Verena Andric for their professional handling of the book.

Special thanks likewise go to Ludovic Balland for the editorial work and the design concept. As the editor he played a vital part in the conceptualization of the book and shaped its contents with additional image work. Our gratitude to Annina Schepping for the close cooperation in realizing the content and the design: her constantly clear and reliable approach assisted us in many of the design decisions.

The photographers Christian Aeberhard, Georg Aerni, Mathilde Agius, Yves André, Ludovic Balland, Michael Blaser, Basile Bornand, Andrea Diglas, Daniela Droz & Tonatiuh Ambrosetti, Luca Fascini, Rory Gardiner, Bruno Helbling, Daisuke Hirabayashi, Maris Mezulis, Mark Niedermann, Michel Pretterklieber, and Ruedi Walti provided us with their pictures, for which we warmly thank them.

We also express our thanks for the external visualization work by ArtefactoryLab, Bildbau, bloomimages, Filippo Bolognese Images, CYAAN, loomn architektur kommunikation, and maaars architektur visualisierungen, and for the urban-planning illustration by the artist Éva Le Roi.

We would like to thank Hans-Jörg Walter for contributing his work and his ideas that, in collaboration with Ludovic Balland and Annina Schepping, constitute an important part of the Workshop chapter.

Our gratitude also to the photographer Alexander Rosenkranz, who together with Ludovic Balland photographed our team with great sensitivity. It was a wonderful day for all of us.

Special thanks go to the two authors Tibor Joanelly and Urs Stahel for their well-articulated texts. We likewise thank Franziska Schürch and Isabel Koellreuter, as well as Oliver Schneider, for the accompanying historical texts to the selected buildings.

Organizational responsibility for the book in the office rested with Natalie Zeitz: she steered the processes behind the book project with skillful discrimination. The monograph was additionally supported by the work of Sylwia Chomentowska. Both of them meticulously worked their way through our archive and compiled the content material. Internally, Natalie Zeitz was also responsible for the copy-editing. Bosco Ferreira refined the plans with patient precision, as well as acting as an assistant, researcher, and corrector.

Our sincere thanks to the copy editor Sandra Leitte, who carefully edited all the texts.

Our gratitude also to translator Thomas Skelton-Robinson, who critically engaged with the texts and gave them a similitude in English.

A wholehearted thank you goes to our most important supporters, namely our invaluable team—our current and former employees who have applied themselves with untiring enthusiasm for our collective architecture and have developed and realized it with a great dependability.

Many, many thanks likewise to out clients, whose open-mindedness and indispensible trust made the development and realization of our buildings possible in the first place.

Imprint

Edited by
Ludovic Balland

Concept
Daniel Buchner, Andreas Bründler, Ludovic Balland, Annina Schepping

Content editing
Daniel Buchner, Andreas Bründler, Ludovic Balland, Annina Schepping, Natalie Zeitz

Coordination
Natalie Zeitz, Sylwia Chomentowska

Co-editors
Natalie Zeitz, Sylwia Chomentowska, Bosco Ferreira

Plan editing
Bosco Ferreira, Clara Alsedà Rodríguez

Design and typesetting
Ludovic Balland and Annina Schepping
Typography Cabinet GmbH, Basel

Font
Plain, François Rappo, Optimo

Paper
Cover: Peyprint smooth satin, Vienna Fabric
Werkdruck 1.8 90 g/m^2
Condat Périgord 115 g/m^2

Copy editing
Sandra Leitte

Translations and proofreading
Thomas Skelton-Robinson

Historical research
Franziska Schürch and Isabel Koellreuter
Schürch & Koellreuter, Basel
Oliver Schneider, Zurich

Pre-press
Widmer & Fluri GmbH, Zurich

Printing and binding
DZA Druckerei zu Altenburg GmbH

© 2022 Buchner Bründler Architekten AG, Basel, and Park Books AG, Zurich
© for the texts: the authors
© for the images: the artists/see image credits

Park Books
Niederdorfstrasse 54
8001 Zurich
Switzerland
www.park-books.com

Park Books is being supported by the Federal Office of Culture with a general subsidy for the years 2021–2024.

All rights reserved; no part of this publication may be reproduced, stored in a retrieval system or transmitted in any form or by any means, electronic, mechanical, photocopying, recording, or otherwise, without the prior written consent of the publisher.

ISBN 978-3-03860-252-1
German edition:
ISBN 978-3-03860-251-4